RISE OF THE
CAJUN
MARINERS

RISE OF THE
CAJUN
MARINERS

THE RACE FOR BIG OIL

WOODY FALGOUX

Skyhorse Publishing

Skyhorse Publishing books may be purchased in bulk at special discounts for sales
promotion, corporate gifts, fund-raising, or educational purposes. Special editions
can also be created to specifications. For details, contact the Special Sales
Department, Skyhorse Publishing, 307 West 36th Street, 11th Floor, New York,
NY 10018 or info@skyhorsepublishing.com.

Skyhorse® and Skyhorse Publishing® are registered trademarks of Skyhorse
Publishing, Inc.®, a Delaware corporation.

Visit our website at www.skyhorsepublishing.com.

10 9 8 7 6 5 4 3 2

Library of Congress Cataloging-in-Publication Data is available on file.

Cover design by Rain Saukas
Cover photo credit: iStockphoto

Paperback ISBN: 978-1-5107-6990-8
Ebook ISBN: 978-1-5107-1846-3

Printed in the United States of America

Contents

———∞∞∞———

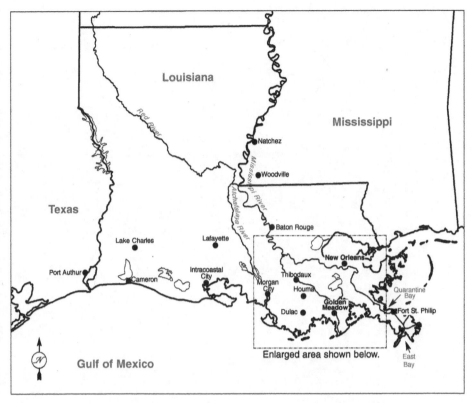

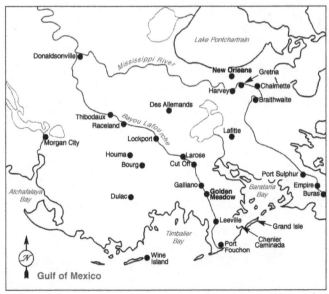

Introduction

Back in 2001, I underestimated this story. I knew that its colorful, real-life characters took extreme risks to build their industry, but I didn't anticipate how much their oral histories would entertain me. These oilfield boat business pioneers told tales that made me gape, laugh, cringe, and almost cry. Their rise and race to the top of their profession formed a book first published in April 2007 and reprinted multiple times thereafter. Now, almost ten years after the first printing, it is time to update their story. For this new edition, I revisited with the featured families and have written a new Afterword.

It's difficult for me to believe it's been fifteen years since my first interview. On that day, November 27, 2001, I drove down a flat, winding road along Bayou Lafourche to Golden Meadow, a tiny Louisiana town about seventy-five miles southwest of New Orleans. Staring through the willow trees at the docked shrimp boats and oilfield tugs, I tried to recall if I'd ever heard of my first interviewee, Bobby Orgeron. I'd grown up less than an hour up the bayou from Bobby's hometown of Golden Meadow. While I knew many of Bobby's contemporaries in the oilfield, Bobby's name didn't ring a bell. I had no idea what to expect of him.

Bobby's son Lee Orgeron wanted an author to write about the early days of the marine oilfield, a story that up until that point had been almost completely undocumented. I knew that although the oil and gas industry is the planet's largest business, much of its inner workings remained a mystery to most people. There had been very few popular books and films on the subject.

The lack of media attention has been particularly true in regard to the offshore oilfield, which only seems to earn significant coverage in the wake of an epic disaster like the BP Oil Spill of 2010. For instance, in Daniel Yergin's 1991 Pulitizer-winning book, *The Prize*, the definitive work on the history of oil and gas, Yergin makes only one reference to the Gulf of Mexico, the birthplace of offshore oil.

Yet, make no mistake, the global economy is dependent on production from offshore rigs. In the United States, offshore mineral revenues account for the largest source of federal income outside of the treasury department. In many third-world countries, offshore petroleum provides the majority of the nations' income.

I also knew that this lucrative industry cannot exist without workboats. These vessels can be as small as the 20-foot crew boats that transport workers to the rigs on shallow inland bays, or as large as a 360-foot supply boat, which hauls equipment and provisions to oceanic rigs operating in ten thousand feet of water depth. These capable vessels, which now sail the seven seas, began as something simple, a Louisiana shrimp boat, oyster lugger or fishing skiff, a wooden hull with a low-power engine. The small vessel and its Cajun captain were the geneses of what became an enormous business.

Given the industry's wide scope but almost unknown history, Lee Orgeron's project intrigued me. Workboats had piqued my interest ever since my boyhood. All my life, I'd admired the regal vessels as they glided down our waterways like marine chariots. When I'd pass by the boatmen's mansions along Bayou Lafourche, I'd hear bits of their improbable stories and wonder just how they had achieved their success.

But writing an honest account about the boat business worried me, too, and I expressed my reservations right away to Lee. Growing up on the bayou, I knew how corrupt the oilfield used to be; I didn't want to write the book unless I could also be fair to the reader and depict the industry's dark side, too. When I brought up this issue to Lee, he shrugged. He didn't see any reason why the boat barons couldn't tell the whole story.

And to the boatmen's credit, most of them did. After interviewing many of the industry's pioneers, I settled on four of them, all of whom were native French speakers and who had risen out of a poor, unlettered culture. They lived along lower Bayou Lafourche in and around tiny Golden Meadow. From the bayou, they blazed the world's seas. In so doing, they walked a line that constantly teetered between fortune and financial ruin. Their stories exemplify how the Cajuns established their place in oilfield history, right alongside the Texans and the Russians, the Rockefellers and the Rothschilds, and the Shahs and the Shieks.

Who are the Cajuns? Today, we are a people from a mix of ethnicities with mostly French surnames who inhabit a triangle of rural land bordered by southeast Texas on the west, the suburbs of New Orleans on the east and the center of Louisiana on the north. Either we speak French or our parents or grandparents did. The term "Cajuns" derives from the Acadians, the people whom the British forced out of Acadia, what is now Nova Scotia, Canada, in 1755 and dispersed all over the world. This expulsion, *Le Grande Derangement*, is the tragic and inspiring heart of our culture.

In truth, the only way to know the people who developed the offshore oilfield is to understand the Acadian story, which began in the mid-1600s when thousands of mainland French immigrated to eastern Canada to escape France for reasons that ranged from violent clashes with the Protestants to starvation to witch hunts. The settlers initially found peace in Acadia. Politically, the Acadians did their best to stay away from the ever-present French and English conflict as Acadia changed hands between the two crowns nine times during the seventeenth and eighteenth centuries. Although the Acadians were French at heart, they were neutral in fact.

In the 1750s, during and after the French and Indian War when Acadia was in English hands, the British governor of Acadia decided he could no longer tolerate the Acadians' neutrality. The governor demanded the Acadians sign an unconditional oath of allegiance to the British crown. By signing the oath, the Acadians would have essentially agreed to, if commanded, take up arms against their mother country and against their friends the Indians and also to possibly give up their Catholic religion. The Acadians refused the oath and soon felt the consequences.

In 1755, the British began an effort to rid Acadia of the Acadians. The Brits detained the people, then burned their homes and crops and confiscated their land and cattle. As the soldiers herded the Acadians onto navy vessels, their motive was not simply to uproot and deport the Acadians. It was to break the family unit and destroy the culture. In some cases, the British placed parents and children on different vessels.

The English navy scattered the Acadians across the globe, taking them down the Atlantic seaboard to the American colonies and across the Atlantic to English prison camps. Many braved a brutal winter while on board cold, crowded ships, and as smallpox and other afflictions entered the vessels' damp, cramped holds, hundreds of Acadians died before reaching their destination.

For those who survived the voyage, some became indentured servants on plantations; others endured disastrous resettlement schemes on remote places like the windy, sterile South American Falkland Islands and the disease-ridden Santo Domingo. Those who did not succumb to sickness still had to cope with separation from their people, land, and culture. In some instances, the deportation permanently separated nuclear families, meaning wives would never again see their husbands, and parents would never again lay eyes on their children.

In the years that followed, the once unified Acadians settled all over the world and watched their culture begin to die from assimilation. For instance, in the British colonies of Maryland and Pennsylvania, Acadians became frustrated as they witnessed their children adopt English as their primary language. As the Acadians' separation and identity anxieties increased, they sought a refuge where they could maintain their culture. Word soon spread that an ideal place of reunion and resettlement was Catholic Louisiana, a then-Spanish, formerly French, and still Francophone colony. Beginning in 1766, after the Acadians arrived in the southern reaches of the present state of Louisiana, their descendants established one of America's only truly homegrown cultures, combining with mainland French, German, Spanish, African and Native American people to create their own language, cuisine, music, and architecture.

Honestly, I didn't consider the Acadian/Cajun history when I first sat down with Bobby Orgeron in his old paneled office across from the docks on Bayou Lafourche. He acted as if he had no story, telling me, "I don't know why you want to know about boats." But his words belied the tales told by his own appearance. His tall, slender body had obviously lived a hard sixty-nine years, enduring beatings by the sun, the waves, and the fast pace of oilfield days and nights. He didn't have to say another word without me knowing that his wary eyes had seen much.

During that first interview, it took us a while before we even discussed his career in the boat business. He spent hours talking mostly about growing up in Golden Meadow in the 1930s, where the dominant language was Cajun French, the sole religion was Catholic, and the tension was thick between the Cajuns and the invading "Texiens," the English-speaking Protestant oilmen from Texas and other parts of the American South. In our first sitting, Bobby and I never discussed workboats in any great detail because there was too much to learn about the background of their captains. These were people who were delivered by midwives, treated by faith healers, and raised on "the fat of the land," without electricity, indoor plumbing, or any of modern conveniences we cannot live without today.

After the interview, as I drove home alongside the bayou's oyster luggers tied up next to oilfield supply vessels, something hit me. I realized that it was the Cajun culture that formed the men who built an industry that now helps fuel the world, and that I couldn't write a marine oilfield history without telling it through the eyes of the Cajuns.

From Cajun generation to generation, strengthened by their Acadian exile, the Cajuns became masters at adaptation, particularly when it came to designing and operating boats to meet the needs of their changing world. Whether it was crafting a "grocery boat" narrow enough to navigate the slim bayous that snaked through the trapping leases that covered the Louisiana marsh or adapting a seafood vessel to work as an oilfield tug, the Cajuns made it possible for the marine oilfield to launch from the shallow inland Louisiana bays across the globe to the deep treacherous waters of the world's oceans.

With the Cajuns raised on fighting hurricanes and having to rebuild their post-storm lives, they were well prepared to battle the unpredictable whims of the oilfield, including the alternating boom and doom years of the 1950s and 1960s, up to the roaring 1970s, down into the 1980s' bust and through the changing realities of the 2000s. Consequently, this book *had to be* the story of four interwoven Cajun lives with a plot that would turn most often on the life of Bobby Orgeron.

Bobby, as a young man, was a tall, wiry whip, who bounced with frenetic energy and operated at breakneck speed. Bobby launched his career as a sixteen-year-old crew-boat captain for his overbearing father Juan. Juan's oppressiveness would actually motivate Bobby's climb through the business.

Like Bobby, Minor Cheramie received his start on the deck of a boat. As a young man, Minor looked and moved like a rugged matinee idol. He was obsessed with cleanliness, women, and alcohol, though the drink could turn Minor's fun-loving, Dr. Jekyll personality into that of a mean Mr. Hyde. Despite Minor's dark side, he was a doting father and a zealous philanthropist. He was also ambitious, determined to develop the industry's ultimate supply boat.

Unlike Bobby and Minor, Nolty Theriot never captained a boat. Nolty, a tan, handsome, fireplug of a man, was constantly moving forward, literally and figuratively. His mind bristled with new boat concepts. He would eventually design, build, and operate the seminal oilfield tugboat to ply the North Sea. Nolty was also more educated than his contemporaries; he'd graduated from high school and even attended college for a time. But Nolty's drive was arguably greater than that of his less-refined brethren. His spark came from a near-death experience in World War II.

Unlike Bobby, Minor, and Nolty, Sidney Savoie made conservative decisions. Sidney, a little man with big, owl-like eyes, advanced slowly and steadily. Sidney also refused to participate in the out-of-control oilfield entertainment scene. The issue was whether he could turn down all the drinking, whoring, and gift giving and still succeed.

The seedier side of the oilfield haunted all of the boatmen. But dealing with dark temptations was only one of their challenges. While they would ultimately rake in millions of dollars and help make the multibillion dollar offshore industry what it is today, their first and most basic goal was simply staying alive.

Survival, I realized during my first interview with Bobby Orgeron, was central to the *Cajun Mariners'* story. And I would learn much more about what "surviving" fully meant for Bobby in my subsequent interviews with him; it wasn't simply enduring but also escaping, whether it was running away from the Guatemalan navy, evading a Louisiana game warden, or dodging death in one of his nine totaled-vehicle car wrecks. As the following pages reveal, it would take all nine of Bobby Orgeron's lives to tell his tale, one that was certainly worthy of preserving.

Woody Falgoux
Thibodaux, Louisiana
August 11, 2016

Bobby Orgeron's first boat, *Davey Lou No. 4*.
(Courtesy of the Orgeron family)

Prologue

Part One: Prelude in the Gulf

Bobby Orgeron was under attack. Rain pelted him. Waves bombarded him. With each big breaker, his small crew boat rose into the air, and then slammed into the Gulf of Mexico.

As the water slapped his face, he spit out the salty spray and wiped his burning eyes. His boat tumbled, and he struggled to keep his balance. Suppressing a shiver, Bobby reached for the radio.

His *Davey Lou No. 4* was anchored, but in this weather the anchor wouldn't hold much longer. He wondered what he was still doing out here on the water. The rig's boss, the toolpusher, didn't seem to care that a hurricane was coming. The rig was right there, only a few hundred yards away from Bobby, but he couldn't see it in the dark storm. He could make out whitecaps and not much else. Despite the conditions, the pusher had asked him to stand by.

But this was something Bobby could barely do. As Bobby could, surely the pusher smelled the ozone. Surely he could feel the cool wind and hear it howl. The pusher knew this black, angry storm already had a name, Flossie, and it was obvious that she was coming right for them. If the pusher had any compassion, he would have ordered Bobby to attempt to pick up the rig's crew and take them to shore. However, when Bobby had made this offer, the pusher's answer was no. Now, Bobby could only worry about his own life. If he evacuated now, he had a chance to survive.

He was just off Wine Island Pass, not that far from the good, safe earth of Terrebonne Parish, Louisiana.

His chance for escape was now or never. He certainly didn't want to ride out Flossie alone in a 41-foot boat. While he was generally not afraid of high seas and believed his lean, six-feet-three, twenty-four-year-old body could do anything, Flossie definitely had him thinking.

The last thing he wanted to do was push the pusher. You didn't do that in the oilfield. You catered to the drillers and the operators. You showed them you'd try anything. He radioed the rig and told the pusher, "Man, I'm standing by out here. It's getting rough. I just can't stay out here by myself in this boat. Can you let me go inside the pass?"

"No, you gotta stay with the rig," said the pusher.

This was ridiculous. It would be at least two days before they could even think about drilling again. Bobby told the pusher, "Y'all on that rig up there. Y'all not being shaken. I'm being shaken to hell out here."

"Look, if you leave the rig, you lose your job."

Bobby knew that this was coming, and because this was the oilfield, he figured it would come that bluntly. But there wasn't much he could tell the man. This *Davey Lou No. 4* was his first and only boat, and this was his first and maybe his only chance to make a name for himself in the boat business. He had notes to pay and a new wife to feed. He'd finally started to prove to his father, his father-in-law, and the rest of his doubters that he might become someone. Of course, he was a long way from proving it completely. But he was planning to be a millionaire by the time he was thirty-five, and he didn't want this pusher to stop him.

The *maudit* oilfield, he thought. Rush, rush. Run, run. Drill, drill. If you're not drilling, you're not making money. That was all that mattered. To hell with everything else—hurricanes, lives.

Maybe Bobby would go into protected waters and wait. Because of the poor visibility, the pusher might not even notice if Bobby slipped inside the shoreline. But Bobby couldn't do that without saying something first. He pressed the receiver button and spoke, "I'll go inside the pass, where it's not so rough, and I'll anchor there."

"No," said the pusher, "I need you to stay."

"I can't."

"Well, if you leave, you lose your job."

"Well, I'm sorry. I'm not gonna lose my life for a job."

That's it. *C'est tout. C'est finis.* He couldn't look back. He decided to pull up anchor. He started to climb from the deck onto the gunwale. He had to walk along the side to get to the anchor at the bow's tip.

As soon as he put his foot on the gunwale, a wave crashed against the boat and knocked him to the deck. He got up, steadied himself, and looked at the bow. While the distance to its tip was only a few feet, it seemed like miles. With the breakers pounding the boat, he didn't see how he could walk the length of the gunwale to the anchor, pull it up, and then make it back to the cabin.

How big were these waves anyway? Eight feet. Twelve feet. Fifteen? It was too dark to tell. But hurricanes could throw up thirty to sixty footers, and the way he was anchored, a much smaller wave could easily flip him.

Until now, he'd been doing so well. His one-boat company had a steady job with Standard Oil Company of Indiana (Stanolind) making $40 per day. During a typical hitch, he'd work for thirty days, and then pay someone to relieve him for three days.

For the most part, the work was manageable. On a normal day, he'd run the drilling crew to and from the rig to the Stanolind dock in Dulac, twenty-five miles inside the shoreline.

But the job's schedule could also be taxing. At times, the oil company would abruptly shift his crew changes from days to nights, throwing off his sleep patterns. And whatever his routine, he was on call around the clock. If the rig needed him to make a one-passenger run in the middle of the night, transporting a mechanic or a special tool, Bobby had to wake up and leave as soon as his cargo arrived. He understood the crucial nature of these trips: without a necessary tool or specialist, the rig couldn't drill; the company couldn't make money; and, in a greater sense, the oilfield couldn't function.

This job with Stanolind was Bobby's first offshore work. His assigned rig, the *Mr. Charlie*, was the world's first transportable, submersible drilling barge. But the rig's landmark novelty didn't offer any thrill to Bobby; he was indifferent to the type of rig he serviced. He was only concerned with doing his work and whittling down his note.

Before today, Bobby hadn't seen anything unusual or particularly hazardous about working off the coast, especially just barely off Timbalier Island, only thirty miles southwest of his hometown, Golden Meadow. It was no different from running to the rigs on the inland bays.

But now, as Hurricane Flossie whirled toward south Louisiana, the danger of offshore work was engulfing him. He was only a couple of miles from safety, but he wasn't sure how to take the first step. In truth, he had no idea what to do. He'd pissed off the pusher. He'd lost his job. Maybe he'd ruined his reputation.

Whatever he'd done, he had to put it past him. Before that final, lethal breaker hit, he had to find a way to reach the anchor.

Part Two: Preface to a Decision
September 1956

What was happening to Bobby during Hurricane Flossie was no different from what Sidney Savoie was facing. At the time, Sidney, his two deck-hands, and his 55-foot tugboat were pushing two barges out on Timbalier Bay, a few miles west of Bayou Lafourche; and the storm's rain bands stood between them and home. While the tug was making her way up the little channel that ran through the bay, she seemed to be running only on fate. The waves were so high the bay might as well have been the deepwater Gulf. Sidney couldn't see anything but driving rain and whitecaps.

It was an odd feeling because, when behind the wheel, Sidney was used to really *seeing*. His eyes were large, more circular than oval, full of hazel light and always wide open. At five-feet-six with his hairline receding, the forty-four-year-old man had the appearance of a little wise man.

But his sagacity, both in look and in reality, was not very useful now on the bay where, most of the time, he couldn't tell the rain from the waves. It was as if he was inside a washing machine, with the only thing visible being tumbling water.

His vessel's radar might have warned him of any structures and an occasional channel marker, but it couldn't come close to delineating the channel's true boundaries. Sidney could have been inches from running aground. He had no way of knowing. With Flossie's bands turning Timbalier into an overflowing cauldron, he didn't want to chance riding out the tempest in the mud. When the brunt of Flossie entered the bay, the storm surge might fill up his boat with wave-wash and rain. Or it might turn her over. He wasn't taking any chances.

So he forged onward, praying, guessing, and feeling. When he felt the slightest bottom resistance on his port or his starboard, he pulled the other way. He was barely moving; if he sailed any slower, he couldn't have controlled the barges on his bow.

When he made it from the bay to a canal to Bayou Lafourche, he sighed. Then finally, the village of Leeville appeared out of the tumult. Within minutes, he was tied up at the Gulf Oil dock.

Sidney stepped into the Gulf office wet and shivering. Waiting for him was a Gulf transportation superintendent, a man who was both Sidney's client and friend.

"Sid," the Gulf man said, "I need you to go back out." Sidney didn't know how to react.

The Gulf man told him that valuable equipment might be destroyed. He wanted Sidney to retrieve it.

When Sidney asked if there were any people out there, the man said he didn't think so.

Sidney didn't understand. With the storm only growing more violent, this was a ludicrous request for anyone to make, much less his friend.

During Sidney's seven-year relationship with Gulf Oil, he had answered the company's call many times. In fact, he'd never, ever told them no. But did Gulf really expect Sidney to risk his deckhands' lives for some lifeless equipment? Why would one friend place another in peril for the futile pursuit of salvaging a bunch of metal?

It was the oilfield at its most insane, and it didn't matter whether Sidney heeded or refused the Gulf man's orders. Either way, he stood to lose.

Part Three: Precursor to Bankruptcy
1959

Losing was exactly what was happening to Nolty Theriot in the late 1950s. In his case, the loss was financial. Frankly, in the spring of 1959, Nolty's business was drowning. It wasn't only the banknotes, but the past-due accounts with his suppliers, everyone from the insurance companies to the paint store to the grocery. Some invoices were six months past due, and Nolty had to convince his vendors to give him more time.

The fact that the suppliers trusted him defied good business sense. Although the confident thirty-four-year-old had the ability to make people believe in him, that spring, his creditors' trust was beginning to fade.

One of Nolty's CPAs, Dan Carroll, was shocked at how Nolty could linger so long on credit. Carroll, who'd recently graduated from Louisiana State University and was helping his father with the annual audit at Nolty's Golden Meadow office, had never seen anything like it with the firm's other clients in Baton Rouge, which was 130 miles to the north. Carroll's other customers either paid their bills on time or went out of business.

But things were different on the bayou, where, as the oilfield dipped in the late 1950s, it sometimes took the boat companies a year to pay Carroll's firm for the previous year's audit. Carroll would soon learn that when it came to market swings, the bayou's boat companies were a breed apart. Between Theriot and some of his other boat clients, he'd sometimes watch a balance sheet jump from a negative $200,000 to a $500,000 profit in six months.

But at times, the companies went bankrupt, and this year, that was exactly where Nolty J. Theriot, Inc. was heading. On some accounts, Nolty was a *full year* past due. In all, the debt was nearly half a million dollars. If his creditors decided to force Nolty's hand, they could bankrupt him on the spot.

For Carroll, verifying all the debt was painful. He was just getting to know Nolty and thought highly of him. He winced when he thought about the man having to close his business.

Then, in the middle of the pile of pink paper and red inky mess, Carroll heard someone running up the steps. Nolty, with a huge grin on his face, bolted into the room. How could he be smiling?

Of course, Nolty constantly grinned. He always sported a handsome, healthy look, with his dark pirate skin, his happy eyes that squinted dramatically when he smiled, and his barrel-chested, five-feet-ten-inch frame that was always edging forward, always ready to pounce on the next prospect.

An outright jubilant Nolty looked at Carroll's father and said, "Mr. Carroll, Mr. Carroll, come over here and let me show you something."

The Carrolls followed Nolty to the window and looked down on the narrow parking space between the office and the highway. A blazing new

1959 Cadillac filled their vision. Her trunk wings were flaring and her rocket booster taillights were shining. Nolty explained that he'd just driven her off the lot in New Orleans.

Carroll's father looked aghast. "Nolty," he said. "What in the world are you doing buying a new Cadillac? You owe everybody up and down the bayou. You can't afford to buy a toothbrush, and you buy a brand-new car?"

"Mr. Carroll," said Nolty. "You know that, and I know that, but *they* don't know that."

"Huh?"

"They don't know that I'm broke. If I drove an old rusty Chevrolet, they'd worry about their money. But with me driving this car, they're not worried about their money."

They, Nolty explained, were the transportation men at Brown & Root, a big oilfield construction contractor in Houston, where Nolty was headed with his Cadillac.

Dan Carroll listened to Nolty talk about his plan to woo more business. He couldn't believe how self-assured the man was; it was as if he were Howard Hughes. Somehow with only negative money to his name, Nolty had convinced the car dealership to sell him that winged Cadillac. But Carroll wondered how Nolty would buy the gas to get to Houston and find the funds to take his clients out to eat.

He doubted Nolty could make it through the trip, much less save his company from insolvency. Nolty J. Theriot Inc. would be lucky to live through the summer.

Part Four: Preview to a Price
1952

The challenges facing boatmen like Nolty also affected their wives. In the early 1950s, Minor Cheramie's wife, Lou, realized that she had to share her husband's commitment to the business. Mostly, she supported Minor's efforts to sell his company and his personality because it was his charisma—not his vessels—that set him apart.

Often, the jockeying for business went on at night, and because the oilmen were at the Golden Meadow bars, Lou recognized that Minor had to be there, too. She understood his impact in a public place and knew firsthand that when Minor moved, people watched. Physically imposing and handsome, Minor was a tapered six-feet-two with a long, deep face and what she called a thin "Errol Flynn mustache." He was a more muscular version of Flynn, a rough-cut, bronzed movie star. But it wasn't just his blue eyes and deep raspy voice that attracted attention nor was it his thick black hair with the trademark curlicue at the peak. It was merely his presence.

Sometimes, Lou asked Minor if she could accompany him to the bars, but he usually said no. It wasn't as if she could go these days; she had an infant daughter to look after. But before Deanie was born, she had certainly been game. She'd still like to get out once in a while and have her mother watch Deanie. And why would he not want to take out his cute, petite, brown-eyed wife? But Minor didn't want her in a barroom. He had too much business to do there.

Lou, however, sensed that her husband wasn't all business at the Glo Room and his other haunts. He'd been a ladies' man when she'd met him, and he still was. The perfume on his clothes was too strong to think otherwise. The feminine scent overpowered even the rankness of male body odor, smoke, and Scotch whiskey. As for the drink, Minor had a problem with that, too. If he drank beer, he was a fairly happy drunk. But anything stronger and he could become out of control. He would sometimes come home sloppy, slurry, and sporting a black eye, then go back out the next night like nothing had happened.

But oh Lord, Lou thought, look at how sweet he is with Deanie. He loves his little peanut. He's so gentle and kind and careful with her. Maybe Deanie would change him. Maybe her presence would make him realize how much he had here at home and how little he had at the bars.

But as the months passed, Lou was not so sure. One particular night, she was sleeping peacefully. One moment, she was dreaming. The next, the dream was breaking. She didn't know what roused her at first. Perhaps it was the jostling or his ear-opening voice, or maybe it was the mingling odors of cigarettes, whiskey, and other women. Whatever it was, her husband wanted her up to make breakfast.

He turned on the lamp, and the light stung her eyes. As her ears began to tune, she could hear voices in the living room. Minor had brought home friends again, or was it clients, or was there a difference?

She could hear Texiens jawing their twang in the den. She could only groan, knowing she'd have to get up before they ransacked the kitchen and woke up little Deanie.

"Come on, *allons*," Minor rasped.

"I'm coming. Don't you wake Deanie up."

She rolled out of bed and threw on her robe, splashed some water on her face, and put her hand on her hair. It was of no use. She didn't have time to gussy up.

When she walked out into the hall, she heard all the predictable words from the smoky men as she made her way to the refrigerator. Sometimes, it seemed as if these oilmen were the only friends she could have. While Minor had the freedom to make friends with anyone and everyone, it was difficult for Lou to find time to maintain a friendship. Lou's old friends? Out of necessity, they'd grown apart. Lou's new friends? Minor would introduce her to the oilmen's wives. They'd have plenty to talk about.

The oilmen were spitting their drunken blather now. At least a plate of breakfast would quiet them. Of course, Minor could make eggs and bacon. He loved to cook, him. But in front of these men, he wanted a servant.

He took pride in full service and that didn't stop at the boat dock. It extended into his home and required his wife to be on call, too.

Lou felt like a robot whipping these eggs in the grease. She was so sleepy she could barely smell the bacon fat. She could only go through the motions and put the plates in front of the smiling heathens, who tore into the food.

Her attention then shifted to Minor. And after a few bites, she got a reaction. "Needs a little mustard, *bé*. Not enough of it in the batter."

Not enough. Too much. Undercooked. Overcooked. He was going to say something. For now, she'd let it lie. With these dignitaries around, she didn't want to say what she was thinking. Instead, she put a bottle of mustard in front of him.

As the men gulped, Lou watched her husband hold forth, telling a story that was actually funny, and she wondered where he was going with it. With all of it. They had some money now. They had boats. Minor was still looking for another angle, but when he found it, would that be enough? When he was bubbling over with boats, hopefully, he would then stop the drinking, carousing, and the early morning breakfast demands.

The potential was there. He was so tender with Deanie that you would never think he could be like he was now. But when Deanie wasn't present, and he was drinking, it was as if he didn't care. Of course, he didn't have to take the evil potion. Perhaps real success, whatever that was, would make him stop.

Lou wanted to succeed, too. She was aware that she was a big part of Minor's team. So she'd give the oilmen seconds, if that was what they wanted. She'd pour them more coffee, pick up their plates, and clean up their mess.

One day, they'd want Minor's boats so badly she wouldn't have to be jolted out of bed. But until then, she'd rise early and light the stove.

Lou and Minor Cheramie (Courtesy of L & M Botruct, Inc.)

I

The Launch

Guidry & Savoie's *Susan G* makes waves in 1951.
(Courtesy of Central Gulf Towing, Inc.)

Chapter 1

The Boy

August 1937

⸺◦◦◦⸺

Bobby Orgeron had always thirsted for boats. Even at age five, he felt their pull. He loved their shape and their power. He relished the brush of their bow wind, the hum of their engines, and the smell of their exhaust.

These boats in front of Bobby traveled on a seemingly limitless waterway. A trip down this Bayou Lafourche could lead him twenty-two miles to the Gulf of Mexico and, from the Gulf, to the world.

But to go anywhere, he needed a boat. The railroad didn't reach Golden Meadow. The bayou road's pavement ended at the town limits, and the rest of the highway north was far from smooth.

The water, however, flowed deeply and freely. On its tea-black surface, white boats glided like swans.

On these boats, things happened. People were moved. Seafood was harvested. Waters were parted and waves were conquered.

With a boat, an illiterate man could make a living and buy a ticket to almost any life.

Bobby's father, Juan Orgeron, was such a man. Juan was completely unlettered, having had just three days of schooling. The only thing he could write was his name. The only language he could speak was the local French. But his new boat gave him hope.

As Juan's year-old, 48-foot-long *Herman J* approached the bank, Bobby watched in admiration. The *Herman J* was a wooden, round-bottom, pointed front hull with a 30-horsepower diesel engine. Juan's presence dominated the wheelhouse. At six-feet-six-inches, he was a giant in a land of smaller Gallic men.

He was also, in many senses, a hard man. Mentally and physically toughened, he was sometimes harsh and often unyielding. His rough edge came from his hunger; he'd felt the pain of an empty stomach and the shame of poverty. When Bobby, his second son, was born on January 19, 1932, Juan couldn't even afford to pay the skilled midwife. Tante Ca-Ca pulled the baby expertly from his mother's womb, but when it came time to pay her $3 fee, Juan could only scrounge up $1.35.

Before Bobby's birth, times for his family had been even worse. His grandfather had taken the whole clan to Violet, Louisiana, east of the Mississippi. They'd gone in search of a shrimping fortune and come back starving.

Bobby's father's starvation hadn't ceased. His belly might have been full of fricassée, but somehow he was still hungry. Bobby could see this as Juan parked the *Herman J* and immediately started cleaning it. As he hosed and scrubbed, he seemed to thrive on the sweat pouring from him. Bobby, of course, jumped on the boat and helped him.

This boat may have been called a shrimp boat, but her nets were rarely used. Her real purpose was to serve as a *glacier*, an iceboat, which was really a floating shrimp wholesaler and grocery deliverer.

Bobby remembered making these pick-up/delivery trips with his father that summer. He could still see the smiling faces of the shrimpers on Timbalier Bay, just west of Bayou Lafourche. These people were the happiest alive when Juan delivered their food, packed their shrimp in the *Herman J*'s icy hold, paid them for the difference between their catch and the cost of the groceries, and then began taking new grocery orders.

Bobby remembered how, when his father took an order, he didn't scribble down words like some people. He drew symbols. If a man had big ears or a big nose, Juan drew an ear or a nose; if he had a crew cut, Juan would draw a crew cut. If the shrimper made a special request other than the usual amount of bread, beans, salt meat, and rice, Juan drew a picture of the request or simply remembered it.

Memory, Bobby learned, was everything. It was not just for grocery orders, but navigation, superstition, religion, and recipes. It was also medicine. While a formally educated doctor had been in town since 1928, most of the people didn't visit him. They either couldn't afford him or used other methods. They saw a *traiteur*. Bobby's grandmother, his "Mémal," was one of these folk healers. She healed from memory with prayers and home remedies. Everything around her, even the tobacco she chewed, was medicine.

When Bobby had an earache, Mémal either blew smoke in his ear or patched it with tobacco. When he had a cold, she put the fatty *coin* of salt meat on his chest and smeared it with mustard and salve. The odor itself seemed to kill the cold. It was so strong he didn't want to breathe, much less cough. For other maladies, Mémal had innumerable poultices and words of faith.

Faith was what Bobby had in his father and in his father's boat. There was a practicality in the capacity of her hold, in the buoyancy of her hull, and the pitch of her propeller. Bobby knew, even then, that boats were money.

As far as he could tell, school was not. School was a living nightmare. The teacher barked a strange, harsh language. This English was far from the melodic singsong of his native tongue.

Bobby quickly learned that a few French words out of his mouth would land him on his knees in the corner. But how was he supposed to avoid this predicament when almost every word he knew was French and he had to use words to communicate?

In the winter, school got worse. His father moved the family for the trapping season to a tar-paper shack camp that skirted the Bayou Sauvage marsh. The closest school was in Gentilly, in the outer reaches of New Orleans. To Bobby's schoolmates there, he was more than a non-English speaker, he was a Boogalee, a New Orleanian's derogatory term for a *Cadien*, or Cajun.

The city boys teased Bobby about his hand-me-down coveralls and his shirts made from salt sacks. They laughed when the teachers punished him and his relocated Cadien friends for huddling together and whispering in French. Times were hard that winter in Gentilly and, really, no softer that summer back in Golden Meadow. In both places, there was no electricity, no telephone, and no indoor plumbing.

But Bobby Orgeron had hope. And it was more than the nautical promise that floated right by his dock. It was in his town's very name, Golden Meadow.

The oilfield booms in Golden Meadow in the 1930s.
Top: A road ravaged by oilfield trucks as derricks loom in the middle of town.
Bottom: A well blows out just outside of town.
(Photos courtesy of Lafourche Heritage Society)

Chapter 2

The Golden Meadow

The trailblazer was Bobby's ancestor William Riley Williams. He was the father of Joseph, grandfather of Rosella, great-grandfather of Juan Orgeron, great-great-grandfather of Mavis Orgeron, and the founder of what became Golden Meadow.

When William Riley Williams arrived on Bayou Lafourche in 1842, he was only eleven years old and, presumably, an orphan. He traveled with a man named Lusk and a woman named Brant. They were the first three white settlers on what would become the Golden Meadow ridge. But he, the boy wonder William Riley, would always be known as the town's father.

Back then, of course, it wasn't even a town. What William Riley Williams found was a far cry from the hilly Victorian city he had come from, Natchez, Mississippi. He'd departed the dry, red dirt and landed in moist, black mud. He'd left the cottony lair of the Protestant-landed gentry and moved to a wet, wild country once ruled by pirates and now inhabited by Catholic Cadiens. Here in lower Lafourche, he discovered a mystical place, with dragonflies that hovered like fairies over a luminous green wilderness. It was as flat as flat got, and in every sense, it was much newer than his old Natchez hills.

It hadn't been very long since the land itself was created. Less than a millennium before, the Mississippi River had shifted its bed westward from the Chandeleur Islands and started dumping sediment here, extend-

ing the continent out into the sea. Spring after spring, the river over-
flowed its banks and dumped virgin, level earth. From that new ground
sprung tropical growth, gnarly live oaks, bright flowers, and thick brush.
Even after the river pushed its bed back east, the tributary it left, Bayou
Lafourche, continued to flood and create new land.

And it was this ever-changing landscape that greeted young William
Riley Williams. What he found on Bayou Lafourche was a mile of ridge
stretching from the bayou in each direction. And where the dry ground
stopped, miles of verdant marsh extended beyond the horizon. The
marshland appeared to be a panoramic field of winter wheat. But on closer
observation, it wasn't a great meadow, but an endless soggy system of
floating pasture, broken occasionally by ponds, bayous, or isolated oak
ridges.

Here, William Riley Williams would grow into a man. He would
lose his Anglo ways and become a Cadien. He would marry a girl from
coastal Cheniere Caminada and socialize with the Cheramies and the
Doucets. When the Civil War broke out, he would don the uniform of
the Confederacy and go into battle. It was not as if he shared the Confed-
erate cause. States' rights? In this remote frontier, neither the state of
Louisiana nor the United States really governed him. Slavery? He probably had no slaves and no need for them. The local trades were seafood
and fur trapping. All the great sugarcane plantations were several miles
up the bayou. Nevertheless, William Riley Williams served in the Rebel
Army and, at his service's end, returned to lower Lafourche to see his
children grow up and grandchildren come into the world.

When he died in 1899, his land was part of a small village with fewer
than eight homes. But within the next sixteen years, William Riley Williams' descendants would watch the little village transform into a town
with more than one thousand people.

The transformation began in 1903 when Yankee settlers arrived in
lower Lafourche hoping to make an agricultural fortune. These Michi-
ganders got off their boats, looked into their crystal balls, and predicted
a golden crop yield. They gazed at the fields and sighed at the glimmer of
wild goldenrods, gilding and yellowing the earth. This glowing, sun-
swept nirvana, they apparently concluded, had to be called "Golden
Meadow."

Golden Meadow's new residents attempted to drain the marsh and grow rice. They dug a waterway the locals dubbed the Yankee Canal and planned a future Holland. But these *Americains* paid no attention to the marsh's below-sea-level elevation or to its resistance to staying dry.

The locals looked at their new neighbors' farming experiment and predicted failure. And they were right. It wasn't long before the Yankees gave up their dream and left their Golden Meadow.

In 1915, as the Yankees departed and headed back north, Cadien newcomers arrived from the south. They were fleeing the marsh town of Leeville, after having started their migration twenty-two years earlier in the coastal community of Cheniere Caminada. During this period, they had survived a string of Biblical disasters.

The first was in 1893 when a hurricane destroyed Cheniere Caminada, a peninsula located on the Gulf of Mexico, twenty-five miles southeast of Golden Meadow. On October 1, 1893, roughly 1,500 people lived on the Cheniere. One day later, more than half of them were dead.

Many of the dead bodies were so mangled they were unrecognizable. In some places, human remains completely covered the ground. The people had no choice but to dig mass graves and bury hundreds of corpses.

Almost all of the living would leave Cheniere Caminada. While some families scattered throughout southeast Louisiana, many of them headed directly across the marsh, a few miles west to the Bayou Lafourche hamlet of Leeville.

By 1904, the Cheniere storm survivors had turned Leeville into a town of 1,700 people. Then, one year later, another catastrophe struck. In 1905, yellow fever drifted into Leeville and ravaged for forty days. Dead bodies piled up so quickly that a new cemetery was created.

In 1909, nature battered Leeville again. A hurricane ransacked the town and killed an infant. Everyone else escaped only because their boats, formerly powered solely by sail and by paddle, now had gasoline engines.

These same *gazzolines* saved them again in 1915 when an even larger hurricane hit Leeville. This storm's 140-mile-per-hour winds destroyed ninety-nine of the town's one hundred buildings.

Many of Leeville's people decided they could no longer risk living so close to the coast. They motored up the bayou to Golden Meadow and settled on a ridge only two feet above sea level, but ten miles further from the Gulf. Their arrival gave Golden Meadow a large population boost and provided the community with an influx of skilled and storm-tested mariners, hardened by all the years of peril and tragedy.

The hurricane refugees soon mixed with and married the descendants of William Riley Williams. Then, in the 1930s, Williams' town, for so many years a refuge for mourners, would finally experience a stroke of good luck. In 1931, oil was discovered in Leeville, and in 1938, the black, bubbling crude made its way into Golden Meadow when an oil derrick was erected on the Falgout property.

The progeny of William Riley Williams did not fully realize at first what this new development would do for them. But they did know that it was attracting a new clan of people, *les Texiens*. They came from Texas, Oklahoma, Arkansas, north Louisiana, and other parts of the redneck South. These Texiens didn't speak French or practice Catholicism.

While most descendents of the father of Golden Meadow found the Texiens to be a nuisance, Juan Orgeron discovered that he possessed something that they desperately needed.

In 1941, on a busy spring day along the banks of Bayou Lafourche, Juan saw an *étranger* approaching him. The outlander had to be a Texien. He walked with the assured, springy step of the oilman, and except for a very few Yankee Americains, all foreigners in Golden Meadow were Texiens.

This particular *maudit* Texien, this damn oilman, wanted to talk, but Juan had little time for chatter. He was consumed with preparing his *Herman J* for the brown shrimp season. Up and down the bayou, almost everyone else was doing the same thing. Their boats were moored to the string of homemade docks, forming a hodgepodge grove of booms and bows, nets and decks. They shared the narrow bank with icehouses, shrimp sheds, canneries, oyster and crab factories, bars and businesses, some of which were on pilings over the water.

When the Texien stepped into this bustle and came up to Juan, he started drawling away. Juan understood that the man's name was "Cole," and that he was from the Atlantic Refining Company. But because this man spoke a language Juan did not, Juan had trouble understanding him.

He didn't trust this Texien or any other. They were so different from his Cadiens. Before they came, everyone was the same: French-speaking and Catholic. It didn't matter if your last name was Williams, Crosby, Rebstock, or Picciola, or even if there was a little Filipino or Chino in your blood—there was still enough French in the mix to make you Cadien. The full-blooded Indians in the area lived south of town, and the blacks up the bayou came into town only to shuck oysters and were outside the city limits by dark.

The Texiens, though, were different, and what Juan had seen and heard of them, he didn't like. He didn't care for their English, their Baptist culture, or their slovenly ways. He'd heard the local women talking about how the Texiens didn't keep house and didn't iron their clothes, about how they ate cold sandwiches for lunch instead of a hot meal. They even had the audacity to eat meat on Friday and get publicly drunk in the middle of Lent. And the Texiens were hypocrites—their religion told them not to drink whiskey or dance, but there they were drinking and dancing with our *jolie filles* on Saturday nights.

So what could this Texien Cole do for him, except steal his wife or take his daughter? Despite Juan's uneasiness, Cole was saying something that told him he needed to listen. Juan couldn't really speak English, but he could understand it well enough to talk basic business. He'd picked up a little of it while doing some roustabout work, mostly unskilled labor, in the Leeville Oil Field, helping the oil companies build board roads in the marsh.

From what Juan could tell, Cole was saying that he was in town to hire boats to run "shooting crews" for Atlantic Refining Company. These crews would shoot dynamite for oil exploration purposes. As Juan would soon learn, the way the process worked was that the TNT-induced explosion sent a seismic wave into the lake bed, which ultimately bounced back toward the surface and was logged on surveying and recording vessels. As the wave crossed the different layers of earth, it created a profile of each layer, which helped determine the location of mineral reserves.

This seismic work required several boats, but the *Herman J*'s sole purpose would be to shoot the dynamite that created the seismic waves. Her crew would be lighting charges on the coastal inlets all over southeast Louisiana, from Timbalier Bay to Lake Pontchartrain and Lake Catherine. The boats would work ten days on and five off.

To take this opportunity, Juan would have to close his shrimp wholesaling company, and this wasn't an easy prospect. He'd worked five years at establishing the business, and now he'd have to give up his hard-earned customer base for a Texien dynamite expedition.

But when the Texien Cole offered his price, Juan was surprised. He did the numbers and realized he could make twenty dollars a day profit from this new operation. Twenty dollars per day for just driving the *Herman J* around the bay? Sure, there was more to it than that, but he knew he couldn't make that much shrimping.

Juan asked the man if he could still trap in the winter.

No, said Cole. Atlantic would keep him on as long as there was work and as long as he did his job. But if Juan walked out on his contract during the winter, Atlantic wouldn't hire him back.

This was a difficult condition for Juan. He'd always felt some security from having two seasonal trades. During a given year, if a poor shrimp yield threatened to ruin him, a good fur crop could save him. Or in another year, a high shrimp price might offset a low muskrat price. Now he was relying on one business, on one very foreign occupation. Instead of peddling a product, a barrel of shrimp or a sack of muskrat pelts, he was suddenly selling a service. Most of the people on the bayou made money by hawking tangible objects, be it seafood or fur, groceries or hardware, a cooked meal or a bottle of beer. Other than boat builders and carpenters, there were very few people making money selling their skills.

Further, in Juan's case, his last three years of trapping had been good ones. The high price of muskrat had allowed him to go from poverty to paying off his note on the *Herman J*.

He also enjoyed the work. He had fond memories of the winters spent at the Gentilly trapping camp on the clamshell road off of US 90. He and his fellow bayou trappers called the road Rue Torchon, "Dishrag Street." Before the winter, the families of the Rue Torchon would hold *boucheries*, where they'd slaughter hogs, use every inch of the animal, and divide the spoils. Afterward, they'd stretch the pig's lard as far as they could—frying it to make tasty *gratins*; or using it as cooking grease, as a preserve, as lamp oil, in medicines, or mixing it with ashes to make soap.

When the families would arrive on the Rue Torchon, the men would help each other build their camps and dig the narrow *trainasses* through the marsh to access their leases. The marsh had always filled their table with food like fresh *poule d'eau*, ducks and duck eggs from the marsh ponds, *gros bec* from the cypress trees, and redfish from the Bayou Sauvage. They'd eat dishes like bouillabaisse, gumbo, and canned Autin sausage with onions and potatoes. It all tasted so good—especially out there, the food, the community, the camaraderie, it was too much to give up for this Texien woodpecker chase.

And no matter how good the oilman's proposition sounded, it was still speculative. It wasn't as *certain* as the trapping life; it wasn't as sure as Juan getting up at 4:00 a.m. and making coffee, frying a marsh hen he'd caught in a trap, putting that meat and some bread in an empty coffee can, grabbing a jug of water, and walking out into the cold to his pirogue.

But then there were the hardships Juan experienced: his legs churning as he trudged through the marsh in his hip boots, checking his lines; the weight on his back of the *homme bras sac* full of muskrat, coon, otter, and mink; the callouses on his hands as he push-poled up the trainasse. And then there was the end of each run, when his boots finally touched the planks of the back porch, but he still had to work until dark curing, drying, preparing, and sorting the pelts and extracting the teeth to be sold as ivory.

Moreover, Juan had always wanted to cash in on this oil. In every direction in Golden Meadow, he could see oil derricks rising above the flatness. These steel trees, the pumpjack grasshoppers, and the slush pits had made their way almost to the bayouside. They were in clamshell parking lots, on front lawns, even in the yard of the Catholic church.

Oil had literally exploded through town. Wells had erupted in school yards, covering the buildings and the trees with black muck. Oil tanks had blown up and destroyed outhouses. Almost daily, puddles of sludge leaked from the pits and accumulated in the town lanes. And the smell, the sharp whiff of crude and drilling mud, depending upon the direction of the wind, could be as acrid and as prevalent as cow dung.

For all Juan knew, the black crude could be coursing beneath his own land. But how would he trust the Texiens to pay him correctly on that? He'd heard about how the local people were already having their trouble with the oil companies.

But it stood to reason that if oil pooled under the ridge land, it existed under the marshes and bays. The oil companies had proven their ability to drill a well over open water as far back as 1911, when the world's first "offshore" rig was established in Caddo Lake in northern Louisiana. From there, it took the industry three decades to succeed at erecting a freestanding, producing platform in a coastal sea, finally getting there in 1938 when a well started gushing a mile and a quarter off the coast of Cameron Parish in western Louisiana.

Now the Texiens were trying to drill over water all across the state, and Juan Orgeron knew they couldn't service these platforms—which held the drilling rigs, and, later, the production equipment—without boats. As far as he could tell, this boat business was sound. He knew what he'd be getting paid. And he sure knew how to handle a boat. Yes, he would be driving around crews of Texien "trash" from north Louisiana, Oklahoma, Mississippi, and other parts of the Texien world. But these *cous rouge* dynamite shooters would be on *his* boat.

And he realized that if he declined the Texien's offer, there were dozens of men and boats in Golden Meadow that could and would take this job.

So Juan told Cole he had a deal. And when Cole told him he needed two additional boats, Juan directed Cole to his neighbors and his Callais cousins, who had shrimp boats that were perfect for running seismic crews.

Sure enough, once Cole saw the Callais' boats, he agreed they'd make good seismic vessels. Cole and Atlantic Refining could now start blasting lake bottoms.

That first summer, Juan Orgeron was driving his crews around the lakes, making money faster than he ever had in his life. It was as if silver coins were shooting up in the plume of water that rose from the dynamite explosions.

And while Juan had to tolerate the Texiens' turkey calling and toe-nail picking, he learned to get along with them. He felt they weren't as bad as people made them out to be and, in any event, they weren't going away. Some Texiens weren't merely renting Golden Meadow houses, they were buying pieces of *la terre famille*. They weren't just flirting with local waitresses at the Kit Kat Café, some were even marrying them and making mixed-blood babies, proving a woman could fall in love with anything, even a Texien.

Even if Juan occasionally did draw an unsavory Texien crew member, this line of work was so much simpler than anything else he'd done. He was sure it couldn't be this easy.

And indeed, less than one year later, Juan's work did become more difficult, but not in a way that he expected. During the spring of 1942, a world war began to disturb his usually peaceful evenings on the water. At first, it was only the unsettling talk of war. Next, some of Juan's Texien crew members began either enlisting or getting drafted. Everyone, it seemed, had family members going overseas.

Then, during that summer of 1942, the war came right to Juan and his crew. On the horizon, occasional fiery flashes began to taint the perfect purple skies of Timbalier Bay. From the Gulf, loud explosions began to disrupt the *Herman J*'s quiet dinners of salt meat, beans and rice. These booms gave Juan the *frizzons*. And he had little doubt that the Nazis were making the noise.

Since May, he'd heard that German *submarins* had been spotted off the Louisiana coast. The story was that these U-boats had been blowing up merchant ships in the Gulf. His ten-year-old son, Bobby, had told him of a sailor's body he'd seen on the beach at Timbalier Island, twelve miles west of the mouth of Bayou Lafourche. He'd also heard that swastika-emblazoned torpedoes had been washing up on the shores of Grand Isle, an inhabited barrier island thirty miles south of Golden Meadow. In the month of May alone, these torpedoes had sunk forty-two ships in the Gulf.

Juan may not have been able to read the newspaper, but he knew that the Nazis were trying to dismantle the US war economy. He also knew that a big part of American commerce was oil exploration and that oil was the fuel behind the war machine. The Nazis would love to destroy any boat dedicated to this effort, and the *Herman J*'s hold full of dynamite made it especially tempting as a target. Juan didn't even want to imagine what a torpedo could do to her.

Juan had few choices, however. This was his living. Even when Atlantic Refining laid off the boat for a few weeks, Juan would then supplement his income by returning to the same water to shrimp. All he had to do was reload his old nets and boards onto the *Herman J* and hit the bay. In fact, one night, after a day of shrimping, he'd anchored his boat inside Little Pass when he watched the Gulf sky ignite. He had no doubt that the glow meant another tanker was burning. It wasn't the most comfortable moment—his son Bobby was on the boat with him, spending a little summer vacation time out on the water. But there wasn't much Juan could do about it. He could only hope that the U-boats would remain several miles offshore.

But there was talk of the U-boats coming closer, of sneaking into Grand Isle's Barataria Pass and lurking along the beach. The U-boat gunmen had already sent bloody merchant sailors to the local hospitals, creating heavy tension in Golden Meadow. On July 9, that tension turned into terror when a U-boat torpedoed an oil tanker, the *Benjamin Brewster*, two and a half miles off the Cheniere Caminada, only twenty-five miles from Golden Meadow. The tanker's hull, which was full of aviation fuel, exploded so rapidly and thoroughly the crew didn't have time to send a distress signal.

By the time the twenty-seven fatalities were counted, the people of lower Lafourche were in a state of outright panic. If Hitler could come that close, he could come even closer.

Chapter 3

U-Boats and Crew Boats

July 1942

As the tankers burned, the Lafourche mariners tried their best to ignore the Nazi threat. But the Germans' presence was all around them. By day, Army K-9 units canvassed the local beaches, where thick oil slicks continued to wash ashore. By night, Navy blimps hovered over the coastline, shining spotlights. During the dark hours, whether the people were at home in Golden Meadow or in their boats, they had to abide by a mandatory blackout. Coastal lights had allowed the submarines to slip into the Gulf of Mexico and creep north toward Louisiana. Now the US government was trying to keep the nighttime traveling U-boats from spotting the coast.

The US military was also trying to quickly build up its fleet. In need of boats for coastal patrol, the Coast Guard borrowed vessels from the locals, randomly taking their oyster luggers, fishing skiffs, and shrimp boats. The military also conscripted some shrimpers and fishermen and turned them into Coast Guard ensigns, forcing them to pull sailors' bodies from seas of burning oil.

With the military commandeering the area's man- and vessel-power, it was difficult for the oilfield to function. But there were still working rigs on the coastal bays, drilling under steam power around the clock. While the rig crews also had to operate at night without lights, summertime heat lightning would periodically light up the sky. The natural light source allowed the U-boat captains to spot the oil platforms and the workboats that supported them.

But Nazis or no Nazis, this was still the oilfield, and the industry's intensity and pace kept its workers occupied with their jobs and their minds mostly away from the U-boats.

Nevertheless, the *submarin* attacks continued in the late summer of 1942, and many people in Golden Meadow feared the worst. What was to stop the Germans from dispatching ground troops? If the Japanese could send suicide bombers into ships, what would that maniac Hitler do? Some believed he would try to destroy everything from the tankers in the Gulf to the derricks in the Leeville oilfield to every oil vessel in between.

Judging by Hitler's tactics in Eurasia, this belief made some sense. The radio reports said the Germans were trying desperately to secure the oilfields of the Russian Caucasus. Likewise, if the Nazis could gut enough of the Allies' petroleum supply in the United States, they would gain an obvious tactical advantage.

The people of lower Lafourche couldn't help but think these things as the radio reports blared in homes and wheelhouses up and down the bayou. They kept their eyes open for Nazi conspirators.

In fact, Juan Orgeron's nephew Melvin Bernard would one day go on record as saying he and his father, Alcide, saw conspiracy in action. Alcide Bernard worked in close proximity to the U-boats; he and his brother ran the Gulf Oil camp on Timbalier Island. One summer day in 1942, Alcide's son Melvin said that he, then only a boy, and his father looked out into the Gulf and saw a U-boat emerge no more than two miles off the beach. Alcide grabbed his binoculars and told his son that a local shrimp boat was approaching the sub. Alcide then watched the trawler meet the U-boat, hand over groceries, and then pump fuel to the sub from some drums on the shrimp boat's deck.

The rumor was that the shrimper was receiving instructions from a coconspirator on the shore, who some believed to be Father Francis Weiss, a Polish priest with alleged Nazi sympathies, who was reportedly communicating with the U-boats via shortwave radio. While some people in the community believed the story of a priest-shrimper-Nazi conspiracy, others thought it was a hoax. Years later, doubting historians, particularly U-boat expert C. J. Christ, would point out that the U-boats did not need local support; the large ones had a cruise range of eleven thousand miles and the smaller ones received provisions from large, midocean supply subs. There was no reason for a U-boat to risk direct contact with a local, either by radio or in person. Nevertheless, to Melvin Bernard, the shrimper's tale wasn't born out of illogical paranoia but grounded in fact. While he could never prove the priest's involvement in the subterfuge, he swore that he and his father saw the treasonous transfer with their own eyes, and on the day following the U-boats' supply run, they found what they believed to be the sub's trash washed up on the beach, everything from bread wrappers to empty oil cans.

The point, at least as it relates to this story, is not whether or not the U-boats made direct contact with the *Lafourchais*, but that the Nazi threat and the resulting local fright were palpably real.

Despite the Nazis' shoreline maneuvers, the Germans never made the land attack the people feared. But they did send torpedoes at nearly one hundred Gulf of Mexico ships, sinking fifty-six of them and killing an estimated five hundred people.

Fortunately, by 1943, the U-boats were gone. The war, however, raged on. The defense effort preoccupied the nation's oil companies, who didn't have the time or the resources to focus on marine oil development. The war also created a steel shortage, which helped prevent the oil industry from continuing its push offshore.

But the war held back the Gulf oilfield for more than economic reasons. Psychologically, the people of south Lafourche were still full of wartime anxiety. While the U-boats had vanished, there were now German POW camps all over south Louisiana. Along Bayou Lafourche, the people could see German prisoners working in the fields, including some at a camp just nineteen miles from Golden Meadow in Valentine and others further north in Thibodaux and Donaldsonville; there were also two POW camps thirty-five miles to the west in Houma. This German presence and the fact that many natives were dying abroad, particularly during the Battle of the Bulge in December 1944 and January 1945, made the people nervous, and many were still suspicious of Father Weiss, the Nazi-sympathizing priest.

One of the priest's altar boys, Dick Guidry, a teenager from just north of Golden Meadow in Galliano, knew all about the community's suspicion. And if he had any doubts about how the people felt about Father Weiss, they evaporated one night as he rambled down the bayouside shell road in his father's 1939 Plymouth, approaching the Sacred Heart Catholic Church in Cut Off, only a few miles north of his home. He was on his way back from Lee Brothers Dance Hall, still juiced up with jitterbug sweat and the perfume of young *jolie filles*.

When the churchyard filled his windshield, Dick's eyes bugged. The scene was at once baffling and unmistakable. A lynch mob had gathered in front of the rectory. There must have been 150 to 200 people. Someone had tied a hangman's noose to the power pole, and the people were banging on the door, calling for the priest.

Dick pulled off the road. Looking at the mob, Dick thought Father Weiss had almost tied his own noose. One Sunday while Dick had been serving as an altar boy at the St. Joseph Mission Church in Galliano, Father Weiss had stepped on an American flag that had accidentally fallen to the ground near the altar and said, "When the war is over, this is what Germany will do to the United States." He then wiped his feet on the flag.

One female congregant, who had just lost a brother in combat, walked up to the altar and slapped the priest.

While Dick didn't support the priest's views, he liked the man. He appreciated Father Weiss's practice of passing a collection at funerals and splitting the take evenly with the altar boys. And to Dick's knowledge, no one had proved the priest's participation in any treason.

Now, with the lynch mob raging, Dick decided to wheel around to the back of the rectory. No one was there. As he turned the knob on the back door, he was surprised that it opened.

When he looked inside, he found Father Weiss, as white as a bedsheet, shaking, pointing a double-barrel shotgun directly at him. The priest flinched, then recognized Dick and pulled the gun away.

Dick led Father Weiss to his car and helped him into the trunk. When he passed the front of the rectory, the mob was still roaring, but the lynchers did not look his way. Dick brought the priest home to his father, who then drove Father Weiss to the chancery in New Orleans, arriving at Bishop Rummel's doorstep at 5:00 a.m.

Father Weiss's affiliation with Sacred Heart Church would not survive the war. He signed his last baptismal certificate there in January 1945.

Despite all the tension, the war generated a surge of nationalism on the bayou. The south Lafourche Cadiens, some of whom flew the French flag as late as the turn of the century, were now fervently American. Throughout the war, the Lafourche country was awash with American flags, as well as red, white, and blue signs and boat awnings. Up and down the bayou, "victory gardens" grew in V-shaped rows.

The heightened patriotism and the presence of a common enemy also eased the Cadiens' problems with the Texiens. While the Texiens were still foreigners, they certainly weren't Nazis. They didn't carry torpedoes but thick wallets.

And because of their money, the local merchants were now courting their business. Some of their attempts at making English signs were, STOP AN EAT, WE FIX YOU UP and PANTS PRESS WHILE YOU HIDE.

The Cadiens' English might have still been a little rough, but their business sense was sharpening. When the veterans returned home, they brought with them a better knowledge of English and a deeper understanding of the outside world. Many of them were also beginning to see oilfield opportunities on the postwar horizon. When the war ended, Juan Orgeron—and, later, young Dick Guidry—would try to seize a growing bounty.

But to Juan Orgeron's surprise, there was no postwar boom. In 1945, Juan discovered that no one had a need for his boat. The country was in a recession due to a low steel supply, and the oil companies were adjusting from lending their men and equipment to the war machine.

As for offshore drilling, the states and the feds were engaged in the Tidelands Dispute, a battle over who owned the coastal seabed. Their fight stymied leasing and, in turn, thwarted production.

With all this uncertainty, Juan returned to what he knew. He couldn't wait on the boat business and starve. He could deal with the existence of U-boats in the Gulf but he couldn't tolerate a cessation in income. So he turned back to trapping. His new muskrat lease was only ten miles down the Leeville Road from Golden Meadow.

Not only was the price of *la muskarat* high, but Juan's costs were much lower. He was benefitting from built-in, free labor. His oldest son Herman "Bouillien" was sixteen, old enough to help him full time, and his son Bobby could pitch in when he wasn't in school.

Soon, Juan lost his need for his boat and sold the *Herman J*. But then in 1946, Bouillien reminded him that while trapping was a good living, the oilfield was a better one. Bouillien told his father things were picking up and convinced him to buy a 36-foot wooden crew boat with twin Chrysler engines, which was working for Texaco out of Lafitte, twenty-five marsh miles to the northeast of Golden Meadow.

Juan made the purchase with the money he'd saved from the sale of the *Herman J* and, in so doing, returned to the oilfield. With the new boat, Juan's company began running crew from Lafitte to the Texaco wells in a nearby bay. Bouillien became the primary captain with Juan as relief captain.

As for Bobby, Juan kept him on the trapping lease. Soon, Bobby would quit school and be of more use. Bouillien had left in the ninth grade and so would his little brother. While the Orgerons were doing well, they weren't making enough money to have their youngest son waste his time in a classroom. Besides, the real education was in the marsh.

But Bobby didn't want to be in the marsh in February of 1948. He had no desire to paddle his pirogue in the cold and check his traps with freezing, stiff hands. Instead, he wanted to be in the oilfield, driving a boat with a big inboard engine. He'd often dreamed of owning a workboat fleet as he paddled down a marsh bayou. While he'd never have the education to be a doctor or a lawyer, while he didn't have the bloodlines to be an Indian chief, he could become a boatman. Boats would lead him to wealth and to some intangible sense of purpose that seemed impossible to obtain now.

It was unattainable only because his father wouldn't let him get started. Bobby didn't understand why his father favored his brother. He couldn't comprehend how his brother actually told his daddy what to do, but when Bobby spoke, he was told to shut up.

One day, Juan would have to listen to him. One day, when Bobby talked, everyone in the room would open their *maudit* ears.

While Bobby Orgeron was stuck in the marsh daydreaming, the oilfield was extending from the bays well into the Gulf of Mexico. In November, 1947, the industry sailed into virgin waters. That month, a contractor erected the world's first oil rig situated well beyond the sight of land, several miles south of the central Louisiana shoreline below Morgan City.

Now in 1948 all over the coast, oil companies were hiring tugs to tow rigs into the bays and deep into the Gulf. The movement caught the observant eyes of thirty-six-year-old Sidney Savoie, a tugboat man who lived a hair north of Golden Meadow in Galliano. The new activity made the typically steady Sidney antsy; he felt as if he should be capitalizing on all the action instead of working as a captain on one of his father-in-law's boats. Their current client, Texaco, was not paying him near what it was paying the captains on the Texaco-owned tugs. While Sidney was usually easy to please and unemotional, he had finally lost his patience with his lack of just pay. He decided to confront the Texaco superintendent and ask for a raise.

When the superintendent refused, Sidney quit.

Although Sidney had thought through his decision, he was still concerned. He had a wife, two children, and no lead on a future job.

Nonetheless, he had an excuse to do what he'd dreamed of doing. He could leave his father-in-law's company, empty his savings account, and build his own boat.

Vessel ownership would crown a progression for Sidney that was typical of a growing number of Lafourche boatmen, who had moved from the seafood industry to dabbling in the oilfield to making a full-time career out of workboats. But for Sidney, there was a twist. Until he'd met his wife, he'd never even taken the wheel of a boat.

Before 1938, Sidney was strictly a land man. After quitting school in the seventh grade, his first job was to work on his family's sugarcane farm in Larose, seventeen miles up the bayou from Golden Meadow. On the farm, he spent long days walking and guiding a mule-powered plow through the fields, cutting cane with a machete and loading it onto barges by hand.

Then one night in 1933, his farming future began to fade when he met Mathilde Eymard at the Lee Brothers Dance Hall. As he two-stepped with the smiling girl from Galliano, the rhythm of his life began to change. He went from the hardwood of the dance floor to the marble of a church altar, from a single man to a married one, from a mule-driving farmer for his own family to a lugger-steering oysterman for his in-laws. Life on a floating, motorized lugger was quite different than on a animal-drawn plow; the wooden vessel had a nice wheelhouse in the back and a long, spacious foredeck used for harvesting oysters from the sides of the boat and storing the shelled "crop."

Sidney's transition to oystering became easier when he learned the new trade would double his dollar-a-day farming salary. And with his father-in-law, Duard Eymard, introducing him to the world of water, Sidney received more than an increase in pay. There was adventure, too. Steering a 65-foot cypress lugger through a maze of dark canals and bayous was both scary and exciting; guiding her through the swirling eddies of the Mississippi River was exhilarating and sometimes downright frightening. On occasion, the river pulled the vessel in whatever direction it wanted, completely overpowering her little 60 Atlas engine.

Whatever the conditions, Sidney mastered the art of navigating the lugger from the Eymard oyster lease to the wholesale dock in New Orleans. He had big eyes that seemed to spot things that other captains couldn't—a very useful trait in his new career.

In 1939, Sidney's vocation became even more lucrative when Gulf Oil approached his father-in-law about using the family's luggers as tugboats on a periodic basis. The Gulf men had seen the luggers passing by the Gulf dock on the Harvey Canal, across the river from New Orleans. It was a good opportunity for the family, who could only make money oystering during the October–April harvest. Moreover, the family didn't have to invest any capital into converting their luggers into tugs; they only needed some stronger ropes.

As the Eymard luggers began to push barges loaded with freshwater and oilfield tools down the turbulent Mississippi, Sidney jumped at the chance to do the extra work. He was anxious to do anything to raise enough cash to build his own home, move his family out of his father-in-law's house and, maybe one day, buy a car.

In the meantime, he and Mathilde did what they could to save. They owned two rental houses, which they leased to Texien families. They'd also gone into partnership on a small grocery store with Mathilde's sister.

One goal was to set aside enough money for Sidney to start his own business, and now, in 1948, he was suddenly there. His plan was to take advantage of an industry gap. For the past year or so, he'd noticed several big rigs sitting idle in fabrication yards, ready to be moved offshore. The rigs that were actually in motion were being moved inefficiently by fleets of five or six tiny wooden boats. Sidney had seen very few steel tugs. It was as if the oil companies were letting a pack of skinny hounds do the work of one strong mule.

Sidney would build a steel tug that would move these rigs much more quickly. First, though, he needed a partner. While he had an impressive $14,000 nest egg, he needed to double that amount.

So he made a pitch to his brother-in-law Elfer "Faro" Guidry. Faro was the husband of Romanda "T-Man," Mathilde's sister, and he was called Faro because he liked to dress up and thought of himself as cool (*faraud* could mean both well-dressed and a braggart in Cajun French). In addition to being a snazzy *vanteur*, Faro was one of the first younger men in the area to own a car. While Faro had a bit of an ego and could be difficult, easygoing Sidney got along with him just fine. Moreover, the couples were already partners in the grocery store, and Faro was also a boatman, having recently converted his shrimp boat into an oilfield tug.

When Sidney told Faro about his idea, Faro didn't even hesitate. "*Allons*," he said. Let's go. And off they went to forge their steel mule.

As a live-eyed Sidney headed to Texas, he left the world of wood. He'd already mentally shifted to steel, and steely images were stirring him and driving him toward the state line. He was thinking of rivets and divots, of sheet metal and steel bolts, of silver welds and blue flames, of rods and wrenches, of pipes and winches. He'd been consumed with metallic dreams ever since he first thought about building his tug.

He couldn't construct her on the bayou. While the Lafourche wooden boat craftsmen were plentiful and masterful, they weren't yet molding steel. It was why he was riding with Faro Guidry in Faro's new black Chevrolet, a sleek, humped-hooded gangster-machine, as they cruised down US Highway 90, through the rice fields of southwest Louisiana. Their destination was Burton Shipyard in Port Arthur, Texas. Although there were steel-wielding shipyards in Louisiana, Sidney had passed by Burton one day on an unrelated trip, and he'd seen what he wanted.

That particular tug was similar to the one Sidney was seeing now, just as he and Faro pulled into Burton. She was a sculpted mass of metal, fifty-five-feet-long by sixteen-feet-wide, very close to the molten mule Sidney had envisioned. It was a big boat built by a tall block of a man. Mr. Burton, a German American who spoke with a *Deutsche* accent, told them they could buy that very hull, which was still under construction.

Sidney realized they could afford her and two 165 GMs to power her. So yes, they'd take the whole package for $28,000.

The ride home was a breezy dash. They talked nonstop of what they'd need and what they'd do. The first step was money; they didn't have any cash left for operating capital.

So Sidney applied for a loan a short distance north of his Galliano house at the Cut Off branch of Citizens Bank. He and Faro had to each borrow $6,000. This was a giant step for Sidney; he'd never sought a loan, and he'd grown up during a time when lending wasn't a big part of the local culture. You worked and you saved, but you didn't borrow from a bank. Sidney himself used green cash to build the only house he'd ever need.

Nevertheless, he was sure he'd get the loan. His collateral was too large to think otherwise. He arrived at Citizens Bank in his pressed khakis, and he greeted a Mr. Ducos, a tie-wearing banker with a conservative countenance.

After the men sat in leather chairs, Sidney carefully laid out his plan. During the beginning of his pitch, he watched Mr. Ducos smile here and there and nod his head. As Sidney continued, Mr. Ducos quit nodding and started to fidget. Sidney pressed on, but he was distracted by Mr. Ducos's uncomfortable body language.

Finally, Mr. Ducos took a deep breath. "*Mais* I don't know, me," he said, shaking his head.

"What?" asked Sidney.

"Well, that boat can sink."

"Sink?"

"Yes, it can sink."

"It's not gonna sink."

"But it *can* sink. I can't loan you money on something like that. It's too risky."

"That boat's worth almost $30,000, and it's paid for. We're only asking you for $6,000 each. I don't see the risk, me."

Sidney saw the sweat starting to bead on Mr. Ducos's forehead. The banker was almost writhing in pain. Sidney looked at him and asked, "Well, what can I do?"

"I don't know. You'll have to talk to Mr. Sims in Thibodaux."

Up the bayou in Thibodaux, at the Citizens Bank main branch, Sidney met Mr. Sims. This time, Sidney thought he'd strengthened his pitch. But as soon as he mentioned the word "boat," Mr. Sims grimaced.

When Sidney heard the word "sink," he knew his loan had sunk.

Mr. Sims finally told him, "Let me look at your file." He went into the other room and came back with a manila folder. He flipped through it and told Sidney he saw that he owned a home. He said if Sidney could give him a mortgage on his property, he'd lend him the $6,000.

Sidney agreed, and when he went to the Cut Off branch to draw the money, Mr. Ducos still looked as if he had sand in his shirt. He winced as his employee transferred the funds.

The banker's reaction, however, was nothing compared to Mathilde Savoie's. The moment Sidney told her he had to mortgage their home, her normally gay expression left her face. "You did what?" she asked, fussed in her French. "How could you give them our house?"

"I didn't give it to them, Mathilde. It's just collateral for the loan."

"But that means they can take it."

"They can't take it unless we default."

"What about if you do?"

"Oh, you think the boat will sink, too?"

"Yeah, no. Anything. Anything can happen, and if it does, they gonna take all that we have."

"Mathilde—"

"You know how hard we worked for this house? I had to put up with them Texiens taking all the lightbulbs out of the rent houses and all that foolishness. I had to work all those hours at the store with T-Man. You know how many times I scrubbed and cleaned that store dreaming about this house? You know how many times I swept and mopped this floor you standing on right here? Just to have Mr. Ducos and those people in Thibodaux take it?"

"Honey—"

"I can't believe this. I can't believe you'd put up our house just to run your boat."

Sidney saw that it was pointless to argue. He knew Mathilde would vent her frustration, and after all the words came out, she would be quiet and *boudé*. And *boudé* she did—for days.

Until Mathilde's disposition improved, Sidney knew he couldn't spend the money. But the days kept passing, and her mood stayed the same. In her own way, she was clutching her house, putting her arms around each of her big cisterns and holding them tight.

Meanwhile, Sidney's business stayed docked.

Three weeks later, Mathilde was still moaning. She wanted the mortgage's black hand off her house. She had $5,000 in US savings bonds, and this sum represented every penny of their retirement, but she didn't care. Sidney could have it for his boat. As for the remaining $1,000, her daddy had already said they could borrow it from him.

So Sidney crossed the bayou and walked into Citizens Bank. When he saw Mr. Ducos, the banker's face shrunk. But as soon as Sidney explained to him that he wanted to cancel the loan, to give the bank back the money, and to pay off any owed interest, a light came into the banker's eyes. He was so happy he told Sidney he wasn't charging him *any* interest.

Back at home, Mathilde was doing better, too. While she and Sidney might have been throwing their life savings at a floating piece of steel, at least no one could take her kitchen.

With peace returning to the Savoie household, Sidney could focus on his business. He and his partner Faro Guidry named their new boat the *Ajax*, after the name of another successful vessel recently built at Burton Shipyard.

Faro and Sidney took delivery of the *Ajax* in November 1949. When they brought her down Bayou Lafourche, traffic on the highway stopped. People climbed from their cars. They left their front porches. They dropped their hammers and their nets. Everyone crowded to the bay-ouside and gawked. There may have been a few other steel boats on the bayou, but there certainly hadn't been any 55-foot steel tugboats like this one.

At the end of this impromptu one-boat parade, Sidney and Faro tied the boat up at the Eymard dock and began to outfit her with bumpers and furniture. For the next few days, they could hardly get any work done. Automobile traffic on the adjacent highway slowed as it approached the boat, and some of the cars came to a complete halt. People, friends and strangers alike, got out and admired the giant. They complimented the owners and asked questions, a common inquiry being, "Where you got the money to pay for this?"

The people talked about the *Ajax*'s sophisticated rigging. The hookups were far different from the basic cleats and small ropes of the lugger. The *Ajax* had steel cables, bigger ropes, and fancy winches. The people touched the new equipment and stroked the hull's surface, as if to make sure it was really cold, hard steel.

When all the foolishness stopped and the *Ajax* found its way to the Harvey Canal, Sidney started looking for work. Since the war, Harvey had changed. Its canal corridor had taken on a distinct new-fabrication odor. It smelled of the creosote pilings piled up at Harvey Lumber and tasted of the gritty sandblasting coming from the contractor J. Ray McDermott. Construction was beginning to boom with the whap, whap, whap of pile drivers building docks up and down the canal.

Harvey was a natural hub. From downriver, freight came from all over the world. From upriver, pipe and other steel products made their way from the Pennsylvania and Ohio mills. At the Harvey docks, the steel wares either met their final destination or were loaded on barges and shipped through the Intracoastal Canal to shipyards and oilfield installations throughout the Gulf Coast.

On the loud, pulsating canal, Sidney Savoie found fast work for the *Ajax*. He stayed busy with a lot of little jobs that might last a few hours or a day or a week. He did whatever they asked—move rigs, push barges loaded with freshwater, supplies, drilling mud, or whatever else was inside the big rectangles. It wasn't ideal work because it was by the hour, as opposed to a flat-day rate of eighty to eighty-five dollars per day. Day work meant the client picked up most of the expenses, but with hourly work, Sidney and his partner paid for everything.

Mainly, Sidney operated through brokers, who found him work with California Oil, Humble Oil, and Gulf. A river barge broker steered him to non–oilfield jobs moving big hopper barges full of plastics, grain, and God knows what else.

The first couple of months were fast and blurry. They were like the swirls of dust that were gathering on one unseasonably hot spring day. On this afternoon, Sidney was standing at a dock, and his pressed khakis were already wilted from the heat. Sidney looked up through a dusty cloud and saw a man in a button-down shirt and tie coming down the street. Sidney said to himself, now that's a salesman.

He was correct. The man's product was insurance. He introduced himself as John Mead, and he started talking and talking, finally asking Sidney, "Do you have insurance on your boat?"

"No," said Sidney. He said this because it was true, not because he understood what it was or why it was relevant.

This John Mead kept running his mouth. Sidney could hardly believe what he was hearing. Mead told him that if something happened to the boat, insurance would replace the loss and make Sidney's company whole.

As Mead continued to talk about the finer points of insurance, Sidney wasn't really listening. He was focused on the fact that this insurance seemed necessary, and he'd *never heard of it.*

Oh, he knew about life insurance, but marine insurance? Where did that come from? In all the years his father-in-law ran luggers for the oilfield, he never had insurance. They'd never even talked about it. When Sidney went to Citizens Bank, the word insurance had never been uttered. Obviously, an insurance policy would have addressed the lender's concerns about the boat sinking. And what about the boat brokers and oil companies? Never once had they asked Sidney if he carried insurance. In Sidney's near decade in the oilfield, he had never, ever heard the word insurance.

Consequently, Sidney wasn't completely sold on what John Mead was telling him. They finally agreed to meet for supper at a mutual friend's house in Cut Off.

By the end of the meal, John Mead had sold Sidney the insurance. Presumably, he was better off. But for the time being he was also poorer because the insurance came with a steady premium. To pay for it and avoid a financial sinking, Sidney had to find better work for his steel mule.

The *Ajax*, a landmark tugboat on the bayou in 1949.
(Courtesy of Central Gulf Towing, Inc.)

Chapter 4

Major Minor

January 1949

As Sidney scrounged for a better opportunity, up and down Bayou Lafourche many young captains were trying to become boat owners. They were doing everything they could to borrow, barter, and budge their way into the boat business. All they needed was a little seed money, the right-sized boat, and a dependable character. Formal education and family name weren't even considerations. These men may have been minor players in society, but they could now become major economic forces.

In 1949 in Galliano, Sidney was watching one of his neighbors, twenty-year-old Minor Cheramie, work his way into the business.

Like others trying to secure their own boats, Minor didn't exactly have an Eastern pedigree. A ninth-grade graduate, he was the son of a respected but relatively poor barber and oyster bar owner. Despite Minor's lack of wealth and education, he was determined to become a millionaire, and that all started with a boat, which he was now somehow building at Duet Shipyard in Golden Meadow. Here amidst the stacks of cypress boards and mahogany planks, among the wood chips and the sawdust piles, tall, well-muscled Minor was running around the yard, pointing his left finger and twitching his Roman nose. His blue eyes were darting as he ran his hand through his thick hair.

As he rubbed his mustache, he looked at his 32-foot wooden lugger. He knew the boat's upcoming launch wasn't just about him. It was really the story of six people, all magnetized and manipulated by Minor.

The first was "The Wife," Lou, his cute *ti buton*, who was not only his mate but his fellow painter and caulker. She was there with him every night when the yard closed and the smells of varnish and wood glue still pervaded. It was there that she and Minor would save money by doing the *calfeutrer* themselves. The *calfeutrer* involved pulling sausage-like cotton strands from a pack and sticking them into every crack in the hull, then stuffing them in with a small chisel. The strands would help seal the boat when the wood got wet and swelled. A tedious process, the cracks swallowed the *calfeutrer*, requiring more and more of it, testing Lou's threshold for boredom and the stamina of her fingers. Nonetheless, her twenty-year-old hands were prepared for this task. They hadn't exactly been hiding in white gloves all her life. She'd put them to work after she left school in the sixth grade to waitress at Golden Meadow's Kit Kat Café and, before that, in her father's garden.

On this night, as Lou stuffed the *calfeutrer*, she looked over at her husband, who was grimacing. He didn't like the *calfeutrer*. It was messy work. Being a fanatically clean person, he much preferred a smooth, spotless surface. Lou knew, though, that Minor had to be doing what he was doing; he wouldn't have lasted with any boss. He had such a *tête dur*, him, and any hard head had to be his own man.

But what a handsome man he was. She remembered the first time their eyes met in the summer of 1947. They were with dates at the Niche Dance Hall in Golden Meadow, and their dates happened to know each other. When Lou looked into Minor's bedroom blues, her heart swelled. That first evening, he asked her to meet him at the same place the very next night, and after their second rendezvous, that was it. In less than a year, they were eloping, traveling an hour up the bayou to Thibodaux to get married before a justice of the peace. They moved in together, sharing milk from cows that Minor's mama had milked, and, suddenly, she'd gone from being herself to being Mrs. Minor Cheramie.

There were details here that would have troubled some. First, Minor was freshly divorced from a brief marriage. The marriage had left him with a son, Minor Jr. While three-year-old "M. J." was a good little boy

and no trouble at all, Minor had problems in other areas; he had a difficult time ignoring pretty women. They seemed to drift toward him. How
would he resist them, especially since he had a tendency to change personalities when he drank too much? His inebriated persona could lead
him to another woman's bedroom or a bar fight or both.

But Lou was sucked in by Minor's magnet. It was what made her
tolerate his obsessive cleanliness and his demands to keep his shoes shined
and to prepare his meals just so. It was why she was helping to give him
this opportunity, along with five other key people.

The second person was "The Teacher," Faro Guidry, Minor's old
boss and Sidney Savoie's current partner. Faro had taught his former
deckhand Minor how to cook and make the roux dark and rich; how to
run a boat, to trawl, and push and pull barges. But in so teaching, Faro
had ridden Minor mercilessly. He'd been the epitome of what the Texiens called a "hard ass."

What he'd really given Minor was hard, cruel motivation. Faro had
the gall to tell Minor he'd amount to nothing. But Minor was not yet
twenty-one and here he was building his own boat.

Of course, Minor would not be here without person number three,
"the Captain." This particular customer, Otto Candies, was where the
boat business started for many men. Any story about the industry couldn't
be complete without Otto Candies, who was known as "the Captain," the
godfather of the business. At one point or another, every boatman seemed
to link to the Captain, and Minor's connection took place one day at the
dock in Leeville. Here, Captain Otto saw Minor and told him, "If you can
get a boat, I can get you a contract." These words were all Minor needed.
A verbal promise from the Captain was as sure as bank tender.

In fact, an oral agreement had been how the Captain originally got into
the business. In 1942, Otto Candies was a thirty-one-year-old struggling
fisherman. He was barely supporting his wife and two little boys and
feared the bank would soon foreclose on his house.

Otto's town of Des Allemands was in the freshwater country. It was
forty-five miles up the Barataria Basin from Golden Meadow, and it

wasn't a salty, marshy coastal place like lower Lafourche but a catfish, fur, and logging village perched on a bayou between two cypress lakes. It wasn't quite as Cajun as Golden Meadow, either.

While French was still spoken in Des Allemands, Candies, who was born there, would never learn to speak it. His Italian surname was originally spelled either Candesi or Candice, but his real influence, as the *allemand* name of the town suggests, was German. Des Allemands sat on Bayou Des Allemands, which ran out to Lake Des Allemands, which was the northern border of La Cote des Allemands, the old German coast between the lake and the Mississippi River. Candies' mother was a full-blooded Swiss German American, and she named her boy accordingly.

Candies grew up as one of five sons in a house headed by a father who worked as a paddle-wheel steamboat captain on Bayou Des Allemands, towing barges of swamp-timbered logs. Not long after Candies finished his final year of school, the seventh grade, he went to work for a local furrier and catfish wholesaler. Candies' job during the winter was to make lugger runs to the trapping camps on his employer's leases, delivering groceries, and picking up muskrat pelts. In the summer, he seined or ran trotlines for catfish and sold the fillets at his boss's market.

One sweltering day at the fish market in 1942, Candies looked up through the scales, ice, and slime and saw three strangers approaching him. They introduced themselves and told Candies the names of their employers, as if these company names might impress him. But Candies had never even heard of Humble Oil or Brown & Root.

The men asked him where they could rent a boat to go up Bayou Des Allemands to look at a recently dredged waterway, which would become the Humble Canal and a future drilling location. Candies borrowed one of his employer's boats and took them. But when the group found the waterway choked with water hyacinth, the oilmen's faces cringed.

Candies saw his chance and offered to clean the canal, then maintain it for $12.50 per day. The men agreed to the rate but on a "no-cure" basis. If the canal was impassable when they returned, he would collect nothing.

The problem was Candies had no boat and no money. So he called his wife Agnes's uncle, who'd taken in Agnes as an orphan and raised her.

Agnes's uncle lent the couple $500, and Candies used every dime of it to purchase a secondhand, 30-foot wooden skiff powered by a Ford V-8 with a dry exhaust and an automobile gearbox.

The unorthodox boat proved to be reliable. Candies soon cleaned the Humble Canal into a shimmer of open water. He then built a floating lily boom at the canal's entrance to hold back the hyacinth and minimize his cleaning trips.

When the three oilmen returned in ninety-three days, Candies escorted them to a tea-colored sheet of water and demanded payment in cash. The men asked him if he could take a check.

"No," said Candies. He didn't trust a check. So he drove them eleven miles to Raceland Bank, where they cashed a check and handed Candies a wad of money, about $1,100.

Candies then made another offer. He told them when the rig construction was finished, he could run crew to the site for $12.50 per day. The Humble man accepted and talked about how Humble would need a base of operations. Candies offered up a portion of his small home, which sat right on the bayou. But as Candies started to convert his living room into the Humble office and his wharf into the Humble dock, Humble "misplaced" the rig by losing contact with the tug, towing it toward the canal. Candies offered to search for it and found it mired in a lake, lodged outside an unmarked section of the channel.

Candies then called his *podnah*, a local fisherman, who came to the site with his lugger, jerked the barge from the muck, and towed it to the canal. For the salvage job, Candies paid his friend twenty dollars per day and charged Humble twenty-five. It was Candies' first broker contract and a clear sign of the future.

After the war, Candies, now called the Captain and firmly entrenched with Humble, could hardly build or buy boats fast enough to meet the demand. He had a knack for finding broker prospects and used his connections to satiate Humble.

In 1948, the Captain had no doubt that he had found an excellent boatman in Minor Cheramie.

But Minor, despite the Captain's endorsement, needed money. His quest for funding began with key person number four, "The Partner," his older brother Lefty. In truth, Lefty offered little more than cash. He knew nothing about boats and had shown no interest in learning, and he lacked Minor's flamboyance and salesmanship. Lefty's present job was to run the Rebstock Theater in Golden Meadow. But Minor had an unusual bond with his brother, and he'd always believed that if he was going into business, he wanted his brother right there with him, fifty-fifty.

Between Minor and Lefty, they could come up with $2,000, but they would need $5,000 more, and this was where person number five came into the picture. "The Benefactor" was Lefty's father-in-law, Jeff Rebstock, the theater's owner and a community leader. By opening the theater in 1922, Rebstock had brought the first glimpse of the outside world into the isolated, largely illiterate town. He then showed a flare for capitalism when he encouraged two ladies to sell homemade ice cream at the theater's entrance and compete against each other. He would later diversify his interests and open up other businesses, including his largest operation, the international Rebstock & Reeves Drilling Company, an early Cajun/Texien partnership between Rebstock and Bob Reeves.

In lending money to Minor and Lefty, Mr. Rebstock had made it clear that he wasn't doing it just because Lefty was married to his daughter Betty. His decision had nothing to do with the boat's future name, *Betty Lou*, named after Lefty's and Minor's wives. Mr. Rebstock thought his loan was solid because he truly believed Minor would make a good businessman.

Despite Mr. Rebstock's faith, Minor didn't want to be in his debt for $5,000. He had to find a way to reduce the boat's price. But boat builder Edmond Duet was giving him the lowest price possible. Edmond and his brother Leonce Duet had made a smooth transition to the oilfield by making a few adjustments to their mental specs for the luggers, which had been designed to carry minimal people and loads of seafood in the hold. For crew boats, the Duets lengthened the cabin to allow the boat to carry more passengers, and for tugs, they widened the hull to make it more suitable for pushing barges. But when it came to Minor's price, they could adjust it no further.

This was where Minor's mind had to move, and move it did, convincing Edmond Duet to let him do some of the work himself. Duet, "The Dream Builder," and key person number six, allowed Minor to personally paint the boat and to do the *calfeutrer*. This would shave a whopping $1,000 from the price.

But Minor, who was still working full time as a captain, couldn't do the work all by himself. To finish the boat on time, he needed key person number one. Minor's future depended on Lou, and they both knew it.

Lou had put up with his drinking and womanizing because he had that rare light in his eyes. She knew Minor and this boat were going somewhere, someplace beyond a March 1, 1949, crew-boat job for Captain Otto Candies and Humble Oil.

And as she wore herself out doing the *calfeutrer*, she did her best to make their trip a faster ride because, so far in her life, her journey hadn't been so smooth. She'd grown up sharing beds in a crowded house of nine kids, and her father had needed every vegetable in his large garden to feed them. As a small-time trapper and handyman, her father had never made enough money to give them any luxuries. Well, Lou Cheramie wasn't much interested in the finer things like mink coats or the yacht Minor told her he was going to buy one day. She would like some comfort, though, and a little excitement.

And *calfeutrer* be damned, this was exciting.

After a Nordberg gas engine sent the *Betty Lou* on her maiden voyage, Minor and Lefty, the left-handed Cheramie brothers, soon established their *modus operandi*. Minor ran the boats and the company. Lefty had little to do with the operations or the clients; he simply continued to manage the Rebstock Theater and to tend to his nonmarine interests. While Lefty might have been a silent partner, on certain issues Lefty was anything but quiet. Lefty was constantly talking his younger brother out of building or buying another boat. Perhaps that was why Lefty was involved. Maybe Minor had unconsciously gone into business with his brother to give himself a conscience, so that he would think twice before he borrowed his way to another vessel.

Minor's operations style was similar to that of his old boss Faro Guidry. He demanded and demanded, barking raspy orders and pointing his left finger at this and that. Everything had to be clean and shining. If he saw a tiny mark on the dashboard, he would tell a deckhand to wipe it away. If a deckhand was painting the gunnel and opened a new can of paint, but there was still a residue of paint in the old can, Minor would say, "Look at you. You wasting. Get it all out of that can there first. Scrape it clean."

But if you kept all things immaculate and did your job, Minor would treat you like a grand deckhand. He would find a way to like you. If Faro Guidry could be his friend now, which he was, then anyone could.

As the seasons passed, Minor's sparkling boats were consistently working. His relationship with Captain Otto Candies was still strong, and the Captain was now even stronger. The Captain's big break had come when he was able to secure a special insurance policy from his broker John Mead that no other boatman or broker had been able to secure. When the Captain presented the insurance certificate to Humble, Humble told him he would be the company's sole supplier of boats in its southeast Louisiana division. Any boat company working for Humble had to work through the Captain and pay him a brokerage fee. This was an arrangement that would exist for decades and would help cement Otto Candies' sons' and grandsons' relationship with the company.

While the new contract cut off the other boat companies from making 100 percent of Humble's day rate, it was a good deal for the Captain's close associates like Minor Cheramie. Minor now had a better chance of finding jobs with the oil giant.

In addition to the Captain, Minor also had a great connection with theater-owner-turned-driller Jeff Rebstock. His relationship with Rebstock had given him the impetus to build his first steel hull in 1951.

But Minor wanted to leave the bosom of Rebstock and the Captain and find his own niche. If the Captain had set himself apart by securing a special insurance policy, then Minor would give the oil companies a unique engine, a distinctive hull, or something that no one else had. Whatever it was, he would find it.

By 1950, the expanding marine oilfield had yet to reach its potential. Stunting its growth was the nation's perpetual war itch; now the Korean conflict preoccupied the American industrial machine. And if the US factories weren't manufacturing munitions, they were mass producing automobiles. As the automotive industry and the Korean War consumed a large portion of America's steel supply, the oilfield continued to suffer from the Tidelands dispute; the state-federal legal battle still limited the number of offshore leasing opportunities. So while the oil companies were building offshore rigs, they weren't exactly screaming for workboats. It wasn't as if, as Sidney Savoie learned, a boatman could build a novel vessel and have the oil companies fight over her.

Despite Sidney's unique *Ajax*, he'd yet to secure the daily steak that he craved. Instead, what he'd been doing was picking at table scraps in Harvey, working by the hour and grabbing whatever was thrown his way. If Otto Candies wanted him to push a barge for Humble Oil for a couple of hours, off he went. If Joe Domino asked him to move thirty barges out of a fleet to retrieve that one grain-laden barge, then Sidney was there.

This hourly work had been challenging and exciting, but also unpredictably nerve-racking. The pay was only ten dollars per hour, and Sidney had to pay for everything—deckhand wages, insurance, fuel, and other consumables. In some months, he made a profit. Others, he broke even. On a few, he hit the red. He had no way of knowing what the month or the day would bring. His existence was literally hour to hour.

Then one day, a Gulf Oil man called him to do some hourly work. Go move this rig. All right, now move that one. For two weeks, day after day, Sidney moved rigs and more rigs.

Then on one cool, golden morning on the Harvey Canal, the Gulf man asked him, "Sidney, you want a steady job?"

Sidney's wide eyes opened wider. Of course he did. Not only was the man offering Sidney a flat eighty-five-dollars-per-day rate, but he was also telling him that Gulf Oil would provide him with all of the boat's fuel, lube, grease, rope, and freshwater. The boat company only had to pay for the crew, including Sidney's captain's salary, the insurance, groceries, and repairs. Fifty percent of the day rate would go to these expenses and 50 percent would go to the boat itself, almost all of which was profit for Guidry & Savoie, for Sidney and his partner Faro.

And the profits added up quickly. Sidney, ever the prodigious penny-pincher, soon saved enough money for he and Faro to pay cash for another Burton behemoth, a 62-foot by 16-foot twin-screw tug powered by two 6-110s. They called her the *Susan G*, after Faro's daughter.

While the new vessel was under construction, strange things started happening to Sidney. The first was when one day at the Port Arthur shipyard, a Houston banker approached him. He wanted to loan money to Sidney. Sidney's big eyes bulged, then crinkled. The banker didn't care about Sidney's land holdings; a boat was enough collateral. It was just two years since Sidney's previous banking experience.

Sidney was puzzled. He and his partner Faro were building this boat with cash; they didn't need a loan. When he explained this to the banker, the banker talked about the next boat. But Sidney didn't have any plans for a third vessel, and he sure wasn't going to borrow money to build one. He didn't want to work just to pay a note.

After he and the Houston banker had a nice chat, Sidney declined the banker's loan offer. He didn't have time to think about a third boat, anyway. He was too busy running his first. He wasn't just the boat's captain, but her chief cook and engineer. He had to maintain the boat's engines and feed his two deckhands. He had to keep up the butane stove, butane refrigerator, and the cabin's 32-volt battery electrical system.

In the kitchen, Sidney produced a steady stream of good groceries. He cooked T-bone steaks, baked chicken, and white beans over rice with sausage. He whipped up all the local sauces, including fricassées (a dark roux), gumbos (a lighter roux), stews (cooked down in onions but with no roux), and etoufées (smothered with onions). On Fridays, his Catholic crew stuck to their religion's no-meat diet. Sometimes, this meant fresh seafood, but usually Sidney fed his boys spaghetti with boiled eggs.

He also had to constantly tend to his boat's chain-and-sprocket steering system. The mechanism operated like a bicycle chain with the sprockets resembling little pulleys with teeth on them. The chain began at the back of the captain's wheel in the pilothouse two stories above the deck and snaked its way all the way back to the rudder. It was full of moving parts and bearings that had to be repeatedly greased and regreased. If one sprocket rusted, it could lock up the entire steering function.

The all-mechanical manual system could also be difficult to maneuver. When Sidney turned the wheel, he had to swing it around with all of his might. As soon as he had it turned as far as it could go, he'd push down on the throttles, using the engine's full power to make the vessel complete the turn. He had to put all his strength into holding the wheel because the propellers' thrust was pounding on the rudder, desperately trying to straighten it, which meant the steering wheel also wanted to recoil against his hold.

Once, Sidney had let the wheel slip, and it immediately started spinning like a high-speed fan. The whipping wheel caught his middle finger and broke it. On another occasion, this same tornado-like wheel action dislocated his relief captain's shoulder. While the captain grabbed and successfully stopped the spinning wheel, the force of the catch almost pulled off his arm.

Given the hazards of trying to stop the wheel, Sidney knew that if the thing started to spin, he had to let it go—even when the boat was connected to a tow.

On one summer evening in Harvey, Sidney held his wheel and made up, or hooked up, to his pipe barge and started pushing it down the river. Below New Orleans, fog set in, and as it thickened, Sidney tried to stay calm. As usual, he pulled out his coupon book of cigarette paper and rolled himself a fresh cigarette. After lighting up and taking a long drag, he sipped from his cup of black coffee.

But the fog soon grew so thick that he lost his bearings. It got to where he couldn't even detect light or shadow and certainly couldn't make out a boat. As his sight blackened, his other senses sharpened. His nose started picking up smells like the diesel fumes, his cigarette smoke, his steaming coffee, and the trees on the banks. In his feet, he could feel the currents trying to whip the *Ajax*. But unlike in his early days, he was used to the river's temper because he rode it every day. Its changes were too gradual to shake him. Still, it was a bit unsettling to battle the eddies while blind. Without any visual recognition, he couldn't really tell the location of the other vessels' foghorns. He blew his own horn one long and two short, but that didn't mean the ships could tell where he was, either.

Too confused to continue, he made a careful turn toward what he believed was the bank and eventually ran the tow into the soft mud. He tied up to a willow tree and felt the chill of the fog, which turned the Mississippi cold, even in the stifling summer.

Once the tie-up was secure, he told his men to go to sleep; he'd personally stay up and watch for the fog to clear. This vigilance gave Sidney his edge. It was what made the toolpushers think he ran in the thick fog. He loved to pull up to the rig with the rising sun imperceptible and the fog still in pieces. The pusher would look at him all wide-eyed and ask him, "How'd you get here so fast? You must've run in that stuff, huh? Cawww."

Sidney would smile. He wouldn't run in fog like this. But he made sure he or one of his men stayed up and watched for it to thin. Most other tug captains wouldn't do that. They'd hit the bank and everyone on board would go to sleep.

But a few months later, Gulf Oil would tell him about something called radar that would give him a new pair of eyes, allowing him to run in dense fog. Gulf wanted him to install this new device on the *Susan G.*

"Radar?" said Sidney. He'd never even heard of it. The Gulf man explained that it had been used during World War II. The radar worked by sending out radio waves from an antenna on top of the pilothouse, and the waves wouldn't stop until they hit something on the water, be it a boat or possibly a piling. The radio waves bounced off whatever the object was and came back to the boat. The radar then measured how long the distance was between the boat and that object. Based on that distance, the object's location appeared on a little screen on the dashboard.

Sidney couldn't believe something like this could work. How in the world could he trust a dot on a screen? A dot wasn't a ship or a rig. It sure couldn't tell him the shape of a rig, and it wouldn't pick up an underwater wreck.

He didn't see the need for this dot machine. His eyes were good enough, much better than most. If his eyes couldn't spot something, it wasn't there.

But the oilman made it clear that unless he installed the radar, his boat would not work for Gulf Oil. Sidney would, of course, install the device and make Gulf happy. But he wasn't going to use that thing.

There were days after he installed radar on both of his tugs that either with the dot machine or with his own eyes, Sidney could see fine, but he didn't need his vision to know where he was. Instead, a south wind blowing upriver would tell him his exact position the moment he detected the stench of the North American pogy. One whiff of the little mealy, fast-rotting fish and Sidney knew he was just north of Empire. The river town was home to an empire of pogy production. The pogy, or menhaden, was harvested for its oil to make everything from margarine and fertilizer to cat food and lipstick. But the raw, rank pogy smelled nothing like any of those products.

One day, the offensive odor increased the closer the *Ajax* motored to Empire's pogy boats and pogy plants. In the pilothouse, Sidney covered his nose and momentarily held his breath. Soon, he would be breathing only when necessary.

The *grot* made him remember a previous pogy encounter. Once at Fisherman's Canal, a pogy captain had flagged him down. Sidney obliged and turned the *Ajax* toward the stinking boat. The closer he got, the more he thought about turning away. Perhaps it was something the priest or his mama had told him that kept him going. Had he lacked religion or a decent upbringing, he would surely have turned back. Instead, he eased right up to the boat and tied up.

"Hey," the captain told him. "I been broke down here three days. How about a tow?"

Sidney heard a noise and turned around to see one of his deckhands tossing his breakfast over the side of the boat. The other deckhand immediately followed suit. Had Sidney not skipped the meal, he might've joined them.

The pogy captain and his deckhand were just watching the *Ajax* crew, completely unaffected. They might as well have been standing in a rose garden. Taking off his cap, the pogy captain asked again, "What you think?"

"Uhhh." It was all Sidney could say.

"Look podnah, you bring me to Empire. I'll pay you good."

Sidney listened to his deckhands. They were dying. He had to level with this man. "You give me a million dollars. I still can't pull you to Empire."

He couldn't subject his men to deliberate torture. Their conditions were already difficult. They were away from their families. They had to live on a boat, sleeping away from their wives in bobbing bunks, passing through the engine room just to take a shower or go to the toilet. Inhaling diesel fumes was one thing, but three-day-old pogy *grot*? Conscience or no conscience, Sidney couldn't play Good Samaritan.

Luckily, the days out on the river and just east of it on Quarantine Bay weren't all filled with foul smells. For one, there was the fraternity of tugboatmen, and then less often, Sidney would run into crew-boat people and mix with them, too. One family he saw from time to time out on Quarantine Bay were the Orgerons, Juan and his two sons. He especially liked Bobby, who Sidney would later recall as "a joyful man. Bobby was always laughing and joking. He didn't care about a thing."

While nineteen-year-old Bobby Orgeron was usually happy-go-lucky in 1951, he was also deeply concerned about his future in his family's company. The company itself was doing well, so well that Bobby had finally obtained a captaincy on one of his father's crew boats. By this time, Juan Orgeron's one-vessel operation had expanded to three 36-foot wooden hulls, each powered with twin six-cylinder Chrysler gas engines.

For the most part, Bobby enjoyed his work. He embraced the non-stop pace, working for thirty days straight on Quarantine Bay, then taking three days off back home in Golden Meadow. He didn't mind the long hours or the lack of luxury that came with sleeping on the boat and "feasting" on meals of Vienna sausage and potted meat. He could consume nothing better because the boat had no stove. Food was not important, though. Opportunity was, and at last Bobby had one.

But there were two problems. One, his brother Bouillien called the shots and Bobby absorbed them. While Bobby appreciated that Bouillien had taught him how to skillfully handle a boat, Bobby didn't think his brother, only four years his senior, should have been his boss. Two, Bobby wasn't making any money. His father provided him with food, clothes, and shelter, but no car and no salary to buy one. If he needed money, he had to beg his father as if he was a child. On the other hand, the old man had given Bouillien plenty of spending money and had bought his elder son a brand-new 1951 Rocket 88 Oldsmobile.

The bottom line was if the Juan Orgeron Boat Company was earning $105 a day out on Quarantine Bay, then Bobby should make *something*.

The situation finally came to a boiling point in August 1951. On one steamy afternoon, Bobby was having a difficult time just steering his boat. Inside the sauna-like wheelhouse, he was trying to keep his cooked and wilted body erect. He'd spent the past four straight days and nights at the wheel and had hardly squeezed in a catnap. Now he could only look at the wavering willow trees behind the levee and anticipate his first real night of sleep in ninety-six hours. As he closed on the dock, he saw something that made his eyes widen. It wasn't the sight of his brother Bouillien that bothered him. Bouillien was supposed to be there; it was the start of his shift.

What was making Bobby's chest rise was the can of Vienna sausage Bouillien was holding. Bobby knew the sausage was his supposed dinner and knew exactly why his brother was grinning. Undoubtedly, Bouillien wanted Bobby to cover his shift for the fifth night in a row so Bouillien could take his girlfriend up the road to a New Orleans restaurant. Most of the time, this was a favor Bobby could handle. But for the last four days, he hadn't seen anything but little weenies, mosquitoes, hard-leg roustabouts, and the inside of a boat.

After docking the vessel, Bobby looked straight up at his brother. He gave him a harsh greeting and told him, "I ain't working at night any more for you."

"You serious?"

"You damn right I'm serious."

"I'm gonna go call the old man," said Bouillien.

By the time Bouillien picked up the phone, Bobby was sure of what would happen. Whatever his brother said, his father would believe. Whatever Bobby said, Juan would doubt. But this time, believed or not, Bobby would say what he thought.

After Bouillien pleaded his case to his father on the telephone, he handed Bobby the phone. Bobby grabbed the receiver and listened to his father rail him in French, telling him, among other things, "Son, you ain't worth a damn. And you never will be."

This wasn't the first time Bobby had heard this from his father. But it was the first time he'd given him this response: "Well, Pop, if that's the way you feel, you run your boat yourself. I quit."

Bobby hung up the phone, hopped the ferry across the river to Buras, walked to the Popich Hotel, checked in, and collapsed. When he woke up the next morning, he decided to quarantine himself from the oilfield. He hitched the first ride north to an Air Force recruiter station in New Orleans, where he filled out his enlistment papers. During his interview, he deliberately lied about his medical condition. He didn't tell the Air Force about the serious nerve damage in his left pinky, which he'd sustained in a childhood hunting accident, or about the asthma he'd had as a boy. He couldn't let anything keep him from getting into the military and away from his father's big hand.

However, basic training did not go as well as Bobby had planned. Not long after his arrival at Lackland Air Force Base outside of San Antonio, Bobby felt as if he was choking. He was having difficulty simply drawing a breath. The doctor diagnosed him with severe asthma; it was the worst asthma attack of his life.

At the base hospital, a respirator restored Bobby's breathing, but his condition was serious enough to warrant a lengthy stay. One day, while in the hospital in a big room full of about thirty sick soldiers lying in beds, Bobby looked up and saw his father's giant figure fill up the place. Juan was accompanied by Edmond Duet, the boat builder. Mr. Duet was along because he and Juan had planned to go to Houston to look at some engines for a new boat he was building for the Orgerons.

When Bobby saw his father and Mr. Duet, he perked up. Their presence and their French added a little color to the sterile hospital ward. But his father had a certain look on his face. Bobby felt the old man was up to something.

After the three made small talk, Juan told Bobby that they'd come to take him home. Bobby didn't understand. He was the property of the Air Force; he couldn't just walk out of the hospital and into his father's custody.

Juan explained that he'd talked to Bobby's commander and worked out a medical discharge. Bobby was shocked. For one thing, his father couldn't speak much English, and Mr. Duet wasn't exactly a professional translator. But after awhile, Bobby realized his father was telling the truth. Somehow, as strange it sounded, this Cajun, through broken English, had negotiated a medical discharge. If Bobby wanted out of the military, he was free to go.

Bobby told his father in French, "I'm not going home."

Now his father was surprised. Did Bobby really want to go to war? Juan told his son he was building another boat, and that he needed him.

Bobby reminded Juan that if he needed him so badly, he should've paid him a salary when Bobby worked for him.

Juan told him things would change if he came back. He said he might even give Bobby a stake in the company.

Bobby didn't believe him; he didn't think his father would treat him any differently if he returned home. He refused to be voluntarily discharged. Juan and Mr. Duet left without him.

After spending twenty-one days in the hospital, Bobby was transferred to Davis-Monthan Air Force Base in the desert of Tucson, Arizona. If his asthma persisted in this ultradry country, he would invariably be discharged. But it didn't. In fact, the condition disappeared altogether.

At Tucson, Bobby trained to be a heavy equipment operator. He also decided to take night classes at the University of Arizona in preparation for the General Equivalency Diploma test. Despite having only a ninth grade education, he passed the test and ultimately received a diploma from Golden Meadow High School.

While his diploma was an accomplishment for someone with his uneducated lineage, the parchment wouldn't give him much protection where he was headed. He was shipping to Taegu, South Korea, and going to war.

Chapter 5

Paratrooper

Spring 1952

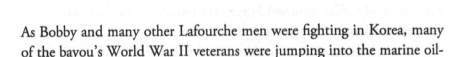

As Bobby and many other Lafourche men were fighting in Korea, many of the bayou's World War II veterans were jumping into the marine oilfield.

One veteran, twenty-seven-year-old Nolty Theriot, didn't need the industry, but he wanted it deeply. Nolty had grown bored working at his father's shrimp shed and before that at Theriot Motors, a dealership co-owned by his father and his uncle.

At both places, Nolty often found himself behind a desk, where his legs would constantly shift back and forth. In fact, everything about his mannerisms, appearance, and his fast talk showed that he needed to move. His dark, robust body was more suitable for his current plan; he was about to convert one of his father's shrimp boats, the 65-foot *Nolty T*, into a tugboat.

In watching Nolty make the conversion, many people had told him that he was *très fou*, flat-out crazy. They said that he had no clients, pointing out that it wasn't like the 1940s when the Texien oilmen were hiring out trawlers, luggers, and Lafitte skiffs because nothing else was available. Now the shipyards were turning out actual oilfield workboats. There was no reason now for an oilman to hire a converted shrimp boat and a man with no tugboat experience.

Nolty shrugged. He believed he knew exactly what he was doing, and besides, *nothing* worried him. First, he and his father, Paris, would convert this trawler into a first-class twin-screw tug because a tug was a boat, and they could build *any* boat. His uneducated father not only constructed his own shrimp boats, he'd also learned how to design sleek fishing yachts.

In fact, boats were deep in the Theriot roots. In 1902 in Leeville, Nolty's grandfather Leon Theriot had created the area's first motorized vessel when he installed a 3-horsepower tractor motor in his 1854-built trawler, *Petit Caporal,* named for Corporal Napoleon Bonaparte. During the 1915 hurricane, *Petit Caporal* had kept the Theriots safe as they fled Leeville forever, motoring up the bayou and not stopping until they had hit the Golden Meadow ridge, where Leon herded his family into a covered barge. When the storm subsided and the family emerged unscathed from the barge, Leon looked at the land he was facing and eventually bought the two-by-forty-arpent tract (a French arpent is about 192 English linear feet) and settled.

As Leon and his eight sons built houses on Theriot Street, almost all of the sons took their turn captaining the *Petit Caporal.* As the brothers grew older, the family began to build more boats. Most of the vessels were one-man operations, with one set of arms pulling in the nets all day long. Then, every evening, as dusk settled over Timbalier Bay, the brothers would begin looking for the boats with the Theriot red and white flag. Then they'd rendezvous, tie their boats together, and cook a big communal meal on the boat with the kerosene stove.

While almost all of the Theriot brothers lacked a formal education, they displayed a unique entrepreneurial savvy. Leo, the only high school graduate, co-owned the car dealership and owned a marine insurance agency, a bookkeeping service and finance company, and was in the process of cofounding the State Bank & Trust Company, right at the head of Theriot Street. In the same area, Leo's brother owned the Theriot Hotel.

All of the Theriot men, especially his father Paris, were role models for Nolty. He'd watched them operate in and around Theriot Street, building each other boats and houses, usually for no charge, and treating their paying customers the way they treated family. At Theriot Motors,

Nolty picked up the art of dealing with everyone the same way both out of humanity and out of financial necessity because he learned that you never knew who might be your next buyer. And if he could convince an old-timer who'd been brought up with a horse and buggy to suddenly buy a big scary car, then he could sell an oilman on the *Nolty T.*

It was a sales pitch Nolty was anxious to make. He couldn't have been more grateful for the opportunity. In truth, he was lucky to be alive. Anyone who stares down a firing squad should be dead.

It had all begun with his restlessness, his *envie* for excitement and his ide-alistic sense of duty. At the time, it was 1943; he was a business student at Loyola University in New Orleans. He was one of the few sons of lower Lafourche privileged enough to go to college, and Loyola's Jesuit-built walls had protected him from the war. But Nolty wanted in on the action; so he dropped out of school and enlisted, becoming a paratrooper with the 101st Airborne.

Like many of the Cajuns in World War II, he qualified as a French interpreter, which made him an ideal scout in the French-speaking part of Belgium.

In January 1945, during the Battle of the Bulge, Nolty had helped his platoon move from farmhouse to farmhouse as he gleaned intelligence from the locals.

On one snowy day in the hilly, forested Ardennes, the visibility had been too poor for Nolty and the other paratroopers to execute a drop. Instead, they were slogging on foot through the drifts, with Nolty and two other scouts well ahead of their platoon. The snow was falling so heavily that Nolty never saw the approaching Nazis. Then, suddenly, five guns emerged from the whiteness. The sight of the barrels paralyzed Nolty and his fellow Americans, who could only throw up their hands in surrender.

At the Nazis' prodding, Nolty and the others began to march through the snow. Then, at some point, the Germans stopped them, lined them up, and started shooting them for no apparent reason. The Nazis' guns bucked, their barrels flashed, and Nolty knew he was going to die. He felt a bullet knock him to the snow. A second later, he realized he was alive, with a gunshot to the leg, right beneath his groin. He heard more machine-gun fire, spraying the little pile of Americans. But apparently, the body on top of him had protected him.

Nolty decided to play dead, keeping his head down and his eyes closed, even after he sensed the Germans were long gone, even as the blood poured out of his wound into the snow and the icy cold began to sting and freeze him. He knew his platoon wasn't too far behind him. Fortunately, after what could've been minutes or hours, he heard in unmistakable American English, "This one's still breathing." Luckily, someone in the platoon knew to pack his wound with snow and stop the bleeding.

Nolty had no idea what happened to his fellow scouts. He presumed they were dead, but it would take him a long time before he could process what had happened, and by that point, he was in a hospital tent.

At the medical unit, a doctor talked about amputating his leg. Nolty shook his head and refused. The doctor eventually relented, and, after extensive treatment, allowed Nolty to be wheeled out of the temporary medical facility and ultimately, in April 1945, shipped back to LaGarde General Hospital in New Orleans.

In Louisiana, Nolty called his parents and told them to bring his childhood sweetheart, Bea Alario, with them to the hospital.

When Bea Alario walked into Nolty's hospital room, she had no idea how he'd been wounded or why he'd called for her. While he'd written her letters during the war, they weren't officially boyfriend and girlfriend. It didn't work that way with her family and their culture.

But she sure liked Nolty. Her friendship with him had begun almost the instant she'd laid eyes on him in the second grade. Their teacher had paired them for the school play because they'd looked good together, and ever since then, they'd been matched up in plays and dances all the way through their high school graduation. They'd always been good friends, but she'd only been on chaperoned dates with him.

Nolty asked her to push his wheelchair into the hospital floor's kitchen for a private discussion. When he asked her to marry him, she was shocked.

Later, Nolty would tell her that she never actually said yes; she just went about making plans for the wedding, which Nolty wanted to happen as soon as possible and which was quickly set for a few weeks away on June 23, 1945. In preparing for the big event, Bea realized she couldn't buy a full-length dress because the train could trip Nolty on his crutches, which he wasn't even supposed to be using. But he'd refused to approach the altar in a wheelchair.

He'd also refused to stay long on crutches or on a cane, shedding all the wooden helpers by that Christmas, though his injury would cause him to always walk with a little hitch in his step. While Bea learned how determined her husband was, she also realized there was a lot of mystery behind the man. As she and Nolty moved into his parents' house, she saw how the family worked. His father, Paris, was a friendly, easygoing man who always had a cigar in his mouth and a wad of $100 bills in his pocket; sometimes, he'd slip the parish priest a few hundreds and tell him to go have a little fun in New Orleans. On the other hand, Nolty's mother, Arteniska—"Nica"—was a strict drill sergeant who ran the household. During Nolty's childhood, the mother had insisted that her son always wear starched shirts and dress shoes; she never let the boy wear tennis shoes. Together, the father and mother were cordial but not affectionate, which was completely the opposite of Bea's parents.

Bea also learned that Nolty's mother suffered from what the Cajuns called the *paisons*, exceptionally bad nightmares. Bea had once watched her mother-in-law sleepwalk into the kitchen and grab a butcher's knife, terrified that someone was about to steal her shoes. On another occasion, she saw her sleepwalk over to the drapes, pull them off the wall, and roll them up so no one could take them. Mrs. Theriot would wake up the next morning not knowing what she'd done.

Bea soon learned that Nolty also suffered from the *paisons*, but his were worse. He would roll around in bed with a look of pure terror in his eyes, sometimes hitting her, sometimes trying to get away from whatever was trying to get him. Between Nolty and his mother, Bea dreaded the coming of nightfall.

One night, when Nolty tried to grab Bea and force her out the window, she'd had more than she could stand. When Nolty woke up the next morning, Bea, who'd not been able to go back to sleep, told him, "We have to talk." She explained what he'd done to her and asked him, "Do you hate me? Do you want to kill me?"

"No," he said "I get flashbacks."

"What about?"

"I don't like talking about it. And I still don't want to talk about it, but I feel like I owe you an explanation."

He proceeded to tell her the detailed story of what had happened to him during the war. For the first time, she saw Nolty break down. He had trouble finishing the story and told her he was sure he'd have more bad memories.

He also told her, as he would many times, "*C'est tous lagniappe*, Bea. *Tout est lagniappe*. Everything is extra. I'm living on borrowed time because I should have been dead that day." He would tell her again and again that he should have been one of the more than nineteen thousand Americans killed at the Battle of the Bulge. And because he did not die in the snow, to him, every moment was pure *lagniappe*.

While the *paisons* were part of that *lagniappe*, Bea learned to cope with them. When a *paison* would wake her up, she'd stand back so he wouldn't hit her, then tell him, "*Tu avais un paison*, honey. It's only a *paison*." He'd look at her with glassy, wild eyes, but he would eventually calm down.

In addition to the diminishing but still present *paisons*, Bea discovered Nolty had also inherited another problem from his forebears, this one being from the Theriot side—bleeding stomach ulcers. One night, less than a year after they were married, Bea heard a noise coming from the bathroom. She got out of bed, walked to the bathroom, and found a woozy Nolty lying on the floor. Apparently, the bleeding in his stomach had caused his blood pressure to drop, and he passed out and hit his head.

Despite the ulcers, the bum leg, and the *paisons*, no matter how Nolty felt at night, he was ready to plow into the morning; that was never more true than when he converted the *Nolty T*. He'd not only enjoyed the challenge of retooling the boat, he relished the unpredictable nature of the venture. He was forever leaving the world of steady paychecks and secure family businesses.

He was also satiating his combat-seasoned need for risk by pursuing the Gulf's most dangerous game, pipeline construction anchor handling. Nolty had learned that to build an underwater pipeline, a tug had to unearth and precisely move a large construction barge's anchors. Often, the anchor-handling crews had to work in rough seas, not stopping even to take on new crew or supplies. If the entire oilfield was rushed, the construction operation was especially frantic because their field was producing, but not making maximum money until the oil company could efficiently ship the product through a pipeline to the shore, where it could be sold. Consequently, the pipeline contractors wanted to show how fast they were, but they couldn't operate at any level of speed without the assistance of fearless anchor-handling tug crews.

Nolty knew he'd enjoy the company of the anchor captains, the marine equivalent of paratroopers. He himself would've liked to have handled the anchor controls, but he believed he'd be more effective running the roads, selling his company, and, hopefully, designing more boats.

As he, his father, and some of his uncles rolled the *Nolty T* into Bayou Lafourche, Nolty had to grin at his achievement. The boat, which only months ago had been pulling shrimp off the bottom of the bay, was now ready to jerk up barge anchors for Nolty's first client, J. Ray McDermott.

While the boat's fresh red and white paint would eventually fade and peel, right now in 1952, everything was gleaming.

By 1954, Bobby Orgeron had survived his own bout with war. Spending fourteen months in Korea, Bobby's job was to service US jets by filling them with fuel and machine-gun belts. While he'd seen no hand-to-hand combat, he was often shot at with tracer bullets at night. Although his risk was minimal because he was usually shielded inside a revetment, he had seen his share of bleeding, dying soldiers being carried from the barricade back to camp on stretchers.

But in truth, the Air Force had been a grand adventure. Overall, the military had been a break from his adolescent drudgery and his father's dominance.

Now back in Golden Meadow on a fifteen-day furlough, Bobby saw no reason why he'd have any trouble with his father. Juan no longer had control over him, and, if anything, Bobby felt his father would be nice to him with the hope of luring him back to the boats when his four-year hitch ended. Bobby simply planned to enjoy his mother's cooking, his friends' company, and the bayou's nightlife.

But too much partying ultimately ruined his trip. Late one Saturday night, Bobby was driving home from the bars in his father's new 98 Oldsmobile and speeding along the bayou road in excess of one hundred miles per hour. At some point, he veered off the asphalt, *jumped* over a small boat tied up to a dock, and landed in the bayou. Luckily, he was able to struggle out of his seat into the cold, black water and swim to the shore.

When Bobby's father arrived at the accident scene, Bobby couldn't read him. He didn't know if Juan was upset by the accident, worried about Bobby, or mad about his Oldsmobile. And he wouldn't know until the next day when his older brother Bouillien told him about a conversation he'd had with their father.

Juan had called Bouillien to tell him about the accident. He'd described what had happened but had offered no details about Bobby's condition. Bouillien then asked, "Well, how's Bobby?"

"You should see my car. It's no good no more."

"Well, Bobby, how is he?"

"My car ain't no good just like that somebitch is no good."

After Bouillien told Bobby the story, Bobby packed and left, ending his fifteen-day furlough at home in seven days. He also terminated any thoughts he had about returning to the boat business.

During the summer of 1955, Bobby began his final military assignment, a three-month temporary duty hitch in Morocco. The minute he arrived in north Africa, it was as if he'd landed in a desert mirage. The city of Marrakech was a *mecca paradiso*.

Not only did the *bon vivant* ethos prevail here, but the sweet French language predominated, drifting through Marrakech's Moorish arches.

Bobby loved the Francophone city of warm weather and well-seasoned food.

By day, his job was breezy. As a French interpreter for an American colonel, he simply spoke the languages that ran through his head like two rivers.

By night, Bobby got to speak in his native tongue in a place that was somehow both familiar and wonderfully exotic. Every evening, he went out and sampled the local delicacies. At the Hotel Lamamounia, he ate his first pheasant under glass. The taste traveled to his memory bank and stayed there; he wanted its cognac flavor to linger forever. The dish was a symbol of all that he wanted in life and, before this moment, could not have.

The fine Moroccan cuisine, the beautiful women, the local dry climate, and the overall *joie de vivre* made Bobby consider reenlisting. He could stand a lot more than three months in Marrakech. In fact, if the army could have guaranteed him that he would stay in Morocco, he would've re-upped on the spot. But in another sense, he was twenty-three years old and, in many ways, he was ready to start pursuing his dream. He wanted to make so much money that he could afford to eat pheasant under glass every night.

From what Bobby could tell, things had settled down back home; he was no longer feuding with his father or his brother. Bobby inwardly acknowledged that he'd made some mistakes in the past himself, and that it was time for him to give his relationship with his family a fresh start. Moreover, Juan had continued to talk about offering him a stake in a boat. Juan hadn't exactly specified when or how this would happen, but Bobby wanted to believe he'd become a boat owner quite quickly. While he still harbored some doubts and knew that he was giving up a carefree existence in the military for the stress of the Juan Orgeron Boat Company, he forged ahead anyway.

He arrived back in Golden Meadow on August 29, 1955, and, two days later, he was behind the wheel of a crew boat, earning the going captain's salary of $300 per month. His father's operations hadn't grown much in four years. He still had only the three crew boats working for Gulf Oil Company. However, the boats had been repowered with diesel engines and had also been moved; the Orgeron base of operations was now close to home at the Gulf dock in Leeville.

On Bobby's first day back on the job, he pulled his craft away from the dock and down Bayou Lafourche. The captain's wheel felt as if it had been made for his fingers. Driving a boat was just like dancing; it came right back to him. Heading down the bayou with green, sunlit marsh on either side of him, he reminisced a little about his last trapping season in Leeville as a young teenager. Back then, he'd check his lines and dream of getting away from trapping and buying an oilfield boat. Now he believed he was close to achieving that goal.

His work schedule soon became erratic. Sometimes he worked days, sometimes nights, sometimes both. During the calm, clear days, the job was easy. But when the night or the weather altered the visibility, the routes became more challenging. Bobby learned to compensate for poor conditions by plotting a course in which he synchronized compass setting changes with running times. He recorded the plans in detail in his notebook. He then meticulously followed them; on a particular course, he would run the direction of the compass for a set number of minutes at so many revolutions of the engine, then change directions when his notebook told him it was time to do so. In favorable conditions, he would recheck his plans to maintain their accuracy.

During this period, early radio wave technology existed, but the Orgerons didn't have radar. Bobby especially wished he had it on one cool, foggy night. He was heading toward a rig in Timbalier Bay, and he could hardly distinguish the pilings that marked the path. Moreover, when he left the line of pilings, he knew it would be more dangerous in the open bay, which was studded with rigs and wellheads. If he hit a structure, he would surely injure or kill all of his fifteen-person crew.

But to Bobby, waiting out the fog wasn't an option. The rig needed its crew to drill, and the rig's company man fully expected the crew to arrive at the rig on time, fog or no fog. In truth, he didn't have much choice anyway; if he didn't learn to handle the fog, a typical hazard of his profession, he'd have to find another career. So he decided he might as well follow his notebook and take his chances.

But as he motored further into the soup, something wasn't right. A short time after he left the line of pilings, he nearly hit a wellhead and realized that he was completely off course. It didn't make sense. Yesterday, he'd checked his calculations in the bright sunlight, and they'd been perfect.

He futilely tried to figure out his location. He then turned his eyes toward the compass and discovered his problem. He'd left a screwdriver on the dashboard, and the metal screwdriver had acted as a magnet and pulled the compass needle toward it, destroying its accuracy. Though he knew a screwdriver or a wrench could pull a compass, he'd been working on a windshield wiper while at the dock and had simply forgotten to stow the screwdriver. The compass wouldn't do him any good now because he had no point of reference. Everything was a cloud.

He killed the engine and listened for the sound of the rig. He couldn't see anything, but he could hear the rig.

Bobby cranked the engine and idled toward the noise. His eyes were straining for rigs or pilings or shell piles, but all he saw was fog. He killed the ignition again. He could hear a hum, yet now the sound was more distant.

The water was playing tricks on him. With no chart, there were no certainties. Bobby could only put-put around the bay, stopping and listening, making correct turns and then incorrect ones, zigging and zagging until he finally found the rig right around daybreak.

By the time he idled up to the derrick, he was several hours late. After his crew disembarked and boarded the rig, the rig's pusher walked toward the boat and gave Bobby a good tongue-lashing. There was not much for Bobby to say in his defense; he could only prepare for his trip back through the soup to Leeville.

On the way home, Bobby told himself there were easier ways to make a living. Still, if he was to achieve his goal of owning a boat, he had to take these chances. One way or the other, he had to take advantage of a bustling local economy.

Golden Meadow had been popping when Bobby left for the service in 1951; now it was roaring. The town, which had become one of the bayou's few incorporated municipalities in 1950, was brimming over with activity and new establishments. Since Bobby's departure, Golden

Meadow had added a jail, a town hall, the Lafourche Telephone Company, the solid State Bank and Trust Company, and the KLEB-AM radio station.

The town's Texien population had mixed and married with more of the locals. This blending, along with all the new infrastructure, had resulted in a more settled, less wooly Golden Meadow. But the town had still not lost its feverish, gold rush feel. In fact, there was an even greater urgency to explore for marine oil. The surge was a result of three factors, one being an end of the steel shortages caused by World War II and the Korean War. Two, there was an increase in the demand for fossil fuels brought on by the nation's rising population of automobiles and airplanes and its soaring need for power generation, home heating fuels, and synthetic rubber. Three, the Tidelands Act of 1953 ended the state-federal offshore leasing dispute and enabled the oil companies to lease waters farther and farther away from the coast.

The favorable regulatory climate also provided the impetus for technological improvements. Advanced seismic exploration allowed operators to find mineral reserves at greater depths, which, in turn, spurred developments in offshore rig design. The post-World War II rigs were almost all small fixed platforms supported by floating tenders, most of which had been converted from war surplus vessels. But these tenders created mooring problems in rougher waters. Consequently, in the early to mid-1950s, the industry began to design all-in-one, self-supported, self-contained drilling rigs, which were mobile and more stable.

The new technology justified building more rigs. And more rigs meant more boats. This trickle-down effect was a boon to marine oil hubs like Golden Meadow, and the economic frenzy did more than keep the area's boat companies busy. It also kept in business the town's inordinate number of family grocery stores, restaurants, and bars.

To Bobby Orgeron, it seemed as if Golden Meadow had at least thirty barrooms, many of them on the bayouside, up on pilings out over the water. And on Saturday nights, Bobby lost himself in them. He might have been in a ramshackle, lean-to saloon or a sturdy, cypress dance hall, but during his first couple of months home, whatever the stops, his routine was usually the same—drink, dance, and fight.

It was as if a part of him was accepting his father's lifelong words that he would never amount to anything. Another part of him was just letting out his *joie de vivre*.

Bobby's whirlwind steadied one night in late October 1955 at a Halloween dance. He looked across the hardwood floor of the Golden Meadow High School Gym and saw a petite, brown-eyed beauty. Wasting no time in asking her to dance, he learned that her name was Myrtle Charpentier and that she was from a short distance up the bayou in Galliano.

While Bobby enjoyed his dance with her, he couldn't pursue Myrtle—he was going out with another girl. But he also couldn't get Myrtle out of his head. The next time he saw her, it was one night at the Bellevue in Cut Off. When she walked through the door with a bunch of girls, a friend of his pointed her out and said, "Boy, the guy that would get her, right there. She would make a wife." Before his friend finished his compliment, Bobby was asking her to dance. After they danced a few times, he asked her for a date. She said no.

Unfortunately, Bobby couldn't prevent Myrtle from learning of his wild reputation. But it wasn't fair. He didn't steal. He didn't hit anyone who "didn't deserve it." But he did enjoy drinking and fighting. He did get arrested for drinking- and fighting-related offenses, even though he was never convicted. Really, this was what he was supposed to do.

He realized she didn't need a troublemaker. She was a respected young lady, a college graduate of the Southwestern Louisiana Institute and a home economist at Louisiana Power and Light. She didn't want to burden herself with an immature, rogue boat captain with crazy dreams.

Bobby didn't listen to the logic. On another occasion, he asked her for a date a second time. Again, she said no. But he kept talking, finally telling her, "You're in love with me."

She started laughing.

"But you are in love with me. You don't know it yet, but it'll come to you."

"I'm not in love with you. I don't even want to go out with you."

But she did finally give in, going with him to a drive-in movie. And as the weeks passed, Myrtle softened, and Bobby started to win. He couldn't stay away from her. And it began to seem as if she had to be near him, too. There was only one thing left to do.

He visited Myrtle's father, though he didn't know the man and had only been dating Myrtle for a short time. Still, he felt it was time to ask Mr. Charpentier for his daughter's hand.

The proposal, however, offended Mr. Charpentier. He didn't want his daughter to have anything to do with this brash young man. And he didn't buy into Bobby's self-serving character defense. In Mr. Charpentier's mind, there was nothing for them to discuss; his answer was no.

As 1955 drew to a close, Bobby's personal and professional frustrations continued to mount. Professionally, he'd decided he could no longer tolerate simply being an employee. He was ready for more than a salary. One night, he asked his daddy to sit down with him in the family living room. He preferred to speak to his father when Juan was sitting down, his six-feet-six frame tucked into a chair.

He then told his father he was ready to buy into one of the company's boats.

Juan told him he wasn't ready.

Bobby reminded him that he'd been promised this opportunity.

Juan told him to keep working and, eventually, he'd *give* him a piece of a boat.

Bobby asked when that would happen.

Juan told him to go back to work, and happen it would. Bobby said it had to happen now.

Juan told him to talk to his brother. Bouillien was doing well now. Bouillien might give him a shot.

Bobby did talk to Bouillien. In the past, his brother had been the brains behind the family business. Now that he had his own company, maybe he could give Bobby what Bobby wanted.

When Bobby made his pitch, Bouillien was all smiles and head nods. Bouillien said he wanted his brother involved. He agreed to a partnership on a boat, and they shook hands. Bouillien was giving his brother a piece of his 51-foot steel vessel called the *Spitfire*, which was working for Chevron, Bouillien's big client. The boat was known as an Equitable crew boat because it was built at the Equitable Shipyard in New Orleans.

Bobby was amazed. While he still didn't quite trust his brother, he was finally an owner.

Bobby Orgeron in the Air Force during the Korean Conflict.
(Courtesy of Bobby Orgeron)

In the four years that Bobby had been away, Bouillien had made his company boom. He was a certifiable millionaire. He owned a large home, a fleet of Cadillacs, and a single-engine Cessna airplane.

Part of the reason for Bouillien's success was his fearlessness. Unaffected by financial or physical risk, Bouillien made sure he had the fastest 51-foot crew boats in the Gulf; consequently, he designed his hulls to plane on the water as quickly as possible. During this time, crew boats were sometimes called "speedboats." With rigs being drilled farther and farther away from the coast, a faster boat saved precious travel time. And though swift-flying helicopters were beginning to ferry crew members to the rigs, the chopper would never completely replace the crew boat, which could carry more people than a helicopter and operate in much poorer visibility.

The oilfield's demand for versatile vessels and daring captains suited Bouillien Orgeron. His crew boats' names reflected his fiery, go-getting personality. His *Spitfire, Starfire, Swampfire,* and *Wildfire* were well known on the bayou, and their owner was as personally wild as his boat titles.

With one lung and a hole in his back, it was as if Bouillien was living on borrowed time. When he'd had the lung removal surgery as a boy, the doctors told his parents he wouldn't live to be fifty. They said that even a simple pneumonia could kill him. So Bouillien was making up for the years he would supposedly lose. He flew his plane like an acrobat, landing it on narrow levees or in the middle of a wooded island on the Mississippi River. He'd shoot a gun through a roof with no warning. He was more reckless than his brother and much more unpredictable.

Given Bouillien's penchant for making spontaneous, sometimes irrational decisions, Bobby wasn't surprised when his brother suddenly reneged on their agreed fee split and revoked their "partnership." The business relationship hadn't even lasted a month.

Bobby realized now that he couldn't count on his father's or his brother's promises. While he believed he could run a boat company as well as anyone, he had no real prospects. He was told by local bankers that he didn't have the cash or the credit to build or buy a boat. And while he was in love and ready to settle down with Myrtle, her father still wouldn't bless the marriage.

A new year was coming, and Bobby was prepared to start his life, if the world would only give him a chance.

The original *Botruc* plies the open water. (Courtesy of L & M Botruc Rental, LLC)

Chapter 6

The Botruc Brigade

1956

———∞∞∞———

In the mid 1950s, as rookies such as Bobby were attempting to break into the business, veterans like Minor Cheramie were trying to distinguish themselves. Minor had developed a reputation as more than a mere lady-killing charmer. He'd now proven that he was a man of action. In six years, he'd bought or built seven vessels, quickly selling one of them to a company servicing the early 1950s boom in Lake Maracaibo, Venezuela. Despite his ability to grow his fleet, he still hadn't pocketed much money because he'd been pouring his profits into expansion. He was also running the company out of his house with no office employees. He wanted something better for his family.

One day in 1956, all of Minor's thinking, planning, hustling, and networking led to a conversation with Merrill Utley, a Chevron transportation superintendent. Utley told Minor about a recent vacation he'd taken in the northeast where he'd seen an interesting passenger and automobile ferry. The ferry had a pilothouse located all the way at the bow and had a long, broad afterdeck. Utley thought the ferry's design could be adapted to an oilfield workboat, what he envisioned as the first self-contained supply boat.

Minor agreed. He'd never seen a supply boat with a completely open stern deck. The current supply boats were either converted World War II surplus vessels or lugger-style tugs that usually carried the rig's supplies by deck barge, meaning that without the barge, the boat didn't have a deck large enough to carry what she needed.

Utley gave Minor the name of the shipbuilder, Luther Blount of Warren, Rhode Island. Minor immediately called the shipyard and asked for Mr. Blount.

Ironically, Blount was ready for the phone call. Despite being located in New England, a world away from the oilfield, the thirty-nine-year-old Rhode Islander had *already* adapted his ferry design into an offshore supply boat. He called it a "Botruc," the pickup truck of the oilfield. Like a truck, the Botruc had a cab located at her front followed by an open back deck.

He'd learned about the idea in 1954 when a Morgan City, Louisiana, businessman, Parker Conrad, had hired him to build an oilfield seismographic vessel. In visiting Conrad, Blount had toured the yards and docks of south Louisiana and observed the current oilfield boats. He noted that the vessels usually carried bulky drilling tools and long drill pipe by barge. While he saw one boat that was sort of being used as a bargeless supply vessel, he thought the boat was too narrow for its length and could be improved.

Blount believed he could design a 65-foot Botruc with enough width, twenty-three feet, to make it especially stable. He would mold and curve the hull's lines like his ferries so the boat would better absorb the pounding of heavy wave action. This would be an improvement on the lines of many of the current oilfield boats, which weren't consistently sloped all the way to the back, but were more of a square barge connected to a bow and a stern. Blount also changed the boat's exhaust system. Instead of having the exhaust come through the stern transom, which was the norm, he discharged it straight from the engine room through the boat's side. That meant the exhaust had a much shorter, more efficient path because it didn't have to pass through a bulkhead and an extra compartment in the hull.

Remarkably, Blount had dramatically improved the offshore supply vessel despite having almost no contact with the oilfield. But to Blount, it wasn't any big thing. He'd grown up in a New England family similar to the boat people of south Louisiana. In fact, when he saw the little yards along the bayous with the boat builders using tree limbs to hoist up bulkheads, it reminded him of his upbringing. His forebears were oystermen, and whenever they needed a new oyster boat, they built her themselves. When Blount was a teenager, he'd experimented with the craft himself, building several duck boats.

Blount then polished his mechanical aptitude by obtaining an engineering degree from the Wentworth Institute of Technology in Boston. After graduation, he went to work as a thread engineer, designing threads for parachute cords, army uniforms, dental floss, sutures, and for other uses. He would secure his first US patent by designing a novel thread. Many more patents related to boats would follow, as, beginning in 1949, he built everything from ferries to fishing long-liners to molasses tankers.

By the time of the Botruc, Blount had obtained a couple of patents on his boats but did not attempt to patent the Botruc. Unbeknownst to him, a fledgling company out of New Orleans called Tidewater was building a similar cab-forward, open-stern deck boat around the same time in 1955. Tidewater's *Ebb Tide* was designed by Doc Laborde, the same man to conceive the world's first transportable, submersible drilling barge. But the *Ebb Tide* was a slightly different animal. At 127 feet, she was much longer and proportionately narrower, and her lines weren't as smoothly molded as the Botruc. In any event, both vessels were a major industry breakthrough and their cab-forward, spacious afterdeck design became the standard for supply boats.

Blount had surely believed he was onto something. He'd asked Parker Conrad about sales prospects and Conrad referred him to the George Engine Company over in Harvey. Technically speaking, George sold marine engines, but they also brokered boat sales to shipyards and provided financing. In this case, the people at George were confident that the Botruc, powered by a pair of Detroit Diesel 6-110s, would sell, and they told Blount they would finance two of the boats.

Encouraged, Blount decided to build four Botrucs. In constructing them, Blount had to follow a new set of federal regulations, Public Law 519, which passed in 1956 and brought all previously uninspected commercial vessels that were more than fifteen gross tons under inspection laws. The inspection laws not only meant actual Coast Guard inspections, but could mean additional manning and licensing requirements and other expenses. So the key was for Blount to keep the Botrucs under fifteen gross tons. "Tons" didn't mean the vessel's actual weight but, theoretically, the amount of water it displaced. "Gross tons" referred to all of the vessel's enclosed space. Fortunately, there were exceptions to the rule. For instance, ballast tanks were exempt from the tonnage calculation. So Blount made sure almost every compartment on the boat, outside of the engine room and the pilot house, had the ability to pump water in and out of it and become a ballast tank. He created tonnage openings by placing tonnage doors on the deck and in bulkheads, a process that was called "letting the tonnage out."

All of Blount's calculating and crafting impressed Minor Cheramie. He loved Blount's tonnage tricks, the boat's pickup truck function, and her svelte, molded lines. After talking to Blount, he pounced on a purchase, heading to Harvey to give George Engine a $1,000 deposit for one of the Botrucs and financing the rest of the $72,000 price through George and the Yellow Manufacturing Acceptance Corporation, a General Motors subsidiary that was primarily in the business of financing taxicabs. Eventually, Minor took his brother and partner Lefty and their wives up to Warren, Rhode Island, to visit Blount and trade their Cajun accents with his heavy New England clip, to eat fresh mussels, lobster, and clam chowder, and, of course, to see the Botrucs being built. At the Blount yard, which bordered oyster businesses on the pitched and steepled Warren waterfront, Minor marveled at the Botruc hulls, which some people had compared to the shape of a wooden Dutch shoe, and at the high wheelhouse, which gave the captain a clear and commanding view of the water.

Minor bought three of the four boats, the original *Botruc* and two others, which he would name *Cheramie Botruc II* and *Cheramie Botruc III*.

Blount delivered the seminal *Botruc* personally, putting his station wagon on her back and taking his wife along for the ride down the Atlantic Intracoastal Waterway to the Gulf Intracoastal Waterway all the way to the Harvey Canal. Before taking his station wagon back to New England, Blount accepted Minor's invitation to take a helicopter ride out to a Gulf oil rig and then head back to Minor's Galliano home for dinner. That night, Blount slept in the Cheramie household, froze in the heavily air-conditioned guest room, couldn't gather enough covers, and caught a cold overnight.

As Blount coughed, sneezed, and sweated his way through the next day on Bayou Lafourche, he received an enthused pitch from Minor. Minor wanted him to build many more Botrucs, starting with another eight. Minor would give him 10 percent down and pay the rest upon delivery.

Blount, however, didn't like the idea of taking such a risk. He'd built the first four Botrucs basically on spec because he was hungry for the work. But he didn't want to get into the habit of gambling on the oilfield. To meet Minor's demands, he would have to enlarge his yard and go into debt. He wouldn't mind taking the risk if Minor agreed to make progress payments, which was the norm on the East Coast. But while an installment deal might've been the custom in New England, it wasn't the rule in the risk-taking Gulf oilfield.

Blount couldn't see going into debt that deeply. His conservative father had always told him not to go into the boat-building business, warning him that, "You'll go bankrupt sure as hell." His father's proclamation had made him cautious.

But Blount's caution didn't curb Minor's enthusiasm. When Minor took the *Botruc* down its maiden Bayou Lafourche voyage, the people crowded the bayouside and drew deep breaths. They didn't appear to know what they were seeing. "What is that?" they'd ask. To many, the boat with the barrel-chest bow was the biggest thing to come down the bayou. While Sidney Savoie's *Ajax* had made quite a stir, it wasn't quite as long and wasn't nearly as wide or as big-bosomed as this well-endowed *Botruc*. For days, she would be the topic of talk in lower Lafourche.

And as Minor had hoped, the oil companies gave the boat a similar reception. Ten companies tried to lease her. After Minor had hustled to sell his services to so many oilmen for several years, now the oilmen were pursuing him. While he decided to lease the boat to Chevron out of loyalty to Utley, there would be plenty of Botrucs to go around.

In buying two more identical Botrucs from Blount, Minor had his plan in place. It didn't matter whether Blount would build future Botrucs because Minor would find someone to build them. The important point was, Minor owned the first ones. From this day forward, he would place the name "Cheramie" and "Botruc" side by side, and they would become synonymous.

While Blount had invented the design and coined the name, Minor's personality and his ability to promote his product would make it famous in the marine oilfield.

In a scaled-down sense, Minor was mass producing a product and establishing a brand name just like many American companies were doing in other industries in the 1950s. At the time, McDonald's was making multiple hamburgers, General Motors was cranking out identical automobiles on the assembly line, and Holiday Inn was introducing the concept of the hotel chain. With the help of Blount and other shipbuilders, Minor planned to develop the Botruc as the industry-standard supply boat.

He not only had a unique vessel, but also a novel name that would stand out from the litany of boats named after children, wives, and baby sisters. In his mind, all he had to do was build more Botrucs, and his promotional and operational skills would do the rest.

As the Botrucs ran supplies around the Gulf, Minor's wife Lou began to take a larger role in the company. After she and Minor bought their first house, she set up a little office there, where she was a one-woman show. She was the secretary, bookkeeper, and dispatcher. She'd talk to the boats and take their orders for groceries, parts, and whatever else was needed. She did everything she could to help the company while trying to also raise her six-year-old daughter Deanie.

As the business began to prosper, her relationship with her husband became more and more complicated. Their problems had a definite cause—despite nearing their ten-year anniversary, Minor still hadn't lost his affection for the drink. It was now clear that Minor was an alcoholic.

Moreover, Minor did not try to hide his affairs with other women. Sometimes, a jealous girlfriend would call Lou and tell her that Minor was with *another* girlfriend. And despite his philandering, he still expected Lou to shine his shoes and iron his clothes. When she finally decided she could no longer stand his open adultery, she confronted him.

That night, he came home smelling like the woman he'd been with and woke Lou up and told her to fix him breakfast. This time, she refused. In Minor's drunken state, he couldn't take a no. As she persisted in her refusal, he shouted and eventually grew violent. He beat her that night, and he would hit her on other nights when he was under the influence. When inebriated, it was as if he sometimes couldn't distinguish between his wife and a man at the bar. Apparently, he couldn't see through his drunken blinders that his sweet, loving Lou was the one taking the blows.

The next morning, after he woke up, it was as if none of it had happened. It was if, in his suddenly sober mind, he had no memory of what he had done. He'd go back to being a generous, fun-loving man whom everyone loved, who'd never harm anyone.

Of course, his sober good deeds did not excuse his drunken transgressions. And sure, Lou wanted to leave. Even though she was as much a part of the Cheramie Botrucs as he was, she wanted to get away from him. When she'd threaten to go, he'd warn her that he'd find her, telling her there was no place on earth that she could hide. And it wasn't only her fear that made her stay with him. She'd also worked for their success and was not about to give up her half of the company. In the beginning, she'd cramped her fingers stuffing that first wooden boat with the *calfeutrer*. Now all day long, she was dispatching and working the books and sweeping the floor. Sometimes in the middle of the night, she'd wake up to answer the phone, and because Minor was off entertaining an oilman, she herself would have to take care of some oilfield emergency. She alone was the vital link to the oil company and its service companies' desire for a twenty-four-hour-a-day profit stream and the necessity of keeping up with the energy-dependent world's constant demand for fuel.

Even when Minor would start to hire office employees and she would technically become a full-time mother and housewife, Lou would never cease serving the Botrucs. She was as responsible for Cheramie Botruc's success as Minor, and she wasn't going to give it all to another woman.

And there was always the hope that Minor would change. When he was sober, he never laid a finger on her. In fact, he didn't even so much as raise his voice in her direction. If he'd give up the drink, she knew her life would be different. If he would stop drinking, he could do anything.

One starkly blue wintry morning in January 1956 in Golden Meadow, Bobby Orgeron looked at the bayou and saw a boat that he had to have. This *Davey Lou No. 4* was forty-one feet of shiny steel, powered by twin 671 diesel engines. The crew boat's owners and namesakes, Davis Theriot and Alvin Louviere, wanted to sell her for $23,000. That price, Bobby knew, was more than fair. He calculated the potential day rate and banknotes and believed he could make a nice profit right away. He was sure that this boat, pleasingly long and taut, would help make him a millionaire.

By himself, even with a bank loan, he couldn't buy the boat. He could secure $8,000 from Citizens Bank in Cut Off, which had changed its boat loan policy since refusing to accept Sidney Savoie's "sinkable" *Ajax* as collateral in 1949. Despite the bank's newfound acceptance of marine loans, Bobby still needed to come up with the remaining $15,000. When his brother told him he'd kick in his signature for another $8,000 and they'd be fifty-fifty partners, Bobby was leery but agreed as long as he controlled the income distribution.

Still, for the bank to finance the purchase with no money down, Bobby needed to produce another credible cosigner for the first $7,000 borrowed.

Bobby hated to ask his father, but Juan owed him. When he finally approached him, his daddy looked weary. He must have been tired of listening to Bobby's demands to buy into his company. Juan grimaced and grunted, but his fight was gone. He signed the note, and Bobby was in business.

Once Bobby tied up the *Davey Lou No. 4* to the Orgeron dock, he wasted no time putting her to work. Within a week, she was working for a drilling contractor out of Caillou Island. Then, a short time later, Bobby offered his boat to Gulf Oil in Leeville, and the company immediately added the vessel to its fleet. Gulf would pay him a rate, fifty dollars per day, that would help him shrink his debt and finally make his own way.

As Bobby began to establish himself professionally, he was also ready to settle his most pressing personal matter. He wanted to marry his "moose," Myrtle Charpentier. Moose, spelled differently, meant love in Korean slang. And the way Bobby saw it, Myrtle would be the only woman he ever called "my moose."

He also saw no reason why Mr. Charpentier wouldn't now let them be married. Bobby was a boat owner and was making a decent living. And besides, they were in love. Myrtle told him she'd talk to her father.

Myrtle made another plea, but Mr. Charpentier wouldn't change his mind. To him, Myrtle was still the little baby who crawled on his chest, who once looked at him as if he were the only man in the world. How could he turn over his sweet, brown-eyed fawn to this *cochon sauvage*? The pig called his daughter a "moose." How could he make a term of endearment out of an ugly *Canadien* cow with antlers?

But as time passed, it appeared as if this Orgeron was going to win. Mr. Charpentier had never seen his daughter so smitten and so sure. This was normally a logical girl who had always been all books and good sense. But she'd lost her mind here. And if Mr. Charpentier didn't allow the wedding, he feared these two young *couillons* would elope. If it was going to happen, then let the priest bless them. Let the Catholic Church sanctify it. Maybe God would help them.

Suddenly, the wedding was dead ahead—April 16, 1956, at St. Joseph Church in Galliano. Bobby could let Myrtle focus on the plans, and he could concentrate on his boat.

Bobby didn't reserve his time for only the *Davey Lou No. 4* and Myrtle. He had to keep up with his podnahs, too. After living the drinking, partying life for four years in the service and then back home, he couldn't stop now just because he was getting married. One evening, three days before his wedding, he was practicing those old habits, barhopping with a friend, ending the night at 2:00 a.m. hard by the marsh at Bouzigard's Restaurant on the bayouside in lower Golden Meadow. They were laughing and eating steaming bowls of gumbo. They'd been trading barbs with a group of Texiens. One of the Texiens was a big

Indian, perhaps a Cherokee. Whatever he was, he was taller and thicker than the local Houma Indians who lived along the marsh road and on its chenieres.

At some point, the Cherokee had enough. He walked up to their table, turned over Bobby's friend's bowl of gumbo, and then asked, "What are you gonna do about it?"

Bobby didn't give his podnah a chance. He popped up and said, "All right. If he don't do anything about it, I will."

"Oh yeah, what's that?"

"Why don't we go outside?"

Outside they went, squaring off in the oyster shell parking lot. Bobby started his dance in the shell dust, jabbing and popping the Indian. But both he and his opponent were a little too drunk to fight effectively, and they ended up sloppily wrestling in the shells, both walking away bruised and bloody.

Bobby was too full of adrenaline to feel any pain, but sporting a black eye and a swollen nose, he knew Myrtle would be horrified. No amount of makeup would make him look any better for the wedding.

When Myrtle saw his battle wounds, her reaction stung him. She hit him with so much guilt that he didn't think he'd survive it. Her words and her crying pounded him, and then her silence burned him. How would she forgive him in just two days?

But on their wedding day, despite the swelling and discoloration in his face, despite the cut on his nose, Bobby was all pride on the altar. He was initially a little embarrassed, but his shame vanished when he saw the lady in white. He could hardly contain his feelings as Mr. Charpentier escorted a veiled Myrtle down the aisle. He'd never seen anything as beautiful as his bride, getting closer and more real with each step.

They stopped before him, and Mr. Charpentier lifted the veil and kissed his daughter.

Bobby extended his hand toward his soon-to-be father-in-law. Mr. Charpentier refused it.

Bobby and Myrtle absorbed the snub and smiled at each other anyway. Their long gazes locked. The priest anointed them. And Bobby married his moose before God, Galliano, and Golden Meadow.

Bobby and Myrtle Orgeron on their wedding day.
(Courtesy of the Orgeron Family)

Despite God's blessing, the people of Galliano and Golden Meadow didn't think Myrtle could change Bobby; she might be a smart girl, her, but she couldn't tame that boy. Sure, Bobby heard their negative predictions, but let them watch what would happen. He would show them what he and Myrtle could do together.

II

Abyss

Frisco Gisclair, Sidney Savoie, and Emmett Eymard stand aboard the *Alamo II* in 1963.
(Courtesy of Ted Savoie)

Chapter 7

Don't Worry About Nothing

September 1956

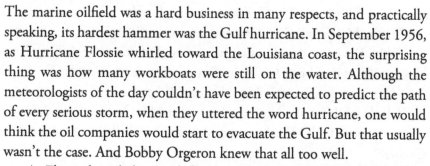

The marine oilfield was a hard business in many respects, and practically speaking, its hardest hammer was the Gulf hurricane. In September 1956, as Hurricane Flossie whirled toward the Louisiana coast, the surprising thing was how many workboats were still on the water. Although the meteorologists of the day couldn't have been expected to predict the path of every serious storm, when they uttered the word hurricane, one would think the oil companies would start to evacuate the Gulf. But that usually wasn't the case. And Bobby Orgeron knew that all too well.

As Flossie barreled toward the shore, Bobby was alone in the *Davey Lou No. 4,* at anchor in a roiling, boiling sea. He might as well have been paralyzed. He'd just had an argument with the rig's pusher and told the man he refused to stand by any longer. The pusher had responded by telling him if he left his post, he'd lose his job.

But presently, Bobby wasn't thinking about money or reputation. He was focused on survival. If he stayed out here much longer, his boat would probably capsize. But it was too rough for him to walk to the bow and pick up the anchor. He'd tried a few times only to be knocked to the deck by waves.

His position seemed hopeless. After thinking and praying, he decided to crank the engines. While keeping them in neutral, he pulled out his pocket knife and opened the windshield. He started to climb out and was quickly pummeled by rain and wave spray.

Then, holding his knife, he crawled out as far onto the bow as he safely could while still keeping his legs inside the window panes. Extending his arm, he could just reach the tight anchor rope with his blade. He cut it, abandoning the anchor.

The *Davey Lou* drifted free, but her freedom soon turned into a problem. Bobby had to scramble back into the cabin and turn the boat toward the waves. If the *Davey Lou* turned sideways, a big breaker could hit her broadside and flip her over.

As Bobby slid back through the panes, he grabbed the wheel and kept the bow aligned with a crashing wave. Then he put the engines in gear and rode the breakers all the way to the sea buoy. Once inside the ship channel, he remembered he had no anchor. So he beached the boat in the marsh bank and, at last, was able to let out a long breath.

A little while later, he heard over the radio, "*Davey Lou No. 4, Davey Lou No. 4*. This is the *Mr. Charlie*. Come back, skip."

"Yeah, *Mr. Charlie*," said Bobby, returning the rig's call.

"Skip, I'm sorry. I realize that here where I'm at, I ain't shaking. You by yourself on that boat. Go on in. But stay inside on the radio."

"That's a roger," said Bobby, shaking his head.

A little while later, a big cargo boat passed him in the channel, heading toward the Gulf. The boat soon returned with the crew of the *Mr. Charlie*.

Bobby sighed. Somehow, sense had prevailed.

Bobby's experience during Hurricane Flossie was eerily similar to what happened to forty-four-year-old Sidney Savoie. Even though Sidney had guided his crew through the storm to safety at the Gulf Oil dock in Leeville, the Gulf man had asked Sidney to go back out into the tempest to retrieve some equipment.

Sidney knew what the Gulf man was thinking—the company could lose millions of dollars in assets. But the man also had to know that he should have safely mobilized his equipment after the first warning of a hurricane. Sidney had seen the oil companies lose equipment before in a storm because they had not taken the proper precautions. Because of the lack of preparation, the companies hadn't only lost equipment, they'd also lost precious work time during the post-storm salvage operation.

Whatever Gulf Oil's predicament during Flossie, by this point, Sidney couldn't help the company. He told the Gulf man, "I'm not going."

These were strange words—it was the first time Sidney had actually turned down a Gulf request. Many times, Gulf and other companies had given him a long list of jobs that they'd wanted completed before the end of his hitch. Sidney would look at the list and shake his head. He knew there was no way he could get those jobs done in time. He was often tempted to tell the company men how unreasonable they were being, but he'd only hold his tongue and keep working.

Sometimes, the oil companies requests weren't just onerous but dangerous. Not that long ago on a Gulf Oil job in Venice, a storm had turned the Mississippi River's current into one big whirlpool. Sidney had been sitting safely in port when the Gulf man told Sidney that there was a tugboat pushing a big dredge upriver that couldn't make it to The Jump, a spot on the River near where it emptied into two passes. She literally couldn't overpower the wind and current. The Gulf man asked Sidney to go help the tow.

Sidney didn't even hesitate, saying quickly, "I'll go." Yes, it was risky but there were lives at stake. So he left port and headed downriver, barely able to control his tug. When he reached the tug in peril, he struggled hooking up his hawser to her, and once hooked up, he had trouble plodding back upriver. But Sidney succeeded in bringing the tow into port. He'd never even questioned his decision to risk his life for the sake of other lives.

Now, however, with Hurricane Flossie blowing toward Timbalier Bay, the Gulf Oil man couldn't tell Sidney whether there were any men out there. Well, no men, no Sidney. He told the company man, "I'm sorry. I can't go back out there."

"Well," the man sighed. "Stay tied up. We'll see."

Within the next few hours, Flossie closed quickly. It soon became clear that any salvage missions would have to be delayed until the storm passed. By that point, the equipment would be blown all over the bay, up on the land, into the marsh, or into the open sea.

Through the Gulf Oil's office windows, Sidney watched Flossie bend a tree all the way to the ground. He was wondering why the Gulf transportation man hadn't fired him on the spot. Maybe it was because he and the man had become close friends. Or maybe it was because the big oil company wasn't as fierce as it threatened to be.

Whatever it was, he'd called the oilfield's bluff, and it had backed down.

Hurricane Flossie had also forced Bobby Orgeron to challenge his big oil client, and luckily, he'd survived intact with his life and his career. After Flossie, it wasn't long before Stanolind Oil moved him and his *Davey Lou No. 4* to another job much farther west in Intracoastal City, a tiny marsh community thirty-six miles south of Lafayette. Because Intracoastal City was a four-hour drive from home, Bobby was going to have to spend most of his entire thirty-day hitch away from his new bride, Myrtle.

In the eight months that he and Myrtle had been married, Bobby had done an absolute about-face. He'd gone from drinking and fighting to being all work and all Myrtle. His podnahs could have their bars, their fights, and their loose women. He had a *real* woman and a real career.

By 1957, Bobby had settled into daily life in Intracoastal City, where his boat rested at the Macabar Mud Company dock. His view included some tin sheds, storage tanks, cattle pastures, and a hog pen. The most common smells were of cow dung, pig odor, and drilling mud.

Bobby grew to accept his existence of one month of working, eating, and sleeping on the boat, and then three days of Myrtle's cooking, conversation, and warm body. Nevertheless, he could barely tolerate Intracoastal City's chilly winter evenings, which he had to pass in his boat's open cabin because he was constantly on call. Sometimes, a call from the rig woke him up in the middle of the night and asked him to stand by for a hotshot truck, an express delivery vehicle, on its way to deliver a tool the drilling crew needed right away.

While Bobby still made regular crew changes and the occasional supply run, he spent a lot of time simply sitting at the dock waiting for a call. He often passed the time by slowly teaching himself the finer points of his boat's mechanical system. He took apart his engines and put them back together so many times that he could overhaul them with his eyes closed. When not dissecting his 671s, he read voluminously. He devoured stories about the Civil War, murder mysteries, and anything else, from *Mein Kampf* to the books of Winston Churchill.

Whenever his hitch ended, he couldn't get back to Golden Meadow fast enough. He and Myrtle had been trying to get pregnant since their wedding night but, for some reason, they couldn't. If he could just put in enough time to pay off his note and acquire another boat, he could make a little more money and buy a little more time at home.

But his grand plan burned to pieces one morning in the spring of 1957 when his boat caught fire in a marsh bayou. While Bobby made a safe escape, the *Davey Lou No. 4* turned into an inferno. As the smoke rose over the tree line, Bobby could only stand safely away in the muck of the marsh and curse. He was only two or three payments from owning the boat outright, just a few months away from building or buying another vessel, from growing his company. Now, all of a sudden, he was back to being boatless.

As Bobby pondered his dilemma, across Bayou Lafouche, Nolty Theriot was building boats as fast as he could. He appeared to be dealing with his troubling wartime flashbacks by immersing himself in the present, by burying himself in the growth of his business. By 1958, he'd long since expanded his one-boat operation. He'd added two more tugs, identical 85-foot anchor handlers. When he saw potential work for a fourth boat, but couldn't borrow enough money to afford her, he convinced a friend to buy two more tugs, which Nolty would build and then operate.

Nolty also moved out of his father's small boat-building space and created his own little shipyard across the bayou on Highway 308. He bought the wooded tract and cleared enough trees to assemble one tug at a time.

While Nolty hired a team of talented men to execute his designs, he remained the creative force. His mind churned constantly with new ideas; he'd sometimes wake up in the middle of the night to jot down a thought. Never bothering to hire naval architects or draftsmen to prepare formal blueprints, he simply sketched the boats' major components on sheets of notebook paper, adding dimensions when appropriate. Nolty would then bring the sketches to the shipyard, where a craftsman would use them as a guide in cutting the steel into bulkheads, engine foundations, shafts, and other components.

Nolty never gave his men any precise orders about the exactitude of the boat's curves and lines. He'd just tell them to "eyeball it."

Nearly every day, Nolty came by and made an inspection. Not needing Coast Guard approval in those days, Nolty himself would make sure every element was exactly as he'd conceived. Sometimes, he would climb a tree for a bird's-eye view to determine whether to make an adjustment.

When Nolty gave the boat her final "okay," the craft then had to travel across the highway to Bayou Lafourche. This was always an event, always drawing an audience to the woods. The spectators would place bets on how long it would take to launch the boat and whether she would float or sink.

The performance began when the boat was lifted with railroad jacks and placed on top of long blocks, which sat atop rollers. The Theriot crew then pushed the boat with a truck and pulled her with two tugs from the bayou. It was a tedious three-hour process of guiding the boat, adjusting the rollers, and making sure the new tug didn't fall off and smack the asphalt. But inevitably, she did fall. Invariably, she would crash into the road and take out a section of Highway 308. In fact, it seemed like every time Nolty launched a boat, he'd end up paying the highway department a few thousand dollars in repairs.

To some, Nolty's insistence on building his own boats caused too much trouble. At times, his wild ideas led him astray. After he'd built a few offshore tugs, he decided he'd try his hand at a river push boat, the tall giraffe-like vessel shaped roughly like a triangle turned on its side. The advantages of the push boat were her height and her straight-up, ninety-degree pilothouse, which allowed the captain to see over the flotilla of barges he was pushing. While her tall center of gravity meant that she could easily topple over in a rough sea offshore, she was the perfect craft on an inland river. Nolty decided he would design an especially large one, tall enough to see over the highest hopper barge and strong enough to push a sprawling flotilla.

Despite Nolty having few contacts in the river barge industry, which had little crossover with the offshore oilfield, he built his giant push boat and put her to work. Not long after the big giraffe took to the Mississippi, the push boat industry took a downward turn and pushed Nolty, the river rookie, back to his dock. With the big craft idle, her loan's high interest and short-term note threatened to capsize Nolty's entire company until, finally, he sold her.

Aside from the push boat disaster, Nolty's building of his own vessels was more than a creative outlet and a cost savings. He also wanted to make sure his boats were up to the metal-stressing task of anchor handling, of moving pipeline construction barges by winching anchors up from the seabed in sometimes rough conditions. Additionally, he had to be able to answer even the most detailed question about his equipment to keep up with his competitors.

By the late 1950s, the anchor-handling market had become crowded. At times, Nolty found himself standing in line behind other boats for work. With some of his boats tied up and making no money, his debt kept mounting. While he hadn't filed for bankruptcy, he was definitely insolvent.

A few miles up the bayou, tug man, Sidney Savoie, was feeling a similar crunch in the rig moving market. In 1958, it was as if the offshore dictionary coined a new word: *competition.* The concept had barely existed until the late 1950s. Before then, veterans like the keen-eyed, conservative Sidney didn't have to solicit business. The oil company simply gave them an agreeable price, and they went to work.

On August 8, 1958, Sidney was standing outside of St. Joseph's Church in Galliano, sweating in his tuxedo. He wasn't at the church to pray for an increase in business. He'd already done plenty of that. He was there for a welcome distraction. His daughter, Helen, was marrying Larbow Cheramie, Minor's distant cousin.

Luckily, Sidney had saved enough money to pay for a nice nuptial celebration for his only daughter. But he wasn't saving much now. He was, for the first time since he started the business, doing everything he could just to keep his boats floating. During the previous year, he and his partner Faro had paid cash for a third, similar-sized offshore tug, the Galliano-built *Ted*, named after Sidney's only son.

No one was prouder of this new gleaming red masterpiece than her namesake. However, what neither teenage Ted nor his father expected was for the *Ted* to make their fleet top-heavy. During the previous year, Sidney and Faro had partnered on another new tug, but Sidney got nervous and sold his interest in the boat to his father-in-law.

As for borrowing money to build a boat, such as everyone seemed to be doing now, Sidney had no interest in it. His philosophy was that when he built a boat, she belonged to him, not the bank.

He had reason to be cautious. Even with his company's outright ownership of three tugs, he was still struggling. It started not long after the launch of the *Ted*. Guidry & Savoie had quickly gone from doing steady day work for Gulf and California Oil to scrambling for any work, much of it only by the hour. They found spot work with the big contractors Brown & Root and McDermott, and for the fist time, Sidney pushed butane barges from points in Texas across the Intracoastal and other inland waterways to Bainbridge, Georgia.

They also located work through the resourceful Donald Bollinger, who had a shipyard twenty miles up the bayou in Lockport and was also a profitable boat broker and owner. Bollinger, a former machinist and a tower of man, had received his start in 1946 by taking a $10,000 inheritance from his boss at a barge company, buying some land along Bayou Lafourche, and purchasing a defunct war-effort machine shop in New Orleans. He tore down the shop's building, hauled its materials and machines to Lockport, rebuilt the structure on his new bayouside property, and opened his own shop. Bollinger then used the talents of his family to diversify the shop into a shipyard. His father Bud was a wooden boat builder, and his three brothers had mastered three different trades— mechanics (Ralph), welding (George), and engineering (Dick).

In 1953, the Bollingers built their first boat, named for their matriarch *Etiennette Bollinger*, and in 1956, the family would finish ten vessels in twelve months. The big year meant Bollinger was finally giving the Lafourche country what it desperately needed—a shipyard that could mass-produce steel workboats. The Bollingers' high productivity and their honest reputation gave local boatmen like Sidney Savoie a boost.

In fact, Sidney hired Bollinger to help him diversify by building him deck barges, one for water and two for supplies. The barge business was attractive because it could result in almost pure profit. When a client rented a barge, the barge owner didn't have to supply any labor, and barges required no fuel and hardly any maintenance. When these slabs of floating steel were working, they earned $600 per month. But when they weren't working, they turned into worthless, rusty rafts.

Despite Sidney's new variety of work, he still couldn't make his revenue pie whole. He and Faro didn't have enough jobs to make a payroll for steady, regular crews. It was bad enough laying off the new employees, but Sidney couldn't stomach laying off the older, loyal ones. He did the only thing he could do to keep them working; he got off the boats and began to pay others his captain's salary.

It also meant he had to find something to do. Sidney had never worked out of an office. He didn't even own a desk. He didn't mind calling on clients and drumming up business, but it was odd not to balance these sales calls with actual wheel time.

Sidney missed the action and comradery of the boat. He often thought about his old crewmen, many of whom he'd had to let go. He remembered funny stories or characters, like one green deckhand who was working for him on a job for Gulf Oil. At the time, Sidney was hauling freshwater. He had to go north into Bayou Lafourche until he found the freshwater line, which was usually in Cut Off, but sometimes all the way in Larose. Then he'd pump the barge full of freshwater and haul it back down the bayou to one of the oilfields, where Gulf would use the water to power the steam drilling rigs.

That day he'd explained to the rookie deckhand how to test the water, telling him to grab a bucket of water from the bayou, then put two or three drops of a special chemical in it. If the water turned gold, it was salty. If it stayed clear, it was fresh. If it was gold, empty the bucket, and Sidney would go a little further north.

Sidney first slowed the tow near where the freshwater line had been on his previous job and waited for the deckhand to come back with the test results.

The hand returned and told him, "It's gold."

Sidney motored up the bayou a few hundred yards. The deckhand came back with a concerned look. "It's still gold."

Sidney shrugged. He pushed down the throttles, sailed a mile and a quarter, and slowed. He yelled out of the pilothouse to the deckhand, "Go 'head."

The hand nodded, half-blank and half-purposeful. Minutes later, he hollered up at Sidney, "I don't understand, me. It's still gold."

This wasn't making sense. The line shouldn't have moved that far that quickly. He pushed the tow much further up and stopped. But the hand came back, shaking his head. "*C'est le meme chose.* I even tasted it, me. It's salty."

"Aw no. *Mais* that water's got to be sweet."

This time, Sidney asked the deckhand to redo the test and he'd watch him. The hand walked over to the bucket and dropped in the chemical.

"Hey," Sidney called down. "You forgot to get some new water."

"Huh?"

"You need some new water out the bayou."

"This is the same water I been testing."

"Since when?"

"Since the beginning."

"You never changed the water in the bucket?"

"*Mais* no."

"You been testing the same water over and over?"

"*Mais* yeah."

Sidney put his hands over his face. He tried not to laugh, but he couldn't help letting out a snort.

Years later, the memory still made Sidney chuckle. But by August of 1958, the humor and the innocence had faded. Green deckhands like the infamous freshwater tester were now mostly unemployed. But for Sidney's family, this financial inability to maintain regular crews did have at least one small upside.

It meant that Sidney's fourteen-year-old son got more work. This was exactly what Ted wanted. When he was a little boy, any time on a tug was like a vacation. It still felt that way. He enjoyed spending his weekends and summers on the boat. He'd come a long way since the first time he'd taken the wheel on the Mississippi as a nine-year-old and snaked the tow all over the river, making his daddy laugh.

Now Ted could drive the boat nearly as well as his father. While he was still officially a deckhand, he had no trouble taking the wheel at any time of the day or night. And grab the wheel was exactly what Ted did right after Helen's wedding. It didn't bother him. He couldn't think of a more perfect ending to the day than to go from serving in his sister's wedding to changing into his coveralls and climbing aboard his namesake.

As for Sidney, the father of the bride wasn't leaving Galliano. He was a largely unemotional man, but this had been an emotional day. In a sense, it epitomized the upside of his time off the boats. This had been a precious period because he'd spent much more time around his family. Having been gone for weeks at a time since 1939, he cherished the continual months at home.

But as glorious as this day had been and as grateful as he was for the quality family time, he couldn't continue to support them without money. Some local operators, who owed big notes on their boats, had already closed their doors. Luckily, Sidney's conservative philosophy had meant he had no notes to pay on the three tugs he co-owned with Faro. If their boat was tied up, all they had to do was protect it from physical decay. But still, he had bills to pay, and he could hardly pay them with the spot jobs and hourly work.

He knew there was an alternative. He'd been watching it develop for the last few years. With there now being competition, the jockeying had begun. Some boat companies had no scruples. They were delivering cars to the oil company transportation men's driveways. They were handing over envelopes stuffed with cash. In Harvey, Sidney had seen a brand-new washer and dryer set dropped off right at the oil company's warehouse. Neither the boat company nor the transportation superintendent had made any effort to hide the gift.

Was Sidney tempted to do the same thing? If playing the game was an issue he debated, he'd never admit it. But he did have to acknowledge something—he was hungry. He had to take *some kind* of action.

Down the bayou, Nolty Theriot had already made his move. In the spring of 1959, he decided to battle debt with more debt. His response to insolvency was to buy a new winged Cadillac, show it off to his fretting employees and fussy accountants, and hit the client trail.

Elfer "Faro" Guidry, Sidney Savoie, and Duard Eymard aboard the *Ted* in 1958.
(Courtesy of Ted Savoie)

En route to Houston, Nolty blew exhaust on his problems and pressed the pedal to the floor. He was flooring it for more than just the joy of speed; his haste wasn't just money—it was survival. While he knew he was at bankruptcy's brink, he blocked out all the red ink, telling himself the same thing he had told his CPAs, his day-to-day bookkeeper, his wife, his parents, and, when appropriate, his banks and vendors, telling them all many times, "Don't worry about nothing."

Don't worry about nothing wasn't just his expression; it was his company slogan and his personal motto. Before it was all said and done, he would stamp the saying on everything he could find—on his letterhead, on his company envelopes, on his paychecks, on bumper stickers, and on the captain's wheel behind his desk. When people looked at him with furrowed brows, tight lips, or crinkled eyes, he would tell them, "Don't worry about nothing, Tiger."

When his employees made a mistake, he did his best to forget it. Once at his shipyard in the woods, his cousin and layout man, Livingston Theriot, sought him out with a look of pure guilt on his face. He told Nolty straight up, "*Mais* cuz, I messed up." He pointed at a bulkhead and said, "I cut it four inches too short."

Nolty never flinched at what was a $3,000 mistake at a moment where he was past due to creditors for untold thousands. He only said, "Don't worry about it. Just cut it up for scrap and make another one."

"You sure, cuz?"

"Tiger, the only man that doesn't make a mistake is the man that does nothing."

So if Nolty excused his employees when they cost him money or his clients when they didn't pay him promptly, then he expected the same thing from everyone else. If he could survive a firing squad and be given a second life, then he could make good on anything and everything. He could always pull out of his yearly financial crisis that started with the darkest of all dark months, February, and ended at a point he couldn't predict but knew would happen. He wouldn't just survive, he'd thrive.

So in 1959, when Nolty—smooth, complected, and smiling—zipped into the Brown & Root facility in the Houston area, his Cadillac was shining and his new Rubenstein Brothers suit was crisp and starched. To some degree, the image worked on the ten-gallon hat Texiens. They wanted to give Nolty a contract, but the problem was, the price wasn't right. Oh, it was probably high enough for Nolty to break even, but what fun was there in just paying bills and chugging along? Nolty wanted to buy his wife a new charm bracelet, and one day, his hardworking father-in-law a new car. He had to build more boats and grow his company. He couldn't do that by breaking even.

So there was no glory in taking that contract even though he didn't have much choice. But after a few months of paying back his vendors but still not reaching anything close to a comfort zone, Nolty asked Brown & Root for a raise.

Brown & Root said no.

Nolty told them he would tie up his boats. Brown & Root said go ahead, tie 'em up.

So Nolty tied them up—and suffered. The vendors and the banks started calling again, and Nolty began to massage them, sending them whatever money he could to appease them. It was getting to where he'd have to cave in and crawl back to Brown & Root.

Then, out of the blue, Brown & Root called and said, "Nolty, name your price."

And the next thing Nolty knew, he was buying his sweet Bea jewelry; his young kids, Pye, Martha, and Rebecca, presents; and taking the whole family to dinner at the Roosevelt Hotel in New Orleans. While in town, he could take the kids to Pontchartrain Beach and the Audubon Zoo and buy himself another suit at Rubenstein Brothers and a new dress for Bea. They'd all spend the summer at Grand Isle, running barefoot on the beach and catching bushels of crabs in the surf. At dusk, the adults would sip drinks on the porch and watch the shrimp boats idle toward the pass.

Nolty knew he had to enjoy that summer because another dark February would come soon enough. Yes, he was grateful just to wake up, be it from a night of pleasant dreams or of dreadful *paisons*, but as long as he had this *lagniappe*, he had to find a way to beat the brutal impending downswings. If Minor Cheramie had his Botrucs, then surely Nolty, with all of his pens and scratch paper, could come up with something that no one else had, something that would make the oil companies pant and drool.

While the late 1950s had decked many people in the tug industry, some of the crew boatmen, like Bobby Orgeron, weren't as affected by the market. But with Bobby's boat burning up, he had his own problem. After the vessel was destroyed, he made an insurance claim. The fire was ruled as accidental with the consensus being the diesel seeped into the bilge and ignited, eventually blowing up the battery and torching the boat.

Bobby took the insurance proceeds, paid off the scant debt remaining on the *Davey Lou No. 4,* and split the rest with his partner and brother Bouillien. Bobby then used his half to make a down payment on a new boat, *his own* new vessel. He was going to have a little wooden crew boat built at Duet's. And finally, the boat and the business would be 100 percent his own.

Before long, Duet's delivered the *Miss Rosella*, which Bobby named after his grandmother, Rosella Williams Orgeron. Then, one week after the boat's mahogany bottom kissed the bayou, on a perfect blue-gold spring day in the late fifties, two men from the Atlantic Refining Company approached Bobby's dock. They told Bobby they were looking for a crew boat. He showed them a brand-new, shiny red beauty at their feet. And they gobbled her up, hiring Bobby for forty-five dollars per day to run an engineer to and from the field in Timbalier Bay, where they were drilling a wildcat well.

Bobby's meeting with the Atlantic Refining men reeked of déja vù. Seventeen years ago, an Atlantic Refining man had given Bobby's father his first oilfield job. Now, Atlantic Refining was advancing Bobby's fledgling career.

Atlantic Refining soon moved Bobby to Barataria Bay, twenty miles southeast of Golden Meadow. At Barataria on a scorching summer day, the drilling company hit pay dirt. Soon, production wells started popping up all across the water. Bobby was again approached by an Atlantic Refining man, and this time the man asked Bobby to build a boat.

Bobby had a 41-foot steel hull fabricated in a tiny shipyard in the cane lands just south of Thibodaux. To pick her up, Bobby rode up Bayou Lafourche in a little outboard *bateau* and towed the hull back down the bayou to Duet's, where they would put a cabin on her.

As the workers at Duet's fit the cabin to the hull, Bobby thought for some reason the boat looked like a San Francisco beatnik. He told people he "hated them sonofabitches (the beatniks)" who were running wild reading their poetry, getting high, and frolicking all over the place. But he decided the name *Beatnik* fit. He'd always shaken his head at how much pride people took in their boats' names. His vessel's new moniker was nothing but a joke, and to Bobby, humor was much better than sentimentality.

With the *Beatnik* at Duet's, Bobby kicked into high gear. His manic energy needed constant release. After he made his runs on the *Miss Rosella* during the day, he hit Duet's at night and piped and wired the *Beatnik* himself. After supper, he would often take a light and climb onto the roof of his house being built in Galliano. He would work on the roof until exhaustion finally overtook him. He had gone from becoming a wild bachelor, a coonass version of a beatnik, to a faithful, married workaholic.

Soon, he hired a captain for the *Beatnik*, and he continued to operate the *Miss Rosella* himself, doubling as a payroll-employee gauger for Atlantic Refining. As a gauger, his job was to ensure the field's proper production levels were maintained. Sometimes, the work was simply going from well to well checking gauges. At other times, it was exhausting; if the tank battery was full of oil, he had to stay there late into the night until enough oil was pumped into a barge.

But the long hours were paying off, and cash was beginning to flow. With the *Miss Rosella*, Atlantic Refining paid him $1,500 a month for the boat rental and a direct salary of $500 a month for his work as a gauger. With the *Beatnik*, he cleared roughly $1,200 a month.

This income was not nearly good enough. With Myrtle finally scheduled to deliver the couple's first child in the summer of 1960, Bobby wanted to be more than a two-bit inland beatnik. He had to stretch his operation beyond the shallow bays into the Gulf's deeper, richer waters. He also had to find the funds to support his new venture.

However, he had never really played the offshore game, and he had no concept of its rules.

In April 1959, forty-seven-year-old Sidney Savoie was fully aware of these not-so-unspoken laws. From day one, he'd refused to play the oilfield entertainment game. He doubted he was even capable of participating. But if he did have it in him, then this was the time to do it. His boats were docked. His bank accounts were nearly drained. His conservative strategy had all but failed.

He had to do something to reverse his fortune. Playing this new game had become tacitly acceptable. It was, of course, okay to bring a client on the best hunting or fishing trip of his life, and, off the record, it was nearly as tolerable to buy a client a lavish gift or to set him up with an expensive prostitute. But Sidney couldn't bring himself to participate in that racket. Sure, there was a company man in Venice who drank beer like water, and Sidney made sure he never visited this man without bringing him a case of Jax. There were other men whom he tried to keep satisfied with bushels of crab or ice chests of shrimp.

He had no trouble taking a man to lunch, but beyond that, he didn't know what to do with him. Sidney, other than being an excellent boatman and an easygoing comrade, didn't fit the new oilfield contractor profile. He just didn't share the same passions as the typical oilfield coonass.

For one, he couldn't take a client hunting or fishing because he'd never been a hunter or a fisherman. As a boy, a hunting incident had made him wary of guns. He and his friend had gone rabbit hunting, and Sidney's gun had inadvertently fired. A piece of the gun freakishly cut Sidney's hand and the discharged shell blew a hole in the ground inches from his friend. No one had been seriously hurt, but the incident made a lasting impression on the cautious boy. It scared and scarred him.

By the same token, he didn't have any great desire to chase other women. His marriage was enough. Even if he wanted to cheat on Mathilde, she packed a mean frying pan. He respected her strong hand and heart and couldn't do it to her.

But Sidney had another trait driving him in addition to his ethics. He was much tighter than the average riverboat-gambling boatman like Nolty Theriot. Sidney didn't enjoy spending money. And a hunting camp cost money. As did the elaborate gifts. As did the partying.

When he started his business, he didn't have to buy a job or buy a friend. For years, the work had just been there. He'd forged relationships without having to give gifts or barter flesh. He listened to the boss man, and he dealt with a partner. But otherwise, he was his own man. When the Gulf Oil Texiens would ask him to come downriver to Gulftown for a goat barbecue, he kept turning them down. He didn't want to go because he had no desire to eat goat. He wasn't gonna taste it just because the company men insisted. But when, after a few refused invitations, it was clear that he was offending them, he went to the barbecue and sampled their goat. And he was right; he didn't like it.

He sure wished he could save his company by simply eating a leg of Texien goat. But it had become much more complicated. It wasn't only about pressure to violate personal or religious ethics, but his freedom of religion, his dear, sacred Catholicism.

Many of the oilmen were members of the predominantly Protestant Masonic Order. They wore Masonic rings and attended meetings at the Masonic Lodge. One of these "Temples of Solomon" had somehow opened in solidly Catholic Galliano. There was a lot of talk in the oilfield about the oil companies pressuring the service contractors, especially the Catholic ones, to become Masons, also called Freemasons. But the Roman Catholic church leadership clearly forbid its members from joining the Masonic Order. For centuries, the Church had excommunicated members who'd become Masons. And even in 1959, whether or not a formal excommunication took place, the Church frowned upon Freemasonry and didn't want Catholic Masons taking Holy Communion.

Sidney wanted nothing to do with the Masons. But he knew it would give him a better chance to fraternize with the oilmen. While he'd watched other Catholic boatmen like Nolty Theriot join the order, he had no desire to follow their lead. He was already a staunch member of the Catholic fraternal organization the Knights of Columbus. He'd joined the Knights of Columbus back in 1939, even though, at the time, there was no chapter in lower Lafourche, and he had to go fifty miles to Thibodaux for the induction.

If the gossip was true, by being a Knight of Columbus he was more than a non-Mason, he was an anti-Mason. The rumor was that Texaco had an unwritten rule that only Freemasons would work for the company. This talk worried Sidney until he met a Texaco executive who was also a Knight of Columbus.

Still, would joining the Masons increase Sidney's chances of getting business with the Masonic oilmen? Yes. Would he do it? Absolutely not.

So what the hell would he do? Once again, he called the oilfield's bluff. But this time, it backfired.

Whatever the cause for his unlucky streak, the industry had left him standing on a teetering altar, the deck of a floating but financially sinking tugboat.

At least, during what had been an economically wretched April, the weather had been pleasant. The air was mostly cool and fragrant, and as the bayouside willow trees fluttered in the breeze, their gold leaves glimmered in the sunlight. In truth, a pretty day and a wonderful family were all that Sidney had.

And that was it—family. Sidney, Faro, and their brothers-in-law would all come to the same conclusion. *La famille* could save them all, the entire extended Savoie-Guidry-Eymard clan. They weren't just a gathering of Eymard in-laws, they were a family of tugboats. They'd all been building their own little fleets. There was Sidney, Faro, father-in-law Duard, brother-in-law Emile, and Emile's son Emmett. They all had their contacts. Sidney had Gulf. Faro had California. Emile had Chevron. And Emmett had Shell.

Apart they were doomed, but together they had a chance. So they united on May 5, 1959, and formed United Tugs, Inc. The company began as a brokerage group that would allow them to profit from each other's sales and help sustain each other's losses. For each job, the company would receive a brokerage fee with that particular boat's owners still receiving the primary fee. At the time, McDermott was brokering boats, as were independent entrepreneurs like Donald Bollinger. If McDermott and Bollinger could do it, then these independent career boatmen believed they could, too.

They threw everything into the venture. One of their first steps was to hire a salesman, a Lockport man who had been working in Gulf Oil's purchasing department. The salesman could exploit his contacts and focus purely on selling, something none of the owners had ever had the luxury of doing.

Eventually, United Tugs would buy and build its own boats, too. With their pooled patrimonies and credit histories, their borrowing power increased. Suddenly, Sidney didn't care about acquiring a boat on credit. The increased spread of risk took away his pain.

United Tugs' first company-owned tug was the *Alamo*, a second coming of Faro's old shrimp boat of the same name and a symbol of what they were doing. They were all inside the same Alamo. They were all taking a stand, and they were slowly driving back the enemy. The Alamo became a theme and a naming scheme. United's next two tugs were the *Alamo Express* and the *Alamo II*. The United fleet may have idled into 1959, but they were charging into the 1960s.

By the early sixties, as the Eymards, the Savoies, and the Guidrys joined forces, many other family-based boat companies were pushing their way into the business. Up and down the bayou, boats were being begotten by all sorts of Doucets, Defelices, and Danoses, Curoles, Collins, and Crosbys, Guidrys, Guilbeaus, and Griffins, with this boatman begetting another, ultimately building one meandering delta of vessels. And finally, all the begetting, whether inbred or outbred, inboard or outboard, mushroomed into a boat balloon that popped when the begotten flooded the bayou with too many boats.

And too many tugs was exactly the problem facing Nolty Theriot in 1960. Unlike Sidney Savoie, who'd developed the habit of putting away money to help absorb industry downswings, Nolty had no intentions of playing it safely. He'd reinvested profits, knowing the only way for him to grow was to spend and borrow money. But it was also an easy way to lose his company.

In the past, he could say, "Don't worry about nothing." But he couldn't say that and mean it in 1960, not with his ulcers eating at his stomach. Under his present circumstances, the only cure for his stomach pains was to save his business. Yet, in a sense, he'd already lost it. It felt that way when he had to lay off most of his employees, including his cousin Livingston Theriot. The creditors had been putting so much pressure on him that he'd had to approach two of his tug crews at a dock near Morgan City and fire all but two of the men.

Nolty's family felt his pain. He realized this when, uncharacteristically, he was approached by his father-in-law J. V. Alario, who was a vice president at the State Bank and Trust Company. Mr. Alario was a principled, private man, but he felt compelled to speak to Nolty, telling him, "Nolty, you know I don't talk about business. I don't discuss anything that goes on in the bank. But I know that things are not going great for you. I hear stories. If there's anything I can do. I don't have a lot of money. But I can lend you what I have."

Nolty was appreciative of the gesture, but he had to be frank with his father-in-law. He told Mr. Alario, "Well, to help me, you'd have to rob the bank, and I still don't think you'd have enough to get me out of this hole."

While he told Mr. Alario he would survive, he couldn't lie to Bea. Nolty had to admit that *he, too, was worried.*

Lord knows, Nolty had done what he could to keep the business going. Against his better judgment, he had joined the Masons to fraternize with the oilmen. He initially kept his membership secret from his wife, but eventually he had to tell her. Although she didn't like it, she understood. Still, it was difficult for him to participate, knowing his church didn't approve. It was something he rarely talked about to Bea and never discussed with his father-in-law, an especially devout Catholic and a very active member of the Knights of Columbus.

In addition to joining the Freemasonry brotherhood, Nolty also felt he had little choice but to participate in the oilfield entertainment scene. While he refused to make cash payoffs, he had the usual yacht and camps in the marsh and on Grand Isle, and he, too, gave the exorbitant presents and enjoyed the girlfriends. But where had all the fun, booze, and the gifts put him now?

Ultimately, it wasn't about entertainment and any bequest of a car or a shotgun. What earned Nolty a promising nibble with Brown & Root was his relationship with the vice president of its pipeline division, L. E. Minor. Mr. Minor was becoming a father figure to Nolty. Their bond had nothing to do with materialism, and everything to do with a deep mutual respect. Through L. E. Minor, Nolty could cement his relationship with Brown & Root. This solidification had yet to happen, but in essence, Nolty was banking everything on it.

Nolty J. Theriot (Courtesy of the Theriot family)

Brown & Root had been talking to Nolty about some pioneering pipe-line work. One job was in the Persian Gulf, which was becoming the world's hottest oilfield. The contract featured the world's first purpose-built lay barge, which was named for Mr. Minor. The *L.E. Minor* was 350 feet long, 60 feet wide, and could house eighty-eight men in air-conditioned quarters. Another Brown & Root job was at the bottom of the world off Tierra del Fuego, Argentina; it involved the installation of a pipeline that would send imported oil from an offshore supertanker terminal to the Argentine shore. While the foreign jobs intrigued Nolty, he couldn't afford them. By this point, he needed more than a lucrative day rate. But he could see that Brown & Root really wanted his tugs and his crews for the South American job. Ultimately, Nolty decided rather than sending his assets to the bottom of the planet, he'd offer up three of his tugs for sale.

Brown & Root accepted his offer and agreed to pay a million-dollar-plus sum for the tugs. It was Nolty's first million-dollar deal. While he'd always been ambitious, it had never occurred to him that he would sell some boats for such a high price. He told his wife, "I wish everybody could have the opportunity to sell something for a million dollars."

The hundreds of thousands of dollars Nolty cleared in net profits did more than save his company and allow him to hire back some key employees, such as his cousin Livingston. It gave him real growth capital and borrowing power. He knew that if he'd been better off financially in 1959 and 1960, he could have taken advantage of Brown & Root's plunge into the international pipeline and supertanker terminal market. But that was of no consequence now. Nolty would put his ear to the wind and his pen to his scratch paper, and he'd come up with something the industry really needed.

M.O.N.T.'s *Monte Christo* in 1962. (Courtesy of MONTCO, LLC)

Chapter 8

Game Time

January 1960

Compared to Nolty Theriot, Bobby Orgeron was still in his oilfield swaddling clothes in 1960. He might have been a master of the inland bays, but he was an offshore neophyte. In his drive to go deep into the Gulf, Bobby truly had no idea what to expect. He wasn't even sure how to raise the funds to get the boats out there in the first place. Then, one afternoon, he received a proposition that made his mouth drop. His beady-eyed, diminutive bookkeeper made him an unlikely offer. This small-boned, five-feet-seven-inch desk maven had emerged from his ledgers and told Bobby he wanted to go into the boat business. This Nacis Theriot, a conservative nontalker, wanted to walk in the loud oilfield.

It took a while for Nacis' proposition to sink in. Nacis, who was also his cousin Nolty's bookkeeper, was a Theriot by blood and by business sense. But that was where the similarities stopped. Little Nacis wasn't the bold, brash bowling ball that his uncles Paris and Leo were. He was the opposite of his risk-loving, swarthy first cousin Nolty.

But Nacis did understand financing. He could lend his borrowing power to help give Bobby what he needed to go offshore and to go big—two state-of-the-art 51-foot Equitable crew boats with twin-screw V12 engines. They would have a wheelhouse with radar and a galley and the ability to comfortably carry more than thirty passengers. With two of these special vessels, Bobby would be halfway to his brother Bouillien's four Equitable grand chariots. By selling the baby *Beatnik* and the *Miss Rosella*, Bobby would have his down payment. By using Nacis' number skills, Bobby could get the financing with Associate Discount or CIT. The George Engine Company would not only sell him the engines, but endorse the note to build the boats.

This was enough for Mavis Bobby Orgeron. It was all he needed to go into a fifty-fifty partnership with Nacis. They would call their business M.O.N.T. Boat Rental Service, Inc., named after themselves—Mavis Orgeron and Nacis Theriot. Their first two vessels would also follow this name-derivative pattern, beatnik style. A portion of the means to build the *Monte Carlo* and the *Monte Christo* and the commitment to keep the books were all that Bobby needed from Nacis. It didn't matter that Nacis didn't know the first thing about running boats or fixing them or selling them to a customer. Nacis could stay in his office. Bobby would put the vessels to work.

As for Nacis, he had full confidence in Bobby. He knew that while they were only seven months apart in age, they couldn't have been more different in personality. He was well aware of Bobby's wild youthful reputation. But Nacis had also watched Bobby's steady rise in the boat business. He knew Bobby had something he would never have—salesmanship. Bobby's brother Bouillien had once sold Nacis his first car when Nacis was convinced he didn't even want a car. Bobby had that same power.

Interestingly, Nacis had been raised to stay away from boats. His father, Leopold, ingrained this in him. While Leopold was a Theriot boatman, he trawled because he had to trawl. He discouraged his four children from following in his footsteps; in fact, he refused to take them on the boat. When one of his boys, Livingston, showed interest in shrimping and begged his father to take him, Leopold put him on the boat in the worst weather he could find, kept him out in it for a week, and watched him vomit every day. By the end of the trip, Livingston never wanted to go on the boat again. While Livingston was now building them for their cousin Nolty, he'd shown no interest in being a captain.

When it came to Leopold's oldest son Nacis, Leopold had no trouble; Nacis never wanted to set foot on the boat. After he graduated from Golden Meadow High School in 1952, he first worked for a few months for his uncles at Theriot Motors doing bookkeeping. He pinched away enough money for school. Then in the spring, he enrolled at Nicholls Junior College in Thibodaux. For the next two years, he rode the school bus fifty-plus miles up the bayou to Nicholls and finished with an associates degree in business administration in 1955. While he wanted to continue his education, he ran out of funds and started working at his Uncle Leo's finance company.

Leo's company kept the books for a few shrimpers, and Nacis took over the book work. After a couple of years, Nacis' work load increased, and Uncle Leo allowed him to go out on his own.

By 1960, the Nacis Theriot Accounting and Tax Service had over four hundred accounts. The business was open seven days a week, and Nacis was working nearly around the clock. At all hours of the night, shrimpers were coming into his office in their white boots with bags of cash, hiring Nacis to make the numbers run, to figure out how to pay the groceries and the deckhands and how to parcel out as little as possible to the government.

As much as Nacis enjoyed the grind, he knew he couldn't do it forever. When Bobby Orgeron said he wanted to find a way to go offshore, Nacis made his offer. He would keep his bookkeeping clients as long as necessary, but he wanted to start making passive income. The fastest way to do this on the bayou, other than owning oil land, was the boat business.

So Nacis invited Bobby into his bookkeeping office in the Theriot Building and put his trust in his partner. Bobby would handle the boat operations, the personnel, and the customers. Nacis would mostly sit at his desk, make payroll, do the books, plan the financing, and try to maintain a budget.

M.O.N.T. Boat Rental shared the office building with Nacis' Uncle Leo's insurance agency, Edward Diaz's law office, and KLEB radio.

At the office, Bobby Orgeron would drink coffee with Nacis and neighbors, but otherwise, he wouldn't spend much time there. He couldn't. He was staring at, for the first time in his life, hundreds of thousands of dollars of debt and zero income. He had to make sure the

Equitable Shipyard in New Orleans quickly framed, tacked, welded, and painted his hulls. Equitable couldn't release the *Monte Carlo* quickly enough. M.O.N.T. couldn't make any money until the boat went to work, work Bobby had yet to secure.

Initially, Bobby looked for cush, oil company transportation jobs, but he couldn't find any. His number one client, Atlantic Refining, wasn't yet in the Gulf. His other clients, Stanolind and Gulf Oil, were dealing with the recession. They didn't have a spot for him.

Bobby had to shift his strategy. He looked at the big picture in the Gulf. Drilling and production had tightened, but despite Nolty Theriot's recent struggles, pipeline construction was perhaps a little healthier. Most crew boatmen didn't like to pursue this risky work, which involved hauling men to the lay barge, containing welders who welded the string of pipeline and dropped it to the Gulf's floor, and to the bury barge, housing workers who embedded the line beneath the sea. It wasn't as profitable as running crew members to fixed platforms. But Bobby didn't have any choice; there was nothing else out there for him.

He made a pitch to Brown & Root, and the pipeline contractor gave him a contract. Many crew-boat companies wouldn't touch this work, which entailed running crews to and from anchor-handling operations. It was dirty and dangerous. Bobby didn't realize the potential danger of it, but he learned as soon as he started running crews to the Brown & Root lay barge. It didn't matter if the barge was at anchor laying pipe, having tugs move its anchors, or moving itself from one anchor position to the next. When the foreman on the barge wanted the crew on board, Bobby had to get alongside and unload them. If the seas were rough, he had to find a way to safely make the transfer. He knew that the foreman could not lose a minute of pipe laying opportunity.

It wasn't that Bobby liked the idea of transferring men from a moving object to another moving object in choppy seas, with a string of pipe being constructed only a few feet away. At times it bordered on the insane. But he was willing to try things that no one else would. He wanted to show the Brown & Root people they could count on him.

To execute his plan, Bobby picked two fine captains, the brothers Butch and Benu Danos. The Danos brothers were muscled, rounded men with big ruddy faces. Benu was shorter and had more of a Santa

Claus look than Butch, but both smiled as if the work filled them with joy.

Bobby told Butch and Benu he wanted to change his engines' injectors and install the most powerful ones available. And he didn't care what controls the manufacturer had set. He wanted to open the engines' racks all the way. The more open the rack, the more fuel going into the injector. The stronger the injector, the more fuel going into the cylinder. More fuel meant more speed and more speed meant more work. More work meant more boats, which would mean millions. It was only a matter of time.

Bobby's mad method began to work. He, Butch, and Benu alternated on the *Monte Carlo* and *Monte Christo*, working fourteen on and seven off. But they were rarely off. Whoever was off the boat was on call around the clock as the "port captain," the combination mechanic and courier who had to stand by ready to bring supplies or engine parts or to fix a broken engine as quickly as possible. A broken engine meant a tied-up boat, and a moored boat meant no money every day it stayed at the dock.

Brown & Root worked Bobby's crew boats day and night, often without any downtime for the boat. It didn't matter. The M.O.N.T. vessels were making twenty-seven knots and not a crew boat could catch them. On a job near Oyster Bayou just east of the Atchafalaya River, Butch Danos showed Brown & Root what a M.O.N.T. captain could do with a boat. They were laying a pipeline from offshore to inshore, and the crew had worked their way inland. To get to the small inshore barges, the *Monte Christo* had to run a narrow pipeline canal. There was only five feet from the sides of the canal to the sides of the boat, and Butch ran it wide open!

When the Brown & Root people saw this 51-footer barreling down the string bean canal under complete control, they gaped.

Butch was suddenly doing all kinds of things he'd never done. He'd never used radar, but on the *Monte Christo* he had to use and depend on their Raytheon. It was a strange device that only worked well when the engines were running at a decent clip. When the engines slowed, the picture started to fade.

One night, he was coming into the Fourchon area, and he saw a tiny spot on the screen. "Goddamn," he said aloud to himself. "That wasn't there before."

As Butch got closer to the spot, his maneuvering got trickier. He couldn't go too fast because he didn't want to run over whatever was in the water. He couldn't go too slow because his radar picture would fade. Easing in until he found the safest speed with the highest visibility, he crept and crept until he saw something that made him veer to one side and throw his engines in neutral. Shining his spotlight, he saw two people sharing a life preserver and struggling.

He pulled them on board. One of them had been burned. They'd been working on a Gulf Oil platform when an explosion blew them off the rig. He believed they were okay, but they were so thirsty he wondered how long they would have survived had he not found them.

As Butch brought them to shore, he shook his head at the power of the radar. It would save him many times. When he ran to and from a Texaco rig south of the Mississippi River, he sometimes had to navigate in zero visibility fog. On one soupy night, Butch wove through thirty-six ships in and around Pilottown.

As Butch and Benu built up wheel time, Bobby was trying to work his way through the maze that was the offshore world. When he was not running or maintaining his boats, he was meeting people, priming the company for future work. The Texaco job had been a nice find. Brown & Root was now talking about some work up north. But neither one of these companies could promise him any long-term contracts.

Less than a year after the launch of the first two boats, Bobby returned to Equitable Shipyard and ordered the construction of two more boats. With the launch of M.O.N.T.'s third boat, the *Monte Casino,* in 1961, Bobby had to get off the boats.

He suddenly had too much to manage. He not only had to keep three boats working and inspect the construction of the *Monte Cello,* but he had also decided to negotiate a contract to build four 100-foot utility boats from Main Iron Works in Bourg, just south of Houma. These utility boats could haul crew or heavy supplies. Before ordering them, Bobby hadn't received any requests from the oil companies or service contractors for these boats. It was only a hunch. A feeling. No more than a gamble.

Some people told Bobby he was at the height of conceit. It wasn't as if he had an Exxon milk cow like Otto Candies. Bobby didn't have any guarantees of any kind. The standard crew-boat agreement was nothing more than a thirty-day contract with a twenty-four-hour cancellation clause. That feeble contract, the ever-mounting hock, and the ever-present hunger for millions began to do something to Bobby. Honestly, he didn't see it coming. But before he knew it, he was in the middle of it.

It began innocently. Bobby had no problem with a little client development. He quickly bought the basic coonass–oilfield entertainment vehicles. He acquired a beautifully varnished 41-foot Chris-Craft tarpon-fishing machine, the *Coyote*, then replaced her with the *My Moose*, a 45-foot Hatteras. For duck hunting and inshore fishing, he leased a section of marsh east of Golden Meadow, creating a camp by moving a house from town, placing it on a barge, and rolling it on pilings across the marsh. The M.O.N.T. men rolled the camp right onto a foundation, which they'd built themselves. In addition to the marsh camp and the yacht, Bobby secured a deer lease in Texas.

Bobby didn't mind the hunting and fishing. He wanted to get to know his customers better. He wanted to become their friends. But these friends came with a price.

One day, he was making a call on an oilfield company transportation superintendent. He and the superintendent started to talk about hunting, and the superintendent told him he sure wished he had this shotgun. It took Bobby a few minutes to get the hint but, once he did, he understood the superintendent's words were more than wishful thinking. Bobby bought the man the shotgun. He bought another man a fancy rod and reel.

These were fairly inexpensive items, of course. They were as much gifts as free meals or a sack of crawfish, an ice chest of shrimp or a few bushels of crabs. But the rods and guns soon turned into automobiles. While he refused to make any direct payoffs, the gifts, big and small, he had to buy.

If he didn't make these purchases, he knew what could happen. Everyone was talking about how you must pay to play. It was more than a cliché; it was the law of the oilfield. If it wasn't gospel, then why was that goody-two-shoes' boat tied up? That guy had refused to hand over anything, and look at his boat sitting there in Bayou Lafourche. How was that man supposed to feed his family, much less make his note?

Sure, the company men were impressed that Bobby had racked his engines into being the fastest in the Gulf. They appreciated the cleanliness of M.O.N.T.'s boats and the friendliness of its crew, but excellent service was only the threshold.

And the superintendents made it so easy. They would never expect Bobby to cut into his margins. They'd give him a raise on the boat's day rate. If he did the math, he'd make back that Cadillac in a couple of months. After that, the raise was his to keep. Until they wanted something else. But he didn't need to worry about that. They'd just raise him a little more.

The problem was even more involved than tangible gifts. The oilmen wanted to take more from you than money. It was hard to know exactly how this next part developed. It was difficult to remember how these beautiful women invaded your beautiful marriage. Did it come with the appearance of a long, toned leg? Did it start with mere words, with a simple request by the oilman for a "girl?" Did it begin with the whores or the girlfriends? For five years, you were a faithful husband, a hardworking crew-boat man. All you did was top-notch, tedious work, and that was good enough for the oilmen. You didn't have to worry about the company man's toys or his sex life. You were a simple man who followed straightforward, ethical instructions. What were you becoming now?

It was all blurred by darkness and drink. It was hazed over with clear vodka, dabbed with gin-soaked olives, muted with martini glasses filling and clinking. There was a lot of smoke in the New Orleans barrooms, and it was difficult to see who was who and where was where. But one thing was very clear. These oilmen didn't want you to just buy them a whore and wait for them in the car. They didn't want to chase these skirts all by their lonesome. They didn't want you to have just a few drinks with them at the Kings Room and go home. You couldn't meet them at the Absinthe House, then not go with them to the Playboy Club.

Even if the oilmen left you alone, it became difficult to look the other way. If your good President John F. Kennedy had the beautiful, perfect Jackie and still strayed with the voluptuous Marilyn Monroe, what could you do? Was there *any* man that could turn down the repeated advances of attractive, willing women? Maybe one night. Maybe several. But not forever. Not if you wanted those boats to work. Not if you wanted your wife and children to have the best of the best. Yes, you were providing for them and betraying them at the same time, but this was your career. You would have to separate business from family. But how was that possible when you were in the shipyard all day, inspecting and haggling, and you came home bone tired, then the phone rang at 11:30 p.m.? It was the oilman, and he wanted you at the Playboy Club. You wanted to tell him not to bother you, to let you sleep with your pregnant wife. You wanted to see your two-year-old son in the morning. But if you didn't go to the French Quarter, you might not have a job for that new boat coming out. That oilman might not be able to help you knock back that big note.

You didn't want the note to swallow your sleeping wife. But when you looked at her peaceful angelic face, the guilt swallowed you. Everything was eating everything else. You might as well get dressed and pretend you could eat the most.

But it couldn't help gnaw at you on your way to the city. They kept wanting more. It got to where buying a woman here and there wasn't sufficient. You had to buy them in bulk. But of course, the women were human, too, and after a while, you refused to call them whores or even prostitutes. You would only refer to them as ladies of the night.

These ladies and your clients needed rooms, but it had become too expensive to keep renting them at the Montleone Hotel. You had to rent an apartment on Conti Street in the Quarter. Your wife couldn't know about it. It was a secret you and the boys shared.

You wondered if they shared your guilt. You wondered if they paid your price.

By 1961, Sidney Savoie had reason to believe he and his United Tugs partners had risen above the recession. Sidney had proven he could make his way without taking part in all the oilfield sleaze. He might not have been making millions, but he was his own man and had what he needed. In December 1961, he was especially happy when United Tugs notched a big job with the supposedly Masonic-only Texaco, through a contractor called Offshore Gathering, Inc. It was a nice Christmas bonus for United Tugs. In all, United would put five tugs on the job, two owned outright by United and three brokered by the company. The tugs would be performing various tasks for Texaco's South Pass Gathering System, a massive offshore-onshore pipeline construction job at the mouth of the river near Venice. It was arduous but good, heavy day-rate work that would keep the bulk of United Tugs' fleet working for six months. And with Texaco's big pocket backing everything, United Tugs looked to have a record first quarter in 1962.

The project was far from the usual, run-of-the-mill rig-moving job. Offshore Gathering, United Tugs, and the dozens of other subcontractors would all have a hand in building a vital link between the offshore mines and the onshore petroleum consumer. To construct the gathering system, Offshore Gathering would lay pipelines from three offshore well sites to a fourth site, and from the fourth site to an onshore fuel separation facility.

The ten-mile-long pipeline would consist of an offshore line buried in the Gulf of Mexico's bottom and an onshore line trenched into the marsh and under the ridgeland all the way to the facility. The product entering the facility would be a mixture of oil, gas, and water, with the facility then separating the fluids and sending the oil into a common carrier pipeline, an interstate highway–like system that stretched far up into North America.

While Sidney and the men of United Tugs were proud of their contribution to the mechanized continent, their real rewards were much closer to home. They expected to bathe in the extra pay. Just as the gathering system would help inject America with oil, their five-boat contract was covering their ledgers with heavy black ink. After surviving the drought of the recession, they deserved to dip into a little gravy. And as the windy months of January and February passed, they were swimming in it.

At some point, Offshore Gathering started making late payments and then stopped paying altogether. It soon became clear that Offshore Gathering was in financial trouble and was probably incapable of making *any* payments. So Sidney and the United Tugs' board convened and decided that their president, Emmett Eymard, had to pay Texaco a visit. On March 24, 1962, Eymard drove to New Orleans and met with Texaco executive, James "Jimmy" Gibbens.

Eymard told Gibbens that he knew Offshore Gathering was in danger of going bankrupt, and he needed Texaco's guarantee that Texaco would pay for their work. If Texaco wouldn't agree to pay United Tugs, the company would have to immediately remove their boats. Of course, such a removal would bring construction to a halt.

Gibbens assured Eymard that United Tugs would be paid. Nine days passed, and United Tugs still hadn't received a check. On the tenth day, Sidney accompanied Eymard to meet with Gibbens again.

During this meeting, Gibbens told Sidney and Eymard, "Go to work. Don't worry about it. You'll be paid." Gibbens seemed sincere. Besides, he was a Lafourche man himself, from the central part of the parish. If this man said a check was coming, then it was coming. When Eymard returned to Texaco's offices a few days later to pick up his check, a Texaco employee told him the check was being delayed for "bookkeeping reasons."

The men of United Tugs had heard enough. The United Tugs board members asked their attorney, Edward Diaz of Golden Meadow, to contact Texaco. Diaz told Texaco he was filing a lien on the pipeline, and he did on April 3, 1962. Texaco asked Diaz to please delay enforcing the lien, claiming it was trying to work out a payment procedure.

Diaz and United Tugs waited until May 10, then Diaz wrote Texaco that it had to send a written guarantee that United Tugs would be paid within forty-five to sixty days. If Texaco failed to make such a guarantee, United Tugs would remove its vessels from the job.

Texaco made a sudden about-face. The company informed Diaz that it had no liability to United Tugs. When Diaz claimed Texaco had made repeated promises to United Tugs that it would pay the company for its work, no matter what the circumstance, Texaco denied making such an agreement. Sure, Texaco had benefitted from United Tugs' work, but that didn't mean the oil company had to pay for it.

United Tugs promptly pulled its tugs off the job.

Meanwhile, general contractor Offshore Gathering was still in a fix. The contractor needed to earn the remainder of the money for constructing the pipeline, which was almost finished. Offshore Gathering couldn't do it without tugboats. The contractor convinced United Tugs to return to work by paying them on a day-to-day basis.

For United Tugs, this day-to-day pay didn't solve their problem. Construction of the pipeline system was completed on May 28, but

United Tugs was still owed tens of thousands of dollars. The job had tied up a large portion of its fleet, and they needed the money. They had no choice but to file suit on August 8, 1962, against Offshore Gathering, Inc., Texaco, and Texaco's bond insurer. While the men had formed United Tugs to take a stand against the recession, they now had to make their second Alamo and take a stand against, of all people, a good, wealthy client, a multibillion dollar oil giant.

To fund the litigation, make up for the losses sustained on the job, and to keep going, Sidney Savoie and United Tugs would have to hit the road and scavenge for work. They had to forget about the bad taste Texaco had left in their mouths. They all had families to feed. This meant doing whatever was necessary, including finding a way to create some cash flow. To that end, the company decided to sell the *Alamo Express* to Minor Cheramie and his L & M Botruc, Inc. The sale would at least buy them some time.

After Minor Cheramie purchased the *Alamo Express*, he immediately changed her name to *Cheramie Bo-Truc 6*. He'd held fast to his plan to mass-produce the Botrucs, even though he'd stopped ordering them from Rhode Islander, Luther Blount. Now, American Marine out of New Orleans was building most of them, with the Japanese American naval architect Y. K. Mock stretching Blount's original 65-foot design into 85 feet, then to 107 feet and beyond.

As Minor launched more Botrucs, he had no trouble proving their worth to the oil companies. In addition to their spacious cargo capacity, the Botrucs were also smooth operators and loaders.

For instance, before the Botrucs, Shell had hired a company with wooden luggers to service its rigs in the East Bay area near the mouth of the Mississippi River. When the wind kicked up the bay into choppy water, the flatter-bottomed luggers took a beating, making it difficult to efficiently load crew or supplies, particularly the wireline units that cleaned the paraffin and other junk from a clogged well.

But the Botrucs, with their deep V bows and molded lines, cut right through the waves when navigating through the grid of well jackets.

Their molded lines also prevented the stern deck from popping up and slapping the water when backing into a rig. Additionally, the Botrucs' versatility solved the loading problem. Hoisting the wireline units from the wooden luggers had been difficult because the well jackets, which were like miniature rigs, were too small to support a crane. To solve the problem, Minor hired an engineer, and the two of them took advantage of the Botrucs' expansive deck and affixed a small boom right behind the cabin, which could efficiently load and unload the wireline unit.

Minor's link to Blount's Botruc design also helped him secure the job as the operator of prominent drilling fluids company Baroid's expanding fleet of Botrucs, which began with Blount's 85-foot *Baroid Express* in 1959 and would lead to a series of 132-foot vessels. These were mud transportation boats, which were outfitted with tanks that carried drilling mud to the rigs. In the well hole, the mud had many functions. As it traveled downward, it lubricated and cooled the drill bit and sealed fissures in the hole's walls; as it flowed back up to the surface, it helped clear the hole.

With Minor adding mud transportation to his areas of expertise, his reputation grew. In late 1962, he finally moved his office out of his house and into a separate building. While he had to share a building in Golden Meadow with the Owens Department Store, he at least had a headquarters. He could relieve his wife Lou of her duties, hiring his first administrative employee, a good-natured, number-crunching man named Linwood "Woody" Terrebonne as his office manager and dispatcher.

As Terrebonne put his organizational and accounting skills to work, Minor continued to add little nuances to his Botrucs. On Gulf Oil's request, he added a front landing platform to *Bo-Truc 8* and *Bo-Truc 9* so the vessels could come into a rig bow first and unload crew.

Minor's boats weren't only novel. They had to be, in his mind, the cleanest vessels in the Gulf. As the years passed, he became even more maniacally meticulous. His boats not only had to look good, they had to have good hygiene. When someone stepped on his vessel, he wanted them to see their reflection in the steel and to smell bleach on the deck and Windex on the windows.

He firmly believed his reputation for cleanliness helped him generate business. As successful as he was, Minor couldn't keep pace with the other big promulgator of the cab-forward, open-deck supply boat—

Tidewater Marine Service, Inc. Tidewater, which was based in New Orleans, had gone public in 1956 and had exploded its fleet in the 1960s to more than one hundred vessels. Of course, it wasn't that Minor or any other family operator was trying to become a public company; collectively, the independents still ruled the boat business. Nevertheless, Minor would have liked to have been doing better.

If he had nine Botrucs, he wanted nineteen, but many things held him back. The first was his partner and brother, Lefty, who had never had an active role in operations. He'd left the bayou and moved to the New Orleans Westbank town of Gretna. Lefty was more interested in looking after his other business interests than in running a boat company. While he'd occasionally go to American Marine to check on the progress of a boat, he remained mostly a silent partner. However, Lefty was anything but silent when it came to Minor's constant expansion plans.

As Minor craved growth, Lefty resisted it. If Minor wanted to build three more boats, Lefty didn't want any. When they'd finally compromise and order one boat, Lefty would still *boudé*.

As conservative as Lefty could be, he was not always budget conscious when it came to his own salary. While Minor preferred to take less of a wage and spend the extra profits on growth, Lefty would sometimes insist on raising his salary. If Minor didn't agree to a raise, the sparring would begin.

When Minor started drinking, these relatively calm arguments turned violent and usually ended with Lefty connecting his trademark left hook with his younger brother's face. Minor was never sober enough to give Lefty much of a fight. One night at Golden Meadow's Glo Room, a drunken Minor took to extreme measures, pulled out a knife, and cut his brother's stomach. The gushing blood brought Minor to his senses, and he rushed Lefty to the hospital.

On the operating table, the doctors actually discovered that Lefty's appendix had ruptured before the fight. Perhaps in stabbing his brother, Minor had, in a sick and bizarre sense, saved Lefty's life.

Many people questioned Minor as to why he didn't buy out Lefty, who cut his profits in half and, by this point, arguably contributed almost nothing positive to the company. While some claimed Lefty's devil's advocacy kept Minor from spending the business into bankruptcy, others believed Lefty was nothing more than deadweight. Minor didn't want to hear it. He'd always wanted to go into business with his older brother. He thought he was supposed to share everything with Lefty. While they might have had drunken brawls, in the morning, it was as if nothing had happened. Even if Minor was sporting two black eyes, he forgot about the fight and hugged his brother.

During this period, Minor also continued to drink, and alcohol increased his impulsiveness. One evening at a bar, he told a man he couldn't wait to buy his daughter, who was only thirteen, a new Corvette convertible. Of course, young Deanie was a couple of years away from the legal driving age, but Minor was looking forward to the day he could spoil her with the extravagant gift. When the man told Minor he couldn't afford that kind of purchase, Minor took a swing at him. The next morning, he took a larger swing by ordering the Corvette.

On another occasion, Minor got into a drunken tangle with a man who grabbed his foot and twisted it, eventually breaking his leg. Despite having to hobble around in a cast, Minor kept drinking, always pushing his luck.

During one Mardi Gras night, Minor spent an evening with the drink, which led to losing another fistfight with two men at Golden Meadow's Wagon Wheel. After the fight broke up, his two opponents left the bar. Unaffected, Minor stayed on his bar stool and continued to drink. Eventually, he left, staggered out to his Lincoln Continental, and attempted to drive home. When his car reached St. Pierre's Restaurant, Minor lost his depth perception, steered off the highway, and went airborne. He landed in the middle of the bayou.

Across the road, two men were watching the car lights go down in the water. They'd been sitting by the window at St. Pierre's and, as the Continental sunk, they ran out of the restaurant and jumped into the cold water. Swimming out to the car, which was almost submerged, they kicked a hole in the back window, swam in, and pulled the near listless driver through the hole. By the time they swam him to the shore, he'd apparently swallowed some water and had lost consciousness. But he was still breathing. Someone from St. Pierre's then shined a flashlight in the man's face.

One of the men cursed. Neither could believe the man they had rescued was Minor Cheramie, the no-good sonofabitch they'd just fought at the Wagon Wheel. One of them said, "If I'd have known that was him, I would've let him drown." But the man did save Minor, who regained consciousness.

Considering the circumstances of the night, Minor felt he had every reason to believe he was indestructible, and, despite his family's wishes, he had no plans to stop drinking. He was not one of those all-day drunks anyway. He didn't start drinking until, at the earliest, four o'clock, and he was never one to let his clients drink alone.

While Minor wasn't worried about alcohol, the increasing competition in the boat business presented a real challenge. When he'd started in the late 1940s, seafood still ruled the bayou. By 1963, that had changed. Oil was now king, and people were continuing to pile into the boat business, much more so than the 1950s rush. What was worse, now anyone could build a cab-forward, open-stern-deck supply boat. While Minor still believed in the uniqueness of his adaptations of Blount's Botruc design, there were a lot of oilmen that didn't care if the boat's special molded lines cost Minor 25 percent more than if he'd built a squarer but rougher riding hull.

Like everyone else, he understood that the oil companies wanted more than a grade A boat. While he could woo them with his marsh camp near Catfish Lake and with his Grand Isle camp aptly named the "Playpen," while he could run them all the girls they wanted, so could many other boatmen. Once again, Minor needed another advantage.

Bobby Orgeron and company christen a crew boat in the 1960s. From left, Goldie Danos, Clarabelle "Cabo" Gisclair, Bobby and Myrtle Orgeron, Butch Danos, and Lorris "Chief" Gisclair. (Courtesy of the Orgeron family)

Chapter 9

Speeding

1963

From the beginning, Bobby Orgeron knew he was in a race. Still attempting to become a millionaire by age thirty-five, he was trying to beat both his competitors and the clock. At age thirty-one, he wasn't there yet.

Whatever he was truly worth, he didn't have time to think about it. While he still showed up at the office in the early morning and examined the books, he was only trying to keep up with the weekly profits and losses.

He had too much on his mind to try to calculate his overall financial portfolio. He had to get to Main Iron Works on the Intracoastal Canal and see how the last of those four new boats he had ordered was coming.

To Bobby, it had been a flash of welding sparks and a cacophony of drills, hammers, and presses. Main Iron Works had blitzed through the building of the *Monaco, Morocco, Mondero,* and, lastly, the *Montego.*

Bobby appreciated the shipyard's pace but wasn't looking forward to his conversation with the yard foreman, Lawrence Mazerac. He and Maz, who was a heavyset man with a great shock of white hair, had been verbally sparring for the last year.

At the yard, Bobby entered the big fabrication shop and greeted Maz, who squeezed his client's hand hard. Bobby increased his squeeze, too, and then looked over and saw his own port captain, Butch Danos, who'd been at the yard since dawn.

Bobby didn't waste time. He told Maz, "You charging me too much for the hydraulic steering."

"That's my price, Bobby."

"It's too high."

"No, it's not."

And there the argument started, leading to cussing, shouting, and fingers in the face. Bobby had to have hydraulic steering; he couldn't deal with the old chain-and-sprocket system, which wasn't nearly as smooth or as easy to maintain as the hydraulic. The old system had too many bearings and levers to keep greased and moving, while the new system only meant adding oil. Bobby didn't want his captains to rip their arms off holding the wheel. He had to be able to tell his customers he had the hottest, best products, but he wasn't going to have it at Maz's price. So they got in each other's faces, and despite Butch's pleading, Bobby wouldn't back down.

Finally, Maz told him, "Get out of here," and then looked at Butch. "You can stay, but he's got to go."

Butch finally escorted his boss away. "Let it go, Bobby. Come on, let it go."

Bobby would leave, but he couldn't let it go. It was his edge. It was what pushed him. It was what made him desperate to find work after a new boat was launched. They were launching quickly now. In addition to the first eight being built, M.O.N.T. was buying two and building three more. Things were moving so fast that the first half of the 1960s was flying by like a flock of blue-winged teal darting past the duck blind.

Darting was exactly what Bobby was doing. He was constantly moving from a boat being built to one being repaired, from haggling with a vendor to schmoozing a customer. Always making transitions, he'd shift from an early-morning duck hunt with customers to a midmorning office meeting to an afternoon in a shipyard to a dinner with his family, only to be jerked out of bed into a wild night in New Orleans. Then, in the predawn hours, he had to leave the flesh pile to get ready for a fishing rodeo that weekend. Often, the week would end in church at Sunday

Mass with the family, with Bobby sometimes praying for a slower, more peaceful existence. Keeping up this pace, his sleep was often compromised. He liked to get four hours of shut-eye. Five was a luxury, and if he only got one to three, he could deal with it.

Really, he would contend with anything. When a boat's engine broke down, if at all possible, Bobby wanted to be there. He would leave his meeting in New Orleans, dressed to the cuffs in one of his many Rubenstein Brothers suits. After arriving at the dock, he would astonish his employees by throwing off his coat, walking into the hold, and putting his hands right in the grease.

Bobby's employees saw his dedication and responded. The good loyal ones—guys such as Butch, Benu, and Chief Gisclair—would do anything Bobby said because he *asked*. He usually didn't demand things but solicited their opinion and watched them perform, which they did because he performed.

After a boat was launched and Bobby didn't have a job for her, he'd go to New Orleans, Houston, or Lafayette and start calling. He would put his feet up on clients' desks and take them to lunch. He'd talk insightfully about the oilfield, or he'd party with them until they'd had enough. Sometimes, his effort was propelled by a panicky feeling that a tied-up boat could create. The mounting unpaid interest would keep him away from home, sometimes for a week or two, until someone gave in to his charm and persistence and handed him a contract.

Of course, it was only a thirty-day contract, with a twenty-four-hour cancellation clause. And that, more than anything else, was what made him keep the accelerator pressed to the floor.

He didn't have time for the speed limit. Between Bobby and his right-hand men Butch and Benu Danos, they were averaging somewhere around one hundred speeding tickets a year. The citations, even when they couldn't fix them, were worth it. A ticket was the only way they'd get an engine part to far-flung Cameron or Corpus Christi and send the boat back offshore. Saving one day on a day rate would more than pay for the tickets, which brought them to their clients faster and created a little more time at home, too. Exceeding the speed limits gave Bobby a few more moments with his little boy and girl or an outing on the Gulf with his favorite fishing partner, Myrtle.

At times, excessive automotive speeds were necessary to take care of special problems. Once in the middle of the night, Bobby and Butch were racing across the Florida Panhandle, blowing through the dark pine thickets. Bobby had already been stopped three times by drawling state troopers in Mississippi and Alabama, and he still couldn't afford to slow down. One of their boats was being held up by the Coast Guard in Clearwater because their captain had a license that didn't contain a proper endorsement. When Bobby heard about the mess, he couldn't get a flight out that night, so he and Butch had jumped in his long Lincoln Continental, his boxy Mafia machine, and buried the needle.

When Bobby was stopped for the fourth time and was again called "son" by a redneck cop, he'd had enough. He told Butch, "You drive."

But after Butch picked up another ticket, Bobby said, "You driving too fast. I'm gonna drive."

Bobby took over and promptly zoomed by a sheriff headed in the other direction.

"Bobby, that was a cop."

"No, that was a sheriff. Sheriffs don't give tickets."

Butch looked at the speedometer. "Even if you going one hundred and five miles an hour?" Bobby heard brakes squeal behind him. He looked in his rearview mirror. The sheriff was doing a U-turn. The cop chased them down and wrote them up. With tickets littering the back of the Continental and yawns emerging from their throats, Bobby and Butch pulled into Clearwater just after dawn.

As soon as they stopped at the Coast Guard station, Bobby leapt out of the car, threw open the office door, and told the receptionist, "I want to see your commander."

When the commander emerged, Bobby was not as lucid as he would have liked to have been. His eyes were red and heavy. Mentally, he was already on the defensive. He didn't like this bureaucracy, especially when it got in the way of a day rate. Within seconds, his discussion with the commander turned into an argument. The commander passed the buck, telling Bobby the Tampa station could be of more assistance.

At the Tampa office, Bobby asked to see the commander, and the receptionist told him, "Do you have an appointment?"

"I don't need an appointment. I'm Bobby Orgeron."

She looked at him incredulously. "I'm sorry."

"I'm Bobby Orgeron. Y'all are tying up one of my boats. I need to talk to your boss."

"You still need an appointment, sir."

Bobby blew up, and a Coast Guard officer asked him to leave. When he and Butch got back in the car, he asked Butch to take him to the airport. "You stay here and untangle this mess." It would take Butch three days to get the Coast Guard to release the boat.

The Coast Guard, the police, and other government agencies were little more than nuisances to Bobby. Early on, he decided the government could only stop him if they caught him. It was only natural that this was his philosophy. He came from a seafaring culture that for years and years, all the way back to the turn of the century, was barely touched by any government. Then, when the federals moved in and began enforcing prohibition, the Cajun skiff captains quickly became experts at rumrunning. No *American* federal could reasonably think they'd run down a Cajun in lower Lafourche's maze of marsh bayous. And they rarely did.

But the law that the Cajuns had always had the biggest problem with was the one on game limits. In the early days, there was no such thing as a limit. The Cajuns took what they needed to eat. God had given it to them, and they wouldn't waste one speckled trout or one duck. In fact, they needed every last morsel of every animal to thrive.

This was the way it was when Bobby was a boy. That was how his family existed at the trapping camp on Bayou Sauvage. This was why it was difficult for him and for countless other Cajuns to follow the stricter game regulations in the 1960s.

On one warm evening on the M.O.N.T. marsh duck lease, the day before teal season, Bobby and Butch were, as usual, ignoring the laws. Their first breach was hunting mallards out of season. Of course, they were only doing what their grandfathers had done, taking summer mallards during the Indian summer. Their second offense was hunting over a baited pond. They hadn't even buried the rice; they simply put nine open rice sacks out there, and the ducks were eating the rice right out of the sacks. Their third transgression was going way over the limit. But again, they'd make sure they'd eat every last one of these sixty-six ducks.

Their fourth violation was they'd shot most of the ducks after legal shooting time. *Mais* wasn't that the best time to get them?

When they heard the game warden's helicopter hovering toward them, they forgot their logic and their arguments about historical entitlement. They knew the game warden wouldn't believe this was all a "misunderstanding." They knew they only had one option—*to run*.

Bobby, who'd been hunting on the levee, grabbed his shotgun and bolted like a madman down the bank. He looked back and watched the chopper sit down briefly on its pontoons, drop one game warden off at the pond, and then rise up into the air and head right for him like an angry *guêpe*, a big, mad wasp. Bobby had no choice but to plunge into the brush. As he thrashed through the *roseaus* and the *mongeaus*, the chopper hovered above him. The more he ran, the more the brush cut him up, and he was soon covered with blood.

When the sky grew dark, the chopper finally gave up on him and turned back toward the pond, back toward Butch.

Butch, who hadn't been near the levee when the chopper pounced on them, had looked for an escape. He couldn't run anywhere without being easily spotted and captured. So Butch had buried himself into the soft mud of a *flottante*, oozing into it like an alligator, leaving only his face exposed so he could breath, covering his head with grass.

The chopper landed almost right on his gun and *bidon*, a shell bucket. He watched the man get out of the cockpit and start looking through his *bidon*, pulling out his shells and his wallet and examining his driver's license. *Mon dieu,* Butch thought. He held his breath as the warden trudged through the muck, picked up the ducks, and took pictures of the open rice sacks. The wardens had overwhelming evidence. While they'd retrieved the bait, the bodies, and the "murder weapon," they didn't have the suspects.

After the helicopter touched down near Butch, the wardens canvassed the area till it was pitch-black. They passed inches from Butch. They looked right at him, but they never saw him.

When the chopper flew back toward the highway, Butch emerged from the ooze and Bobby from the brush. Bobby was nearly as bloody as Butch was muddy. They cleaned up at the camp, and when they got back to the front, Bobby called the sheriff at the courthouse annex in Galliano and complained that Butch's wallet was stolen.

When the deputy asked him what happened, Bobby said it was stolen from his duck camp. The deputy then asked if he had any idea of a suspect. Bobby's response was, "I don't know who stole it. But it had to be the same one that's shooting up my pond."

Despite Bobby's pitch to the sheriff, three days later some game wardens came to Butch's house with a warrant and picked him up. He played dumb at first; then acted overjoyed when they showed him his wallet. He'd been looking all over for it. What was it doing in that *bidon* with those shotgun shells and that little bottle of whiskey? That wasn't his *bidon* or his shells. He didn't drink that brand of bourbon. How did his wallet even make it to the company duck camp? Somebody must've taken it from the office. Some salesman, some *maudit Texien* who snuck onto the duck lease, must've stolen it and put it in his shell bucket. That was it. That *bidon* belonged to a Texien. You could tell, Butch told them. They don't even make those kinds of *bidons* in south Louisiana.

Butch, he wouldn't be caught dead with a *bidon* like that. That Texien had to still be at large. He was probably in the marsh, lost and near death. Now was the time to find him and take him.

The wardens listened and laughed. They told Butch he could tell that story to the judge.

He did give the judge that story, and when the judge looked at this young, innocent rosy-cheeked Santa Claus, his honor didn't find proof beyond reasonable doubt. He let him go.

And Butch was off and running again. As was Bobby. This time it was with Butch's brother Benu. They were zipping back across the sandy rises and piney dips of the Florida Panhandle. They were doing their best to spot the troopers and adjust their speedometer accordingly. But they couldn't decelerate too much because they had a boat that wasn't just losing money; she was abandoned.

A shrimper had called them and said their *Monte Christo* was at anchor off Alligator Point. He said no one was on the vessel. She was simply floating there, pulling against the anchor rope.

The news hit Bobby so oddly he couldn't believe it at first. When his boat's predicament sunk in and the shock wore off, his head filled with his blood and his foot hit the floorboard.

At Alligator Point, Bobby had to hire a skiff to take them to their boat. When they stepped aboard the *Monte Christo*, Bobby's shock returned. He'd never seen such a sight. The inside of the boat was ripped up. The furniture was in pieces. The whole cabin was a ravaged, dirty mess; even the galley was full of rotting food and dirty dishes.

Bobby could hardly stand the smell. Benu would have to drive the boat back to shore for repair. All Bobby could do was get back to his Continental and race back home. He would grind his teeth thinking about the captain who'd abandoned his vessel, but all the gnashing and cussing in the world wouldn't do him any good because the damage was already done.

Perhaps the reason the *Monte Christo* had been abandoned was because she was cursed. Soon, in another incident, this same boat somehow found a way to ram into a rig south of Dulac. The collision turned the side of the boat that struck the rig into scrap metal. Later, when the unsteady captain walked into the M.O.N.T. office in Golden Meadow, Benu told him, "Get your clothes and get out of here."

"Why?" the shaken captain asked.

"You better leave. He's coming."

The captain didn't have to ask who the "he" was and rushed out of the office.

When the "he," Bobby, showed up, he had to do his best to forget about the accident and any other unfortunate occurrences because, as always, he had somewhere to go—and somewhere to collide. In all, he would total nine automobiles and walk away from every one of them. The collisions caused him to have significant spinal troubles, and even though he had a spine full of herniated discs, he wouldn't let the doctors operate on him for that. They'd cut on him enough— hemorrhoids, gall bladder, kidney stones. Between the collisions and the operations, he hardly had any ass on one side. After his second hemorrhoid operation, he had to wear a woman's tampon and sit on newspaper to keep from bleeding all over his seat.

He also had to take Darvocet to deal with the misery. Of course, he knew he had to watch his medication intake; his brother, Bouillien, had already gotten hooked on pills. But Bobby would take a few to get through the pain in his seat and keep going.

Aller, to go, was the only thing he knew. And one night, he and Butch were going toward home, coming back from New Orleans. They were speeding down US 90 near Boutte, trying to get back to their families. Without any warning, Bobby drifted to the middle of the road. His Continental's hood emblem crossed over the center of the double line, speeding no less than 110 miles per hour.

And here came a truck. Butch, who was half-sleeping in the passenger seat, saw the eighteen-wheeler steaming for them, and he sat straight up in his seat. It was too late for him to do anything. He was hearing the truck horn and was trying to move or speak, but it was not up to him.

The truck swerved and missed them.

Butch looked at Bobby's face. It hadn't flinched. He asked, "Bobby, you sleeping?"

"No, why?"

"*Mais* you almost hit that truck."

But he didn't hit it. As long as he didn't make contact, or as long as he collided but walked away, he would keep speeding. If he got sleepy, he would drink black coffee or smoke a cigar. If he was still sluggish, he'd purchase speed in a bottle, the little amphetamine pill that made him go. There were millions to make, and he didn't consider himself a millionaire. He had to get there in time.

They said you couldn't buy time, but maybe Bobby could. The faster he traveled, the more moments he acquired. These were extra hours the slowpokes didn't have. Even if the others had more money, they'd never move fast enough to buy his time.

It wasn't just the boatman who had to manipulate the clock. It was also his wife trying to balance a demanding schedule. Usually, that meant raising the kids and running the house with little help from your man. In other instances, like in the case of Lou Cheramie in 1963, it meant having an oilfield weekend every bit as hectic as your husband's. But on Grand Isle, Lou and Minor's five-bedroom "Playpen" camp was usually anything but playtime for her. When Minor and his latest group of oilmen buddies came in from a night of drinking at 4:00 and 5:00 a.m., she'd get up and cook them breakfast. She'd watch Minor as he filled up his belly, then go to the bedroom and pass out. Later in the morning, while Minor was still sleeping, Lou would have to fix lunch. Then after Minor and his crew went off to fish in the afternoon, Lou would prepare supper and try to entertain the oilmen's wives, many of whom she'd just met.

Lou got used to seeing so many Texiens that their images began to run together. But in the summer of 1963, the Cheramies had an unusual visitor. He was a Texien from north Louisiana, but he wasn't an oilman. To Lou, the man was strange looking—a tall lanky person with big expressive eyes. An oilman friend had brought him by the camp for dinner, and it didn't take him long to make himself right at home, lying down on the Cheramie's couch. As Lou saw this John McKeithen, a former legislator from Columbia, Louisiana, stretch his long legs over the sofa's edge onto a chair, she could hardly believe he was running for governor.

After McKeithen left the camp, Lou told Minor, "There's no way that daddy longlegs is going to win."

Minor disagreed with her. Minor and McKeithen had hit it off, and Minor heavily supported him in the race. He did what he could to make every Cajun he knew vote for the north Louisianan. He knocked heads with Nolty Theriot, who supported McKeithen's opponent, New Orleans Mayor deLesseps "Chep" Morrison. But as Minor and Nolty enjoyed a spirited race, Lou had her doubts. She still didn't think McKeithen would prevail, especially when he made a commercial where he pleaded for the public's support, and instead of saying, "help me," said, "hep me." But the people liked the "hep me" candidate, and they voted him their governor.

As McKeithen took office, he rewarded Minor for his support by giving him a seat on the State Mineral Board, which controlled the awarding of leases on state lands, which extended three miles into the Gulf of Mexico. Of course, the oil companies seeking the leases were the same companies that hired boat companies like L & M Botruc. If an oil company competing for a lease wanted Minor's support, it wouldn't hurt that company to give L & M Botruc a supply boat contract or two. Suddenly,

Minor had added a position of power to his arsenal of natural personality and his Botruc speciality. At the Mineral Board office, he hung up a big picture of a Botruc and hobnobbed with hundreds of oilfield executives and industry insiders.

While voters in other states might have considered Minor's appointment a conflict of interest, in Louisiana, hardly anyone batted an eye. The only people that really complained were some jealous boatmen, but they weren't calling Minor's appointment unethical. They were just envious that they themselves weren't on the board.

After Minor took his oath of office, it was as if he moved to Baton Rouge. He'd leave for a three-day meeting and end up staying eight days at the Capitol House Hotel, where he traded backslaps with all types of oilmen and politicians. During this period, he dressed immaculately, shedding his formerly casual attire for a traveling wardrobe full of the finest threads. He was so conscious of his appearance that he'd make four trips a year to Rubenstein's in downtown New Orleans, parking right in front of the Canal Street store and telling the seasoned salesman to pick out four new suits, with new matching shirts, ties, shoes, and socks.

Although Minor grew used to his dapper threads, he wasn't always comfortable at the board meetings. When the board was in session, he said very little. He was worried about his lack of education and his less than proper English, and he didn't always understand what was being discussed. But as he gained experience, he realized some disturbing things were happening. He confirmed his suspicions with his new confidant and friend, the tall, talkative, and perceptive New Orleans lawyer, Bill Porteous.

Porteous and Minor watched some of their fellow members bribe and blackmail the oil companies. They listened to them glean confidential geological information about certain well sites and use it to their advantage, either by selling the information or by investing in the project. According to Porteous, the graft infuriated Minor, who would say nothing until the board members retired to the bar at the Capitol House Hotel, where he'd confront a "black hat" one-on-one and light into him. Minor thought that as a board member, he had a responsibility of stewardship over the industry and thought he could help improve Louisiana's reputation as a place where political officials used their power to gain profits. Those in Minor's inner circle believed that he would never even consider telling an oilman that he would give the man's company a vote if the oilman gave him a boat contract. This is why it was difficult for Minor to witness some of his fellow board members cheat so openly. One of them would even end up in jail for the oilfield equivalent of insider trading.

Minor's tenure with the board was a good example of his unusual brand of honesty. On the one hand, he detested the sneaky cheating and the defiance of public trust he saw going on at the board because, among other things, it was dishonest. Then, in staying true to his nature, he did not lie to his wife about his marital infidelity. While he was ignoring his vows and causing Lou great pain, he was also telling her the truth. Other boatmen, and any cheating married man, would of course try to hide the girlfriends from their wives. Minor didn't. His candor about his extra-marital affairs did not justify his behavior, but it was consistent with his conviction of being honest.

By the same token, Lou knew that, despite her husband's bad habits, he loved her and didn't want her to leave him. He wanted her to have a mink coat, fine jewelry, and whatever else he could buy. She was too frugal and practical to ask for anything luxuriant, but, at times, he doted on her. He couldn't stand for her not to have the nice things. He told her that she deserved them, that she'd worked for them as much as he had.

He also wanted Lou to do as little work outside the home as possible. He made sure someone did all her grocery shopping for her. He had employees pick up her car and change the oil. If she needed something, anything, he told her to call the office and someone from the company would take care of it.

Although these might have been thoughtful gestures, they also made Lou a kept woman to some degree. She developed the habit of staying home and hardly going anywhere. And yes, if he was drunk and she argued with him, he still sometimes resorted to violence. Why he did it made no sense. As far as Lou could tell, Minor had loving parents and a good childhood. His father was a well-liked man and to her knowledge did not share Minor's dark side. Consequently, neither Lou nor anyone else could explain his inebriated antics, other than it was something in the drink that triggered them.

When sober, Minor was still exceptionally generous. He gave jobs to many extended family members. He donated money to the church, even though he had no interest in attending Mass. When an ailing shrimper tried to get into the Mariner's Hospital in New Orleans to receive free treatment, Minor would help him gain admission by doing something out of character, lying, saying the shrimper worked for him and was, in fact, a member of the merchant marine. He justified the lies because the shrimpers were taking as many risks at sea as the more traditional commercial mariners. But really, Minor signed the application because he wanted to help the shrimpers. He made it a practice to assist whomever he could, giving money to complete strangers for burials or for groceries.

He'd proven that he could be a prince as easily as he could be a pig, with the determining factor being how much alcohol was in his system. But no matter what his state of mind was at night, when he woke up in the morning, he was determined to build his company and protect his people.

In September 1965, Minor's family and many others would need protection from Hurricane Betsy, which roared from the Gulf up Bayou Lafourche, devastating many of the homes in its path. It would prove to be the worst hurricane to hit the Lafourche Country since the Leeville storms near the turn of the century. While Minor kept his family safe by herding them onto one of the Botrucs, when they emerged, their house was destroyed.

Despite his wrecked, unlivable home, despite an oilfield economy that was showing signs of recession, Minor's maneuvering had kept his company and his family riding high. The other boatmen could sweat the downturn. For the time being, Minor the Mineral Board man was impregnable.

A little ways down the bayou from the Cheramie house, Nolty Theriot had no illusions of indestructibility or immortality. In the early 1960s, he still firmly believed he was living on borrowed minutes. So when he was in a vehicle, he had the same attitude as his good friend Bobby Orgeron. He couldn't get there, wherever there was, fast enough.

After the tug sale to Brown & Root had pulled Nolty out of hock, he'd treated himself to a sleek gold Chrysler. He loved the car's golden gleam, but when he'd gun it, its back end would shimmy. Nolty fixed the problem by going to his shipyard and putting a few boxes of welding rods into the trunk. With the extra weight, his Chrysler could finally hold the highway.

As fast as the Chrysler moved, it didn't compare to the speed of the ideas zapping around his brain. His latest creation was what he believed to be the world's first self-propelled submersible rig. He'd begun thinking of the idea back in the late fifties, forming a separate corporation on June 15, 1959, called Offshore Submersibles, Inc. At that time, he'd had too much to do just keeping his business afloat to figure out how to design a submersible that was part motorized boat and part drilling rig. Now he finally had it figured out.

With this project, he knew the oil companies would want a naval architect's stamp on it. Nolty worked with an architect, made a design that he believed would work, and then, as the sixties progressed, finally found a way to fund the special vessel. Many people thought he was crazy; he was a tugboat man, not a rig designer. Moreover, while non–self-propelled submersibles had been around since the early fifties, they'd had their share of trouble withstanding a rough sea. Some had even capsized. Just who did Nolty think he was?

As usual, he paid no attention to his doubters. Instead, he studied and restudied the submersible's basic design of a platform mounted on bottle-like tanks, which were flooded and sunk to stabilize the submersible in place. He adapted this model to create his *Unit 10*, but he also added an engine and propulsion system. The rig would motor offshore under its own power; then the crew would fill up and sink its four sixty-foot-high tanks called "cans." Once the platform was stabilized, the crew would work over the drilling rig, which usually meant cleaning the paraffin wax deposits out of the wells. Then, when the *Unit 10* was ready to move, the crew would pump out the cans and move to the next location.

Nolty gained confidence in his idea after he hired an ex–Chevron employee, a tall Mississippian by the name of Charlie Sanders. Everything about Sanders was large and loud, from his heavy, six-feet-five-inch frame to his crushing, mitt-like hands, to his deep piney woods voice.

While Nolty knew his Cajun captains might have some trouble with a non-French speaking Texien as their VP of Operations, he knew they'd forget about the cultural difference when they realized how astute Sanders was. When Nolty shared his *Unit 10* idea with Sanders, Sanders bought into it and believed they could sell it to Chevron.

As Nolty's shipyard crew began to piece together the *Unit 10* in the woods, onlookers scratched their heads. They looked at the strange cans, the barge-like platform, and a cabin topped off with a helicopter pad. Eventually, the gawky superstructure sat on top of the cans, and the *Unit 10* protruded over the trees like an awkward spaceship. The people said it looked like a monster. It soon developed a nickname, the Purple People Eater, after the hit 1958 song. During the monstrosity's launch, its cans cracked the asphalt on Highway 308, and it lumbered into the water, flooding the banks with big waves. After all the commotion, the *Unit 10* actually floated. Dominating the bayou, it looked every bit the "one-eyed, one-horned, flyin' purple people eater."

As some people in the crowd cheered, others shuddered and laughed. They didn't believe an oil company would spend money to rent this freak of iron.

Well, Nolty would prove that the Purple People Eater could fly.

With new gimmicks launching and new companies forming in the 1960s, the boatmen, whether knowingly or unknowingly, were drafting an unwritten code. The Code, which no one actually knew as a code, held that while the boatmen competed feverishly for contracts that were up for grabs, they couldn't call on each other's established clients. The Code was a strange thing in America, the home of the free market and a government that blocked only the most extreme monopolies. The United States was not only the land of the free and the home of the brave, but the stomping grounds of John D. Rockefeller and Andrew Carnegie. It was a place where Ford and General Motors bought up city trolley systems across the country in an effort to abolish them altogether and establish the automobile as the nation's dominant method of transportation. The goal of US companies seemed to be to conquer and own the market.

The goal of the independent boatman, on the other hand, was to live by the Code and share and share alike. Bobby Orgeron had learned about the Code at any early stage. When he'd broken into the business, he'd placed his inland crew boats with Gulf Oil, Stanolind, and Atlantic Refining because there was no competition for those jobs. Even as boats crowded into the market, he would never have dreamed of going after a job currently taken by someone like Nolty Theriot, Minor Cheramie, or Anthony Guilbeau and Albert Cheramie's C. & G. He was friends with a superintendent at C. & G.'s big client, Conoco, and perhaps he could've beaten C. & G.'s price, but the Code prevented him from even thinking about it. These were his friends, sometimes his relatives, and in lower Lafourche, always his fellow Cajuns.

Throughout history, the Cajuns had stuck together, going all the way back to their Acadian days in Atlantic Canada when the only way to farm the Bay of Fundy tidelands was to drain and dike the marsh. Without a communal effort, the Acadians simply couldn't have accomplished the arduous task of constructing the dikes. The dike building forged a unique bond among the Acadians. In the twentieth century, this unusually strong brotherhood was still in place when the Cajuns worked closely together in helping each other dig marsh *trainasses* and build skiffs.

The Cajuns had worked hand in hand for more than two hundred years; they weren't about to work against each other now in the boat industry. As for Bobby, instead of competing with people like Andrew Martin and Kip Plaisance, he befriended them. He was the *parrain*, the godfather, of his "competitor" Martin's son, Andy. Bobby would throw elaborate *boucheries* at his home with boatmen making up a large portion of his guest list. He hunted and fished with them, took trips with them and their wives to the annual Lafitte Pirogue Races and to the Roosevelt Hotel in New Orleans, and, later, to Las Vegas. He'd sometimes meet Minor, Nolty, and other boatmen for a drink at the Glo Room, where they would openly talk business as if they were all on the same board of directors.

Even in a more complicated relationship, the Code was still honored. For instance, Bobby considered himself to be one of Minor's friends; but because of Minor's penchant for getting out of control when drunk, Bobby wouldn't invite him to his *boucheries*. Nevertheless, Minor still brokered one of Bobby's boats to Shell. Later, their relationship would be tested one night when they got into a fight at the Glo Room. After the tussle, Minor called Bobby and said he wanted to talk. Bobby went to Minor's house a little shaken up, packing his pistol, and telling Minor, "If you touch me again, I'll kill ya."

Minor, who'd sobered up, said, "No, no. Look, I just want to be friends with you."

The next day, Bobby went to Minor's office, and the two shot the bull. Minor kept Bobby's boat working for Shell as if nothing had happened. By the same token, despite the fight, Bobby didn't consider going around Minor and trying to sign a contract directly with Shell.

Of course, Minor and Nolty and the gang were Cadiens and fellow *Lafourchais*, but in the boat business, the Code could extend beyond the bayou. For example, after Bobby became good friends with a Texaco vice president, he had an obvious lead with the company. But because Texaco used Arthur Levy and Tony Guarisco out of Morgan City, Bobby never made a pitch. He wasn't as close to Levy and Guarisco as he was to his Lafourche brethren, but he respected them too much to attempt to steal their clients.

Bobby firmly believed, as many of the other independents thought, if everyone treated one another fairly, there was enough work for everybody. He still wanted his millions, but he thought he could make them right along with everyone else. And while there would always be rogues who didn't care about the Code, surviving by being client thieves, he sure wouldn't be one of them.

Chapter 10

Sovereign State

February 1964

———— ⊷∞⊶ ————

The 1960s hadn't done much to change Sidney Savoie. To him, the decade could have its counterculture, its flower children, and the mop-headed Beatles that had just hit the American shores. But neither the British rock invasion nor any rush to design new oilfield gizmos would have any effect on Sidney. He was as even and dependable as he'd been in 1942 when he was sharing the coastal waters with marauding U-boats.

In early 1964, Sidney's business was moving fairly steadily. He was surviving despite his battle with Texaco in federal court and the hint of a recession on the horizon. Luckily, his original venture, the *Ajax*, was still working by the day for Gulf Oil. The relationship had lasted fourteen years with little interruption. This *Ajax*-Gulf alliance, along with the formation of United Tugs, had kept Sidney afloat.

In early 1964, the *Ajax* was sailing mostly out of the Plaquemines Parish town of Venice. While Sidney's work there had been going smoothly, he was starting to hear some troubling news.

An organization called the Venice Boat Association had been formed by some of the Plaquemines Parish resident boat owners, and their apparent goal was to drive from the parish all non-Plaquemines boat companies. The man behind the organization, whether officially or unofficially, was parish boss Judge Leander Perez.

Sidney knew all about Judge Perez. The man had controlled Plaquemines Parish since before Sidney started running lugger tugs there in the late 1930s. Perez's reign extended beyond Plaquemines to the whole twenty-fifth Judicial District, which also included St. Bernard Parish. This meant that Perez ruled all the land in the Mississippi River corridor south of the urban sprawl of New Orleans. There were many oilfield towns in this stretch, including Buras, Port Sulphur, and Venice.

Judge Perez, who was only briefly a real district judge, carried the official title of district attorney, but he was really the dictator of the delta. In this region, Perez had more power than either the US president or the Louisiana governor.

Judge Perez had a hand over every detail in his district. He ran the levee boards that granted the oil leases; he commandeered the elections, the school boards, and jury selection.

Perez apparently now wanted to control how the oil companies doled out the workboat jobs. One of his organization's tactics was sabotage. Although Sidney had yet to witness these acts of subversion, he had reliable information they'd been taking place. Out-of-parish boats were experiencing engine trouble because sugar had been poured into their gas tanks. "Foreign" captains and crew members were being stopped on a speeding ticket and placed in jail for a couple days, which would prevent them from making a timely crew change. And warning shots had been fired over the bows of non-parish tugs.

This harassment had come up out of nowhere. While Sidney knew full well that Judge Perez did whatever he wanted in Plaquemines, the Plaquemines residents had never seemed interested in the workboat business. They were shrimpers and trappers, and in the decade-plus that Sidney had been operating there, he'd always gotten along with the natives.

By 1964, some Plaquemines residents had begun to realize the cash-cow potential of the oilfield boat business. Rather than bide their time for the already spoken for local jobs, their solution was to simply take them.

In this environment, Sidney was approached one day by the local Gulf Oil transportation man. The boss told him, "I'm gonna have to let you go."

Sidney was stunned. "Why?" he asked.

"Perez. He wants to put a boat in your place."

The transportation boss didn't have to say much more. By this point, Sidney understood. Still, he had a hard time accepting that the Perez machine could snip a fourteen-year relationship with such ease. Sidney decided to visit the Gulf Oil big boss at the Elks Building in New Orleans with some other out-of-parish tug owners, but the vice president backed up his superintendent's story. Judge Perez wanted them out of the parish, and Gulf Oil didn't have much choice but to oblige. Because Perez controlled the local mineral leases, if Gulf didn't respect his wishes, the judge might keep them from getting a lease interest in the oil-soaked parish.

Sidney left the Elks Building shaking his head. The only positive was that Gulf Oil hadn't officially pulled the *Ajax* from the job. But still, he couldn't believe what was happening. It didn't feel like he was in the United States. Geographically, he was; politically, he wasn't. In fact, Judge Perez had once cut at the soul of American government by saying, "Democracy—I hate that word." Perez detested democratic rule so much that he'd single-handedly removed it from the parish, stripping Plaquemines citizens of their most personal, powerful democratic tenet—the right to vote. His imposed voting blockage on the parish's black citizens was outward and obvious. In 1952, of the thousands of blacks in Plaquemines, *none* were registered to vote. Even after a federal district court had ordered Plaquemines to register black voters, by the landmark civil rights annum of 1964, only 97 of the parish's 6,500 blacks were registered to vote.

When it came to voting, whites were nearly as powerless as blacks. While Perez "openly" allowed the white man to vote, he monopolized the white vote, too. A classic case of this control and the ultimate example of the area's sovereignty involved the plight of Salvador Chiappetta, a resident of lower Plaquemines. Chiappetta, a highway maintenance foreman, had once complained to his fellow workers that Perez had used state highway labor to build himself a private road and pond. Chiappetta was promptly fired. After he obtained another job in the parish, he was quickly fired again.

Chiappetta decided to fight back by voting against the Perez machine. But he'd never actually registered to vote, and when he drove to the parish courthouse to register, he couldn't even find a registrar of voters office. Chiappetta made the trip five more times but could never locate the registrar, whose practice was to drive through the parish randomly registering people. Chiappetta then sent the registrar a letter but never received a reply.

After Chiappetta hired a lawyer, the lawyer wrote the Louisiana attorney general, who in turn queried Perez. Perez never responded. Chiappetta then wrote the president of the United States, but the president's counsel, an assistant US attorney general, told Chiappetta that registering to vote was a "local" affair. Chiappetta had no apparent recourse. All paths led back to Perez.

The incident proved that Perez controlled every affair in the parish—local, state, national, and private. There was no way to beat him. What was Sidney Savoie supposed to do? He couldn't file suit against the Venice Boat Association in state court. Perez controlled the district's judiciary and every jury selected to a panel. If Sidney could find a federal claim and bring suit in federal court, he'd have to put up with the association's sabotage while the suit was pending. And if Sidney prevailed, who would enforce the federal court order?

Perez had already proved that military force had little effect on his power. In 1943, Louisiana Governor Sam Jones had even sent the National Guard into Plaquemines. The incident arose when Governor Jones appointed the Plaquemines an interim sheriff through a Louisiana law that allowed the governor to appoint a sheriff after the incumbent died with less than one year remaining in office.

On the same day the Plaquemines sheriff died, Perez quickly appointed the parish coroner to take the sheriff's place. Perez then claimed the governor should allow a special election for the interim position, with his main reason being that he didn't want the governor's man to have access to boxes of incriminating "public" records stored in the courthouse.

But Governor Jones wasn't going to stand for Perez's puppetry; he and Perez were old enemies. While Perez had been a dedicated disciple of former Louisiana governor and assassinated US senator, Huey Long, Governor Jones was an anti-Longite dedicated to trying to clean up Louisiana politics. Given their rivalry, Perez had anticipated the governor would try to send someone into the sheriff's office at the courthouse in Pointe a La Hache. Consequently, he surrounded the courthouse with parish deputies.

When Governor Jones learned of Perez's actions, he mobilized two Louisiana National Guard units. In response, Perez strengthened his defenses, erecting a wooden barricade around the courthouse and recruiting a dozen vigilantes to join his deputies. Eventually, Perez officially created a "wartime emergency patrol" and started rounding up troops, which included all members of the American Legion Vidocovich Post Number 193.

Meanwhile, in Baton Rouge, four hundred guardsmen were drilling, preparing to go into Plaquemines. After Governor Jones appointed Walter Blaize, a Buras man, as interim sheriff, Blaize drove south to Plaquemines. At the parish line in Braithwaite, Blaize saw armed men wearing badges stopping a car in front of him. He turned around and headed back toward New Orleans.

All the while, Perez was using the court system to keep Blaize out of office. The matter would stay tied up in the courts for four months as Perez kept the courthouse and parish lines guarded with his militia.

Losing patience, Governor Jones sent Perez a telegram asking him to surrender the sheriff's office to "avoid the possibility of bloodshed." Perez's reply telegram said he could not comply with the governor's order "as district attorney and as an American and as a man."

On October 9, 1943, Governor Jones declared martial law in Plaquemines. He sent in the National Guard that morning to stop "insurrection and open rebellion." The governor's force barreled toward the parish line in thirty armed army trucks, led by two armored cars mounted with machine guns. At Braithwaite, three Plaquemines deputies attempted to stop the convoy, but the guardsmen disarmed and arrested the men.

Driving southward, the Guard pushed aside a tractor-trailer barricade and burned a massive oyster-shell barrier and shoveled it from the highway. The few Plaquemines vigilantes the guardsmen had encountered had retreated.

As the National Guard plowed toward the parish seat, the courthouse was in chaos. In command there was Judge Perez, wearing a helmet and hunting camouflage and barking orders to his defense forces. Perez and his men were hastily removing dozens of file boxes from the courthouse. They then boarded a ferry and retreated to the west side of the river.

When the guardsmen arrived at the mostly deserted courthouse, they escorted the interim sheriff into his office. The Guard's general then set up an impromptu military district.

As the weeks passed, the interim sheriff Blaize could get little accomplished. Perez had cut off Blaize's access to parish funds, preventing Blaize from paying his deputies. Perez also frustrated Blaize's efforts by filing lawsuit after lawsuit against either Blaize, the governor, the Guard officers, or any other possible member of the "enemy." All the while, Perez's man, the coroner Slater, was also acting as a sheriff, paying deputies with a "loan" from the police jury, an organization similar to a county board of commisioners. With an election approaching, the interim sheriff's position was about to expire.

By the time of the race, Blaize's presence had hardly been felt in the parish. He lost the election to Slater by a four-to-one margin. Before Slater officially assumed office, Governor Jones withdrew the remaining guardsmen and revoked the reign of martial law. For all practical purposes, nothing much had happened. The governor, the guardsmen, and their guns had occupied Plaquemines, but Perez had still been in control.

Remembering this infamous incident and many others, Sidney Savoie knew his plight was fruitless. It was kind of ironic. Sidney was fighting the global superpower Texaco in court, and he stood a decent chance of winning. But here in Plaquemines, neither Sidney nor an international oil company nor any outside government stood even the slightest chance of defying Leander Perez. If Perez wanted Sidney out, he was out.

At this point, neither Perez nor any member of the Venice Boat Association nor Gulf Oil had taken the *Ajax* off the job. Sidney and his partner, Faro Guidry, decided to keep the *Ajax* working until Gulf Oil ended the contract. Of course, if they became the victims of sabotage, they might reconsider.

One spring Sunday, Sidney was finally approached by a member of the local establishment. The man, Paul LeBouef, may or may not have been a member of the Venice Boat Association; but he was a Buras resident, and he and his brother, Donald, were starting a tugboat company. LeBouef was a Lafourche name, and Paul and Donald LeBouef apparently had Lafourche roots. But they were Plaquemines residents now and considered locals. They weren't exactly turncoat coonasses, but in this wacko totalitarian climate, it seemed that way.

After Paul LeBouef shook Sidney's hand, he told him point-blank, "I heard that y'all are gonna get run off."

"Yeah." There wasn't much else for Sidney to say.

"Do you want to sell the boat?"

Sidney asked the price.

LeBouef quoted a number that had to be somewhere near market value. "I don't know," said Sidney. "I'll have to talk to my partner."

Later, Sidney and Faro mulled their options. As soon as the Perez machine produced a substitute tug, Gulf Oil would terminate their contract. Day-rate work wasn't nearly as plentiful as it had been in the mid-fifties. Sidney and Faro didn't want to eke out a by-the-hour existence in Harvey, at least not with the *Ajax*, which had always been their prized pig. While the boat was worth more on a day-rate job than it was for a lump-sum price, without a steady job, the lump sum was preferable. The money from the sale should tide them over until the Texaco suit was resolved and the economy picked up.

Sidney contacted LeBouef and agreed to the sale. On April 14, 1964, Paul and his brother, Donald, formed P and D Tugs, Inc. On the same day, the new company purchased the *Ajax* from Guidry & Savoie, Inc. and the *Ajax* never left the Gulf Oil job.

To Sidney and Faro, it was as if they were selling their old, lovable hound. Only someone like Perez could make a man sell his dog.

By the summer, Sidney was glad he'd pulled out of Plaquemines. That August, Perez's despotic shenanigans took a medieval twist. One afternoon, he unveiled to visiting press an interesting site on the lower east bank of the Mississippi, a place that was accessible only by water. Perez guided the media via shrimp boat to Fort St. Philip, which had been built by the Spanish in 1746 to guard the entrance to the river. The fortress had also been used by the Americans in the War of 1812 and the Confederates in the Civil War. Now it had been claimed by the one-man government of Plaquemines Parish.

Perez told reporters he had converted Fort St. Philip into a prison. He intended to use it as a civil rights concentration camp for unruly blacks and for freedom-fighting activists who dared to venture into the parish. Really, the fort was nothing more than a trumped-up cattle pen, with the old bricks buttressed by nine feet of hog wire topped by electric strands. Surrounded by water, marsh, and swamp, mosquitoes infested the dank cells, which were transformed old powder magazines.

As Perez led the media around the prison, he proclaimed, "This place isn't for Negroes only—it's for anarchists, those who come here to overthrow the legally constituted government."

Would Perez classify a Cajun tugboat owner as an "anarchist?" Had Sidney stayed in Plaquemines, would he have ended up in Fort St. Philip with Ivy League activists as cell mates? He could have been subjected to an onslaught of philosophy and a barrage of mosquito bites.

While Perez didn't throw the Lafourche tugboat owners in Fort St. Philip, his machine did retaliate against some of them. Sidney continued to hear stories about the sabotage. He once visited his fellow lower Lafourche tugboat owner, E. J. Lee, at Lee's office. Lee, who'd had several tugs operating in Plaquemines waters, told Sidney that Perez supporters had shot at him. They'd opened fire on Lee's car when he was driving down a Plaquemines highway.

"If they shoot me again," Lee told Sidney, "I'll shoot them back." Apparently, Lee never got his chance. Perez convinced the oil companies to force Lee out of Plaquemines.

While the sale of the *Ajax* settled a potential catastrophe for Sidney and Faro, it did nothing to resolve a developing internal problem. In 1964, Sidney's son, Ted, had become a licensed captain. Although Ted had been hanging around the company since he was a child, his official entry into the business soon changed his *Nonc* Faro's treatment of him. When Ted was a boy, he would accompany his uncle on business trips to Texas or to southwest Louisiana. Faro had almost been like a second father.

As soon as Ted joined the company, both Ted and Sidney felt as if Faro was criticizing Ted's every decision. He was always after Ted about something. Even though Ted was a certified diesel mechanic and Faro knew little about engines, Faro claimed Ted didn't know how to fix an engine.

Most of the time, Ted silently absorbed his uncle's criticism. He rarely defended himself to his elder. But Sidney, who could let almost anything roll off his shoulders, grew tired of his partner's chiding. Many were surprised that Sidney had coexisted with Faro for as long as he had, but that coexistence was coming to an end.

After a few years of dealing with Faro's tirades against Ted, Sidney told his partner, "Well, if we gonna keep on like that, we gonna have to split."

Faro didn't argue. They divided up the boats they owned between them, and Faro sold his shares in United Tugs. Curiously, Faro kept the *Ted*, named for Sidney's son, and Sidney kept the *Susan G*, named for Faro's daughter.

Change, in one form or another, took place more often in the oilfield than in other industries that weren't as volatile, rough-edged, and fast paced. One boatman not afraid of undergoing a metamorphosis was Nolty Theriot. Nolty had not only changed his strategy, he'd mutated his equipment into a steel monster. When Nolty showed his monstrous *Unit 10* submersible to Chevron, the oil company was convinced the submersible could turn into a purple paraffin eater and hired it. Before Nolty knew it, he'd paid off the note on this supposedly unusable space creature.

Even though the Purple People Eater was an initial success, Nolty never built another self-propelled submersible. Even with the *Unit 10's* novelty and utility, it was ahead of its time in one sense and behind the times in another. On the one hand, the oil companies weren't demanding fleets of self-movable work platforms, and, by the same token, a better self-propelled platform had already been invented. Over on the east side of the river in Chalmette, an ex-welder named Lynn Dean had created the first prototype for what he called an "elevator boat" and what would later be termed a "liftboat," which like the *Unit 10* submersible was a self-propelled platform. But liftboats had legs instead of cans, and the legs jacked up and down hydraulically, which was much more efficient and effective than pumping the cans full of water to sink them and pumping them out to raise them. Liftboats, not submersibles, were the wave of the future.

Moreover, Nolty had also run short of the resources needed to upgrade and market self-movable platforms. He'd once again overextended his company by venturing unsuccessfully into the supply-boat business. He'd soon learn that supply boats, the submersible, and his past fling with the push boat were unnecessary, expensive diversions from his anchor-handling tug specialty. When he began to truly focus on his company's ability to handle anchors, he discovered an interesting opportunity. He believed he'd finally found a way to escape the maddening financial swings of the Gulf of Mexico and to ease his ulcers, which had gotten so bad the doctors had to surgically remove 80 percent of his stomach.

Alas, he thought he'd truly discovered a way to send his company skyward.

III

Resurrection

Celebrating Vegas-style, from the bottom left, Norma Guilbeau across from
Anthony Guilbeau, Myrtle Orgeron across from Bobby Orgeron, Bea Theriot
across from Nolty Theriot, Mae-Rita Ayo across from Yule Hitt, Mary Cheramie
across from Albert Cheramie. (Courtesy of the Orgeron family)

The *Rebecca Theriot* in Great Yarmouth Harbor, England, in 1966.
(Courtesy of Pye Theriot)

Chapter 11

Nolty on the North Sea

1965

It began in the mid-1960s, when Brown & Root started talking to Nolty about a perilous but potentially profitable venture, a rare virgin oilfield opportunity in the North Sea. At the time, North Sea oil and gas exploration was only in the planning stages. During 1964 and 1965, Brown & Root and its then Dutch partner, Heerema, were installing the sea's first small platforms off the coast of Germany. Despite the unprecedented event of drill bits breaking up the German seabed, there had been no commercial oil discoveries.

Nevertheless, some of the major oil companies had big plans for the area, which were fueled by the European nations' desire to become less dependent on Middle Eastern oil. The North Sea could not have been more conveniently located; it bordered England, Scotland, France, Belgium, Holland, Germany, Denmark, Norway, and Sweden. With such sweeping coverage and potential, the Brown & Root/Heerema partnership had already invested millions in equipment, including the summer 1965 launching in Rotterdam of a mammoth derrick barge called the *Atlas*, which was 350 feet by 100 feet by 25 feet and carried a five-hundred-ton revolving crane.

While Brown & Root could adapt its engineering practices for the North Sea, its derrick, lay, dredge, and bury barges depended on anchor-handling tugboats. Brown & Root quickly learned that there weren't any suitable anchor-handling captains or tugs in the North Sea region. Despite the grand traditions of the British navy, Dutch naval architecture, Norwegian navigation, and Danish marine engineering, the Europeans didn't understand the oilfield. Even though the unpredictable, rough North Sea was the Europeans' stomping grounds, they didn't understand how to handle anchors in it.

Consequently, Brown & Root turned to its bayou-dwelling tug man, Nolty Theriot. Nolty almost immediately decided he would make the North Sea the new home for his fleet. When he imagined these storied European waters, which some Cajuns called the Queen's Sea, with nary a single oil or gas pipeline, he anticipated something he'd never seen in the Gulf of Mexico—real stability and endless opportunity. He imagined automatically renewable, year-long contracts for ridiculously high day rates. And he saw very little, if any, competition. When Brown & Root asked for a quote, he estimated his costs and doubled them, and then took that number and doubled it. Brown & Root accepted it, and Nolty prepared for the biggest financial windfall of his life.

But to Nolty, the North Sea was about much more than monetary gain. As he would say many times, "You can only spend so much money." What really attracted Nolty was the challenge. If no one had built a pipeline in the tempestuous North Sea, then he would help Brown & Root build the first ones.

His plan to eventually send his entire fleet to the North Sea was considered by many, including his trusted CPA, Dan Carroll, as much too risky. The oil companies had not exactly committed to permanent exploration there. By the summer of 1965, not one of the companies had found any commercial deposits of oil or gas, and the conditions had made exploration difficult.

In the North Sea, the weather stayed cold nearly year round and, with hardly a moment's notice, the wind could kick up a flat sea into a cauldron with 40-foot waves. The waves could climb to 70 feet before the barge even had a chance to return to shore. In the southern North Sea, depths were relatively shallow, from 30 to 150 feet, which meant the swells were closer together and steeper, and the dangerous shoals weren't always obvious. In the north, the sea was much deeper, the waves higher, and the temperature much colder, sometimes turning rain to ice the instant it struck a vessel's handrails. In the Gulf of Mexico, the occasional tropical storm might shut down work, but in the North Sea, it was apparently difficult to get *any* work done from November through March. One British Petroleum official would later say that wintertime pipelaying in the North Sea was "financial suicide."

What made the work more difficult was the sea's hard clay bottom, which was full of shale and dotted with boulders. Brown & Root had already experienced problems sinking jackets evenly into the clay; in the Gulf of Mexico, these jackets would simply settle under their own weight into the Gulf's soft mud. The North Sea's hard bottom would also present problems for laying pipelines. In Nolty's case, his crews would need an ungodly powerful winch to jerk a thirty-thousand-pound anchor from the clay.

Compounding the problem was the presence of Nazi mines left over from World War II. The North Sea was still full of them, and striking one with an anchor or a section of pipe could injure or kill everyone on the barge and the adjoining tugs.

These conditions cast doubt on the financial prospects for exploration. In 1964, one British oilman called the North Sea a "massive gamble . . . played with multimillion dollar dice."

But Nolty didn't worry about the risk, and he didn't shy away from the dangers of the sea or the potential logistical nightmares of moving his operations across the Atlantic. In fact, in spirit and in ancestry, Nolty had crossed the Atlantic many times, and he was well aware of his family's history with this journey.

The voyage had begun in the 1600s, when the Theriots left France to settle in Acadia on the east coast of Canada. It continued after 1755 when, during the French and Indian War, the British expelled the Acadians from Acadia and dispersed them throughout the world. Some were imprisoned in England for the duration of the Seven Years War.

After the war, contingents of Acadians resettled in mother France, only to find out that there was little economic opportunity there. One of Nolty's relatives, Olivier Theriot (then spelled "Terrio"), would lead thousands of his countrymen to find a new home in the Spanish territory of Louisiana.

In 1783, Olivier Terrio was an Acadian exile working as a cobbler on the northwest coast of France in Nantes when he was approached by a native Frenchman, the soldier-of-fortune Henri Peyroux de la Coudrenière. Peyroux was seeking an Acadian intermediary to help him reap a large financial reward by resettling the Acadians from northwest France to Spanish Louisiana.

Terrio wasn't interested in making a profit; he only sought a better opportunity for his people, most of whom had been farmers in Acadia and were unemployable in France, existing mostly on government welfare and charity. Being a cobbler, Terrio was one of the few Acadians in France who had a moneymaking trade and could read and write.

Inspired by the desire to reunite his people in Louisiana, Terrio began circulating a petition in the Acadian slums across the northwest coast to implore the Spanish king to bring the Acadians to Louisiana. The French Acadians had seen one too many failing resettlement schemes, and only five of them signed the petition.

Despite the lack of signatures, the Spanish King Carlos III, who was trying to recruit Catholic settlers to Louisiana, issued a royal *cedula* in October 1783 authorizing the French Acadians' colonization there. Fearing it was a way for the Acadians to avoid paying their personal debts, the Acadians' creditors in France opposed the project. The creditors attempted to detain Terrio, who avoided incarceration by going into hiding.

While Terrio used his Spanish royalty connections to have the arrest lifted, he was far from safe. His resettlement drive confused some of the Acadians; a hostile minority believed it was an attempt to discontinue their French government dole. After surviving a knife attack, Terrio pressed on and assisted in negotiating an incredible deal. He and Peyroux convinced French King Louis XVI to pay the Acadians' debts in exchange for the termination of the dole, and King Carlos III agreed to assume their dole until the date of the Acadians' departure. Additionally, the Spanish crown would not only fund the Acadians' transportation to Louisiana but also would provide them with support upon their arrival in New Orleans.

By securing these propitious terms, Terrio convinced more than 70 percent of the Acadians in France to join the Louisiana expedition. Ultimately, between May and October 1785, Terrio and 1,595 of his *confrères* boarded seven ships bound for south Louisiana.

In marshaling the passage, Terrio had done more than help his people; he'd also put his stamp on American history by organizing, as historian Carl Brasseaux has noted, "the largest single migration of Europeans into the Mississippi Valley in the late eighteenth century."

Despite Terrio's achievement, the mission left him bankrupt. Because he'd abandoned his cobbler shop in 1783 to devote himself to the colonization project, he'd amassed debts that he couldn't satisfy. Nonetheless, in the communal Acadian tradition that would continue for centuries, Terrio's people took care of him, giving him the necessary financial assistance before he left France.

In Louisiana, Olivier Terrio settled along northern Bayou Lafourche near the Mississippi River. His descendants would, over the years, descend the Lafourche, eventually settling on the Gulf of Mexico at Cheniere Caminada until the series of horrible hurricanes drove them north to Golden Meadow. Then, as the Acadian Terrios became the Cajun Theriots, one of their own would transport their people back across the Atlantic.

Astonishingly, in developing the North Sea, Nolty Theriot was bringing the Cajuns back to the shores of their British oppressor. They were traveling to the east coast of England, just across the island from the old Acadian prison camps in Liverpool. While the irony of it all was not lost on Nolty, he wasn't coming to Britain to show the British that their forefathers' attempt at Acadian genocide had failed. Many of the Acadians had already redressed their upheaval, to some degree, by aiding the American cause in the American Revolution. In Louisiana, some of the very Acadians expelled from Acadia would help Andrew Jackson and Jean Lafitte route the redcoats in the Battle of New Orleans during the War of 1812.

But the greater irony was that Nolty Theriot had defended the British in World War II, fighting alongside thousands of Brits in the Battle of the Bulge. His return to Europe certainly wasn't about avenging the past sins of the British Empire. In both world wars, England, especially Nolty's future English base of Great Yarmouth, had suffered enough. In World War I, the German zepplin airships had bombarded the medieval town. In World War II, the Nazi Luftwaffe struck Great Yarmouth again, causing more damage than in any other coastal English city.

Nolty's current mission was to help fuel England and the continent and, in so doing, grow his own company. But more than all the wealth building, Nolty wanted to show Europe what his boys could do. He would prove that there wasn't a mariner on earth that could match his Cajuns, not the descendants of Leif Erickson or Christopher Columbus, not any modern-day Lord Nelson or Captain Cook.

For Nolty's boys to strut their talent, for Nolty to help build steel cities and pipeline highways in seas that had previously contained only hostile waves, he needed better equipment. He realized he didn't have one boat in his fleet that could handle the North Sea. His 85- and 90-footers weren't long enough, their engines weren't powerful enough, and their hulls were too thin for the icy conditions.

Surely, Nolty would meet his need by building his North Sea vessels in the great shipyards of Rotterdam or Bremerhaven. Undoubtedly, he'd hire the best Danish naval architects and Norwegian marine engineers. This time, he'd have to commission an elaborate set of plans for the hull, the engine room, the refrigeration, the piping, and the electricity. If Brown & Root/Heerema was building barges in Holland, then Nolty should construct his tugs there, too.

Whatever the conventional thought might have been, Nolty didn't build his North Sea tugs anywhere in Europe. He planned to fabricate them in the woods in his Golden Meadow shipyard. His only blueprints would be scratch paper and whatever spatial formations existed in his brain and in the minds of his craftsmen. Their only guides would be their collective eyeballs.

Nolty also realized that his lot in the woods couldn't finish the tugs fast enough. After he started construction in Golden Meadow on the first, the *J. V. Alario*, a 100 X 27 iced-class mule named for his father-in-law, he found a shipyard to build three additional identical boats. They would all contain four 16-71 GMs, with each pair of engines laid out back to back, "in tandem," a clutch in between. The total power was 2400 horses.

To build the *J. V.*'s three sister vessels, Nolty made a deal with Houma Fabricators, which was thirty-five miles northwest of Golden Meadow, to rent a section of its shipyard and some of the shipyard's men. He then sent his twenty-nine-year-old cousin, Livingston Theriot, to manage the construction.

When Livingston showed up at the Houma yard, he met the yard's old salty foreman, who asked him, "Where's the prints?"

Livingston handed him seven sheets of scratch paper. "I got seven bulkheads."

The foreman gave him a puzzled look. He examined the scratch paper and said, "No, I mean the prints, the blueprints."

"These are the prints," said Livingston, pointing at the bulkhead drawings.

"Those aren't prints."

"That's what we use."

"I don't believe that," the foreman laughed.

Livingston looked around the yard at the men staring at him. They obviously didn't know what to make of him and his notebook paper. This Houma Fabricators wasn't exactly the famous Norfolk Naval Shipyard, and these men sure weren't college-educated marine engineers. They were skilled Cajuns like himself, but they were sophisticated enough to believe Livingston was crazy. He could hear one of them saying, "What's that boy gonna do with that?"

No one could believe that this was Nolty Theriot's man. They couldn't accept that they were building a revolutionary North Sea tug by following sketches on scratch paper. This young man from down the bayou was gonna piece them through the building of a boat that would cross the Atlantic? If the hull's seven bulkheads were on notebook paper, would he sketch the engine room on a napkin and draw the cabin in the dirt? They continued to shake their heads in disbelief until Livingston started laying out the steel and marking it.

As he told them where to cut, he noticed that they began to trust him a little bit. As the bulkheads went up and the keel went on, the men realized these Theriot boys knew what they were doing. When the men welded on the thick side plates, perhaps they began to see that this wasn't Nolty Theriot building a boat; this was more like Noah building an iced-class ark. With Nolty's scratch paper–breeding instructions, they were about to give birth to a specimen that was part Clydesdale and part cutting horse.

Now all Nolty needed were the jockeys willing to enter the transatlantic race. When Nolty polled his captains, however, not one of them volunteered. Despite Nolty's boastful pride in his boat handlers, none of them showed any interest in the North Sea. In fact, as the *J.V. Alario* neared completion in the Golden Meadow woods, Nolty couldn't find a captain willing to take her on her maiden voyage.

It wasn't that Nolty's captains were worried about North Sea's waves and cold wind. They were about as scared of a rough sea as they were of a swirling commode, but the men were fearful of leaving home. It was hard enough being away from family during their work in the Gulf, much less crossing the Atlantic for even lengthier hitches. Many of them couldn't even conceive of England. They may have seen the country as cold, gray, and Frenchless. They may have pictured it as a land without duck blinds and redfish holes, a place of bland food and dainty formality, or they may not have pictured it at all.

For some strange reason, many of these same men wanted to go on an Alaskan job. Alaska was the great American frontier. But Great Britain? It was the great, undesirable unknown.

Then, one day in 1966, Nolty's port captain Edless Rousse was discussing the company's North Sea-captain problem with Morris Rebstock, the office manager. Rebstock remembered something. "Hey, you know Tommie Vizier?"

"Yeah, he's *mon amis*, him."

"He's with Twenty Grand, you know."

"I know."

"Well, Tommie, he's gonna go to the Nort Sea."

"How you know?"

"I asked him."

"When you asked him?"

"Two years ago."

"Two years ago? *Mais* we didn't even know we were gonna go over there two years ago."

"Go find Tommie. He's gonna go."

When Rousse found twenty-seven-year-old Tommie Vizier near his Galliano home, it was true. Captain Tommie, who had the look of a salty, cockeyed mariner, did want to go. Two years ago, not necessarily thinking about the North Sea, Captain Tommie had told Rebstock, "If ever you have a boat that's going foreign, I'm gonna go."

And go Captain Tommie did. On April 11, 1966, he took off from Port Fourchon on the newly christened *J. V. Alario*. In part, Captain Tommie's motivation was the money. His captain's wage would be increasing from $45 to $60 per day. Captain Tommie's first motive was the adventure; he'd been up the east coast of the United States and down into the Caribbean Sea but, more than anything else, he wanted to cross the big pond.

He made the crossing with a crew of six: five Texiens and one other Cajun, Harry Pinell. As they headed across the Gulf of Mexico, they met up with the *Gulf Queen*, a similar anchor-handling tug, at the Southwest Pass sea buoy. The *Gulf Queen* was Claude Autin's boat. While Autin's Gretna company was Nolty's competitor, Nolty happily brokered the *Gulf Queen* for Autin to Brown & Root, who needed another suitable tug. Nolty already believed he wouldn't be able to build the big tugs fast enough for the North Sea. So Captain Tommie would share the honors of being the first anchor handler on the North Sea with the *Gulf Queen*'s three captains, Donald "Duck" Ledet, Russell Duet, and Jack Martin.

But after traversing the Gulf and the Florida Straits, trouble developed when the *J. V. Alario* lost her communication. Captain Tommie had read all about their current location, the Bermuda Triangle, with the triangular points at the tip of Florida, Puerto Rico, and the islands of Bermuda. He knew about the planes and ships that allegedly hit the Triangle and disappeared. Apparently, the Bermuda Triangle's powers had already killed the *J. V. Alario*'s single sideband radio.

As the boats approached Bermuda, the Triangle's legend turned real as a sudden storm kicked up the seas and started tossing the boats about. It became impossible to tell the height of the waves. Everything was rumble and tumble. Captain Tommie had been in some horrible weather in his ten years offshore. He'd run from tropical depressions in the Gulf and battled storms off Cape Fear, North Carolina, but the Triangle's seas were rougher than anything he'd seen.

When the seas finally calmed and the boats hit port in Bermuda, the *Gulf Queen*'s Captain Donald came aboard the *J. V. Alario* breathing sighs of relief. He and Captain Tommie were recounting the roller-coaster ride when Captain Donald pointed at the wheelhouse steel door and said, "Look, look, Tommie, look at your footprints right here."

"Naaa," said Captain Tommie. Then he walked over and looked at the door and, sure enough, his shoe prints were all over it. He had no memory of walking up the door during the storm and could never remember a Gulf storm throwing him feet first into the wall. Just what was he getting himself into?

After the boats took on bunkers in Bermuda, they sailed toward the Azores Islands. Having seen only water for days on end, the Azores appeared on the *J. V. Alario*'s bow like a green mirage. The Portuguese-governed islands were otherworldly and beautiful, full of flower-laden hills, blue lagoons, and clean little towns with white stucco buildings.

Captain Tommie and the crews stayed at a nice hotel with hot springs. Exploring the streets, they encountered the friendly but oddly dressed Azoreans. Captain Tommie had never seen clothes like theirs. At one point, he ran across a funeral procession where the pallbearers were carrying a casket-less body on their shoulders on the way to the burial. If there was any doubt he'd left home and was going to a foreign place, the exotica of the Azores dispelled it.

Even the crew's return to the comforting sameness of the sea grew a little unnerving when the weather turned frigid, ridiculously cold for April. Captain Tommie had yet to reach the North Sea, but he already knew he wouldn't be walking around shirtless on the deck.

Passing through the English Channel by the white chalky cliffs of Dover, the men felt the temperatures continue to drop. Finally in the North Sea, the crew of the *J. V. Alario* had gone from the bright, technicolor splash of the Azores to the grays of the English coast. Still, England was a sight, with its big rocks and lighthouses, coves and tidy villages.

When Captain Tommie reached Great Yarmouth, Norfolk, the home base of the fledgling Theriot Overseas, Inc., he wouldn't have believed that the English summer resort town with its beach and quaint row of seafront buildings was going to undergo an oilfield industrialization. He couldn't see this city becoming a Morgan City, Louisiana, with a wharf full of workboats, dry docks, cranes, and pipe yards. Great Yarmouth was too cobblestone for that kind of a makeover; some of its old town walls and towers still stood. Outside of town, there were windmills and a little community with thatched roof homes set around a traditional village green. Although Great Yarmouth's Bure River quay had a salty, shipping feel to it, the quayside had yet to take on the look of an oil hub.

As Captain Tommie wandered through the narrow streets of Yarmouth, he also began to feel a little underdressed. Every man he saw was wearing a tie; even the men who swept the sidewalks and collected the garbage sported cravats.

Oddly, in this formal, old-world place, Captain Tommie did spot one oilfield vessel, a single supply boat. He had no idea what she was doing there, but she must have been servicing the West Sole Field, where British Petroleum had discovered natural gas five months ago in November 1965, marking the finding of the first commercial oil or gas deposit in the North Sea. Unfortunately, West Sole, located just off the coast in UK waters, had already been the site of tragedy. On the day after Christmas, the *Sea Gem*, a converted construction barge used as a drilling facility, was tapping into a hole when it suffered a brittle fracture and collapsed into the sea, killing thirteen people.

In the wake of this catastrophe, Captain Tommie would be piloting the *J. V. Alario* into those same waters. For the time being, the crew would spend a few days in Great Yarmouth, get their land legs, and absorb the culture shock.

And shock it was. Between the flat-tongued Cajuns and the syrupy, twangy Texiens, the people of Yarmouth looked at the new visitors as if they were aliens. Captain Tommie himself had no idea what the Brits were saying. If this was the Queen's English, then why was it so hard to understand? At one point, a Brit looked at the *J. V. Alario*'s smokestack and asked, "Are you Yanks from Los Angeles?"

"Did you say, 'Yanks?'"

"Righto."

"Yanks like Yankees?"

"Why, yes, of course. Yankees."

"We not Yankees. And we not from Los Angeles."

"Then why, might I ask, do you have the letters, L-A, on your chimney?"

"That's for Louisiana, podnah. Where we live. That means we not Yankees. We from the South."

Before Captain Tommie and his crew could acclimate to England, they received orders to head to Rotterdam. Like the transition from the Azores to Great Britain, the great Dutch port was an entirely different place with a totally bizarre language. Before Captain Tommie could get used to these tall people with their guttural sounds and their unpronounceable shipyard, De Rotterdamse Droogdok Maatschappij NV, he was back at sea, working with two Brown & Root derrick barges, the *Atlas* and the *Hercules*, until the company's new pipelaying barge, the *Hugh W. Gordon*, was ready to leave the droogdok.

Right away, Captain Tommie got an idea of what pipelaying in the North Sea would be like while assisting the *Atlas* in building the first platforms in the West Sole Field. The design depth of the platforms' piles was one hundred feet into the seabed, but the barge's sixty-thousand-pound steam hammers could only drive the piles half that distance.

After two months, Captain Tommie and the *J. V. Alario* finally headed off on the North Sea's first pipelaying mission when they picked up the newly christened *Hugh W. Gordon* in Rotterdam. To any oilfield man, the *Gordon* was a woolly mammoth. At 400-by-100-by-30 feet with a displacement of 8,300 gross tons, it was the world's largest operational barge. It had a ten-line mooring system with five thousand feet of two-inch cable, thirty thousand–pound anchors, and a 250-ton revolving crane. One reporter said the *Gordon*'s vast deck looked more like a factory floor than the top of a barge. It could accommodate up to 250 workers, and could lay up to two miles of pipeline per day in good conditions.

Initially, the North Sea didn't give the *Gordon* a favorable working environment. As the *J. V. Alario* towed the monster barge back toward England, a calm sea started boiling into a forty-foot wave whirlpool. The tow was too far along to go back to Rotterdam, and it was too rough to make a beeline for England. Captain Tommie received his first lesson in how to handle an unruly North Sea—hold onto the barge, roll with the waves, and don't think about fighting them until the seas "calm" to twenty feet or so.

On that July day in 1966, the wind was so strong that it blew all of the *Gordon*'s tightly fastened tarpaulins into the sea. Captain Tommie had never seen that happen in the Gulf, and he wouldn't witness it again in the North Sea because Brown & Root would replace the canvas covers with steel. It was difficult to fathom that this tempest was occurring in July, supposedly a relatively calm month.

When the seas did lay down into steep but workable waves, the *J. V. Alario* began to assist the *Gordon* in laying a forty-five-mile line from the West Sole Field to onshore facilities at Easington, East Yorkshire.

To connect the line with Great Britain's existing onshore pipeline grid, all the *Gordon* and the *J. V.* had to do was lay a pipeline for less than two miles under the Humber River in the Hull area. Compared to working on the open sea, this job couldn't have been easier. They were in a city's protected waters. The crews would be working so fast they might even have time to break for a cup of afternoon tea.

Then one day, as Captain Tommie was winching up an anchor, a storm roared up the Humber River. The wave spray and rain became so fierce so fast it was impossible to see. The river turned so wild that the *Gordon* had to stop working in what should've been an impenetrable, sheltered waterway. By that point, Captain Tommie believed that if he were offshore, the *J. V. Alario* couldn't have made it. He'd never had this thought on her, not in the Bermuda Triangle storm and not when crossing the North Sea with the *Gordon*. For that matter, he'd never had this feeling on any other vessel he'd been on in any body of water.

Like all other storms, this one passed, and the *Gordon* and the *J. V.* finished the historic line, with the final welds leading to a celebration of the onshore arrival of North Sea gas. While the pipeline would help convert Britain from coal to gas, ironically, Captain Tommie and the other expatriate captains who moved to England would cook with coal-powered stoves. They would fuel their water heaters with chunks of real coal, which many of the Cajuns had not seen since their days of living in wintertime marsh trapping camps.

In the fall of 1966, domesticity, or the lack of it, was exactly the problem for Captain Tommie Vizier. He was working nonstop, getting almost no relief on the anchors, because no one other than himself knew how to handle them. He'd watched with amazement and a little amusement when he first saw a lumbering British tug grab an anchor not with a winch but with an archaic block and tackle system. It was an incredibly slow and methodical process that resulted in the tug not even pulling the anchor back to the boat. As for the British tug captain, he shied away from getting close to the barge. It was as if he was afraid he'd hit it. To Captain Tommie, it was nothing for him to get a foot from a barge in a fifteen-foot sea while his deck was dancing and bobbing between two anchor cables. He'd long since lost his fear of colliding. If he smacked the barge or popped an anchor cable, so be it.

As Captain Tommie moved anchor after anchor, the North Sea bubbled with the discovery of two more fields in 1966, Leman Bank and Indefatigable. While he considered himself as indefatigable as any mariner, his family in Galliano was getting tired of him being gone; he'd been working for six months straight. He either had to leave the North Sea or bring his wife and four small children across the ocean. Tommie brought them over, not realizing that, in time, his own children would sound nothing like his people. Their English would be the English of the British Crown, or some limey version of it.

Captain Tommie also needed professional relief. While he wasn't exactly handling every anchor in the North Sea, it sure felt that way. But soon, by the start of 1967, he wouldn't have to worry. By that point, his fellow Cajun captains had learned of the extra $15 a day in pay. They'd also heard that after 501 days in England, they wouldn't have to pay US income tax.

Captain Tommie, who'd already convinced his brother Jimmie Vizier to come, knew that when Theriot's captains showed up en masse, they wouldn't just impress the British mariners, they'd overwhelm them.

Back across the Atlantic in Golden Meadow, the master of the Theriot fleet now appeared to be in the best position in his fifteen years in the business. Nolty Theriot had willing top-notch captains and more work than he'd ever seen. Still, he didn't have enough boats. He'd reached the end of his borrowing power. Ultimately, he'd sell his smaller boats and raise more expansion money, but it wouldn't be nearly enough. To satisfy the North Sea's demand, Nolty needed more money, a lot more money.

Left: A Nolty J. Theriot Inc. crew handle anchors on the North Sea.
Right: Two deckhands are tethered to the gunnel to prevent them from being swept overboard.
(Photos courtesy of Pye Theriot)

Chapter 12

Bobby Goes to Washington

1966

———◆◆◆———

Bobby Orgeron needed money, too. And if he didn't get it, he was going bankrupt. It had gotten to the point where his debt load was keeping him up at nights. During one of his bouts of sleeplessness, he was lying in his bed with his lids heavy but wide open, able to do nothing else but watch his wife breathe. He realized that she had no choice but to sleep. Taking care of the home and three small children would do that to any woman. She had little reason to stay awake after a day spent chasing six-year-old Lee and three-year-old Ann while carrying the infant Joseph on her hip.

Bobby wished he could shut his eyes and drift, even for an hour. Yet sleep was not possible when he had several tied-up utility boats sitting on his chest and he was providing for his newborn by exhausting his savings and floating his credit. Relaxation was not an option when he couldn't pay the company's bills, much less make the millions he was supposed to have made by now, his thirty-fifth year. Hell, the oil companies were killing him too—many of them had the habit of taking sixty to ninety days to pay an invoice. That was hard to take when the rest of the world wanted to be paid in thirty days or less. In this terrible climate, how could he expect to make a dollar when oilfield service businesses up and down the bayou were going broke?

As he tossed and turned, he looked at his snoozing wife. He knew what she was thinking during her waking hours. He'd heard about what she'd told the crowd at the corner grocery, where she sometimes visited. When things were rolling, Myrtle would talk to the people there about Bobby making her sign another note for God knows how much money.

They'd ask her, "How will y'all pay for that, Myrtle? What if you can't pay it?"

"Well, if things get bad," she'd say, "we can't even pay for what we owe now. So what's another note? What's another million?"

Of course, Bobby knew that Myrtle now had to be wondering how they'd pay for it all. That moment was coming. The day the bank called their loans for real was approaching. Bobby told himself he couldn't dwell on that. Instead, he should try some trick that would make him sleep.

He'd attempted to count sheep but all he could count were boats—his docked boats. He had tied up nearly three-quarters of his thirteen-boat fleet. Of his seven utility boats, three were still working. How he had found work for them, he didn't understand. It was so bad it was a miracle that even *one* was on a contract.

Then there was the issue of his partner. The way Bobby saw it, Nacis Theriot was blaming him for the company's losses. When they were rolling, Nacis called their boats "our boats." Now Nacis referred to them as "your boats."

Across the bayou, Nacis wasn't sleeping too well, either. He also wasn't happy with the partnership, and he disagreed with Bobby's claim that he was calling these tied-up boats Bobby's boats. For better or for worse, he had always gone along with Bobby, even when he hadn't been sure of what Bobby was doing.

For instance, when Bobby pulled some of their boats that were working a job for Gulf Oil and put them to work for a seismographic company called Harvest Research, Nacis had said nothing. He watched as Bobby's daddy, Juan, fussed at Bobby for taking such a risk. Gulf was steady; Harvest Research was volatile. The old man thought Bobby was *couillon*, and he told him as much.

Sure enough, it wasn't long before the Harvest Research job ended, and there was no Gulf work waiting for them. Where did those boats end up? Tied up, like they were now.

So many times Nacis would have liked to speak out. When Bobby and his old man argued, Nacis would have liked to have taken Mr. Juan's side. Mr. Juan would tell his son, "Why you want to build another boat, Bobby? Don't you have enough?"

Nacis would watch the father and son verbally fight with each other over this issue like snapping Dobermans. Their argument would bounce all over the office and into the parking lot. Nacis would listen to the shouting and sometimes believe the old man had more sense, but still, he deferred to Bobby.

Despite Bobby's pigheadedness, Nacis wasn't blaming him for their present dilemma. He knew it was just the oilfield. He didn't think Bobby should hold their partnership responsible for his unhappiness. He also believed that Bobby needed to take a hard look at his pill habit. It seemed to Nacis that his partner's Darvocet consumption had increased since the boats started finding their way to the dock. Finally, Nacis thought Bobby resented the fact that Nacis wasn't a boatman. Bobby's body language told him he was tired of Nacis just doing office work and wanted him on the road, selling. *Mais* what good would that do? Nacis couldn't sell anything.

But Nacis didn't point any fingers because he still believed in Bobby. Bobby's mind, whether it was clear or clouded with pills or drink, was still quick. His *tête* was still *dur*. He would move them into the black or kill himself trying.

Nevertheless, did Nacis have his doubts, especially lying awake in bed? Of course. Recently, he, Bobby, and Mr. Juan had gone in on a 135-foot cargo boat together. The cargo boat concept had been the rage of the supply boat industry. It had a triple, as opposed to a double cabin, and a much longer deck. It would make them more money than the 100-foot utility boats, but this boat, the *Montco*, had also carried a hefty note.

Nacis saw what that note did to the old man. Mr. Juan, who'd retired from the boat business and wasn't used to its newfound up-and-down nature, didn't last three months in the deal. He quickly sold his interest in the *Montco* to Bobby and Nacis. Nacis was tempted to unload his interest, too.

Nacis wasn't crazy about being at the office these days. They were now renting out his uncle Paris Theriot's old converted shrimp shed, his cousin Nolty's old office. But the place wasn't big enough for the both of them. Still, he'd have to live with Bobby. He damn sure didn't want to run a boat company by himself. He had no desire to go to Lafayette for days on end. He didn't want to manage the flesh pile in New Orleans or stick his fingers in the engine grease. Hell, no. Bobby, he could have all that.

Back across the bayou, Bobby imagined what it would be like to be on his own. He'd love to buy out Nacis, but he had nothing to offer. He needed to focus on something more probable. He needed to *do* something. He'd like to go by the shop and work on an engine, but there was no work to do. He'd like to call on a customer, but that was no use. It didn't matter what he told them or gave them because they had no work for him now, and he couldn't afford to give them anything anyway.

He didn't want to think about laying off loyal employees. They'd given him too much, and he'd worked too hard to keep them. He'd sweetened some of their deals by selling them stakes in boats. While they shared in the profit, they shared in the loss, too.

He had to reverse all of these losses, which were pulling him down from every direction. In devising a strategy, he realized that he didn't have the Mineral Board position that Minor Cheramie had. He didn't have that kind of ace. Surely, though, he could think of something.

Finally, one morning, the grand idea hit him—Vietnam. He believed that the navy could use his four docked utility boats as gunboats in the Mekong Delta. The Vietnam War was only getting more intense. The United States was drafting more of its young boys. It was spending more money.

The conflict was getting more complicated. Uncle Sam had to have these boats.

In fact, he could offer the navy *six* 100-foot utility boats because his friend, Nolty Theriot, also had two docked boats that were holding him back from taking over the North Sea (as the vessels were too small for the Sea's rough waters). Boy, what a deal. In one simple sale to the navy, he could save himself and help build his friend.

Later in the morning, Bobby bought an airline ticket to Washington, DC. The next afternoon, he hopped on a plane. He'd never been to the nation's capital. He'd made no hotel reservations and hadn't made any phone calls. At Dulles Airport, he simply jumped in a cab and asked the cab driver to take him to a hotel that was close to the Senate Building.

Heading up the Beltway, Bobby wasn't really taking in the sights. Before his stay was over, he would pass by them all, but the Washington Monument and the Lincoln Memorial made no difference to him. While he loved to read about history, he had no time to soak it up now. He was busy trying to save his own history. Until he sold his boats to the navy, he would think of nothing else.

Bobby checked in at the Washington Hotel. Early the next morning, Bobby immediately took a cab for the Senate Building. Once inside, Bobby asked for directions to the office of Louisiana senator Allen Ellender. He had decided to go right to the senior Louisiana congressman. He didn't want to waste time with junior senators or mere US representatives. He wanted to push the biggest button possible.

Ellender, despite being short in stature, was a very big switch. He was nearly president pro-tempore of the Senate, was a member of the Appropriations Committee, and would soon be that committee's chairman. Ellender also had the ear of his good friend and former fellow southern senator, President Lyndon Baines Johnson. Ellender had cooked gumbo for LBJ and Lady Bird many times.

This Vietnam War, of course, was LBJ's baby. Ellender, who was initially opposed to the war, had come around to support it, partially out of deference to LBJ.

Bobby knew all about the Ellender-LBJ connection. He also understood enough of Ellender's background. Ellender grew up less than an hour away from Bayou Lafourche on lower Bayou Terrebonne. Like Bobby, his first language was French. Ellender still even carried around a childhood French nickname, *Sous-Sous* (Little Pennies). Sous-Sous was a former Houma attorney who'd risen to political power at the heels of Huey Long.

Unlike some of the other Longites, Ellender had never carried the label of a corrupt Louisiana politician. Ellender was, from what Bobby had heard, a textbook straight shooter, and Bobby planned to shoot straight at him. Having never met the senator, Bobby hadn't made any appointments and didn't even know if Ellender was in his office. If Ellender wasn't there, he'd go see Louisiana junior senator Russell Long. Long, Huey's son, was a power broker in his own right. If Long wasn't present, Bobby would knock on the door of US representative F. Edward Hebert. If Hebert wasn't in, he'd visit Representative Hale Boggs, a rising star who had a House Majority Leader position in his future.

When Bobby entered Ellender's office, he barely paid attention to the pictures of national and international dignitaries that covered the wall from floor to ceiling. The place's history and walnut grandness were lost on him. He looked the receptionist dead in the eye and told her, "I'm Bobby Orgeron."

When she smiled politely but blankly, he said, "I'm from Golden Meadow. That's about thirty miles from Houma. I want to see my senator."

At some point during Bobby's brief conversation with the receptionist, a young man came into the lobby, walking with a slight limp. The man introduced himself as Jim Guirard, the senator's chief of staff. Guirard's words were in French, as if he knew that any coonass from Golden Meadow could speak the same language he'd spoken as a boy in St. Martinville.

Bobby was impressed by Guirard's French and his friendliness. When Guirard took him to meet Senator Ellender, Bobby had the same impression. The little stocky man with a big head and roundish dark glasses was as down-to-earth as he could be. His French was rapid and natural.

Before long, the three Cajuns were spinning away in their native tongue, talking as if they'd known each other for years. As Bobby shifted the conversation to his plan, he showed the men the specs from his four boats. He made sure the senator understood these boats were built in

Ellender's hometown at Main Iron Works, which was owned by a friend of the senator's, Jack Guidry. It sure would be nice to have some Terrebonne Parish–built boats in the navy's fleet.

Ellender looked, listened, and nodded. Before long, he got the Pentagon on the phone. He hung up and told Bobby he'd made him an appointment for that afternoon.

When Bobby walked into the Pentagon, he intensified his tunnel vision. He took a second or two to observe his surroundings. He had seen military facilities all over the world; this place was as sterile as the rest of them. The famous, massive five-sided structure was no different to him than a simple Quonset hut.

Bobby wasn't that awed by his appointment, either. If you'd seen one military commander, you'd seen them all. He was, however, grateful that Ellender had placed him with a man of some apparent influence.

He was scheduled to meet with Rear Admiral Elmo Zumwalt Jr. Within the next year, Admiral Zumwalt would command all of the US naval forces in Vietnam. He was on his way to becoming the youngest four-star admiral in US naval history and Chief of Naval Operations.

Inside the admiral's office, Bobby returned Zumwalt's firm grip, and the admiral gave him a smile full of white teeth. Zumwalt's eyes, which were buried under heavy black eyebrows, were sincere. In a sense, the man was a typical high-ranking official in his late forties, frequently calling Bobby "son" and "young man." But Zumwalt was a little atypical, too. He didn't seem to have the ego that Bobby suspected and appeared to be genuinely nice.

Bobby threw the specs for four of the boats on Zumwalt's desk. He told them about their heavy steel construction and claimed that their decks could hold cannon and big machine guns. They were shallow draft and powered by strong American engines, GMs. These boats would be ideal for the Mekong Delta.

Zumwalt, his eyebrows shifting, his pupils pouring over the specs, said, "I think you're right. We could use these boats in country. How many do you have?"

"I have six ready to go."

"What kind of price are you looking for?"

"One hundred seventy-five thousand apiece. They're ready to go right now." Bobby wasn't exactly pricing the boats to sell. He'd bought his four for only $160,000 apiece. Nolty Theriot had apparently purchased his two for about the same price. Bobby had worked the boats for much of the four to five years M.O.N.T. had owned them. On his four, his total payoff on them was much, much less than his total asking price of $700,000. Bobby wasn't looking just to pull himself out of hock. He wanted top dollar. One hundred seventy-five grand wasn't too much when you considered that the boats could be used in the Mekong Delta right away. Besides, he'd paid his taxes. It was about time the government paid him back.

The admiral, still pouring over the specs, looked up and said, "I think we're gonna buy them."

"I think you making a great deal."

"Can I keep these specs?"

"Sure."

"I have to study them some more. I want to see exactly how we'll use them."

After Admiral Zumwalt escorted him out the door, Bobby exhaled. Could it be that easy?

Of course not. Bobby returned to Golden Meadow and told everyone the navy would buy his boats. The people shook their heads; Bobby never talked to any senator or admiral. *As if.*

After a few days, Bobby realized that he would prove these doubters right if he just waited for the sale to happen. This deal might have been the center of his life, but it was of little significance to a rear admiral and a senior-ranking senator.

Bobby scheduled another trip to Washington. For this meeting, he decided he needed a reinforcement. Most men in his position might have brought their attorney, but Bobby brought someone with negotiating skills beyond those of the average lawyer. His special adviser, Leon Theriot, was yet another well-known member of Golden Meadow's Theriot clan. He was the son of Fedalise, who was the brother of Paris, Leopold, and Leo, and the grandson of Leon, the original captain of the *Petit Caporal.* Leon had learned the insurance business from Nonc Leo but, after having a falling out with his uncle, struck out on his own and cofounded the agency of Theriot, Duet, and Theriot.

Young Leon was, perhaps more than any of the other Leo-named Theriots, a true lion. He was an energetic, grinning, roaring rock of a man. Standing about five feet ten, weighing in at about 220 pounds, with a receding hairline on a big, round head, Leon loved to smoke, cook, and tell stories. While he was never in a hurry, he was always accomplishing something.

By title, Leon was Bobby's insurance man, but he was much more than that. Leon was a notary, a loan broker, a de facto attorney, a confidant, and a deal maker extraordinaire. When Bobby needed to buy a boat, Leon often put together the deal for him. He read the contract, negotiated away the fine print, and negotiated in the protective clauses. Bobby himself didn't read it. He relied solely on Leon.

When Bobby wanted to buy a piece of real estate, Leon or his insurance partners and fellow notaries would draft and pass the act of sale. They'd also pass his auto title and form his corporation. When Bobby ran into a paperwork problem with the Coast Guard, Leon would head to New Orleans and take care of it. Leon did the same job for his other boat clients, be they high-dollar oilfield men or illiterate shrimpers. His only charge to anyone for any of this noninsurance work was the price of their insurance premiums. He didn't make a nickel from any of the notarial work, brokering, or contractual advice. It was all *lagniappe.*

Leon made it all work by constantly reading, doing informal research, remembering names, asking questions, and absorbing details. His favorite meeting place was a new restaurant on Broad Street in New Orleans called Ruth's Chris Steak House. Chris's served the world's most tender, juiciest New York strip, and some weeks, Leon was at Chris's nearly every day. He could persuade anyone with a lunch there—be the person an insurance underwriter, an oilman, a new boat client, a Coast Guard official, or a politician. By the time he was drinking his after-dinner Grand Marnier and smoking his tiny cigar, he had won over his guest.

Of course, up in Washington, DC, Bobby Orgeron was hoping that Leon could repeat his magic. Bobby understood that Leon wasn't exactly a Beltway insider, but thought he could assist somehow.

If nothing else, Bobby thought that there might be a contract for Leon to read. When they arrived in the District, it was clear there would be no contract, not yet at least. When Leon asked Bobby about drafting one, maybe a letter of intent to commit the government to buying the boats, Bobby shrugged it off. He wanted to engender Admiral Zumwalt's trust. A handshake was good enough for him.

Although Leon's presence made Bobby breathe a little easier, Bobby realized that the deal was far from simple. The admiral had talked about a few things he'd like added to the boat. That part was easy. Bobby and his people could do those things themselves. The hard part was successfully traveling from the admiral's oral intentions, through a maze of government functionaries to a clerk cutting a check in M.O.N.T.'s name. That wouldn't happen today, Bobby realized, as he and Leon made their rounds from Capitol Hill to the Pentagon and back.

That night, they ate at a restaurant, The Rotunda, where the star Democrats liked to hang out. After the meal, they were waiting for a cab but it was taking too long. Bobby told Leon, "The hotel is right down from here. It can't be any more than a mile or so. Let's walk. *Mais* I'm sure a cab will pass us by on the way."

They walked a few blocks, but there weren't any cabs. They shrugged and kept walking.

A few minutes later, a police car pulled up along side of them and stopped. The cop looked up and down their Rubenstein Brothers suits. He asked, "Where you guys from?"

"Louisiana."

"Do you know where you are?"

"We not that far from our hotel."

"You're crazy. You could get rolled out here. Or killed."

Bobby looked around. The area didn't look that bad. "What's so dangerous about this place? This is our nation's capital."

"It's also a high-crime neighborhood. Where are you going?"

"The Washington Hotel."

"Get in the car. I'll give you a ride."

When they hopped in the cruiser, it hit Bobby. He was just a coonass in Washington. This deal might take a while.

After returning to Golden Meadow, Bobby made another solo trip to Washington. The third time was far from the charm.

He might have been going backward. Every trip went the same way. He'd hit town and visit Senator Ellender's man, Jim Guirard. When they'd walk into Ellender's office, the senator was overjoyed. He'd spew French as if he'd been holding his breath for hours and was finally exhaling. Bobby walked out feeling like anything was possible. But by the time he left the Pentagon, he wasn't so sure.

Still, he continued to press. For one thing, he was learning Washington. He and Jim Guirard had become fast friends. Guirard eventually introduced him to every member of what might have been per capita the nation's most powerful congressional delegation. He met Long, Boggs, and Hebert, but his most notable meeting was with a young US representative from Crowley, Edwin Edwards.

Edwards was a fellow Cajun originally from the northern edge of Acadiana in Marksville. He, too, could speak French. When Bobby walked into Edwards's office, he had the strangest feeling. He heard this man's language and felt a sense of comfort, but at the same time Edwards made him uneasy. Just looking at the man, Bobby knew he didn't like him.

To Bobby, Edwards was all flash and bull. Bobby wanted to talk politics, but all Edwards could talk about was women. He went on and on about this was the place to go tonight and this was where you go tomorrow night. Every man liked to talk about women, but Edwards seemed obsessed.

After leaving Edwards's office, Bobby told Guirard, "That's all he's in Washington for—women."

Of course, Bobby knew that, by now, he had a womanizing problem himself. He couldn't justify it, but to him, his partying was for a greater purpose.

It kept the boats working and the dollars flowing. He womanized to make money. It appeared that Edwin Edwards played politics to womanize. In Bobby's opinion, their ends and means were flipped.

In truth, Bobby wasn't making ends meet at all. He didn't have the funds to buy his clients any flesh or other gifts. They still dropped hints, though, even though they knew damn well this was a recession.

Really, he didn't have the funds for these trips to Washington. He didn't have the money to stay in the Washington Hotel and eat big meals at The Rotunda. But he couldn't afford not to do these things, either. He had to make something happen. Spending money, creating an image, was the only way to do it.

He also had to be persistent. After four trips to Washington, DC, where exactly was this persistence taking him? Since his first trip to Capitol Hill, his checking account balances had shrunk, and his loan balances had swooned.

As the bleeding continued, at some point, Bobby decided he had to involve his partner, Nacis. No, Nacis wasn't going to talk the navy into writing a check, but Nacis did have a brother-in-law who could provide some assistance. His brother-in-law happened to be a congressman, a North Louisianian by the name of Speedy O. Long. Speedy was kin to the famous Louisiana Longs.

While Speedy didn't quite have his kinfolk's influence, he could help. Speedy got Bobby and Nacis a meeting with the Small Business Association. But what exactly was the SBA going to do for them? Bobby wasn't interested in conquering debt with more debt.

Bobby soon realized that while Speedy O. Long might help, he was going to have to close this deal by himself. This transaction hinged completely on Bobby, on whether he could continue to make headway with the senator and the admiral.

He didn't care who criticized him. He was buying another ticket to Washington, DC. And once he landed, the DC cabbies could get ready. The Washington Hotel could turn down his sheets. He'd be blowing into the lobby at any minute.

While Bobby looked for a "quick" political fix, his old friend from his Quarantine Bay days, Sidney Savoie, was grinding through the sixties. Unlike Bobby, Sidney had no political tricks in his bag. He and his United

Tugs partners finally did have—after five years and five separate state and federal lawsuits—a trial date in their case against Texaco. The case, which had consolidated into one federal court action in New Orleans, would take two trials, one in 1967 and one in 1969, to resolve the matter. The judge bifurcated the case into separate trials because of the dozens of claims and the scores of factual and legal issues, some of which had never been decided by any American court.

In all, nearly seventy parties joined the action. They ranged from giant corporations such as Southern Bell and Ingersoll-Rand to small mom-and-pops such as Vela's Garage and the Barataria Tavern Service Station.

At the heart of the proceeding was the plight of United Tugs. From United Tugs' perspective, Texaco and its bond insurer, Continental Casualty, were trying to make the case more complicated than it needed to be. The corporate powers were trying to file as many motions, write as many lengthy briefs, propound as much discovery, and ask for as many continuances as they possibly could. They wanted to browbeat their little guy opponents into submission and to discourage them from vigorously pursuing their claims. They were trying to bury the real issues in legal morass and take the court's eye away from the crux of the matter: all these companies, big and small, had helped Texaco build a crucial, lucrative pipeline, and Texaco had not fully paid them for their services.

In Sidney Savoie and United Tugs' case, it was the Cajuns versus Big City Oil. It was English-as-a-second-language, undereducated witnesses versus smooth-talking, college-lettered executive witnesses. It was country, Lafourche-accented lawyers versus the New Orleans blue-blooded elite.

Texaco's position confounded Sidney. The oil company and its legal forces had gone to illogical lengths to deny United Tugs just compensation. The principal amount of the debt was $78,066.96, a lot of money to United Tugs in the 1960s and a very small pittance to Texaco. If Texaco lost the suit, it would be forced to pay United Tugs' principal, daily interest from August 3, 1962, plus its costs and attorney fees.

Rather than Texaco trying to make an early, sensible settlement, their attorneys conjured up new and sometimes absurd arguments about why Texaco shouldn't pay full price for a profitable product.

At first blush, the case called for a straightforward application of construction lien law. Louisiana's version of the law, the Private Works Act, protected the people who performed work at a job site or supplied it with materials. The act gave these contractors and suppliers a lien against the site and the structure erected on it.

In the oilfield, Louisiana law also gave certain contractors and suppliers the protection of the Oil Well Lien Statute, which applied the logic and policy of the Private Works Act to oil wells.

Texaco's position was that United Tugs and the rest of the pipeline's subcontractors and suppliers didn't have valid liens against the pipeline under any lien law. Texaco argued that the Private Works Act didn't apply because the pipeline was underground and claimed the act only covered aboveground structures, and the Oil Well Lien Statute didn't apply because, basically, a pipeline was not an oil well even though one structure was physically attached to the other.

The court scoffed at Texaco's arguments and held that both lien laws were applicable. Even if neither lien statute protected United Tugs, Texaco still owed the company money because Texaco had *promised* United Tugs' representatives it would pay them. The court held Texaco to the promise even though Texaco crawfished from its repeated assurances to Sidney Savoie and his partner.

Despite Texaco getting slaughtered at the district court level, the oil Goliath did its best to avoid payment by filing an appeal. Ultimately, it would take United Tugs until 1971—*nine years* after Texaco reneged on its promise to pay them—to win the appeal and finally see a check. The award, which with interest had climbed into six figures, made it much easier to tolerate the wait.

In 1967, judgment day was also approaching for Bobby Orgeron. Bobby didn't have nine years to fix his problem. If he didn't sell his boats to the navy, he was going bankrupt in a matter of months. One day during yet another trip to Washington, as he walked on Capitol Hill among the hordes of suits, he sensed his battle. The Declaration of Independence might say, "All Men are Created Equal," but he knew that wasn't true. He may have looked as equal as anyone here in his pressed Rubenstein attire, but the fact was on this mighty hill, he was an outsider. He may have been able to look over at the Library of Congress with the knowledge that he could read and understand those books as well as anyone, but when it came to comparing wall hangings, he only had a GED.

How could a high school-equivalency graduate compete with a town full of Ivy Leaguers? Even Senator Ellender, who was certainly no elite Easterner, had a haughty degree from Tulane Law School. As for Admiral Zumwalt, he might have been a genteel Californian, but his gun belt was full of decorated notches, everything from prep school to the Naval Academy to the National War College to a breast pocket full of medals. The admiral had honorary degrees and foreign grand crosses in his future. Why would he listen to a self-educated, ex-enlisted man?

Looking around the hill, Bobby glanced over at Lincoln Park and saw the statue of Honest Abe, a great American story if there ever was one. Like Lincoln, Bobby used to read by a non-electric light as a child. Lincoln's log cabin couldn't have been that much different than Bobby's tar-paper-covered trapping camp, but Lincoln would earn a law degree. Bobby didn't even have a college credit.

Bobby could only block out his lack of a lettered background. He didn't care if he was dancing with men who were already in the history books. They were still only men, and they could give him what he needed.

Bobby left the hill and headed to the Pentagon. He left Washington and returned to Golden Meadow. He left Louisiana and flew back to Washington. Was this his fourth trip or his fifth? All he knew was that on this day at the Pentagon, Admiral Zumwalt shook his hand. He told Bobby the deal was done. The admiral, who had been going back and forth about how he wanted to modify the boats, finally told Bobby he was satisfied. He wanted the boats at the naval dock at Algiers, on the Mississippi River across from New Orleans.

Bobby flew back home a little lighter. He was already spending the money. Three weeks passed, and the check hadn't arrived. Bobby had the boats ready for delivery, but he had yet to see a cent from the government. Wasn't Zumwalt a former Eagle Scout? Didn't he give him Scout's honor? Bobby didn't understand.

Bobby scrounged up the money for another plane ticket. He went right to Capitol Hill and pled his case to Senator Ellender.

The Senator's jovial expression disappeared, and his face reddened. Bobby had never seen him like this. Ellender started making calls and eventually got Admiral Zumwalt on the phone. "Look, you told this young man here, one of my boys, you were buying his boats. He has them ready to go. You better have a check for him."

So this was congressional pressure, thought Bobby. Ellender then gave the phone to Bobby and told him, "*Ecoutez bien.*"

And Bobby did listen to the admiral, and he did what he said, bringing his four boats to the naval dock in Algiers. Meanwhile, Nolty Theriot signed over his two boats to M.O.N.T. Boat Rental Service, Inc. Nolty had put the boats in M.O.N.T.'s name on no more than a word of honor.

Oral words were also the only guarantee Bobby had that a check would be waiting for him in Algiers, but it was there. After he signed the government paperwork, a naval officer handed him government paper for a little more than one million dollars.

Bobby then wrote Nolty a check for $350,000 for his two boats. When Nolty, whom Bobby called "Black," tried to pay Bobby, whom Nolty called "Slim," a $35,000 brokerage fee, Bobby refused it. He didn't want to take money from his friend.

After Bobby and Nacis balanced the M.O.N.T. books, they couldn't believe it. Before the sale, M.O.N.T. was $250,000 in the red. Now the company was $450,000 in the black. Most of their boats were working, and the ones that were tied up were paid in full.

Flush, Bobby decided to have the company buy a large tract of east bank frontage on Bayou Lafourche. The land cost $92,000. Oddly, there was still money to burn. For the first time in years, they weren't building or drowning but coasting.

But to Bobby, things weren't right. His stake was worth more than a million dollars and, at age thirty-six, he could finally call himself a millionaire. But something, as strange as it may have seemed, was still wrong. Why was he so damn restless?

Bobby's friend Nolty "Black" Theriot was every bit as antsy. He'd taken the money from the sale of his two supply boats to the navy and dumped it right into his North Sea expansion. Meanwhile, the Theriot shipbuilding operation was in a state of flux. With the company's work shifting exclusively to preparing North Sea vessels, Nolty would have to shut down his yard in the Golden Meadow woods. The little lot on the narrow bayou was now too small to build what the North Sea demanded—vessels of 120-plus feet in length. Nolty closed the yard with mixed feelings. He wouldn't miss climbing a tree with his war-injured leg to examine a boats' lines, yet he didn't like giving up what was near absolute control over when and how a boat would be built. He was now at the mercy of what third-party shipyards could produce.

To lean on the American Marine shipyard in New Orleans, Nolty had sent Livingston Theriot. At this point in 1967, Livingston had completed his work at Houma Fabricators and forever finished his practice of building boats from scratch paper. To build Nolty's new 124-footers, Nolty had hired Matt Kawasaki, one of New Orleans' ace Japanese American naval architects. The new boats would require bigger engines, and the best way to obtain additional horses was to insert railroad power, actual EMD locomotive engines.

Livingston also had to convert the winch engines on the working North Sea boats from 471s with compressed air controls to 671s with electric controls. He then brought the new engines and every spare part imaginable, down to the smallest screw, to Great Yarmouth, where he stayed for seven days, converting one vessel and showing the local port captain how to convert the others.

It was during this seven-day trip to England that Livingston had a revelation. He was riding a little duck boat in the Great Yarmouth harbor out to one of the Theriot boats at anchor. The duck boat's driver told him he was lucky because the seas were calm. Livingston's stomach told him this seven-foot sea was far from calm, and he asked himself, "What the heck am I doing over here?"

Here he was in England when he had three sons and a fourth one on the way back in Golden Meadow. He'd had enough of all the running from place to place, checking on this and converting that.

When Livingston got back home, he walked into Nolty's office and told him point-blank, "Cuz, I think I'm gonna quit. I want to open up a welding shop."

Nolty absorbed the news that his ace shipyard man was quitting without even shifting in his seat. "Tiger," he told his cousin. "Do what you want. I'm gonna miss you, but do what you feel like doing."

Livingston's plan was to rent a bayouside lot owned by his brother, Nacis, and build his business there. He knew that Nacis had just scored a big sale. There was no reason why he wouldn't lease the land to his brother; Livingston would call him right now.

Only three days after taking the call from Livingston about the lot, Nacis Theriot received another phone call, this one from his partner Bobby Orgeron. Bobby asked him to come over to his house. Then, not long after Nacis walked through the door, Bobby told him he wanted to part ways and buy him out of their newly formed MONTCO, Inc.

Nacis said he wasn't interested. Bobby insisted that they split.

Nacis looked over at his partner and realized there was no talking him out of it. He would protest, but it wouldn't do him any good. When Bobby made up his mind, that was it.

Later, Nacis left Bobby's house terribly upset. Yes, Bobby had been driving him crazy. Yes, Bobby's pill consumption scared him. Bobby's brother Bouillien already had a pill problem, and Bobby's Darvocet intake seemed to be approaching the addictive stage. Bobby had even admitted, "Maybe I shouldn't be taking these because I don't have no more pain." While Bobby claimed to have stopped taking the pills, he still liked to drink. But the fact was that Nacis didn't care for the boat business and was not ready to run one himself. Even if he convinced his brother Livingston to go into business with him and not open his intended welding shop, Nacis still wasn't crazy about taking a more active role in sales and operations.

Soon, the two MONTCO shareholders split their newly acquired eight arpents of land, divided the boats, and divvied up the business. Nacis allowed Bobby to keep the company name.

Before Nacis left the office to start his new boat company with his brother, who'd agreed to join him, he decided to make a pitch to MONTCO's number-one employee. If he could convince Butch Danos to come with him, he could remain behind the scenes. Butch could be the point man; he could handle the clients and help Livingston with the operations.

When Nacis made the offer to Butch, Butch told him, "*Merci*, Nacis. That's real nice of you. But I can't take your offer. I started with Bobby. I'm gonna finish with Bobby."

Where exactly was Bobby going? Some people thought he might be setting himself up for failure. With Nacis around, at least someone had been theoretically holding him back by making him consider his partner's position, even if the partner hadn't been especially vocal. At least someone had been crunching numbers and keeping track of things.

Bobby's doubters watched as he built a red brick mansion on his new four-arpent homestead. It was a fancy place with big white columns, a sweeping front yard, and a regal circle driveway. He had a pool and a Hollywood-like pool house, horses, a stable, and a Kentucky-like horse arena. Golden Meadow wasn't used to such extravagance. While up the bayou, there were dozens of plantation big houses, the mansions in lower Lafourche were mostly brand-new structures that had been paid for with oilfield, "new money." Bobby's critics looked at all this opulence and they wondered whether he'd spend himself into bankruptcy.

Once again, Bobby was ignoring the critics. He'd severed his partnership with Nacis because he wanted to make more millions and take more chances, and he thought a partner, be he Nacis Theriot or anyone else, would only hold him back. If he was going to make multi-multimillions, he was going to make them for himself. Along the way, he was ready to spend lots and lots of money.

Chapter 13

Robert Alario and the Cajun Cavalry

1968

By 1968, Nolty Theriot still couldn't find enough money to spend. He needed a mini mint just to keep up with the North Sea's demand. The oil companies and contractors were making frenzied calls for his tugs and his men, and by this time, his cavalry's captains had lost their cultural inhibitions and were charging across the Atlantic Ocean. Despite their sudden enthusiasm about the stories they'd heard, however, no Theriot skipper could quite prepare himself for the culture clash.

Nevertheless, some of them tried to ready themselves. One captain, Bob Savoie, Sidney Savoie's twenty-four-year-old nephew from Larose, did his best to prep himself for his first-ever plane trip by buying his first suit. He paid twenty dollars for the three-piece ensemble at J. C. Penney and proudly wore it to the airport for the transatlantic flight. Captain Bob had heard the stories about all the formality, about how even the English shipyard welders wore ties. Well, he, too, could dress the part.

By the end of his long flight, his clothes were rumpled and his muscles were stiff, and when, at Heathrow Airport, he searched for the Theriot representative who was supposed to meet him, the man was nowhere to be found. Captain Bob had no idea what to do. He tried to talk to some of the airport officials, but he couldn't understand them. When he asked more questions, they looked at him like he was another species. Apparently, they couldn't understand him, either.

He stared at all the frenzy in the terminal and didn't know where to go. It was strange. Many times, he'd been in the middle of the Gulf, well beyond the sight of land, but knew right where he was. But now, in this cradle of Western civilization, he was lost. He said to himself, "What the hell I'm gonna do? A coonass stuck over here."

At least Captain Bob, who finally met his liaison, had made a move that one of the Theriot captains was not so sure about making—leaving the ground in an airplane. Captain Whitey Adams, one of Nolty's most daring skippers, listened to his boss talk about how he'd purchase Whitey a first-class plane ticket, and that once Whitey got to the London airport, a limousine would be waiting for him.

Captain Whitey looked at Nolty as if he was crazy. "*Es-tu fou*? I'm not getting on any damn airplane. That's not safe."

Captain Whitey didn't even like driving his car across the narrow, steep Huey P. Long Bridge over the Mississippi River in suburban New Orleans, and he damn sure wasn't getting on an airplane. The only alternative was to put him on one of Nolty's remaining 90-foot tugs with a navigator and cross the Atlantic Ocean in the worst part of winter.

While Captain Whitey had never been out of the Gulf of Mexico, when he heard the plan, he nodded. He'd take that tug anywhere in any sea. But a plane? There was no chance of that.

As for Captain Jimmie Vizier, he couldn't wait to get on the plane for the crossing. He'd been listening to his little brother Tommie's stories for months. The money had peaked his interest, the rough seas had intrigued him, and he wanted to experience the culture.

When Captain Jimmie had brought his wife and three daughters over to Yarmouth, everything hit them at once. The cars drove on the wrong side of the road. The people's accent was fascinating, almost intoxicating, and their manner was flawlessly polite. Many of their homes abutted each other in row houses, a style that didn't exist in Louisiana. Captain Jimmie's own home had no refrigerator but instead sported an outdoor brick rectangle that made use of the constant cold weather to serve as an icebox. If the weather warmed, he'd toss in a big block of ice.

Inside the home, the sole purpose of one little room was to store coal, the fuel source they were all working so hard to replace.

Another adjustment was the food. For every good and greasy serving of fish and chips there were a dozen other bland staples. There were the tasteless sausages and the ubiquitous boiled potatoes, the roast lamb, the strange little peas, and the Yorkshire pudding. The fare was not all dreadful, but it tended to reduce the custom of the meal into a necessary, mechanical exercise rather than what it was in south Louisiana, a daily celebration. In fact, Captain Bob Savoie wouldn't taste a remnant of home until he sampled a plate of Steak Diane. Savoring the smothered beef, he could hardly believe the British knew how to make rice and gravy.

But to Captain Jimmie Vizier, the biggest difference between the two worlds was their marine cultures. While he admired the stability and power of the Europeans' seagoing vessels and the knowledge of their mariners, his brother Tommie was right when he said they didn't have the slightest idea how to run an anchor tug.

In fact, everything about the way they handled their vessels was different, *foreign*, if you will. In England, Norway, and the other North Sea countries, the captain steered his

The brother captains Jimmie and Tommie Vizier. (Courtesy of the Vizier family)

boat by barking commands to a wheelman, who physically turned the wheel. The European captain didn't so much as lay a finger on the controls. By foregoing the feel of the wheel, the European failed to take advantage of his sense of touch and the benefit of muscle memory, which was as necessary to handle anchors as it was to drive a race car, jockey a thoroughbred, or rope a rodeo calf. Anchor handling was even more tactile than those other endeavors because it involved operating so many controls with so many different textures at once. The Europeans couldn't fathom how, in a roiling sea, the Cajuns simultaneously operated a steering wheel, two engine throttles, two or three winch controls, and two radios, one to communicate with the barge and one, if necessary, with another tug, all while keeping their eye on their deckhands, the barge, the waves, and a possible twin tug.

To Captain Jimmie and the other Cajuns, their actions were automatic. Their hands slid from one control to another without thought. Captain Jimmie himself possessed amazingly deft motor skills developed from years of precise duck decoy carving. It was a Vizier family trait; his father, Odee, and his cousin, Tan Brunet, could carve ducks that looked so real you had to touch them to know they were made of wood. While carving was obviously slow paced and tedious, and North Sea anchor handling could be blistering and nerve-racking, it all boiled down to fine muscle control, poise, and, sometimes on the rough seas, what the Spanish deckhands called *cojones*. It wasn't necessarily hand-eye coordination; many times the captain was so focused on the action below the wheelhouse, he never even looked at the controls; his hands just glided from one to the other.

In addition to all the levers and switches on the anchor panel, the Europeans also couldn't comprehend how the Cajuns could operate a boat from her stern; they'd never seen stern controls. At times, when Captain Jimmie and the others would try to show them how to run anchors, some of the European captains would turn and face the bow and try to operate the anchor controls with their hands behind their backs, on top of their butts. Facing the bow to steer was so ingrained in them that they couldn't get comfortable with their back to the boat's front.

Moreover, while the Europeans could run their vessels in a rough sea with high skill, they weren't used to stopping in such a sea and actually *working* in it. But these Cajuns jumped into the ring like a flat-accented

John Wayne. The Cajuns personified the ultimate American image, the fast and fearless western cowboy. Even with the existence of these storied American legends, it was still difficult for the Europeans to believe what they were seeing. They'd watch in awe as the Cajuns would back up a tug to a barge in a rolling sea with a four-knot current pounding one of the gunnels, then make the stern fit in between two snug anchor cables while keeping the cables out of her prop. Just when it seemed like a cable was about to get caught or the tug was about to gash the barge, the deckhand would hook the anchor buoy, and, pow, the captain would hit the throttle on the winch, whip up the slack, and then hit the throttles on the boat's engines, hoping it was all enough to unearth the anchor. The British couldn't understand how the Cajuns executed this close call so routinely.

The European captains usually recoiled, as any first-timer would, when a Cajun tug bore down on an anchor and the force drove the deck underwater, with the seas rising up to the deckhands' necks. The Spanish and Portuguese deckhands may or may not have been scared, but they never complained. They were tethered to the gunnel, and they trusted their Cajun captains. But the deckhands' predicament startled the European mariners.

In some instances, it was as if the European captains didn't understand the limits of their vessels. One night, the Vizier brothers were running anchors, with Captain Jimmie on the *Rebecca Theriot* and Captain Tommie on the *J. V. Alario*, and a British tug was assisting them by holding onto the barge. The British tug somehow got crossways in a strong current; then one of its hatches popped loose, and it was too rough to close it. The tug's stern, which was hooked to a barge anchor, began digging in. Water began to gush onto the deck, into the hatch, and the force quickly pulled the stern underwater.

The British captain radioed the Viziers, saying, "Come pick up my crew. I'm sinking."

Neither Vizier believed the Brit was sinking, but the captain persisted, pleading over and over, "Come pick up my crew. Come pick up my crew. I'm sinking. I'm sinking."

Both Viziers took off, with Captain Tommie, who was closer, getting there first and maneuvering alongside the barge. He evacuated all fourteen of the crew.

They watched the tug for a while and realized she wasn't going to sink, but only needed to be pumped out, which was what the Viziers had believed in the beginning. Finally, the British captain and engineer got back on their tug and pumped out the water.

Perhaps the most significant difference between the North Sea natives and the Cajuns was that the Europeans were not used to the absurd pace of the oilfield, and the Theriot captains had never known anything else. To Captain Jimmie, it wasn't unusual to have a professional diver swimming under your boat in a turbid sea, with all of its currents, not to mention the presence of two giant suctioning, slicing propellers. He knew he had to follow the divers' bubbles and keep their breath pipes, their actual life cords, out of his wheel. He knew that as long as he stayed behind the bubbles and didn't let down his guard, he wouldn't make a mistake.

The divers knew this, too. It got to where the divers wouldn't jump overboard until they checked the wheelhouse to make sure Captain Jimmie or another Cajun was at the controls. When a diver was diving off of a British tug, Captain Jimmie grew used to the practice of going aboard the tug and tactfully asking the British captain if he could relieve him of his duties. The British captains never posed any argument. They knew the diver would simply not go underwater with them at the wheel.

The British, and later the Norwegian captains, watched the Cajuns with more than admiration. They were also taking notes. This was their territory, and if they could learn how to handle these anchors properly, they could grab *all* of the work. They also talked to their bosses about the Cajuns' efficient anchor-handling systems, and, in response, their companies sent naval architects aboard the Theriot tugs to analyze the anchor-jerking apparatuses. There was no reason they couldn't steal this Cajun/Texien technology.

While the North Sea natives studied the Theriot tugs, the British oilmen couldn't decide what to make of the Cajun tug captains. Many would say what a British Brown & Root employee said in Charles Zewe's 1973 WWL-TV documentary called *Cajuns on the Queen Sea*: "They'll go out in these waters, and they'll do things that a European captain and a European tug won't do. They're the only people we know that will work like that. They can run anchors two hundred percent better than any other tug in the North Sea. In fact, as of yet, we've never had a European tug that I've seen that could run anchors anywhere like them."

Zewe then asked the British oilman, "Do you think that goes back to their experience or do you think it goes back to their gutsiness or what?"

"I think a lot goes back to their experience. They know what they're doing. And either one of two things—they've either got a lot of nerve and a lot of guts, or they're dim and don't realize what they're doing. A lot of things they do, you know, we just wouldn't think of."

Of course, as the oilman acknowledged, the Cajuns were far from dim. Ironically, their bilingual ability made them more effective communicators than their King's English counterparts. Captain Jimmie Vizier's command of French allowed him to pick up the similar Portuguese spoken by his deckhands while playing friendly card games with them. Before he knew it, he was speaking to them entirely in a bastardized coonass version of Portuguese. His French also came in handy when, occasionally, the contractor hired French tugs to help with the pipelaying operation.

During a storm one day, a French tug was helping to hold a barge. As the winds began to subside, the Brown & Root foreman radioed the French captain, telling him in his drawl, "Back off so I can take your tow line off my barge."

The French captain didn't respond.

The Texien barge foreman persisted, "Back up, you know, give me some slack so I can throw your line off."

Even though it was apparent that the French captain didn't understand English, the barge foreman kept repeating his instructions as if by his ever slower, louder repetition, the meaning of the English words would suddenly come to the Frenchman. Finally frustrated, the barge foreman asked Captain Jimmie to translate. But Captain Jimmie had already been racking his brain for the French word for "back up," which in 1960s Cajun French was simply "back up."

Then, out of the blue, Captain Jimmie recalled an image of his childhood, when he'd watch his neighbor plow the field with his mule, and the neighbor would tell the mule, *recul*, when he wanted it to back up. Captain Jimmie hit the radio and said, "*Capitain, peut-tu fait reculer?*"

"*Oh, recul,*" said the French captain. "*Oh, recul, oui, reculer.*"

The captain promptly backed up his tug, and the problem was solved.

To Captain Jimmie, the North Sea was more than a place to demonstrate his language skills and anchor-handling ability. In fact, it didn't take him long to see a bonafide business opportunity. One day, some of the barge's Texiens approached him and asked him if he could pick up a case of Scotch during his next run to port. He said yes, and they gave him a $100 bill. When he made his run, he paid $80 for the case and pocketed a $20 profit. He then hid the Scotch in the hull and, at the right moment when the seas were calm and the coast was clear, one of the barge Texiens boarded the tug and grabbed the stash.

Later, when the Texiens were good and drunk, Captain Jimmie would jump across to the barge and challenge the barge hands to a few hands of *bouré*. At this point, Captain Jimmie had a decided advantage—neither he nor his crew ever drank onboard. Any captain that drank in the North Sea was foolish; a dulling of the senses during an anchor move could result in a fatal disaster. The barge workers didn't have the same responsibility over navigation, so when they could sneak a drink, they sometimes did. And if their liquor supplier wanted them to play that coonass card game with him, then sure, count them in.

The problem was that the Texiens were playing a game they didn't really understand, and they were playing it while intoxicated. The result was that Captain Jimmie took home fistfuls of cash. It got to where he and his family lived off of his *bourée* and liquor broker cash money, and he saved nearly every penny of his paycheck.

The Texien barge men didn't catch on or, if they did, Captain Jimmie's card-playing dominance didn't dissuade them. They kept drinking Scotch, playing *bourée*, and losing money. The plan worked to perfection until the Brown & Root barge superintendent sent a drawling radio message into the *J. V. Alario's* wheelhouse, "Hey, Captain Jim, come over here to my office. I want to talk to you."

To Captain Jimmie, this was a strange request. The head honcho of a lay barge had never called him into his office. In the office, the superintendent started talking to Captain Jimmie about a whiskey problem on his barge. Captain Jimmie acted as if the presence of alcohol was news to him. After some hemming and hawing, the superintendent told him, "If

I ever catch you bringing this whiskey to this barge, I'm gonna send you back to the States."

Captain Jimmie nodded. He knew two things: first, the superintendent knew full well he was the one bringing the whiskey—the men were sober before he left on his run and drunk after he got back; and second, until an army of qualified anchor handlers miraculously appeared on the British shores, Brown & Root wasn't going to get rid of Jimmie Vizier.

Back across the Atlantic Ocean in Golden Meadow, Nolty Theriot had heard nothing but rave remarks about his captains and his boats, but the praise didn't help his problem. He still lacked the borrowing power to build enough boats to satisfy Brown & Root's North Sea needs. He was working on brokering more tugs, but this wasn't easy either. The broker prospects had to be able to finance the building of an expensive ice-class tug, and not many of them could make this kind of investment.

In 1968, Nolty saw a potential solution in his brother-in-law, Robert Alario. Robert had just returned to Golden Meadow from working for Texaco in Haiti, having come home to be with his ailing father J. V., who'd been diagnosed with cancer. In Robert, Nolty saw an intelligent, capable man with an incredibly diverse background for a thirty-year-old. Believing Robert's international experience would help him expand his increasingly global operation, Nolty hired Robert with the initial instructions to locate the necessary money to build more boats. Nolty had no idea about where to look, but if Robert thought he could be of some assistance, then he had the job.

Robert Alario agreed. He was no financier, but he believed his varied experiences had prepared him for almost anything. His training had begun with his upbringing. Like Nolty, Robert was born and raised in Golden Meadow. French was his first language, and he'd worked in the oilfield during the summers of his youth. He had memories of toiling on a labor gang in the sweltering marsh, fighting mosquitoes and handling creosote pilings, not realizing that the chemicals would burn him until he felt his skin turn to fire.

He remembered working as a deckhand for Minor Cheramie and as the boat's young buck, once volunteering to swing from the vessel in a heaving sea onto a rig to grab a water hose. In attempting this maneuver, Robert hit a piece of scrap metal that put a permanent hole in his shin. He also recalled once sitting out on the deck in the middle of the night under a beautiful star scape, just enjoying the absolute quiet while consuming one canned peach after another. He didn't stop eating the peaches until he realized he'd almost finished the whole gallon and would soon have the stomach to show for it.

Growing up, Robert Alario saw many people on the bayou who had the mental capability and the inventive talent to match anyone, but because they were either uneducated or couldn't speak English, they'd never reach their potential. He wouldn't make the same mistake.

He went to college, graduating with a liberal arts degree from the Southwestern Louisiana Institute before heading to LSU Law School. Robert wanted to become a lawyer so he could help his people deal with the oilfield's shysters. He'd seen what some of the Texien oilmen had done to the Cajuns during his boyhood in the 1940s, especially when the Texiens cheated illiterate Cajuns in land leases. After Robert became an attorney, he'd hang a shingle in Golden Meadow and he'd negotiate those leases fairly.

Despite his lawyerly convictions, the romance of international affairs lured him away from law school before his third year when he received a fellowship for a master's degree program in foreign affairs from Georgetown University. Although he was heading to Washington, DC, and giving up a legal career, Robert's two years of law school had taught him how to pinpoint issues and how to resolve them. He'd never be a lawyer, but he'd learned to think like one.

While at Georgetown, Robert worked part-time for the post–McCarthy House Committee on Un-American Activities. The committee job gave him a feel for the fundamentals of government. He saw how the hardworking staff influenced the high-profile politicians and vice versa, and he also learned all about the art of posturing. This was something he scarcely knew existed; now he was seeing it up front on Capitol Hill, then analyzing it as a student.

All of Robert's experience and education would soon crystallize when Robert graduated from Georgetown and took a job with Texaco's international division, volunteering for a post no one else wanted, communist West Africa. When Robert arrived in Conakry, Guinea, he could find no other Americans working in the private sector. He got a taste of his isolation during his first meeting with the oil companies, when he walked into a room full of smoke, rapid-fire French, and a conspiracy. The oilmen, who were all in their forties or older and were veterans of Africa, were busy jockeying for refining and distribution territories for what was then only imported oil.

When Robert, with his boyish face and 140-pound frame, walked into the room looking every bit the American kid, the Shell representative said to his comrades in French, "Who is this altar boy?"

Robert said nothing. He let the men talk and never revealed that he knew any French, even though he understood every word of their conversation. He wanted to learn their plans, especially their intentions of giving Texaco a small piece of the distribution and minimizing the company's allowances from the government.

After the meeting, Robert went to the local US embassy. He discovered quickly how everything worked; the US aid mission gave a check to the government, who turned around and gave it to the oil companies who were supposed to divide it up equally with each company taking a turn at administering the money. Robert learned that it was supposed to have been Texaco's turn, but the other companies had already forced him out of the picture. So he arranged with the US embassy that he would get the check just before it left the embassy.

At the oil companies' next meeting, the representatives couldn't understand why the check hadn't come. Then Robert spoke up in French, telling them he had the check. The grizzly old oilmen were shocked. They realized all at once that the altar boy understood French and had played them. Then and there, he had their respect.

Two years later in 1965, Texaco transferred Robert to Port au Prince, Haiti, which was then under the control of the oppressive Francois "Papa Doc" Duvalier. When Robert arrived in the city, he drove into the center of town and saw a sign that said, BIENVENU À HAITI, and beneath that sign was a dead man strapped to a chair, with his hands tied behind his back and a sign around his neck that said in French, "Beware to Traitors." The very next day, when Robert showed up at the Texaco office, he learned that the secret police had taken away his operations manager and the manager's family. He'd never hear from them again.

Despite the obvious danger and oppression, Robert adjusted. He listened and learned his parameters. What he discovered surprised him. He liked Haiti. While he detested the tyrannical Duvalier regime, he loved the West Indian culture, which was similar to South Louisiana's. After spending two successful years in Texaco's office, he learned of some non-oilfield business opportunities in manufacturing and real estate. He was just about to pursue them when he learned of his father's cancer and returned home to the bayou.

In Golden Meadow, it was probably apparent to Nolty that there was no one on earth with Robert's background, a bayou-reared, hyper-educated, oilfield-savvy, bilingual international businessman with experience in legal theory, federal politics, and third-world survival. What Robert had become was a problem solver. He'd learned how to identify an obstacle and find ways to get around it or knock it down.

When Nolty had told him, "I need to build some boats. I can't get the financing," that defined the problem. Robert then looked at the present financing available to boat companies. The banks didn't have authority to lend for more than five or seven years, and their rates were anywhere from 3 to 5 over prime, depending on your credit, which meant an interest rate floating between 13 to 17 percent. For the finance companies like CIT and GE Credit, the terms could be even less favorable. In a cyclical business like the oilfield, short-term, high-interest loans were hardly workable. In Theriot's case, he'd already extended his credit anyway.

Assessing the situation, Robert quickly realized he didn't have time to change the banking culture in Louisiana or in any other state. He had to find another source of financing. His instincts took him to Washington, DC. His research there revealed there were federal, maritime-related plans, particularly the Title 11 program, that featured long-term loans with a low, fixed rate of interest. This Title 11 also had certain tax advantages, including a provision for a construction reserve fund, which permitted a merchant marine company to take its profits and put them in a tax-deferred reserve account for future vessel construction or upgrade. This would break the chain of workboat companies avoiding maximum income tax payments by deliberately spending end-of-the- year profits on vessel construction, whether they needed the equipment or not. Robert realized if he could qualify Theriot for Title 11, he'd exceed Nolty's expectations.

While the Maritime Administration (Mar Ad) Title 11 loans were available to the merchant marine, the Mar Ad didn't consider the oilfield vessels to be a part of the merchant marine fleet. Not only had the bluewater merchant marine been around much longer, their contracts were longer term and more stable. While a bluewater company might be operating on five-year shipping contracts, the oilfield workboats were working on contracts that ranged from a two-year contract with a ninety-day cancellation clause to a thirty-day contract with a twenty-four-hour cancellation to pure hourly work. Where the bluewater companies had long, detailed financial histories, the oil vessel companies had scant historical information. Their financial statements were weak and misleading because the liabilities columns were full of personal perks like hunting camps, yachts, and an ungodly entertainment fund that was difficult for a non-oilfield man to understand. The oil boat industry only had one significant public company in Tidewater, and there was no real record of proving what the industry had done in the past.

Robert had to convince the Mar Ad and the bigger banks in New York and Chicago that part of the reason for the industry's lack of a financial history was the non-availability of long-term, low-interest loans. But if Mar Ad and the banks extended these kinds of loans to workboat companies, the companies could break the cycle and prove the industry's viability. It was in the government's best interest to help them because, without workboats, the offshore petroleum industry could not function, and without offshore oil and gas, the US industrial machine would lack the fuel it needed to operate at full strength.

In Washington, Robert Alario found himself drawing on his varied experience. He'd first used his legal training to analyze the issue and find the applicable law; he'd then employed his Beltway savvy to work Capitol Hill from both ends, from the grunt staff level of the Mar Ad to the political penthouse, which included the big swingers in Louisiana's congressional delegation. With his roots, he had a knack for communicating his profession's struggles, needs, and value. And when he finally made his presentations, he went back and forth between the big banks, the politicians, and the Mar Ad, convincing each party that the other parties were behind the plan.

To make the plan desirable, to put the New York and Chicago banks in a position where they were actually competing to sell the bonds for the loans, took loads of work. In 1969, the preparation began in a whirlwind at a New Orleans hotel.

At the center of it was Theriot assistant bookkeeper, Benny Bourgeois. Bourgeois was a little, dwarflike man who, at nineteen, was a numerical whiz kid. He'd been at Theriot less than a year and was blown away by the operation, awed by Nolty's personality and managerial skill, by Charlie Sanders' sheer size and booming Texien command, and by Robert Alario's worldliness and broad and beaming intellect. At times, Robert would say a word to Bourgeois, and Bourgeois would just nod, making sure he looked up the word in his dictionary when he got home.

When Bourgeois joined Robert and CPA Dan Carroll at the New Orleans hotel for nights of number crunching, their job was to write the loan amortization schedules and relate them to the company's profit projections. They had to project when the new boats would leave the shipyard, what their costs would be, the amount of their day-rate profits, and factor in depreciation, taxes, inflation, and the rest of the company's profits, losses, and income. Bourgeois had known that Dan Carroll could grind, but Robert Alario was another species. He'd watch Robert wake up at 7:00 a.m., take a seat at the table, and start pounding the adding machine, not stopping until exhaustion overtook him at 2:00 a.m. the next morning. If they needed food, they ordered a sandwich and ate it as they handwrote numbers into the stacks and stacks of ledgers. If one number changed, they had to redo the entire progression. Years later, a computerized spreadsheet would have dramatically shortened their work, but in 1969 and 1970, it was all pencil lead, eraser dust, and strong coffee.

On the other side of the table, the CPA Carroll put in overtime as always, once working through the night with Bourgeois until 4:30 the next morning, even though Carroll had doubts about the venture. He was impressed by Robert's intelligence, but he didn't see how Robert would ultimately convince the banks with nothing but ledgers full of contingencies. It was too speculative and, in Carroll's mind, an over-extension for a family business.

Despite his reservations, when the time came for the final presentation, Carroll grabbed the reams of ledgers and boarded a chartered plane with Nolty, Robert, and the Theriot attorney. On their trip, they would stop in Washington to show their ledgers to the Mar Ad people, then travel to New York City to show the same projections to the bankers and then to the Midwest to make their pitch to the First National Bank of Chicago. During each stop, Carroll marveled at how smoothly Robert handled the politicians and the executives.

In the end, First National Bank of Chicago agreed to do the deal. Robert's paperwork and irrepressible salesmanship had defied the odds and set a far-reaching precedent for the entire industry. The deal worked like this: the bank would sell the Mar Ad government-guaranteed bonds and would refinance the existing Theriot fleet for longer-term loans at an attractive rate of interest; the bank would also lend Nolty the money he needed to build as many boats as the North Sea could handle; and the government would guarantee all the loans.

Now all Robert Alario and Nolty Theriot needed was to receive the loan proceeds. They had boats to build, and the new funds couldn't hit the company's checking account quickly enough.

Now on his own in 1969, Bobby Orgeron could howl at the moon without any interruption. His independence made him feel as if he could fly. He decided to transfer that feeling into reality and bought a single-engine Cessna. He hired a pilot but made the pilot teach him how to operate his new toy. Soon, Bobby began taking the controls whenever he wanted.

When he wasn't gliding through the air, he was flying on the ground in his big Lincoln Continental, looking for new opportunities. Soon, the sensation of being far into the black lost its freshness. He deliberately went deep into hock again. Like Nolty Theriot, he had to build.

Bobby began by ordering two new crew boats from Equitable Shipyard, and as he built those vessels, he looked for other deals. Chevron, who had the *Montco* hauling drill pipe, told Bobby the 135-foot boat wasn't quite long enough to haul two strings of pipe. Bobby then found the perfect vessel, a 155-footer that Bollinger Shipyard in Lockport had built on spec and Donald Bollinger still owned. This *Georgia* looked like she had just been launched. To buy her for $350,000, Bobby put down $50,000, and Bollinger owner-financed the balance.

When Bobby sold the *Montco* to a California company for a premium $275,000, he had the opportunity to pay down his loan on the *Georgia*. He'd paid $250,000 for the *Montco*, worked her, and had her almost paid off. But with these *Montco* profits, Bobby decided not to take the conservative route. Instead, he plunged deeper into construction debt, financing the construction of more crew boats. Over the next few years, he'd build more than seven aluminum crew boats at Camcraft in Crown Point, Louisiana, two 65-footers and five 100-footers, all triple screws.

All this spending was easy. What was difficult was putting the boats to work. It wasn't that Bobby couldn't do it; he did do it. But to keep the boats working, to overcome the lack of security of the twenty-four-hour cancellation clause, he had to play the game full force again. In a sense, the challenge of the Navy sale had been much easier and had been a welcome break from the oilfield race.

During his Washington, DC, blitz, he didn't deal with the flesh market. He didn't have to buy girls from known Mafia. Over the years, Bobby had gotten to know Don Carlos Marcello and his cronies. They were nice to him, and he even reciprocated their friendliness by occasionally taking them fishing. However, when they offered him business opportunities, he turned them down. Always, he kept them at arm's length. Nevertheless, because the Mafia controlled the girls, he had to work with them a little bit. And any dealing with the wise guys felt dirty.

So much of the oilfield was every bit as grimy as oil sludge itself. The transportation superintendents still had their hands out, and the service companies were still obliging. There were some straight rods who wouldn't ask for so much as a sack of crawfish, but to Bobby, it was as if all but one out of three dozen of them were on the take. The company men were not just receiving, they flat out asked, propositioning without any trace of shame.

Bobby found himself paying for obscure things, for refrigerators, for air-conditioning systems. If he didn't, his competitors would. He'd heard of the competition funding everything from mink coats to college educations.

Once, he saw a motor home and purchased it on the spot. Four months later, when a client oilman saw the new recreational vehicle, he told Bobby he wanted it. In the same breath, the oilman said he'd give Bobby a $100 per day raise on each of the three boats that were working with his company, which amounted to $9,000 a month. With the extra money, Bobby could pay off the $18,000 he spent on the RV in two months and keep the raise as long as the boats were still working. If he didn't give the man the motor home, then it was implicit that he'd lose the job and find himself with three boats tied up, accruing interest.

So what else could Bobby do but hand the man the RV's keys?

The oilmen never stopped their demands. It wasn't always good enough to make a duck hunt at the marsh camp. Sometimes, the oilmen had to have the girls there, too. They'd hunt in the early morning, kill a limit of ducks, then catch redfish until noon. After a long afternoon nap, they'd drink and whore all night.

Everyone wanted a piece of Bobby in one form or another. The vendors could be especially tedious. One day, a salesman made the mistake of walking into his office and being pushy. So many had passed through hawking this and that that they'd long since run together. This one could have been selling paint, but it didn't matter. Bobby didn't care. He wanted to get rid of him, and he ended up throwing the salesman out of his office.

Nothing relieved the pressure. It came from everywhere, including family. Even his brother Bouillien was relying more on him now. In the 1950s and into the 1960s, Bouillien had been a big boatman on the bayou, but all the pain from his pulmonary condition took its toll, as did the excessive Demerol and Percodan. It had turned him crazy. He'd abused his wife and neglected his family. Then in the late 1960s, he had sold his company to his partner, left his family, and took off with a lot of cash, hopping around Mexico and the Caribbean and ending up in

Brownsville, Texas. Now that he was back in Golden Meadow, he was finally clean but broke and broken. Bobby and their father supported him and put him up in a nearby rented apartment. Every day, he ate lunch with his parents.

Bobby knew he himself was not immune to addiction. He'd had his bout with Darvocet, but he'd never seen it as a real problem.

Now that he was out of hock and was his own man, nothing could stop him. When his head port captain, Butch Danos, left the company and ultimately ended up working for Minor Cheramie, Bobby was sad to see him go, but he knew Butch's brother Benu could also do the job. He couldn't afford both of them anyway. So he'd trade one Danos brother for the other; swap one ruddy Santa Claus for an even redder one.

As Benu slid into Butch's chair, Bobby unveiled his plan. He wanted to finish the aluminum crew boats under construction and eventually build some more triple-screw versions. For now, he had to get back his boat legs and come up with a more family-oriented scheme, abandoning the old Mont-naming theme and start naming the boats after family members or employees. To celebrate Benu's promotion, he'd name one of these shiny aluminum jobs the *Benton Danos*.

Also, Bobby decided to make better on his promise that his weekends were for family and that those oil company assholes couldn't call him on Saturday and Sunday. He'd deal with them in their office during the week, and he'd sell them on his sleek aluminum triple-screw crew boats as they came off the blocks. *Shew*, they weren't boats, they were three-engine Camcraft cruisers, veritable jets on the water. With Benu's tinkering, these *bébés* would outgun anyone, and they'd do it without bending a prop, scratching a side, or nicking a passenger's fingernail.

The problem was the boats would never be fast enough for the oilmen. Even at light speed, they were no substitute for sex and money. That was why the *maudit* oilmen still called on the weekend. Because they were in a little recession, Bobby had to take their calls and set his course for their playgrounds again.

If they requested a visit to his marsh camp, he had to take them. If they wanted more than ducks and *poule d'eaus*, if they called for two-legged hens, he had to rustle some up.

That was exactly what Bobby and the boys were doing one night while gunning down the Yankee Canal in his old man's wooden skiff with its big V-8 engine. The old hull was loaded with men and whores. They'd all been drinking. Bobby knew he should've watched his intake, and he'd tried. But the customers didn't want a designated driver even though it was black and gaseous out there. The fog smell was so intense it overpowered the marsh's fresh, dank odor. What was worse was that the people at the town dump were burning trash and the smoke was drifting into the canal. But the boat's passengers didn't care about the conditions. They wanted a fearless song leader, not a whistle-blowing, clipboard-carrying camp counselor.

So what was Bobby going to do? Drink an RC Cola? A Barq's? Whatever it was he'd consumed, he was feeling it as he whirred down the Yankee Canal; he knew this stretch well. As long as there were no new obstructions in the water, he could drive it while sleeping.

But there were obstructions. Bobby was headed right for one. He didn't see it. The other men and the ladies of the night weren't exactly looking through their night eyes, either. The boat wind was blowing back their long locks. Everyone was laughing. There was nothing to fear here. This tall, jolly coonass at the wheel could do anything. The faster he went the better.

Until he struck an oncoming boat. Until he bounced from that boat and plowed through a moored *bateau*. After the boat stopped, Bobby looked at his shocked crew. He called over to the driver of the other boat. He was okay, and his boat was still operable. Bobby then examined the wreckage. It didn't seem possible that no one was injured, but then again, Bobby was with them. Wrecks didn't kill him, and he must've passed some of his powers onto his entourage.

But his daddy's old skiff was totaled; the old man wouldn't forgive Bobby for destroying that boat.

Really, it was the last thing Bobby wanted to do. It wasn't as if he was trying to crush his father. He wasn't consciously breaking Juan's beloved possessions to get the old man's attention. But subconsciously, he still didn't feel as if he was on equal status with his brother. Bouillien may be a sad story now, but to Daddy, Bouillien was still the first son in every sense. Now Bobby's brother had sympathy on his side.

Bobby felt sorry for his brother, too, but the dynamic was complicated. Bobby, for some reason, still had to prove himself to his father. He could never do enough to completely win the old man's affection.

Then, one afternoon in 1971, things changed, but not in the way Bobby wanted. The day started out promising. Bobby was putting the finishing touches on the deal for the triple-screw, 100-foot aluminum crew boats, signing the contract at George Engine Company in Harvey when the phone rang. It was his father.

The old man's voice was desperate and broken. He'd found Bouillien dead in his apartment. Bobby told him to shut the door and wait.

Bobby jumped in his Cessna and told the pilot to sit in the back. The pilot would never make the short flight fast enough. He wouldn't fly as low as Bobby needed to fly.

Landing in Golden Meadow, Bobby opened the door to his brother's apartment, the ghastliness hit him. Nothing had prepared him for the sight, not even mangled corpses in Korea. His brother was lying next to a plate-sized puddle of pus, which had pooled on newspaper.

The doctors would say fluid flooded Bouillien's lungs, and he died of heart failure. His body, weakened from operating for so many years on one lung, had finally quit. Herman "Bouillien" Orgeron, *Wildfire* captain, uneducated millionaire, his brother's role model, the brains of his father's early operations, father of four children, died at forty-three.

After Bouillien passed, a strange thing happened. Bobby emerged. His father should've realized that Bobby had stepped up as soon as he'd married and had successfully gone into business for himself or as soon as he'd sired children and delivered a fleet of boats. But at least to Bobby, as long as Bouillien had been alive, Bobby had been second. While appreciative of his new status, Bobby never wanted to be first; he only desired equality. He certainly didn't want his brother to have to die for this to happen.

With his father now looking at him fondly, one might think that Bobby could take it easier. Enjoy all of his success. Even in this recession, he was doing well.

Both his daddy and his wife had been telling him for years, "You got enough. You have enough." And now that he had his daddy, in addition to already having his wife and three children, he knew deep down that he had plenty enough of everyone and everything.

But he had to keep going. Part of the reason was because the times weren't perfect. Another part was that his boats were always having engine trouble. These triple screws, which were now on the water, broke down more than they should have. But even if he didn't have any problems, he still had to build. He also had an unusual desire to please people, especially customers, but also anyone depending on him—his family, church charities, employees, stray women. This need he had to make people happy and to enjoy himself while doing it was almost as strong as his unquenchable thirst for success.

So that was why when he went to New Orleans to pick up a new Lincoln Continental, he couldn't just make a trip into town with a friend and come back soaked in new-car smell. He couldn't do this when his oil podnahs were lurking at the Kings Room. They wanted to check out the new rod and "buy him" a few drinks on his tab.

By the time he left the place, he was in no shape to drive his new car. So for once, he took it easy. Outside of town, on Highway 90 near Boutte, he was cruising. His friend, who'd also kicked back a few pops, was following him in another car.

Despite Bobby traveling well within the speed limit, he wasn't prepared when the car in front of him stopped abruptly at a yellow light that quickly went to red. He barreled into the stopped car, and his friend barreled into him. His new Lincoln was totaled and sandwiched, accordion-style. His friend's car was inoperable.

After Bobby called Benu to pick them up, Bobby then phoned the dealership and told the salesman, "Hey, that car's no good. I don't want it."

"Well," said the salesman. "I've got another one waiting right here for you."

The next day Bobby returned to New Orleans. He decided he couldn't play it safe and simply pick up another Continental. He had to call on clients, and, in this city, it was an insult to visit an oilman and not share a cocktail or two.

And after a few rounds, Bobby was well oiled, and this time he was heading back to the bayou alone. Once he arrived along Bayou Lafourche, it was hard to know what happened. The big, good-smelling car was running smoothly, hugging the bayou road. To his left the cane fields were thick and endless. To his right the bayouside oaks and willows were close and knotted. The Lincoln handled the highway so well.

The next thing he knew he was in the cane field.

The next thing Benu knew the phone was ringing, and Bobby was telling him, "I had a little wreck." Then, on the day after the incident, he and Bobby drove back to the possible accident scene. But the car was so buried in cane, Benu didn't think Bobby knew where he was going. Benu could see nothing but thick rows of swaying stalks.

But Bobby, who'd always had an amazing memory, walked right to the wreckage. When he pointed his finger at the car, Benu's eyes bulged. He asked, "*Mais* how did you survive that one?"

The car's seats were flush with the roof. The vehicle's two sides were almost hinged together, the wheels nearly touching. How lucky could Bobby be?

He was fortunate enough to have lived at least seven lives. In what had to be his eighth or ninth life, Bobby couldn't exist on pure providence. At some point in the early 1970s, he would need his pills because, without them, he lived in constant pain. Colliding with cane fields, boats, and cars may not have killed him, but it had beaten his spine so badly he couldn't move it without wincing and gritting his teeth. In a few years, it would get to the point where he couldn't make it without the strong stuff, Percocet and Percodan.

He couldn't be his happy-go-lucky self if he had to deal with a back full of herniated discs and crushed vertebra. He had too much else on his mind. These new triple-screw crew boats, for instance, were continuing to break down. His port captains were always complaining about the engines. He could deal with their groans, as long as the customer didn't moan.

But the only way the client wouldn't whine was if MONTCO worked overtime, and, if when they weren't working long hours, Bobby was taking the customer's mind off of a broken engine. If the oilmen wanted ladies of the night in Houma, and that would make them focus on how great a guy Bobby was and not on his engine trouble, then he'd deliver.

And if he had a few drinks with them this one night, well, that would make them laugh, and it would ease his pain. Some cocktails would help make him the life of the group, and they'd all have so much fun only the Houma police could kill their party, which was exactly what happened. To the Houma police, if the oilmen wanted to throw a bash with women with questionable careers, they could rent a hotel suite. The police didn't want them making racket in a parking lot in their little city.

The disturbance was enough to get Bobby thrown in jail. Inside the clink, Bobby did something he probably shouldn't have done. He called Myrtle. She undoubtedly heard the inebriation in his voice. She'd had enough of his behavior. If he wanted to act like that, then he could sleep in jail. She wasn't bailing him out. He could call his lawyer.

Bobby called Benu. As he waited for him in the drunk tank, he smelled the snoring bums and listened to the yelling maniacs. What was he doing here? He might have been a drunk, but he couldn't drink away his guilt.

He didn't want this life, and he didn't love these night ladies. Even when he had a non-prostitute mistress of sorts, he'd made it clear to her that he wouldn't leave his wife. The girlfriends came with the territory, but he wasn't like his friends who'd gotten all messed up emotionally and divorced their wives. He wasn't like his podnahs who wouldn't leave their wives but had fallen in love with their mistresses. *He'd never loved anyone else but Myrtle. No woman had even come close to her.* So why the hell was he doing this to her?

He couldn't answer that, really. He could say it was for the money or the career. But at this level, it was hard to say that convincingly. He was consuming the women just like he was consuming alcohol and would consume pills. It was all the same addictive disposition with the greatest addiction being that of making money.

Chapter 14

Lucky Dog

1970

To make money efficiently, every boatman needed a good lieutenant. While Benu Danos was Bobby's man, Benu's brother Butch, Bobby's old right hand, was adjusting to a new assignment with Minor Cheramie. At first, it was difficult for Butch to believe that he was even back in the boat race, working for Minor. After Butch had left Bobby, he'd taken a month off, something he'd never been able to do during his tenure at MONTCO. The one long vacation he'd attempted had been cut short. The family had been at Six Flags Over Texas having a grand time, but Butch couldn't relax. He had to call in constantly. He had to talk the mechanic through repairing an engine and fix whatever other problem he could over the phone until the phone wasn't good enough. Finally, he had to return home.

When Butch had made his decision to leave MONTCO, he looked forward to slowing down. But then late one night around 11:00, Butch heard a knock on his door and opened it to find Lefty Cheramie staring at him. He had no idea what Lefty, of all people, was doing there. Lefty got right to the point, telling him he'd heard that Butch was parting ways with Bobby Orgeron, and Lefty and his brother Minor would love to have him come work for L & M Botruc.

Butch didn't know quite what to say. He didn't understand why Lefty, who he understood was the company's silent partner, was the one making the overture. Lefty explained that Minor would've come, but he was busy with the Mineral Board in Baton Rouge. But still, why the hell was Lefty at his house at 11:00 at night? Lefty lived more than an hour away in Gretna. Why would he make such an inconvenient trip? Apparently, that was how bad L & M Botruc wanted him.

Butch had a hard time processing it all, but he explained that he was flattered, and he would have to think about it. Could he go from working for hard-charging Bobby Orgeron to the harder-partying Minor Cheramie?

Of course, Butch respected the abilities of both men, but their talent was beside the point. After all, this was his life. He couldn't see himself working for Minor Cheramie. For one thing, Minor had recently spent time in jail.

Really, Minor was lucky he wasn't still behind bars. In 1967, Minor was driving drunk in New Orleans when he ran a red light and hit a woman crossing the street. His senses were so fogged he didn't realize what he'd done. As it turned out, the collision broke the woman's leg. Minor had kept on driving until a policeman pulled him over and arrested him for hit-and-run driving.

After a trial, Minor was convicted and sentenced to twenty days in New Orleans' Central Lockup. As soon as Minor went behind bars, a strange thing happened. He took over the jail. He convinced the warden to let him cook a big gumbo and requested a dozen inmates to help him. He gave the jail administrators a grocery list and personally paid for all the food.

When Lou, Deanie, and M. J. visited him, in the middle of the visit, he told them, "I better go. I got to go see about my gumbo."

Minor turned into a cooking fanatic, whipping up anything he could think of to take his mind off of being confined. He immediately won over both the inmates, whom he paid to make his bed and shine his shoes, and the warden, who loved his food.

In fact, Minor put everyone in such high spirits that his sentence was cut in half to ten days on good behavior. When he walked out of jail, the guards followed him all the way to his car, slapping him on the back and hugging him. The warden was right there, too, sad-faced and almost misty-eyed.

Despite Minor's freedom, he didn't have a driver's license. For more than a year, Minor had to put up with a chauffeur. Then, before the end of his license suspension, Governor John McKeithen decided to help his good buddy by giving him his license back prematurely. The press criticized McKeithen's move, and the story ultimately ended up in the August 1970 edition of *Reader's Digest* as part of an article on mobster Carlos Marcello; even though Marcello had nothing to do with Minor's incident, the writer William Schultz cited McKeithen's symbiotic relationship with Minor as one of several examples of Louisiana's good ol' boy network. The point was to help explain how the state's corrupt politics created an environment tailor-made for the Mafia. The article read in part:

> Carlos Marcello has flourished in a political climate unlike that anywhere else in the country . . . Consider the case of Minor Cheramie, a financial contributor to McKeithern's 1964 campaign, who demanded—and received—an appointment to the State Mineral Board. . . . For Cheramie, the job guaranteed prosperity—major oil companies were quick to rent crew and supply boats from him for thousands of dollars a day. Cheramie's friendship with the governor paid off in other ways. Convicted of drunken driving and driving without a license, Cheramie was awarded a full pardon last May by the governor, who restored his driving privileges. "He's a big whiskey drinker but he's a supporter of mine," McKeithen said.

While the article embarrassed Minor's family, he laughed at it, even though he took issue with the statement about the Mineral Board appointment "guarantee(ing)" him "prosperity." Nevertheless, Minor had his wheels again, and he was already rolling on to his next adventure.

Knowing about this incident and countless other near misses, Butch Danos decided to work for Minor anyway. When Butch had arrived at L & M Botruc, he couldn't believe what he found. The company had boats tied up, and some of them were in need of repair. While the oilfield was experiencing a recession, Butch thought Minor's Mineral Board status would have kept all of his boats working. Some of the inactivity was due to the downturn, but Butch could see no reason why the vessels weren't in top shape.

One of Butch's first jobs had been to retrieve *Bo-Truc 7*, which had a broken wheel, from a Morgan City repair yard. When Butch showed up, the yard wouldn't let go of the vessel until Butch paid them first, which meant he had to pay the repairer with his own money before getting reimbursed.

Butch thought part of the problem was that Minor was spending a great deal of time in Baton Rouge with the Mineral Board. When Minor wasn't politicking at the state capital, he was entertaining. In fact, as much as Bobby Orgeron had partied, Minor appeared to entertain twice as much. Of course, given the shaky state of the oilfield, Minor arguably needed to be around the Mineral Board or somewhere with potential clients, doing what he could to drum up business.

To Minor, what his company was experiencing was proof of his clean hands. If Minor's Mineral Board status meant so much, why were some of his boats tied up? If he had joined the board's black hats, surely he would have had the cash flow to keep his Botrucs running and in absolutely pristine condition, without worrying about the cost of repair. The problem with that assumption, according to his board mate Bill Porteous, was that Minor was a white hat and was not trading his vote for a boat job. As the board's black hats counted their cash and risked prosecution, Minor shook his head and dealt honestly with a slow economy. While he still worked the room at the Capitol House Hotel and reaped the indirect benefits of board membership, the recession prevented him from truly cashing in on his prestige.

With Minor in Baton Rouge, in Butch Danos' opinion, there was no one at the company to look after the L & M fleet's upkeep. Minor had put two of his relatives in charge, but one of the relatives was always sick and, in Butch's opinion, the other was unreliable and lacked motivation.

This wasn't like MONTCO, where family worked in Bobby's business but never interfered with it.

Nonetheless, as Butch began to overhaul the boats, he started enjoying his work. He liked working for Minor, who would discuss a job with him and then let him run with it. While Butch believed Minor had some family members slowing him down, Butch saw two others with the potential to make the company better, Minor's son M. J. and his son-in-law Pat Pitre.

M. J. was, in the best way, nothing like his father. If Minor's blue eyes were lively and always moving to the next moment, M. J.'s big blue pupils were sleepy and in no rush. Unlike his father, M. J. was laid-back, low key, and didn't share Minor's penchant for drinking and violence. In fact, when M. J. went out with his father, he rarely drank, knowing he had to stay sober to watch out for his old man. Although M. J.'s lacked Minor's flamboyance, the company didn't need another P. T. Barnum. It needed a steady presence who understood the business and could handle the personnel, and M. J. was on his way to becoming such a man.

M. J. had been raised primarily by his grandmother, but was around his father more than enough to understand the oilfield. After graduating from high school, M. J. had plans to pursue a career outside of the boat world. He'd spent a year in college and a year in trade school learning diesel mechanics. After he'd worked a year in his trade with Brady Engine and was about to be promoted in the mid-sixties, his father had sensed him drifting away from the family company and put on the hard sell, telling him, "You need to come back to work for me. Some day this is gonna be yours."

M. J. then agreed to join his father and soon broke out as a captain on the Botrucs in the East Bay field. Of course, M. J. knew handling a boat was only part of his responsibilities. He'd joined knowing full well about the business's dark side, but he also believed that just because the seediness existed, he didn't have to be a part of it. If, for some reason, he did get drunk and give in, which was unlikely with his conservative personality, he'd decided he wouldn't make it a habit. Before marrying, he knew he had to explain the business to his then fiancée Susan, telling her, "There's gonna be parties. There's gonna be women. I'm never gonna embarrass you. But that's the way things are."

Telling her that was one thing and exposing her was another. One time during the Grand Isle Tarpon Rodeo, a storied big-game fishing tournament and an infamous orgy of prostitution, M. J. and his newly wed bride were on the company houseboat when three oilmen came by and told Minor they couldn't find any women. M. J. and his wife watched his father get on the phone and line up three prostitutes for the clients. Minor then told his son, "Take those three gals and bring them to the camp and stay till they finish." M. J. nodded and looked at his wife, whom he could tell didn't like what was going on, but knew it had to be done.

M. J. realized that she trusted him fully, and, of course, M. J. trusted himself. He knew he could work in the business, still abide by his own ethics, and never turn into his father.

The same could not be said of M. J.'s brother-in-law, Pat Pitre, who initially wanted no part of his father-in-law's company. While he'd fallen in love with Minor's daughter, he was leery of the oilfield. He grew up in a household nothing like the Cheramies'. He observed how Minor was always, always around people, catering to them, ushering to their needs. He watched Minor come home late or not at all.

Growing up, Pat's father, Orleans Pitre, had always come home. The Pitre family had lived a lot like the families in 1950s and 1960s sitcoms such as *The Adventures of Ozzie and Harriet*. While such a lifestyle seemed unlikely in the boating culture of lower Lafourche, where many of the men were gone half the time to trawl or to work in the oilfield, Mr. Pitre was a respected educator, rising from the ranks of teacher and coach to assistant superintendent. His wife was a secretary and housewife. With such steady parents, Pat was used to predictability, not volatility.

He didn't approve of Minor's drinking and cavorting, and he didn't need Minor's money. Minor had the nerve to ask Pat, the son of educated people, to quit school at Nicholls State University and work for him after Pat and Deanie married in November 1970. Pat, of course, refused.

When Minor wanted to give the young couple the house next door to him, Pat's response was, "Yeah, to do what? To tell me you gave it to me so when you want me to do something, you can remind me?"

After Pat and Deanie declined and decided to rent another house, one night Minor showed up at their home intoxicated. Incensed, Pat told him, "The only goddamn thing I wanted from you is your daughter. Nothing else. You didn't have to give me a house and all of this. I don't even want you to come to my house if you're drunk again."

"Pat, I'm sorry," said Minor. "I didn't want to come, but I can't find the bridge. I don't know who to call."

He'd seen the liquored-up and cocky Minor; now he was seeing the slurring, pathetic side of an alcoholic.

Despite's Minor's obvious alcohol-induced flaws, his charisma impressed Pat. He noted how when Minor walked into a place, his presence immediately dominated the room. People stared at him and watched him walk and gesture. He couldn't help but want to see how this man made people follow him and like him. Besides, Pat did need the money. So he decided to work for Minor part-time, which he had done before his marriage. Then when he graduated, he would find his own career and his own way.

A few months into the marriage, things got tough. Pat was only receiving $50 per month from the government for his ROTC scholarship, and between his military obligations and commuting up the bayou to Thibodaux for classes, he didn't have as much time to make side money with the company. Pat decided he had to swallow his pride, quit school, and go to work on the boats. When he told Minor, Minor immediately responded, "No, I want you to finish."

Pat was confused but told him, "Then I'll go work for somebody else."

"You can't do that," said Minor. "You won't get a job on the bayou on the boats. I promise you that."

While Pat believed his father-in-law could blackball him, he also realized how much his father-in-law didn't want him to miss out on what he didn't have—an education. He finally understood how difficult it could be for Minor to spend all this time around executives, legislators, and attorneys with master's and professional degrees while Minor lacked even a high school diploma. The absence of an education really affected Minor.

Ironically, Minor would become one of Pat's most influential educators. Although Pat would take some interesting college classes, although he'd have his share of leadership training in the army, his time working for Minor was very enlightening.

Pat was taken by the man's attention to detail, especially his manic cleanliness. Minor would see a mark on the door and say, "Go get some 409 and clean that smudge." Pat would look at the door and barely be able to detect a spot of any kind. During the fall, Minor would spend the afternoons fishing in the marsh and drinking little pony beer bottles, discarding them into white five-gallon buckets. After he and his clients would fill up six or seven buckets, Minor insisted that those buckets not be only empty and washed out the next day, but Cloroxed until solid white.

Once at the marsh camp, a cheap plastic bowl cracked and Minor made his employee, whom he was paying seven bucks an hour, spend two hours fixing the three dollar bowl. Pat told him, "Minor, it would be cheaper just to buy another one."

"No, Pat, that's not the point."

It also wasn't acceptable for Pat, when working at the camp, to have stained yellow boots. The stains bothered Minor so much that he himself cleaned them with a steel brush, scrubbing them so hard they had holes in them from one end to the other.

Minor, Pat learned, was not afraid of what people thought of his strange ways as long as his method led to a positive result. For instance, Minor installed a phone on his bathroom wall, telling Pat, "You know, just sitting on the toilet, that's where I do my best thinking."

As Minor thought, drank, and fished in peace, Pat, along with his brother-in-law, M. J., learned all about the work it took to keep the clients happy. In the summer, the action was on Grand Isle, at the camp or on the houseboat, culminating during the last weekend in July at the Tarpon Rodeo. In the fall and winter, the entertaining moved to the marsh camp, where Pat and M. J. would work themselves into exhaustion, waking up before dawn to cook breakfast, prepare the pirogues, and take the oilmen hunting. All day long, Pat and M. J. would feed beer, fried trout, and boiled shrimp to the customers, clean ducks and filet redfish, bait the duck ponds, and take clients to hunt and fish. Sometimes at night, they'd run the customers to town. After an evening at the Golden Meadow bars, the oilmen would sometimes get so *cassé* that Pat and

M. J. had to carry them to the dock and pour them into the boat to take them back to the camp.

Also in the fall, Pat, M. J., and Minor, sometimes with the wives, would head out for an LSU football game weekend in Baton Rouge on a Friday night, check in at the Capitol House Hotel, and party all the way through the Saturday night game at Tiger Stadium. On Sunday morning, if the New Orleans Saints were playing, they'd drive more than an hour east to Tulane Stadium, watch the game, and sometimes stay the night at the Monteleone Hotel in the French Quarter. If the Saints weren't at home that week, they'd head to the company's deer camp in the hills north of Baton Rouge near Woodville, Mississippi. Sometimes, they'd throw *boucheries* at the Woodville ranch with the stays turning into four-day drunks where the oilmen would want to hang out all night at the nearby South of the Border Lounge.

During the 1970 Super Bowl, on a cold January day in Tulane Stadium, Pat watched quarterback Lenny Dawson lead the Kansas City Chiefs over the Minnesota Vikings, and after the game, he observed Minor invite seemingly everyone in a French Quarter bar back to his hotel room. Minor had rented his usual corner suite at the Monteleone, which overlooked the river. As the people piled in, Minor was worried about having enough food for them, so he and Pat left the hotel, looking for some groceries. On the street, Minor spotted a Lucky Dog hot dog cart and he told Pat, "Go find out how many hot dogs he got."

The Lucky Dog vendor said he had about six hundred dogs. Pat asked him, "Brother, how much would it take you to come up to the suite with us?"

"Aw, I can't do that," said the vendor.

"Well, how much you want for all the hot dogs?"

"Aw, I can't sell you all the hot dogs."

Minor walked up and told the vendor, "I need them hot dogs."

"It's my best night. I can't miss out on any tips. I can't do it."

Minor offered to buy the cart. The vendor finally gave in and said he could have everything for $1,200.

When Minor accepted, the vendor said, "For that amount, y'all can have me, too."

As the Lucky Dog stand made its way onto the fine marble of the Monteleone's lobby and up the elevator into the suite, Pat watched the vendor beam as he served dog after dog. The man had made the biggest score of his life.

When the party finally ended a day and a half later, Pat told Minor he'd paid too much for the cart.

"But Pat, it's stainless steel," said Minor, who loved anything that didn't rust. Nevertheless, he fell quickly out of love with the shiny cart, selling it to the hotel at a loss in exchange for some credit.

Sometimes, the frenzied partying at the Monteleone would be more than Pat and M. J. could handle. Once during the WorkBoat Show in New Orleans, somewhere around seven hundred people crowded into the suite. Pat and M. J. were trying to simultaneously work the bar, keep the customers happy, and break up fights. They were kicking people out at seven in the morning.

While this year-round partying whirlwind provided some great life experiences for Pat, he decided he'd probably look elsewhere for a career. He would obtain his BS in Agricultural Business from Nicholls and would spend his army tour in hospital administration at Fort Polk. Then, after he would secure his MBA from Nicholls and move into his chosen field. The boat business was interesting and full of surprises, but Pat didn't need all the brouhaha. He'd make his mark elsewhere.

For the time being, Pat's father-in-law was sure enjoying his ride. Minor had long since put his jail time behind him and was experiencing a nice upswing in business. In the office, his manager Woody Terrebonne had the business's finances in order, and on the docks, Butch Danos had the Botrucs gliding all over the Gulf. Of course, there were people on the bayou who said Minor was only making it because of his affiliation with the Mineral Board. That affiliation would almost surely end in 1972 when the new governor would come in and appoint his own man. And sure, Minor knew there were people that predicted he'd finally get his comeuppance when he was no longer on the Mineral Board. Well, they would have to wait and see.

If anyone thought that the North Sea would fail Nolty Theriot, by 1971, those misgivings had vanished. A lull in production at the end of the 1960s hadn't affected Nolty, and in late 1969 when Phillips Petroleum discovered the enormous Ekofisk, a multibillion barrel oilfield off the coast of Norway, Nolty only had to adjust to the move north.

As the Theriot boats pushed the construction barges toward Ekofisk, the captains grew used to long days in the summertime where, sometimes, the sun didn't set. In the wintertime, it was the opposite, with the nights eclipsing the days. Occasionally, while out on the water, the Northern Lights would surreally splash across the sky in swirls of green and dashes of pink and purple, turning everything into a natural kaleidoscope. Some nights, the sky flat rained color, then whipped it, making it appear as if heaven had begun to merge with earth.

Amidst all this natural wonder was a very palpable harshness. In the far north, the air was colder, the winds gustier, the current stronger, and the seas much deeper. If the higher workable wave heights were ten to fifteen feet down south, they were twenty to twenty-five feet in Ekofisk. At times, the captains welcomed a high, hard wave to help unearth the anchor by uppercutting the bottom of the deck and adding just enough force to break it loose. But, as the waves grew past thirty feet, the captains could do without them. In truth, there was no escaping the confrontations.

During Brown & Root's conversion of the three-hundred-foot jack-up rig *Gulftide* into a temporary production facility, Captain Bob Savoie watched in disbelief during a storm when the seas hit the bottom of the rig, which was jacked up *sixty-eight feet* over the waterline. The sixty-foot-plus seas had begun to split the derrick barge. The resulting evacuation was maddening. Captain Bob and his fellow tug skippers had to transfer the workers from the rig and barge, then haul in the barge. Bringing in the barge really meant holding it and hoping it didn't completely break apart before the seas calmed. Between the thrashing waves and the disturbing sound of metal cracking, the noises were frightening. Somehow, despite having to endure the barge's slow and steady rip, they made it into port.

Once, in the same area, Captain Tommie Vizier watched the seas pound a sixty-foot high bridge between two platforms. All he could do was hold his wheel. He knew full well how bad the north could be. He remembered working in the southern sea when bad weather forced him to stop the job. The next morning he'd heard that a German submarine had gone down in the northern sea, killing its passengers. On the same night during the same storm, several fishing vessels had perished. The wave spray hit their cabins and turned instantly to ice, making the vessels so top heavy they capsized, pulling under and killing dozens of people. Eerily, Captain Tommie had heard these fishing captains talking over the radio about the ice. He'd listened helplessly to their cries until they'd lost radio contact.

In the northern sea, fishing vessels went down so frequently that it seemed to be a daily occurrence. The threat of capsizing was always present. Once, Captain Jimmie Vizier got caught in a storm with three other tugs and a pipelay barge. As the designated watch tug, Captain Jimmie ran from side to side, staying two hundred feet off the barge, waiting for the seas to calm so he could get alongside and evacuate more than two hundred crewmen. The other two tugs held the barge as it drifted northward with the current.

Eventually, the wind increased to Force 10 (approximately seventy miles per hour) and the waves began to send the 400-foot barge straight up into the air, sometimes nearly perpendicular to the sea. As the barge threatened to flip, the wave action began to disfigure one of its metal buildings, twisting its big H-beams into junk. Captain Jimmie had never witnessed a sea with such destructive force; he didn't believe the barge would hold up.

The further north the flotilla rocked and crashed, the colder it became. They were slowly being sucked into the Norwegian Sea. If the current continued to push them toward the Arctic Ocean, Captain Jimmie could forget about rescuing anyone.

Just when all appeared to be hopeless, the wind began to die around three hundred miles from the Arctic Circle, and the tugs brought the barge back to safety into Bergen, Norway.

It was storms like these that steered Captain Jimmie and most of the other Cajun boatmen to the Great Yarmouth pubs as soon as they knocked off of their two-week hitch. Despite their seemingly constant heroism, the days of riding steel rodeo bulls began to take their toll. They'd get bleary eyed from dealing with a tricky current that changed every six hours, with the cold, nearly incessant wind, and with waves that were mountains in the north and cliffs in the south.

Even with their immediate families settling in Great Yarmouth, it was hard to live so far from home, to raise kids who couldn't speak French and spoke a British English that their grandparents couldn't begin to understand. Admittedly, the only way many of the captains knew how to deal with their stress was to drown it in mugs of frothy ale and lager.

They had unofficially taken over one of the pubs, the Rumbold Arms, erecting a picture there of the popular Lafourche joke teller, Emmanuel Toups, the owner of Cut Off's Hubba Hubba bar. They'd also imported a jukebox stocked full of Cajun music, and the bar itself was packed with French-speaking expatriots. Still, the Cajuns mixed with their new Norfolk friends, drank the British beer, and played the English games, with Captain Tommie Vizier becoming so good at darts he started winning tournaments.

The Vizier brothers had done so well in the North Sea that they'd pooled their money and built their own 60-foot tug, which they'd hired out in the Gulf of Mexico. If they continued to ride the roll of the North Sea, they believed they could save enough to build a North Sea tug to add to the Theriot fleet.

For the time being, Great Yarmouth had become home for the Vizier families. The place had turned some of their kids' English into that of Little Lord Fauntleroy and Little Miss Muffet. Even Captain Jimmie's speech took on a British tint. In fact, his sentences were such a mixture of accents it was difficult to tell just what and who he was.

Meanwhile, Nolty Theriot had maintained his Cajun accent and his identity, but was broadening his operation. He was officially pulling out of the Gulf of Mexico, leaving Brown & Root's work there to his friend, Otto Candies. As to the rest of the potential business in the Gulf, he saw no reason to pursue those contracts. There were other good people in Louisiana who needed the work.

Nolty was too busy growing his own company, crisscrossing the Atlantic to open up North Sea satellite offices in the green Scottish highlands in Peterhead and among the fir-studded fjords in Stavanger, Norway. He hopped around Europe, visiting with Brown & Root officials in London, calling on an increasing number of European oilfield contractors in the Netherlands, France, and Italy, and sometimes checking on the repair of his working vessels in the naval yard at Bremerhaven, Germany.

Collectively, the North Sea contractors continued to demand more tugs than Nolty owned or could possibly build. To that end, he formed a brokerage group, Offshore Tugs, Inc., on April 8, 1971, and brokered as many boats as he could, including one from his friend, Galliano resident Tomey Doucet.

While the brokering made good economic sense, Nolty's decision to give shares in Offshore Tugs to Doucet and to his key employees, Charlie Sanders and Robert Alario, seemed to be overly generous. Nolty also took some of his own tugs that were working directly for the client contractor and ran them through Offshore Tugs, so Doucet, Sanders, and Robert could share in their profits. Robert told Nolty the unnecessary charity was a mistake. "This doesn't make sense," he said. "You have a hundred percent family-controlled corporation, and you are taking work out of it and putting the boats to work through Offshore Tugs and basically paying somebody else off of *your* boat?"

Nolty only smiled. It was his way of rewarding his loyal friends and employees. In fact, the more the money poured in, the more Nolty spread the wealth. During an audit one year, CPA Dan Carroll noticed that Nolty was buying large quantities of bread and milk from a little grocery down the street in Golden Meadow. He asked him, "Nolty, why are you buying all the milk and bread from the store down here at retail? I bet if you went to the dairy and if you went to the bakery, they would sell it to you at wholesale."

Nolty grew serious, looked Carroll in the eye, and told him, "Dan, those people carried me when I was broke. Sometimes for six months at a time, they'd carry me. I'm not about to change now that I have money."

Nolty rewarded all of his loyal suppliers by staying with them even when it was obvious they couldn't offer a competitive price, even when his advisors would show him how he could save 20 percent if he just paid the market rate. In the end, Nolty didn't want that extra 20 percent, and whether his old suppliers needed it didn't matter. It was payback. It was what he thought was right.

Nolty also believed he should give as much as he could to the Catholic Church, to which his loyalty was immeasurable, even though his relationship with the Church was kind of complicated. Officially, he believed he was excommunicated because of his business affiliation with the Masons.

This conflict with his Masonic membership didn't stop him from doing whatever he could for the Church. At the time, the local parish had to turn over a large percentage of its collections to the Archdiocese, and this frustrated the Our Lady of Prompt Succor pastor and parishioners. To raise money solely for the parish, Nolty helped organize the Bull Club, which held a yearly auction at the Blessing of the Fleet parish fair, where he and many of the boatmen like Bobby Orgeron and Minor Cheramie would try to outbid each other. These men refused to compete against each other when it came to their clients, but the auctions were no-holds-barred.

Once, Nolty paid $25,000 for a gate to a park. On another occasion, he ponied up $10,000 for a live monkey. On another, he paid a few thousand dollars for a stuffed donkey.

While Nolty showered the parish with money, he also contributed to the Archdiocese. He and Archbishop Philip Hannan had become friends and shared the common bond of both being members of airborne regiments during World War II. Although they never met during the war, when Nolty was shot, Archbishop Hannan was also in the Ardennes area serving as a chaplain. Eventually, the two met in New Orleans, and the archbishop learned he could always count on Nolty for a needed donation or for a favor.

When it came to Nolty's employees, he was also generous. If his bookkeepers came to him with a questionable expense on a bar tab with no clients present or for some tool that was probably for personal use, Nolty typically let it go. The expense might have troubled his accountants, but Nolty just shrugged. He didn't want the money. If anything, it was a method for him to give some more of it away.

Every Thanksgiving, he invited over his in-laws, the Alario clan, for a big dinner and made it a habit to stick an envelope under his brothers-in-law's and sisters-in-law's plates. Usually, he stuffed the envelopes with $5,000 in cold cash.

After one Thanksgiving, he told his wife, "I wish it was as much fun for them to receive as it is for me to give."

While Nolty had no interest in making money for money's sake, he was obsessed with growing his fleet and frustrated that he *still* couldn't maximize the North Sea's demand. In 1971, he found an unlikely broker prospect in his friend, Dick Guidry, his district's colorful state representative from Galliano. Dick was the same man who, as a boy, had saved the Nazi-sympathizing parish priest from a lynch mob.

When Nolty told people about his potential relationship with Dick's fledgling American Offshore, Inc., some rolled their eyes. If Nolty thought he was going to grow in the North Sea through Dick Guidry, they'd have to watch that happen.

For one thing, while Dick was a certified high roller, he was a tugboat novice who knew very little about the actual running and building of boats. For another, he'd gone broke four times.

Although Dick had proved he could lose his arse in several businesses, he'd also been resourceful enough to rebuild himself after each failure, and he'd been productive enough in the legislature to get elected three times. With that kind of up-and-down track record, it was difficult to know what to make of Dick Guidry. Of course, Nolty knew all about wavering track records, and he sure recognized a kindred gambler when he saw one. With vessel demand at an all-time high, if Dick wanted to play a little tugboat *bourrée*, Nolty was game.

One thing about Dick Guidry was certain—he'd come from good business stock. Dick's father was John L. Guidry, a community leader who had owned the village center of Galliano, including the all-important bridge, general store, ice cream parlor, saloon, café, movie theater, baseball field, boarding house, a couple dozen rental houses, and a small dairy farm. Mr. Guidry had also operated a grocery boat back in the 1940s, which he'd take on two-week runs to sell salt meat, beans, rice, canned goods, and coal sacks to trappers in the marsh during the winter. The long boat was all cabin with almost no deck and was unusually slight, needing to be narrow enough to fit through the marsh canals. Young Dick would often accompany his dad on trips that covered the marshes from Morgan City all the way to Loyola Drive in the New Orleans area.

From a very early age, Dick worked a variety of jobs for his father's operation. He'd get up in the morning and milk the cows, then do various chores before and after school, including bartering with trappers in the store, waiting tables at the café, sweeping and mopping the saloon, and jerking soda in the ice cream parlor. During baseball season, he'd sell beer and soft drinks in the stands for the semipro team that played in the Sugar Belt League. He had so loathed lugging the heavy crates of bottles in the hot sun that he grew to hate all sports and, years later, couldn't even remember the name of the team that his father owned.

In the warmer months, when the crabs were running on Grand Isle, he'd ride to the island with his family on Fridays, and they'd catch a pickup truck full of crabs to bring back to the bar for a free Friday night crab boil, knowing the salty, spicy meat would make patrons buy beer. Selling beer, ice cream, and other cheap consumables was the only way to generate daily cash because most of the store's patrons bought goods by bartering (usually fur pelts) and through credit.

All the daily dealing, hard labor, and constant movement made Dick grow up fast. He first took the wheel of a car at age nine, and by his junior year at Golden Meadow High, he was already taking his father to the bank to cosign a loan to buy real estate. He acquired a forty- by one-arpent tract and subdivided it, needing his father's signature to sell the lots since he was not yet eighteen. He could hardly believe that people would pay $500 for a small lot when they could have had the whole forty-arpent tract for $4,000. Then he realized the reason: they could easily raise the $500, but had no idea how to borrow $4,000. It suddenly occurred to Dick that business was all about borrowing power. He did well in the real estate venture, selling enough lots to quickly pay off the note and buy a car to drive during his freshman year at LSU.

There weren't many cars at LSU in 1947, and having one made Dick popular on campus. But, the sedentary lifestyle of a student did not fit Dick's personality, and he left school before the end of the first semester. He came back home, rustled up four investors, and built the Jet Drive-in

Theater. Then, in 1951, at age twenty-two, he ran for the state legislature and won. Two years after losing his seat in 1956 he headed up to Kentucky and successfully drilled some wildcat wells.

A wildcat was exactly what Dick Guidry would become, starting a pattern of drilling stretches of good holes, then dry ones, opening and closing movie theaters, winning and losing his seat in the legislature, gaining and alienating investors and voters, getting rich and going broke, rising every morning with wide open eyes at 3:00 a.m. and hardly sleeping at night, running the roads and sometimes steering his car into the bayou.

Once, in the 1960s, Dick bought a Cadillac that featured something he'd never seen on an automobile, straps that went across the driver's and passengers' laps and, disturbingly, *locked.* He pointed at these strange locking belts and asked the salesman, "What the hell are those?"

"Those are seatbelts, Mr. Guidry."

"Take 'em out."

"Oh, Mr. Guidry, I can't take 'em out."

"You gotta take 'em out. You ever tried to swim in Bayou Lafourche with a Cadillac strapped around your waist?"

Luckily, Dick had always managed literally and figuratively to swim out of murky waters. While he'd bottomed out financially four times, he would somehow bounce back and convince someone else to loan him money.

One of those loans financed Dick's entry into the tugboat business in the mid-1960s, first partnering with Andrew Martin. From there, he maneuvered his way in and out of boat deals, buying into partnerships and selling out of them, picking up investors and paying them off, running his tugs all over the Gulf and the Caribbean, in and out of Venezuela and the Bahamas, until Nolty Theriot had approached him with Nolty's North Sea needs.

When Dick learned that he could earn $8,600 per day for a tug, albeit an expensive one to build, it was an easy decision. He'd build some tugs and feed them to Nolty's fleet. How would he raise the money? He would find a way; he was, after all, Dick Guidry, the political fox, the boy barterer, the wildcat on the water. Because of his talent for wheeling and whirling, Nolty would have his tugs.

Ultimately, Nolty's instincts about Dick Guidry were correct. Dick did start sending him tugboats, eventually growing the Theriot fleet by six. In order to meet the international demands of Brown & Root and foreign pipeline contractors, Nolty still needed to build more boats. A new North Sea tug was like a mini US mint; it was as if she was spitting dollars from her propulsion system to the tune of up to $12,000 per day, with the oil company picking up all of the boat's fuel and lube and any underwater damage.

This was more money than Nolty could spend. He'd built a cavernous, California-style yellow-brick ranch house on Highway 308 in Galliano. The place had three full kitchens, seven phone lines, and a walk-in closet stocked with Rubenstein Brothers suits. He'd also put in a swimming pool behind his camp on Grand Isle, a place where there were hardly any pools. He bought two planes, one for the Americas and one for Europe, a new yacht, and God knows how many cars.

Despite having more creature comforts than he needed, he wanted to grow faster simply for growth's sake, and now, flush with the Title 11 loan money, he was trying to produce as many boats as he could. He needed to build them because the shipyard availability was high due to the slumping US oilfield. If the market turned, the shipyards would fill up fast, meaning Nolty might not be able to meet his loan's projections, which depended on new tugs being christened by certain deadlines.

While Nolty's top envoy, Robert Alario, continued to manage the company's financing, he was also busy handling other matters. During this period, Robert met frequently with the Coast Guard, his biggest issue being the agency's new requirement that captains sit for written licensing exams, a rule that hurt Theriot because some of its skippers were illiterate. Although these same captains could handle a vessel better than almost any full master Coast Guard Academy graduate, their inability to read and write threatened their livelihoods. The rule would also create a serious captain shortage in the workboat industry. Robert met with the Coast Guard hierarchy in Washington and convinced them to give the captains oral examinations and, if necessary, to provide a French translator.

When Robert wasn't hammering out administrative matters, he was globe-trotting and stamping out all sorts of problems. Sometimes, he ran diplomatic interference for Nolty's clients. Once, Gulf Oil had hired Brown & Root to build a pipeline off the coast of the Japanese island of Okinawa, but the Japanese were reluctant to grant a business license to the American entities.

Nolty sent Robert to Okinawa to investigate the problem. Robert learned that the Japanese, who had a rich seafaring culture, thought that their own companies could handle the work. Robert believed it boiled down to a matter of Japanese pride and nationalism—while the American occupation of Japan ended in 1952, control over Okinawa would not officially revert back to the Japanese until 1972 and, even then, the United States continued to maintain a large military presence on the island. Robert knew that the Japanese, although excellent mariners, had no pipelaying experience and could in no way handle this job without Theriot's assistance. He was careful, however, not to offend them in his initial meeting. He asked questions, made very few declarations, and mostly listened.

He then flew to Great Yarmouth and asked the Theriot captains for any film footage they had of their North Sea anchor handling. He edited the film, splicing together the scenes with the most violent seas, and hired a Japanese-speaking American to be the narrator. When he showed the film to the Japanese officials, their eyes popped open. The Japanese would admit that anchor handling was much more complex and dangerous than they realized. They acknowledged that until the Japanese captains learned how to handle anchors, they needed the Theriot boats to do the work. Consequently, they granted the license to Nolty J. Theriot, Inc., creating the strange circumstance of the oil company and the contractor working through the tugboat company's license.

As Theriot's tugs moved from the East China Sea to the drug-ridden Pacific waters of Colombia and around the South American continent to Brazil, as they sailed up to Taiwan and down to Singapore, as they motored from the Persian Gulf to the warring shores of Africa, Robert continued to ease their diplomatic path. During a pipelaying job off the coast of the tiny West African republic of Cabinda, a breakaway province of Angola, a Brown & Root vessel had a breakdown and needed parts from the United States. There was no time to apply for a visa, so Brown & Root called Nolty, who dispatched Robert, who grabbed two suitcases so full of parts that he could barely lift them and hopped on a plane to Lisbon, Portugal, then connected to Luanda, Angola. In Angola, he learned he that couldn't get into neighboring Cabinda, where there was a civil war. Apparently, it would take him three weeks to secure a plane that would cross the border.

At the airport, Robert walked around and asked questions, then saw people waiting in line for a plane. He discovered that they worked for Chicago Bridge and Iron, and they were scheduled to take a charter flight into Cabinda the very next day. Robert jumped in line, posed as a Chicago Bridge and Iron worker, and reserved a seat on the flight. But, because he wasn't staying at the same hotel as the Chicago Bridge and Iron workers, he wasn't informed of a change in flight time, and he missed the takeoff.

Desperate, Robert racked his brain and remembered that during his service in Africa with Texaco, he'd met the local chief of police in Luanda. They'd gotten along well. Robert called the chief's office and, sure enough, the chief remembered him and used his connections to book Robert a flight. Later, as Robert was about to board the plane, the handle fell off on one of his suitcases.

The police opened it, saw all of the metal parts, and took him to a back room. They didn't believe Robert's story about the metal implements being oilfield parts. Robert asked them to call their chief, and when they did, to his great relief, he finally was allowed to board the plane.

In Cabinda, he met another Texaco connection at the airport, who smoothly escorted Robert and his suitcases to Brown & Root. After making the delivery, it took Robert a few days to find a flight out of the country. The first one he could secure was on a small Piper cub with a welder who'd been badly burned and was wrapped up like a mummy. After taking off from a gravel runway cut out of a sugarcane field, the pilot made a hard turn and threw the injured welder into the side of the plane onto his burns. The welder started screaming.

Robert asked the pilot, "*Qu'est-ce qui se passe?*"

The pilot said in French, "Every time we leave here, they shoot. Machine gun fire."

Right about that time, Robert heard it—tat-tat-tat-tat, tat-tat-tat-tat. The rebels were shooting at them. The pilot gunned the plane toward the ocean, explaining that if he crashed, he'd rather go down in the sea and contend with the sharks than land in the Congo because in the jungle, the rebels would kill them.

Eventually, the pilot escaped the gunfire. It wouldn't be the last time West Africans aimed their guns at Robert. He also once escaped flying bullets when trying to get out of Escravos, Nigeria, in a helicopter.

After a while, the abnormal became the normal for Robert Alario. If he wasn't finagling his way in and out of a banana republic, he was negotiating a deal in a palatial London office with a member of the inconceivably wealthy Rothschild family. With all of Robert's international dealings, sitting across the table from a high-ranking Rothschild representative was an eye-blinking, dreamlike experience.

He had obviously caught the Rothschilds at a good time. They wanted in on the North Sea workboat business, and Robert was convincing them to go in through Theriot on a supply boat deal. He was aligning his brother-in-law's little coonass boat company with one of the greatest financial resources in Europe. For now, they'd build world-record-sized supply boats, 220 feet in length with seven thousand horses under the deck. Theriot would build the British-flagged boats with Rothschild's money, but Theriot's captains would operate them. With Rothschild's backing, Robert could now help Nolty J. Theriot, Inc. expand into all kinds of things. With the Rothschilds aboard, one day, Theriot wouldn't even need Title 11.

Just as Robert was shaking hands with a cuff-linked Rothschild executive in London, the next moment, he was back in Louisiana, shaking his head over an expense request for a set of false teeth. As Robert reviewed the requisition, which was submitted by a Theriot engineer, he couldn't help but laugh. Things were really getting wacky. He called the engineer, who was back home after a stint in the North Sea, and asked him to come to his office.

When the engineer walked in with a brand-new set of chompers, Robert held up the expense sheet and asked him, "What the hell is this? Why should I be paying you for a set of false teeth?"

The engineer took a deep breath and told him the story. He'd been standing in the pilothouse in a rough sea, when a wave blasted over the bow and broke straight through the pilothouse windows. The water struck the engineer and washed him into the gangway. As he bounced like a pinball from wall to wall, from the handrail to the steps, his mouth made contact with something, and the impact knocked out his teeth. He ended up dazed and toothless all the way down in the engine room.

Robert waited until the engineer finished, then said, "Even if that story's not true, it's worth a set of false teeth."

The stories from the North Sea kept making their way across the Atlantic. It seemed like there was one dramatic rescue after another. Of all the tales told to Robert, few, if any, topped what happened to Captain Whitey Adams who, only in his thirties, already had the swagger of a grizzled old mariner.

In the middle of the night at Ekofisk, Captain Whitey, who still refused to step on an airplane, was commanding his 140-foot tug in a rainy, forty-foot North Sea. When he heard over the radio that a British supply vessel was sinking next to a rig near him, he pointed his tug in her direction and pushed down her throttles.

Pulling up to the rig, Captain Whitey noticed that all of the crewmembers, who were mostly Norwegian, were clinging to a life raft, popping around in the waves. On the supply boat, the captain was still onboard, perhaps minutes from sinking with his ship.

Captain Whitey knew right away he couldn't get close enough to the vessel to make a deck-to-deck transfer. He directed his crew to throw the captain a line, and they pulled him through the waves, reeling him in like a big fish. When the Norwegian skipper greeted Captain Whitey, he hugged him, then fainted.

Captain Whitey then looked at the life raft with fifteen men clutching her side. He knew that he had to get alongside of the raft, but how could he judge a raft in a forty-foot sea? If he didn't hold her just right, his hull could land on top of them and kill them all. Even if he made no technical errors, a rogue wave or a jolt of current could do them in.

Somehow, he eased in and saved all fifteen crewmen, with his Spanish deckhands hurling them aboard to safety.

When the weather calmed, he took the spent men into Stavanger. Like his crew, all he wanted was to rest. As the boat entered port, he saw a crowd of people at the dock. They were pointing at his boat and cheering. By the time he tied up and disembarked, he could hear music. He could see brass instruments reflecting the sun, moving up and down, sliding in and out. Apparently, all of these trumpets, trombones, and pretty blond Scandinavian women were there in his boat's honor.

As Captain Whitey and the sailors made their way into the crowds, he thought that the locals were just happy to see the survivors. In the days that followed, he realized that these people actually thought that *he* was a hero. He was told the Norwegians wanted to give him some kind of medal or plaque, as did the US embassy, the British embassy, and Phillips Petroleum.

Captain Whitey could've done without the fanfare and the hardware. He didn't want to wear a coat and tie and make a speech. He didn't feel comfortable enough with his English to speak it to a crowd. Despite his English surname, Whitey Adams was one of those Cajuns that spoke French at every opportunity and had never mastered English. Luckily, the company would send Robert Alario to translate for him.

As Robert whisked him around Norway, Captain Whitey looked into crowds full of blue eyes and athletic figures, and he did his best to thank them for the honor, letting Robert translate it into his genteel English.

By the final speech at the last embassy or park or square or wherever he was, Whitey's tie was starting to strangle him. His collar was chafing badly and his shoulders were stiff. He and Robert took the podium and Robert asked him what he wanted to say. In his sharpest *Cadien*, Whitey told him, "*Mais* you tell them this. The next damn time I'm out there doing my job, and I get a call that somebody's sinking, and if it means I have to make one more *maudit* speech and wear a *cravat*, those sons of bitches are going down because I'm not going in."

Robert started laughing. He translated the message to the crowd, who roared.

When Nolty Theriot heard the story, he cracked up, too. He needed the laugh. While he was enjoying his success, at times, the demands of his evermore international company was hell on his already impaired stomach. He was tiring from his transoceanic jet lag, and from keeping track of all of his current jobs and his boats being repaired and built in far-flung shipyards. Back in the good old days, he could build and repair his own boats in the woods to his own damn specifications. Now he had to meet the standards of the American Bureau of Shipping, the US Coast Guard, the Norwegian Det Norse Veritas, and the British DTS.

As much paperwork as those shipping nitpickers created, the Mar Ad was worse. The Title 11 loans were getting to be a headache. Although they were making his growth possible, they contained dozens of annoying covenants. He hated legalese and would just as soon forget about it and tell Robert Alario and his accountants and lawyers, "Don't worry about nothing." Which is exactly what he told them, but still, they'd stand their ground.

Of course, Nolty realized he had to follow these covenants. That meant if he wanted a pleasure yacht to entertain his clients and to go fishing, he couldn't buy it with Title 11 money. He was also limited in what he could personally draw out of the company, and that wasn't going to work. So his boys had had to figure out a way around the restrictions, with CPA Dan Carroll advising him to borrow the funds for two new tugs himself. He could own them personally and buy his yacht and make a cool $300,000 in annual personal spending money. Still, these covenants were always telling him he couldn't do something, and no one could tell him that.

What was compounding Nolty's stomachache was a problem with his European manager in Great Yarmouth. His boys in the North Sea, his crack port captains and his matador skippers, didn't like the man in charge, and his men had always come first. But Nolty couldn't take the man's place himself. He didn't mind visiting Europe, but he had to keep his home base on the bayou.

Thinking about possible replacements, Nolty considered his eldest child and his only son, Pye. Pye was about to graduate from Nicholls State University with a business degree and get married to the lovely Janet Bergeron of Crowley. Pye and Janet could leave for Great Yarmouth after their wedding in January 1973. One day, the company would belong to Pye anyway. This was a good way to roll him right into it. And what a honeymoon, huh? On Pye's time off, he and his wife could spend long weekends touring Europe. Pye would be delighted.

❀

Actually, Pye was shocked. In truth, he didn't want anything to do with the tugboat business. He didn't like the industry's swings, which he'd seen too many of growing up. While his father's motto had always been "every day is Christmas," the truth was Santa Claus didn't slide down the chimney every night at the Theriot home. Pye remembered as a boy how things would get tense around the house when the company was doing poorly. He could feel the tension in his own stomach, too. Yes, he also had inherited the Theriot *ventre*, and when the air at home was close and hot, he felt it, developing ulcers as early as grammar school.

Of course, the times would always get better, and Pye appreciated his father's attempt to hide his financial problems from his family. Whenever possible, Nolty doted on his kids. For Pye's and his sister's birthdays, they'd go into New Orleans and eat at the Roosevelt Hotel or Bali Hai, the Polynesian restaurant at Pontchartrain Beach. He took them to the camp at Grand Isle, where they spent heavenly summers bronzing their skin, running barefoot in the sand chasing toodaloo crabs, and catching ice chests full of speckled trout.

But, for every full, bright, and sunny summer, there was an empty, dark, and cold February. Pye recalled his mother saving money by cutting her kids' hair herself instead of sending them to the barber. Pye might have been only a young teen but he understood that if his parents couldn't afford a haircut, things had to be bad. As he grew older, he would sometimes help with the company's bookkeeping. He'd never forget the sight of that big Burroughs, the tank of an accounting machine, spitting out red ink. The world might've heard Nolty say, "Don't worry about nothing," but at home, Pye had seen his daddy sweat.

He also didn't see his father that often. The business had kept Nolty on the road. It kept him out late at night. When he'd been at home, he was a good daddy, but he hadn't been home nearly enough.

Sure, Pye understood that people assumed that he would one day step right into his father's office. In fact, Pye looked like a cross between his father and his uncle Robert Alario; with looks like that, he was born for the business. Despite all this, Pye had never thought he'd be a boatman. Instead, he'd been busy carving out his own niche. He was about to graduate from college and continue a career that he'd recently started. At age twenty-three, Pye was already what he'd dreamed of becoming—a politician. He was easily the youngest member of the Lafourche Parish Police Jury, what might have been called in other places a county commission. Pye hoped his police jury service was the start to a career that ended in a high place in Baton Rouge or Washington, DC, but for the time being, he was already living his dream.

During Pye's childhood, politics had bedazzled him. On Sunday afternoons, he'd religiously listen to local state senator A. O. Rappelet's dramatic radio speeches in French, chastising his real or imaginary opponent. Pye loved going to stump meetings to hear the showboating local politicos like Dick Guidry and longtime Lafourche sheriff Eddie St. Marie.

To Pye, the political scene was all pageantry, romance, and intense competition, which was in sharp contrast to his view of the boat business—an uninteresting, ulcer-inducing, day-to-day grind. While his father didn't really compete with his fellow boatmen, he fought like hell against them politically. When it came to politics, Nolty had even battled his family. During the 1964 gubernatorial election, Nolty supported Chep Morrison, while his uncle, Leo Theriot, was John McKeithen's local campaign manager. Supporting his father's candidate, Pye had poured himself into working the phone banks.

Pye didn't mind any of the work generated by politics; to him, it was all action and excitement. When he ran for police juror, he'd thrown himself into the race, which he wasn't supposed to win as an unknown college student. He did whatever it took, such as writing campaign speeches in English and translating another version in French, a language he understood, but was not used to speaking. He slapped backs at a baby *gros bec* supper at Nelson's Bar at the Pointe au Saucisse. He turned an old Theriot crew change Suburban into a sound truck and drove from lane to lane, passing out cold drinks and shouting over the loudspeaker, "Vote for Pye Theriot."

After he got elected, Pye's first job was one of espionage. At the request of his south Lafourche betters, he began spying on the north Lafourche power brokers. This was a crucial mission because the northern and southern parts of the elongated parish were constantly battling over the distribution of the parish's dollars. The north had the parish seat in Thibodaux, a university, the big hospital, a large professional community, sugar mills, an agricultural equipment plant, a candy factory, and a more-educated populace. Conversely, the south was the undereducated underdog, the rougher-cut world of oil, boat building, and seafood. Between these two extremes was a thirty-mile-long middle ground that could swing either way.

Fortunately for Pye, the northern chiefs didn't know what he looked like. Every morning, Pye would head up the bayou and, before class at Nicholls, he'd eat breakfast just off campus at the Pitt Grill with his back to Harvey Peltier Jr., a state senator and the son of the parish's most powerful man. He'd listen to Peltier and his gang talk about plans for current and upcoming campaigns, police jury issues, and potential appointments to levee boards and other political positions. Then, every evening, Pye would give his report to his south Lafourche elders.

The workings of the police jury itself fascinated Pye. The jurors, including the north Lafourche contingent (who didn't eat breakfast at the Pitt Grill), were the epitome of gentlemen politicians. While the older jurors had taken Pye under their wing, they'd also put him in charge of the Solid Waste Committee. At the time, few people understood what solid waste was, but once Pye learned, he didn't care if they threw him into a pile of garbage, as long as he was holding a public office.

Serving his constituents, taking their phone calls, eavesdropping at the Pitt Grill, meeting interesting people up and down the bayou, Pye was having the most fun he'd ever had in his life.

This was why he was torn when his father asked him to take over in Great Yarmouth. He'd have to give up his police jury seat and live across the ocean from his political base. In Pye's mind, he didn't have a choice. This was a family business, and he was the only son. He saw his father's tiring eyes and the deepening lines in his forty-eight-year-old face. The old man's dark complexion wasn't as smooth as it had been a few years ago. Pye couldn't stand the thought of his father having to take over in Great Yarmouth, not with the company's boats now being built in shipyards from Seattle to New Orleans, being repaired in Germany, and with the active boats handling anchors across the globe.

Eventually, Pye decided to look at the positives. He remembered the excitement of his first long trip away from home. He'd visited the Theriot operation in Okinawa, and the experience had blown him away.

From the Japanese architecture and culture to the impressive US Naval base to the way Brown & Root had wined and dined him, the trip had awed him. If Europe was anything like that, he would surely have a good time.

So, he told his father he'd take the job, never expressing his reservations, never telling Nolty how much it hurt him to put off his political career. He didn't want his father to know that he loathed the tugboat business. He only shook his father's hand and smiled.

As Pye's hiring signified a changing of the Theriot guard in Great Yarmouth, in Baton Rouge, the state's mineral bureaucracy was also undergoing transformation. In 1972, as Edwin Edwards rolled into the Louisiana governor's mansion, Minor Cheramie presumed he was going to roll off the Mineral Board. His fellow Lafourche boatman, Andrew Martin, had been a dedicated Edwards supporter and Minor assumed Martin would take his seat.

That is why Minor was shocked when one of Edwards's lieutenants approached him at his Woodville ranch and offered him a seat on the board, but the offer came with a price. Minor would have to give the man, who was in the insurance industry, half of L & M's insurance business plus a cash payment of $20,000.

As Minor absorbed the man's words, he didn't think about the bribe or about the fact that if he accepted such an offer, his company's insurance premiums would probably rise significantly. His only thought was for his friend Andrew Martin.

"What about Andrew?" he asked the Edwards's lieutenant. "That's the position Andrew wants."

"Andrew's gonna take what we give him," the man said.

Minor couldn't believe it. He later told the man, "If that's the way y'all treat your friends, I don't want to have nothing to do with y'all."

While Minor never asked Edwards personally about the offer, he was confident the new governor had acquiesced to the deal. Minor decided at that point, that unlike most Cajuns, he would not support Edwards.

The matter became even more confusing when Martin took Minor's seat and promptly removed the picture of the Cheramie Botruc that was hanging prominently in the board's office. After that gesture, Minor severed his ties with Martin, too.

Whatever Martin and the Mineral Board were doing, Minor knew he'd lost his influence in Baton Rouge. The positive was that he could trade his fancy vestments for jumpsuits and coveralls; he liked his new clothes so much he would sometimes wear a jumpsuit to a formal boat loan closing in New Orleans. He could also forget about the formalities of the Capitol House Hotel and concentrate on his camps, taking a break from all the politicos and focusing on oilmen and his friends.

But 1972 was not a good time to be losing leverage in the oilfield. While in the North Sea, Nolty Theriot was enjoying the fruits of Ekofisk and couldn't build enough boats, things weren't nearly as good in the Gulf of Mexico, which couldn't approach the low Middle Eastern prices and had turned into a workboat regatta with many of the boats at the dock waiting for a job offshore. Although Minor would have liked to have had more than his fourteen Botrucs, he couldn't exactly shift the oilfield demand the way the Federal Reserve chairman changed the interest rate. All he could do was keep his boats clean and his clients satiated and hope the Gulf oilfield would revive.

Despite this difficult period, the unwritten Code of not poaching clients was still in effect among the boatmen. Bobby Orgeron sure saw no reason to break it, but he did notice that one company was clearly doing business in a different way. By 1972, the public Tidewater had grown so large it didn't remotely resemble the independents. The company had more than 350 vessels and had diversified by acquiring a large gas compression company. With all of those boats, Tidewater had to find a place for them and couldn't be expected to live by the same Code as the independents.

That didn't mean Bobby had to like what Tidewater was doing. While he and his friends were undereducated Cajuns who were personally liable for all of their debts, Tidewater was a giant backed by stock exchange capital and run by New Orleans attorney John Laborde.

Laborde's brother was Doc Laborde, an engineer and the founder and head of ODECO Drilling. Because of the Laborde connection, ODECO offered Tidewater a built-in client. Though the Labordes had French surnames and were originally from the French-speaking parish of Avoyelles, Bobby didn't view them as humble Cajuns. They were, to him, big-city corporate bulldogs trying to take business away from the little man. He seethed when Tidewater cut its price to move in on a client that he saw as belonging to one of the independents. During these instances, he'd look at John Laborde as John D. Rockefeller and Tidewater as the Standard Oil of the boat business.

Of course, the Labordes were just trying to live out the American ideal of market dominance. But, Bobby wondered how much money the Labordes needed to make. Didn't they understand there was enough for everybody to make millions? If Tidewater continued to slash prices and take jobs, they'd run the little man out of the oilfield. What pleasure was there in that?

On the positive side, Tidewater's position as a threatening monopoly gave Bobby a new sales angle. He'd tell the oil companies, "Hey, I'm a little boat owner. I started with one little crew boat and tried to be successful. And come on, you know you gotta buck these big dogs." Sometimes, his underdog pitch helped get him a contract.

But in 1972, his sales pitches were losing their effectiveness. It wasn't that Tidewater was moving in on his clients; his real problem was that the available contracts were few and far between.

Chapter 15

The Contract

April 22, 1972

As the oilfield wreaked its havoc, for at least one weekend, Bobby was chasing peace. One cool spring day, he was driving and, as usual, burying the needle. He was flying down a straight shot of concrete, listening to his tires click over the joints in the bridge, the Lake Pontchartrain Causeway, which Bobby had turned into a twenty-two-mile-long elevated drag strip.

As the lake's blue expanse blurred, he could exhale and be himself. He didn't have to worry about entertaining his passengers. For once, they were not his clients. Better yet, he knew his passengers felt the same way. They could be themselves, too.

Bobby was with his fellow bayou boat barons, Nolty Theriot, Anthony Guilbeau, Albert Cheramie, Morris Rebstock, Tomey Doucet, and Earl Rome. They were booking it toward a Catholic retreat, of all things. For a couple of days, they wouldn't think about the oilfield. They didn't plan to contemplate anything too deeply. They certainly didn't intend to ponder the mysteries of self or of religion. They had a stash of Scotch in the trunk, and they would drink every last fiery drop of it.

For Bobby, Nolty, and the boys, this was the only way to get away. Otherwise, they couldn't throw a party without inviting oilmen. They couldn't have a nonbusiness outing without taking their wives.

239

For once, Bobby wasn't beholden to anyone. He could do or say whatever he wanted and not worry about it, and his actions would have no financial or familial consequences. When he arrived at the Regina Coeli Retreat Center in the dry piney woods in Covington, he could drink the Scotch and forget about the oily world south of the lake.

Bobby was making something called a "Cursillo." He didn't know what Cursillo meant. He had some idea that it was the Catholic version of evangelization, but Catholics didn't really evangelize. They didn't hold revivals; that was for the Bible-beaters. That was for the down-on-their-luck Baptists and Pentacostals looking for some fundamental brimstone that said if they followed the rules, they'd elevate their lives and climb to a special plateau.

Bobby didn't need salvation. He went to Mass every Sunday. He said his prayers. That was enough.

He and the others had told their wives they were going to Cursillo, and the wives loved it. They all had a mutual friend that went to one of these things and quit drinking.

Of course, Bobby, Nolty, and all had another plan. They were anticipating its execution as they turned off the highway into the tranquil Regina Coeli estate. As they motored through the tall pine trees, Bobby could feel his shoulders relax. This place was peaceful, different. He could already taste the whiskey. He could hear the jokes they were gonna tell in their dorm room.

The first event, the retreat general assembly, was just a formality. As soon as they left the building, they'd grab the Scotch. But when the Jesuit priest took the podium, he immediately clutched the audience. Bobby's first impression was "weirdo." The priest had a strange, unnerving look in his eyes, and Bobby could feel the audience, one hundred or so grown men, shift and stiffen. Bobby's relaxed shoulders started to harden.

The priest started talking about his life before he became a man of the cloth. He made confessions about his own drinking and sinning and painted a grim picture. The man was so honest, his emotions so raw, that the audience could feel his struggle. He talked about his calling to become a priest, his decision to quit drinking. As he told of his character change, he moved the audience, transferring his emotion to them.

When the priests asked the people to come up and tell their stories, Bobby experienced an odd feeling. He wanted to leave his seat and at the same time was clinging to it.

The first audience member walked to the front and spoke into the microphone. He told them about the horrible things he'd done. Bobby didn't think these things were anywhere near as bad as his own sins. But still, the man was confessing. Bobby looked at his friends, who appeared to be as startled as he was. None of them knew that they were walking into an open confessional.

Before they knew it, there they went. The boat barons were taking the stage, one after the other. When Nolty Theriot left his chair, Bobby said to himself, "So help me God." As he listened to his friend pour out his soul, Bobby's eyes jumped out of his head. It wasn't that he was aghast at what Nolty had done. He just couldn't believe he was telling his sinful story to a priest and a room full of strangers.

Bobby realized he had to go. Until his butt left his chair, he didn't think he'd do it. He didn't even like to admit his sins to himself. How could he deliver them to a bunch of judgmental faces? But he did, divulging everything sinful he'd ever done in his life. He talked about his chemical consumption and his womanizing. Everything that popped into his mind came out of his mouth. As he wrapped up his story, he had tears in his eyes.

By this point, almost everyone in the audience was crying. When Bobby stepped off the stage, he couldn't take it. He had to get out of the building. He had to take a walk in the dark woods and collect himself. Outside, he paused to wipe his eyes, then looked up and saw a man about his age approach him.

The man looked him dead in the eye and said, "You have to be the worst sinner I ever met."

Bobby didn't know what to say. He didn't know this man. How could the man treat him so harshly after he'd opened up and emptied himself? Bobby felt the blood rush to his head, but he couldn't bring himself to say anything.

"I'd like to make a contract with you," said the man.

"A contract?"

"That's right."

"What kind of contract?"

"You pray for me until you die. By pray I mean you say a Rosary a day until you die. And I'll pray a Rosary a day for you until I die."

"You want me to say a Rosary for you, until I die?'"

"Yep, both of us, we'll pray for each other until we die."

"Why would I do that?"

"Why wouldn't you do that?"

The man was acting as if Bobby couldn't do it. And by God, Bobby could do anything. Don't you dare dare him. "Yeah, why not. Shit yeah, I'll do it." He didn't know if he'd do it, but he wanted to let the man know that he *could* do it.

"Can we shake on it?" asked the man.

"Yeah." Bobby extended his hand.

The man, referenced here by the pseudonym "Johnny Casey," lived in New Orleans, where he was the vice president of a construction supply company. He had a wife named "Erin" and children.

When the handshake ceased, Johnny Casey said, "I want to tell you. You made a bad deal."

"What?"

"You made a bad deal because I only have six months to live. I've got cancer."

Cancer? thought Bobby. *He screwed me is what he did. I don't have to honor the deal because he tricked me. My handshake might be my bond, but not if I've been double-crossed. That man doesn't deserve a Rosary.*

But that night, Bobby said a Rosary anyway. He'd always enjoyed saying the Rosary. The monotony of it didn't bother him. It slowed him down, cleared his head, opened his pores and, maybe, sometimes his soul. The Rosary was especially easy to say here at Regina Coeli.

The place had grabbed Bobby and his friends. After the mass confession, they gave their whiskey to the priest. They hadn't so much as broken the seal. The boatmen forgot about boozing and cutting up. Instead, they folded their hands and got on their knees. If there was such a thing as the fear of God, they'd just received a healthy dose of it.

Bobby spent the next day in prayer and contemplation. It was so quiet here. It was so nice just to walk around on soft pine needles with a clear conscience. For once, he wasn't harboring his usual guilt. For a change, he wasn't being propelled by a maniacal drive for money.

The following day, when it was time to leave, Bobby didn't want to go. He wouldn't admit that. But Regina Coeli's pines were whispering to him, well, not so much whispering as listening. He said a Rosary before he left, but not for Johnny Casey.

To prove that he didn't say any of those Rosaries for Johnny Casey, when he got home he passed a full day without saying one. He was helping his wife get ready for a vacation. He and his family and Anthony Guilbeau, his wife Norma, and their family were all headed for ten days at Disney World. Bobby surely wouldn't say any Rosaries out there.

As he prepared to leave the next morning, the telephone rang. Bobby didn't recognize the woman's voice, but she identified herself as Erin Casey, Johnny's wife. Before Bobby could manage to say anything, she told him that Johnny was at Ochsner Hospital. It didn't look like he'd make it. He was asking for Bobby.

Bobby wasn't sure what to tell her. He said something about leaving for a vacation, something about maybe having enough time for a visit. He wasn't sure, but he was shocked. He was sorry. He'd pray for them. What else was he supposed to say?

On the family's drive to the New Orleans airport, Bobby didn't say much. At one point, Myrtle said something about him being so quiet, but he barely heard it. He was thinking about the handshake. It was working on him. He couldn't renege on a shake. His father and brother both shook his hand, then broke their promises. He couldn't go back on his word to Johnny Casey, even if Johnny Casey had fooled him.

He couldn't take it; he had to stop at the hospital. Erin Casey had told him the room number, and that was where he went. When he stepped inside, he fought the urge to wince. Johnny Casey's throat was opened up. Next to him on a table was a rosary.

Johnny Casey looked at Bobby. Obviously unable to talk, he picked up the rosary and clasped his hands.

"Yeah," said Bobby. "The contract is still on."

When Bobby arrived at Disney World, he asked his wife if he could borrow her rosary, and he told her about the contract; then he started to fulfill it. He said a Rosary every day, all through the trip. He'd missed that one day in Golden Meadow, but he'd never miss another.

After the Orgerons returned to New Orleans and were driving away from the airport, Bobby told his wife he had to visit the hospital.

Myrtle took a long look at him. "It's really getting to you, huh?"

"Yeah. It is."

Bobby turned the car around, toward Ochsner Hospital. When he walked into Johnny Casey's room, it was empty.

He blocked out his worrisome thoughts and went to the nurse's station, asking the attendant, "Mr. Casey, where's he at?"

"Aw, he's gone."

Bobby's heart sank. "Gone?"

"Yes, sir."

"Is he dead?"

"No, he's gone home."

"I don't understand."

"The doctors don't either. They're puzzled. Everything's fine."

When he got back to the car, he told Myrtle what had happened. Her response was, "When a sinner prays for somebody, God listens."

Bobby couldn't argue with her. Later, he called Johnny Casey. They talked, and their wives talked. The Orgerons invited the Caseys to a boucherie, and the families became friends.

Bobby's contract with Johnny Casey transformed him. Suddenly, he couldn't bring himself to drink, chase, and whore anymore. If the oilmen wanted to hire his boats, they'd have to do it for honest reasons. They could have their partying. Bobby had a higher purpose now.

The contract had done more than make him say the Rosary. He returned to Regina Coeli for the next two Cursillos. The priests asked him to wash dishes and mop the floors. He obliged and did whatever else they wanted. He was much closer to their God now. He was listening to the old Man and trying to serve Him.

By some miracle, the Lord had worked His power on Bobby. Now he was someone else, or maybe he was finally himself.

IV

The Sultans

Minor Cheramie, ever the oilfield promoter
(Courtesy of L & M Botruc Rental, LLC)

Chapter 16

All Hail the Arabs

1973

———❈———

Religion wasn't just changing the personal lives of men like Bobby Orgeron. In 1973, it was affecting the world's geopolitics and spinning the international economy. If there were any post-world war doubts that the globe's crucial battleground was not in Europe but in the Middle East, 1973 should have eliminated them. That year, two religion-driven nations, Israel and Egypt, were fighting.

This centuries-old regional, fanatical religious war took a hard, global turn on October 19, 1973, when the United States publicly proposed a $2.2-billion military aid package to Israel. That same day, the Arab nations started their retaliation when Libya declared that it would ban all oil shipments to the United States. Saudi Arabia and the other Arab nations soon followed suit. By the end of 1973, a full-scale Arab oil embargo was in place.

The lack of availability of comparatively inexpensive Arab imported oil drove the price of available crude skyward in the United States. In a few months, retail gasoline prices climbed by 40 percent. The high prices caused a gasoline shortage, and at service stations across the country, long lines formed at the pumps. While this Arab-generated energy crisis increased the stress level of most motorized Americans, it was a boon to Louisiana, the republic that A. J. Liebling called "the westernmost of the

Arab states" in his book *The Earl of Louisiana*. The westernmost Arabian boatmen couldn't have been happier.

The skyrocketing price of oil and the need to find alternative oil supplies drove the big oil companies to pour untold billions into developing the Gulf of Mexico. Suddenly, *every* boatman in the Gulf could do no wrong. In fact, there weren't enough boats to meet the demand. By imposing the embargo, the Arabs had turned the boatmen into Cajun sultans. This irony led WWL-TV to produce a segment about the south Louisiana boatmen, called "Sheiks on the Bayou."

WWL-TV had asked Minor, ever the turbanless sheik, to be interviewed for the story. Minor declined, believing the television feature would only flaunt his wealth. But Minor, too, had heard the sound of the boom and immediately started building Botrucs by the boatload. In five years, he would more than double his fleet of supply boats, increasing it to thirty by 1978. In scrambling to find space at quality shipyards, Minor luckily secured spots at Bollinger, where he built most of his new boats, and at Halter, where he constructed some of the others at their Lockport and Moss Point, Mississippi, yards. Two of the boats built at Halter, the 180-foot-long *Bo-Trucs 33* and *34*, were especially novel because of their triple-screw propulsion systems. Minor had worked with Butch Danos in coming up with the idea, and the two designed the systems with the help of the yard.

While three propeller systems were not uncommon on crew boats and tugs, Minor had never seen them on a supply boat and used the feature in selling the vessels. The "open wheel" triple-screw Botrucs didn't need a center rudder and were particularly maneuverable when backed up to a rig, where the captain could leave his center prop forward to keep away from the structure and use the port and starboard props to move left and right. The boats, with their extra engine, were faster than the plodding twin screws.

Minor loved the new design and had no trouble selling it to the oil companies. In fact, after the Arab oil embargo, he had little trouble marketing any of his vessels. All he had to do was hire enough people to meet the demand. He would ultimately need upward of 450 employees, pulling people from everywhere, including, in 1974, his college-educated son-in-law, Pat Pitre, who was helping the company part-time while pursuing his MBA.

Pat had been working overtime in running crews and supplies from the Galliano office to as far west as Galveston, Texas, with stops in between to attend classes in Thibodaux. Although Pat appreciated his graduate business classes, he'd already invested thousands of hours into learning a real business. By this point, with the Gulf oilfield soaring, he thought it was time to start recouping his investment.

Pat told his wife, "You know, you gonna end up owning part of that thing one day. I feel somebody should be there to look after your interests. Who better than me?"

Deanie's first response was to cry, and when her mother, Lou, heard Pat's decision, she cried, too. More than anyone, they'd seen the worst of the business, and they couldn't stand the thought of Pat taking it into the next generation. Eventually, Deanie accepted Pat's decision and watched him plunge into the company.

When Minor heard the news, he was elated. While Minor was more than happy to have Pat, mixing family and business didn't work in every case, especially now that everyone wanted a piece of his mega-prosperous company. In fact, Minor and his brother, Lefty, often argued about which family members would be included in the business. After Lefty hired his son, Steve Cheramie, Minor clashed with Steve, and their inability to get along ultimately caused Steve to leave the company. Although Lefty remained a hands-off partner, not even wanting his own office space when the company built a new administrative building, he still fought with his brother over the company's expansion. Despite Lefty's pessimism, Minor never even considered buying out his brother. If the success was his, it was Lefty's, too.

There sure was plenty of success. From 1974 through 1978, Minor's Botrucs would have no real major breakdowns, only losing time to routine maintenance. Things were going so smoothly that Minor could have put everything on cruise control, played with his grandkids, and enjoyed a little family time at his camps.

But he wasn't quite ready to become a full-time family man. He still drank to excess. Sometimes, he'd get loaded and become so happy he'd give an employee a hefty raise. While these moves sometimes drew the ire of other employees, when Minor sobered up, he'd keep the raise in place.

When drinking, he also still picked fights at the bars. Some nights, Butch Danos would pull him away from a scene with three guys chasing him into the parking lot. Once, Butch was with Minor at the "Playpen" in Grand Isle when they were entertaining a vice president of a major oil company. Minor got so looped he started picking a fight with the man, who, with one phone call, could've pulled three Botrucs off the job. Butch had to separate the two, pulling Minor away and encouraging him to apologize. It took some coaxing for Minor to tell the executive he was sorry and for the oilman to accept his apology. In typical fashion, a few hours later, Minor had the man laughing as the two of them went on a helicopter joyride over Grand Isle in the middle of the night.

There were some things that Minor couldn't simply patch up and could never justify doing. His disrespectful treatment of his wife, Lou, continued into the 1970s. One night at a Grand Isle bar, Lou had seen enough. Both she and Minor had been drinking when Minor started blatantly flirting with a woman at the bar. Lou walked up and told the woman, "He wants a date with you, but I'm his wife."

Lou's remarks ended the flirtation and their night on Grand Isle. As they left the island and headed back north on the lonely highway through the marsh, Minor, who was driving the car, started chastising and insulting his wife.

Lou could no longer stand the abuse and, out of rage, grabbed the steering wheel from Minor and *whipped* it. At that moment, she didn't think of anyone or anything. She could've cared less about the consequences. As the wheel spun, so did the car, whirling off the road into the shallow water marsh ditch. When the car came to rest in the muck, Lou didn't so much as look at her husband. She opened the door and started slogging through the mud to the highway, losing a high-heel boot in the ooze. Reaching the asphalt, she flagged down a car as Minor stood next to her, unable to talk. After the car stopped, Lou looked at Minor and said, "Are you coming or what?"

He was stunned. When they got in the car, Minor told the young driver, "She's crazy."

She might have made a wild, irrational move, but judging by Minor's startled eyes, Lou was, at the moment, in complete control.

The boom did nothing to curb the oilfield's high-dollar, extramarital entertainment. If competition in a late 1950s recession had helped create the gift-giving and sleazy practices, the almost competitionless 1970s only made the business more unethical. Suddenly, there was more money to spend on hunting, fishing, and whoring, and, naturally, the lower level oilmen demanded more of all of it.

While Bobby Orgeron had experienced a character change after he agreed to the contract in April 1972, within a year, the oilfield brought him right back into his old habits. He'd abided by the contract's terms and continued to say a Rosary every day without fail, but the prayer couldn't insulate him from his bacchanalian business. Even with a ten-pound chastity belt and an iron will, the oilfield wasn't a good place to be a born-again and chemical-free Catholic. As the boom mutated into a seemingly unending gusher, there was no way Bobby could escape its by-product temptations.

At times, he hated himself. Nevertheless, he couldn't stop himself. He'd once again lost his inhibitions in going from client to client and boat to boat. If he didn't pounce on every opportunity during this period, his competitors surely would. So whatever the oilmen wanted, short of an outright cash payoff, Bobby would, once again, give them.

Over in the North Sea, Nolty Theriot and his son, Pye, were trying their best to manage their prosperity. Pye had officially received his introduction to the North Sea coast just days after he married Janet Bergeron. After their wedding, the couple had spent a few days in the balmy Virgin Islands, then flew to Great Yarmouth, landing in a cold January windstorm in 1973. During the first night in the hotel, Pye woke up shivering, colder than he'd ever been in his life, and he'd been buried under thick blankets. He then realized the fire in the coin-operated fireplace had burned out, and the only way to reignite it was to add more coins. As he fished through his pants pockets for some more shillings, he made a mental note to keep plenty of change next to the fireplace.

Eventually, Pye and Janet settled in a nice little brownstone and began adjusting to English life. They had to get used to all kinds of changes, including the shopping. Instead of buying in bulk from an American supermarket, they made separate, daily trips to the dairy mart, the produce shop, the baker, and the butcher. Once, Pye had gone to the butcher with his mother, who'd been in for a visit. His mother looked up, saw six rabbits hanging, and told Pye, "I'm gonna smother some rabbits for us." She then told the butcher, "I'd like the rabbits."

He pulled one rabbit off the hook and started packing it. "I'm sorry," she said. "I want them all."

"You want them all?"

"Yes."

"How odd. I've never had anyone buy more than one rabbit."

Because Pye's mother cooked the rabbits, they were delicious, and that was the secret—importing as much down-home food as possible. So when Theriot sent a boat across the Atlantic, its freezers would be stocked with the south Louisiana specialities, vats of gumbo, bags of Gulf fish, ice chests of duck and venison, and just about anything else from home they could freeze and ship.

Sometimes, the Cajuns couldn't wait for the shipments of home cooking. Once, when Dick Guidry was in Great Yarmouth for a visit, one of his expat captains invited him over for a duck supper. Surprised, Dick asked him, "Where'd you get the ducks?"

"Oh, the Queen got a lake that's full of them."

"What you mean," asked Dick, "you go hunting?"

"Oh, no, no, no. I go by the feed store. I buy me some corn, and the ducks followed me to the trunk of my car. When I got fifteen, I closed the trunk. I brought them home, fed them corn for two or three weeks so I can purge them. Then I wring their necks."

On another occasion, the captain told Dick he caught a "big goose," which eventually escaped. The goose was actually a swan.

At the Theriot Overseas, Inc. office, Pye learned that running the European operation was far different than running a Gulf-based business. When a boatman knocked off of his hitch at home, he was on his own. But in England, when the expat captain and crew got off the boat, Theriot was still responsible. As Pye would say, "Their problems are our problems." He saw quickly that at heart, these men were sailors, and that meant that many of them would drink from the time they walked off the tug until the time they staggered back on two weeks later. On several occasions, that meant bailing a Theriot employee out of jail when he got a little too rowdy at the pubs.

Pye also quickly discovered the value of his captains to the North Sea operation. The skippers had developed a reputation and marked their marine and cultural identity by placing stickers on their tugs with the initials RCA, "Registered Coon Ass," next to a sketch of a raccoon, with a banner at the bottom with Nolty's motto, "Don't Worry About Nothing." Pye had learned that, in essence, the oil companies and contractors had no worries as long as a Registered Coon Ass was behind the wheel.

Pye enjoyed the stories of his captains' bravado and even relished the tales of his skippers playing tug of war with other companies' tugboats. The game started when two tugs backed up deck to deck, hooked up a tow line from one to the other, then pulled against each other, seeing who could out-muscle the other. While Pye was not supposed to know of this practice and couldn't endorse it, he felt a surge of pride when one of the Theriot boats won.

Pye knew it was not all fun and games for the Theriot captains. He realized that the treacherous seas were taking their toll. He saw deckhands come into port shaken from being washed overboard and washed back on; he saw tugs slide into berths, missing their wheelhouse windows and radio equipment, which had blown into the sea. Shortly after the beginning of his tenure, a stressed-out Captain Ronald Gros experienced a heart attack offshore. Fortunately, Captain Ronald survived, but the incident reminded everyone of the danger of handling anchors on the North Sea.

After Pye's first few months in Great Yarmouth, he was relieved when the weather turned a little warmer. But the summer "heat" brought on another problem—tourists. As scenic as the Norfolk coast could be, it still seemed far too chilly to be a resort area, but that was exactly what Great Yarmouth became in the summertime, with its population tripling and thousands of tiny campers invading the seashore parks.

With all the tourists, traffic was horrendous. Pye had to fight the vacationers, the trailers being towed into town, and the series of bridges that, like back on Bayou Lafourche, stopped traffic when they were raised to allow a boat to pass below. By the time Pye would get to his dockside office, he would shake his head at the Brits frolicking in water far too tepid for even the most cold-blooded coonass.

Mostly, Pye was having a ball in Great Yarmouth. Soon, he hired one of his groomsmen to work in the company, his best friend Leslie Schouest, who'd just graduated from LSU; around the same time, another grooms-man, his first cousin Chippy Turnage, transferred to England from Theriot's Bahrain operation. Pye also developed relationships with the large expatriate community; approximately six thousand Louisianians, working in all facets of the oilfield, would make their way to the North Sea. He even got along well with his competitors, who really weren't competition because no one could build equipment fast enough. There was plenty of work for everyone.

There were also plenty of opportunities to play. For Pye, just visiting the other Theriot European offices was an adventure. In Peterhead, Scotland, he strolled the streets of the old town of brick parapet walls and Celtic culture.

Beyond the city were castles on high perches and historic golf courses that fed his passion for the links. Across the North Sea in Stavanger, Norway, Pye worked in a harbor of colorful, wooden row buildings with trademark high-pitched triangular roofs. Outside of town, everything just rose, from the forests of tall Norwegian firs to the sheer mountains of rock to the infinitely climbing northern lights.

When Pye wasn't hopping from company office to company office or calling on customers, he was gallivanting around Europe with his wife or friends or taking plush "business" trips. Even though Brown & Root was his client, sometimes the contractor would take him on trips where they'd charter a fifty-passenger airplane and head to Spain for a weekend of golf in a posh resort.

All the trappings overshadowed any headaches that Pye experienced in managing what had become a forty-vessel North Sea fleet. This was definitely not the boat business Pye had known growing up. While it wasn't nearly as rewarding for him as serving on the police jury, it sure was a blast.

In fact, it was probably easier than working at Theriot's Golden Meadow base, where a new crisis was developing. For Theriot, the Gulf oilfield's 1973 boom had a different meaning.

With the US shipyards suddenly crowded, Nolty Theriot was having serious trouble securing the space to build his tugs. Louisiana's once quiet shipyards were now full of metallic noises. Boat owners were standing in line to have their boats built. Nolty's subcontractor, Dick Guidry, gave up on the domestic yards and found a place in Spain to build two 135-foot North Sea tugs. To find a yard that could deliver a vessel in six months, he had to go all the way to Santander in the Basque Country along the Bay of Biscay.

But Nolty needed more than a couple of tugs. Even though he had plenty of loan capital, he had a hard time finding a place to spend it.

With good fortune sweeping through the 1970s, Bobby Orgeron finally indulged and christened himself. In launching the *Bobby Orgeron*, a 100-foot, triple-screw, aluminum Camcraft crew boat, Bobby had given into his employee's insistence on naming a boat after himself.

But heck, now that he had a *Bobby Orgeron*, he might as well do his name justice and find the perfect job for her. While the work abounded in the northern Gulf of Mexico, Bobby could stand an even sweeter pond to ply.

One day during the post-1973 boom, he received a candied offer from Paul Candies, the second son of Captain Otto. Candies had called Bobby and asked him, "Do you have a job for that new boat?"

"Not really."

"Would you like to go to work in Nicaragua?"

"Yeah," said Bobby. "I'm interested."

"It's out of Puerto Cabezas. I can pay you fifteen hundred dollars a day."

Fifteen hundred, thought Bobby. Where do I sign? That was triple the rate he could get in the northern Gulf. Before Candies had even quoted the price, Bobby knew he would probably accept. To him, the Candies were the best people in the boat business, and in working through them for Exxon, formerly Humble, Bobby couldn't go wrong. Through the years, he'd enjoyed the company of the ol' Captain. He loved to walk into the old man's office and have him peer up at him with his big eyes and say, "Come in. Come see. I want to show you something." He'd then open a ledger that would make Bobby's eyes pop out.

Four million dollars was sitting in Candies' business checking account. All that money was resting there, just lounging around.

Sure, the old man had a good-sized ego, but he was a generous fellow. Bobby couldn't visit him without the Captain taking him to his house for crawfish bisque or crawfish etoufée. With the Captain, Bobby knew he'd get paid every fifteen days, and if he needed an advance, ol' Caps would give him one. He couldn't even dream about getting that kind of treatment from some of the oil companies, who'd sometimes take 120 days to pay an invoice.

When Bobby showed up to sign his contract for the Nicaraguan job, Paul Candies wasn't there. Bobby instead dealt with Paul's older brother, Otto Jr. After he told Otto Jr. about the contract, Otto Jr. asked, "How much did Paul offer you for that job?"

"Fifteen hundred dollars a day."

"We can do better than that. We getting two thousand dollars a day for that boat. We'll give you eighteen hundred dollars a day. That's plenty of spread for us."

Bobby signed the contract but later worried that he'd offended Paul. He called him and explained what had happened with Otto Jr. Paul wasn't the slightest big agitated, telling Bobby, "It's all right. Don't worry about it."

Bobby wasn't worrying about much now, not at $1,800 a day. He could deal with the more complicated crew changes and all the other logistical Central American headaches. His *Bobby Orgeron* was ready to join his moose, the *Myrtle C. Orgeron*, which was already in Central America. At these high rates, nothing could sour the sweetness.

Except unripe bananas. And there were plenty of bananas in Central America, hundreds of species of them. As Bobby soon found out, from Mexico south, this entire world was one big banana bandango. Things were crooked and bent in every sense. The muddy airport runway at Bluefields, Nicaragua, for instance, was on a steep incline; the blasted thing went straight up a hill. As a plane would touch down on a relatively level piece of ground, it would then make a ridiculous ascent. And as it climbed, you felt as if you were approaching the top, where you'd surely fall off the mountain. Then the pilot would kill the engine and wait for the plane to safely stop climbing, before he backed it down the mountainside. The takeoff was even more frightening. The plane had to charge uphill, and when it crested the hilltop, it would make a big drop, a kind of free fall. Your stomach made a sudden descent, too. Then, just before you'd lost your breakfast *huevos*, seemingly seconds before a crash, the plane would lift and fly.

As much as Bobby craved risk, he hated this kind of flying and this pissant airport. The terminal was a fifteen-by-fifteen-foot palmetto-covered shack with no windows, and it was surrounded by dogs, pigs, and chickens. He couldn't go inside without a dog sniffing him and trying to lick him. Sometimes he'd take out his frustration on the chickens, hollering at them, blaming them for their country's backwardness.

While everyone was easygoing in the banana lands, nothing was easy. One day, Bobby decided to fly into Puerto Cabezas to take a look at his boat. He only wanted to make a quick appearance to check on things and make sure everyone knew he was involved. When the pilot landed at the airport, Bobby asked him when the plane would be leaving to go back to the States.

"A half hour," the pilot told him. So Bobby, who was accompanied by Benu Danos, told the cab driver to drive as fast as he could. En route to the dock, the rusty early fifties model Ford engine was misfiring. Benu was shaking his head. He could see what was coming.

When the cab arrived at the port, Bobby jumped out and onto his boat. He made a quick pass of the vessel, shook a few employees' hands, and told Benu, "*Allons.*"

They jumped back in the cab, and the cab really started sputtering. The driver was talking away in Spanish, complaining about something, but the only thing Bobby could understand was "spark plug."

"We gotta go. *Allons,*" said Bobby. "I gotta plane to catch, me. *Vamanos!*"

Again, the only words he understood in the driver's response were "spark plug."

The engine coughed and backfired, made a final burp, and died. After the car coasted to the side of the road, the driver opened the hood and attacked the engine with a pair of pliers. He unscrewed the spark plugs, put them back in their holes, and *hit* them with the pliers.

"What are you doing? Let's go!" asked Bobby.

"*Sí.*"

The driver whacked the tops of the plugs again, and somehow, the engine fired.

The Nicaraguan driver's ingenuity was a little too late. When the cab returned to the airport, Bobby couldn't accept that the plane had left. After realizing the terminal was closed, he started banging on the locked door, but no one answered. He tried to jimmy the lock but couldn't get the door open.

He sighed, realizing he was stuck in Puerto Cabezas until the morning. Benu then took him to a little encampment of round bamboo hunts near the beach. He pointed at one of them and said, "Bobby, you see that thing? That's what you gonna sleep in tonight."

"I'm not sleeping in that."

"There's no place else to stay."

"I ain't sleeping in no bamboo hut, I can tell you that."

"You sleep in there, or you gonna sleep outside with all the mosquitoes and the Mexican *brulots*. You wouldn't believe how big the bugs are out here."

"I ain't sleeping outside, and I definitely ain't sleeping in one of them huts."

"Where we gonna stay, the Hilton?"

"We'll sleep on the boat."

When they returned to the dock, they found that the crew boat had left for the evening. Back on the beach, when night fell, the bugs began their assault. Bobby and Benu were no match for them and quickly retreated to the hut. Inside, Bobby walked on the dirt floor and lay on his thin "mattress." He tried to close his eyes, but it was so hot and still, he could hardly breathe. Soon, his clothes were soaked and salted with sweat.

He looked at Benu, who appeared to be taking his suffering in stride. Having already passed the night in one of these huts, Benu stood up, opened a little hatch, and some water sprinkled on top of him.

"What are you doing?"

"There's some big drums up there. You let a little water out on you. That's how you cool off."

Even with the rooftop shower, Bobby couldn't get comfortable enough to sleep.

The next morning, he told Benu, "Me, I'm going back."

"I can't blame you."

"Why are we out here, anyway? You should tell our boat to come back. I'm tired of this place. We don't need this."

Bobby may not have needed Central America, but he wanted the big profits so badly he couldn't leave. So, he did what it took. Sometimes, he'd insist on handling problems himself. Everyone at MONTCO still had to know that Bobby wanted to be the first one to get into the grease and the first one to dive into the water.

When the *Bobby Orgeron*'s propellers needed changing, Bobby, Benu, and company pilot Penny Robichaux flew to Belize City, British Honduras, with fresh wheels in their hands. They took the boat to a little island where the water was clear and deep enough for the boat, but shallow enough for them to stand. Then they dove underwater, not using fancy scuba equipment, but simple snorkels. Bobby himself did most of the work. He'd personally make sure those wheels were on there good and tight.

While the props were perfect, Bobby noticed the *Bobby O*'s bottom was full of pesky *grabons*. To scrape off the barnacles, he'd have to put the boat on dry dock. Her bottom had to be completely slick to achieve maximum speed to the rig, which was off Punta Gorda, but could Bobby find a trustworthy dry dock?

He talked to the rig's pusher, who said there was a military dry dock across the British Honduran border in Puerto Barrios, Guatemala. "They'll pull you up," he said. "It's a government dock. You got nothing to worry about." So eventually, Bobby sent his namesake boat there and watched the *muchachos* scour and copper paint her bottom.

When the Guatemalans finished painting the *Bobby O* one evening, the human Bobby Orgeron paid $1,500 to the military captain running the dry dock and thanked the man. By this point, Bobby and another one of his port captains, Atoff Danos (Butch and Benu's cousin), were supposed to bring the boat back to Belize City, where a MONTCO captain would meet them. When Bobby told the Guatemalan guard to lower his boat into the water, the guard lowered the boat almost to the water level, turned off the switch, and held out his hand.

In the guard's other hand was a rifle. The constant presence of guns had initially made Bobby a little nervous, but by this point, he was incensed. Something tripped inside him. He wasn't paying the man another dollar. Instead, he grabbed him and pulled him away from the dry dock switch. Keeping his eye on the guard, who was startled, Bobby then told his port captain, "Atoff, get on that boat and crank all three engines when she hits the water. Don't worry about me."

Atoff, eyes bulging, boarded the boat and did what he was told.

Bobby then flipped the dry dock switch, and as boat made her way to the water, he told the guard, "Shoot, if you gonna shoot, but this boat is coming down."

As soon as Bobby heard the last of the third engines fire, he took off running. By this point, he didn't believe the guard would shoot him, and he was so enraged he didn't care whether the guard shot at him or not. He jumped on the *Bobby O*, hit the pilothouse, and put the three engines in reverse. As the boat slid backward, the blocks on which she had been placed started flying up in the air.

Pulling away from the dry dock and into the bay, Bobby noticed the Guatemalans scurrying, jumping into patrol boats, and then he saw exhaust plumes shoot out from the sterns of their vessels. He didn't think they could catch him. The *Bobby O* had three turbocharged GM V12s, brand-new propellers, and a slick bottom with nary a *grabon*.

As Bobby zipped into open water, he easily pulled away from the Guatemalans. Heading back through the Gulf of Honduras toward Belize, he realized he had another problem, low fuel. He looked at his gauges and calculated the miles in front of him, in what would be an all-night run, and concluded that with all three engines running at a decent clip, he'd run out of gas. So he shut one off and hoped that was enough. Fortunately, it was. He drifted into Belize City on fumes, just as the sun was rising over the West Indian–style mansions on Front Street.

While this was a picturesque and peaceful end to a nervous night, it was incidents like these that sometimes made Bobby think that he wanted nothing to do with Latin America. He had enough problems at home. The bigger his business got, the more employees he had to hire. It wasn't like the old days, where his people were either family or good, solid men with familiar Cajun names. Now, he had to take on some people who weren't even from the bayou. Sometimes, he didn't even know what he was hiring. They may have been golden, or they may have been gold-digging. How would he know?

In any event, the more employees he took on, the more likely that one was to get injured on the job. An injury, of course, could lead to a lawsuit under the Jones Act. The Jones Act, in Bobby's opinion, was grossly unfair to boat companies. It allowed these employees, these "Jones Act seamen," to sue MONTCO directly. MONTCO was liable if it committed "any negligence, however slight." This was an impossible standard, and it created a fair share of anxiety when an employee claimed to have been injured.

As bad as an injury in the United States territorial waters could be, an injury abroad to an American was even worse. When Bobby heard that one of his new deckhands had broken his leg on Bobby's boat and was in a Nicaraguan hospital, he told Benu to handle it.

Benu shrugged. He'd fly down there and pick up the deckhand and bring him back to Louisiana. But, when Benu got there, he discovered he was powerless. He couldn't remove the man from Nicaragua because the man had no passport, no driver's license, and no other form of identification. The Nicaraguan officials didn't know that this man was a US citizen. They couldn't release him.

Benu told them that the man spoke English with an American accent. He even looked like an American.

The official was not impressed.

Benu had to go back to Louisiana, retrieve the man's birth certificate, and have someone take it back to Nicaragua; but a certified copy of a birth certificate wasn't enough. MONTCO also had to pay the officials more *dinero*. Of course, this was no surprise. The extra charge was only the tip of one banana plant in a sprawling banana grove. It seemed as if every time MONTCO people left the country, they'd have to slip a hundred dollar bill to a grinning customs official. Ironically, all the big tips were no different than the expensive gifts given to US oilmen; in fact, the government official payoffs were probably cheaper than the money spent on entertainment in the US oilfield. With the money Bobby was making in Central America, he could afford to turn his back on all the third-world shenanigans. Still, he shook his head when he thought of what would happen next to his boats or his men. It sure made him appreciate his US Constitution.

Until his Constitution turned on him. Or maybe what he had just heard from a man working in Lafayette was unconstitutional. Maybe this "affirmative action" was nothing more than inequitable liberal, Black Panther bullshit. Whatever it was, he couldn't believe it came from this particular oil company, which he would never go on the record and name, but it was one he had worked for since the late 1950s. While the company wasn't Atlantic Richfield (formerly Atlantic Refining), it was almost as important to him.

The oilman had just told Bobby he had to cut loose from a job two of his triple-screw aluminum crew boats and replace them with two boats owned by two black men, which were a few weeks from leaving the ship-yard. The oil company was going to give the black men a *five*-year, *non*-cancellable contract.

Bobby didn't understand. Every time he'd built one of his new tri-ple-screw crew boats, this oil company wanted her. He had to ask the oilman to repeat the story. When the man regurgitated it, Bobby knew he wasn't dreaming. He wasn't in Guatemala, but in Lafayette, Louisi-ana, USA.

He asked again, as calmly as he could, "You mean ya'll never gave me more than a thirty-day contract with a twenty-four-hour cancellation clause, and ya'll are gonna take these people and give them a five-year, noncancellable contract?"

"That's right. Look, Bobby, I don't have anything to do with this. This came from New Orleans."

Bobby would go to New Orleans, but before he made it there, he was going to the field in Intracoastal City. He was going to ask the transpor-tation superintendent, his friend, what had happened. He'd personally taken care of this superintendent, even giving him his brand-new motor home. What the hell was going on?

In Intracoastal City, the superintendent was scratching his head, too. He was embarrassed. He had no idea what was happening, but maybe Bobby could straighten it out in New Orleans.

In the city, Bobby hit the company building on Lee's Circle. Looking toward the Circle's center at the towering statue of Robert E. Lee, he felt a little of the general's defiance. High up in the building, he walked into the head notch's office and realized immediately this vice president was a good twenty or thirty years older than him and was obviously a distinguished man. Whatever his status, he better have some answers.

At first, the vice president didn't have much to add to Bobby's knowledge. He could only say, "This is just what the company wants to do, Bobby."

"Uh-huh," said Bobby. "Well, I got two other boats out there. And ya'll are still planning to keep those boats on the job, right?"

"Of course."

"I want ya'll to give me two five-year, noncancellable contracts for those two boats."

The vice president tucked in his lips. "I can't do that."

"You mean to tell me you can take these guys because they're colored and give them five-year noncancellable contracts for two boats, and me, you can't give me a five-year contract for the other two? And you gonna replace two of mine with theirs?"

The vice president didn't seem comfortable. It was as if he wanted to say something, but he couldn't. "Bobby, that's not the best part of it."

"What do you mean?"

"We're also going to finance those two boats for them."

"For the colored guys?"

"Yes."

"They don't have to put up any money?"

"Not much. Nothing, really."

"They getting guaranteed five-year contracts *and* you're financing the boats for them? Is that what I heard?"

"That's right."

"Well, if that's the case, you take these guys, and you tell them to build four boats."

"Why is that?"

"You tell those colored guys to build four new boats because I'm pulling all mine off the job right now."

"You can't do that."

"I can't do that?"

"If you do that, you're going to shut down the field."

"Well, your field is gonna be shut down, or today, I'm gonna walk out of here with two five-year, noncancellable contracts for those other two boats."

"I can't give you that."

"Well, I'm gonna pull them off."

"You can't pull them off."

"I will. You can consider it done. But don't worry, I'm not going to use your telephone to call. I'm going to use another phone."

"You'll never work for us again."

"I don't want to work for you. A company like this, I don't wanna work for you."

Bobby walked out the building and headed for the first pay phone he saw on Lee's Circle. He called his port captain and told him to bring back all four crew boats from Intracoastal City.

Bobby then started telephoning other clients. He didn't go back to Golden Meadow until he found a job for all four of those boats. Under the current conditions, with the Arabs still blessing the Cajuns, it didn't take Bobby long to secure work. He placed two boats with Atlantic Richfield, one with Exxon through Otto Candies, and one with Penzoil.

But his now former client wasn't finished with him, or so they implied. A man from the company called him and told him they wanted to talk. There had to be a misunderstanding. The people in Louisiana wanted him to go to headquarters and talk with a company executive in Chicago.

Sure, said Bobby. He wasn't certain why he was flying to Chicago. He guessed it was because he still didn't understand what had happened. When he was still a boat captain, he'd once risked his life working for the company during a storm. He'd given them the best service and had showered their superintendents with fishing trips; lavish, bunny-adorned parties; and gifts. When these good ol' boys needed something, Bobby would take care of it. What more did they want from him?

After touching down at O'Hare International Airport, Bobby paid almost no attention to the great sprawl of Chicago. He wasn't focused on the stockyards, the maze of ethnic neighborhoods, or the towering buildings on the great sweep of Lake Michigan. He was still a little shocked by what the company had done.

During his meeting with one of the company's national executives, he realized if he harbored any hope that the oil company would apologize and make him feel better, he was mistaken. The executive claimed this order came from even higher than him. But from this office, Bobby could look out the window and damn near look down on the clouds. What place, what person on the oil company earth was higher than this?

Bobby couldn't contain his anger. He started calling the company and the man horrible names, telling him point-blank that they were only giving the jobs to the other men because they were black—only he didn't use that term.

The executive was listening with his mouth hanging open. He didn't have a response.

Even though the top brass was speechless, the superintendents wouldn't go so quietly. Six months later, Bobby received a call from one of them. He actually asked Bobby if he had any boats available.

"No," said Bobby.

"We need you."

"Oh, now you need me."

The man explained that the black men's boat company wasn't working out too well. He said, "If their boats break down on the weekend, I can't get ahold of anybody. Their boats are only six-months old. They might as well be five-years old. I don't like working with these boys. I can't depend on them."

"Well, don't look at me."

"Come on. Screw those people in Chicago. I'll put your boats on."

"I don't want to work for your company."

"Huh?"

"You and I can still be friends, but I'm not working for your company again."

As brazen as Bobby's words had been, he was about to take an even bolder position. He was getting ready to leave the crew-boat business altogether. Since he'd started with the *Davey Lou No. 4* in 1956, crew boats had been his staple.

Now he was going to sell all of his crew boats and focus on buying higher-risk, higher-reward supply and cargo boats, maybe even get into tugs.

But before Bobby sold one of his crew boats, he decided to sell one of his cargo boats, the *Georgia*. He'd paid her off and worked her steady with Chevron for six years. With the Chevron job petering out, he wanted to see what he could get for the boat before finding another job for her. He made contact with a boat broker in Copenhagen. The Danish broker told him there was an Arab who was interested in such a cargo boat. From what Bobby could tell, the Arab was either from Bahrain or Yemen, but the purchaser's place of residence made no difference to him.

Bobby had one price, and it was $775,000. Yes, he'd purchased the *Georgia* for only $350,000, but even if the Danish broker or the Arab purchaser discovered this information, Bobby still only had one price.

When he called broker and gave him the number, the Dane didn't even pause to consider it. He agreed in principle, pending a dry dock inspection at Avondale Shipyard outside New Orleans. Then, after the survey, the smiling broker handed Bobby a check certified by Chase Manhattan Bank in the amount of SEVEN HUNDRED SEVENTY-FIVE THOUSAND AND 00/100 DOLLARS.

The sale of the *Georgia* sparked Bobby's crew-boat auction, and the boats sold like the hottest, latest lava lamps. The old crew-boat business, even with the engine trouble, had been too easy. In need of a new challenge, Bobby was ready to disco into new waters.

But by 1973, his life was much more challenging than his new business venture. All of his rough-riding had ravaged his body. His constant aches demanded palliation, and he was popping pain pills again. This time, he'd graduated into something much stronger than the Darvocet he'd taken in the 1960s. He was now frequently ingesting Percodan and Percocet. And at some point, in what was becoming a hazy decade, he'd admitted to himself that he was dependent on them. He checked into a rehabilitation facility but unfortunately didn't stay for the suggested duration.

His battle with prescription drugs was harshly typical. For stretches, he'd be pill free. Then he'd drift back toward them. One week, he was sure he'd beaten his habit, then the next, he'd succumb to it.

He knew if his family understood how addicted he was, they'd be terribly upset. They had seen what excessive pain medication had done to his brother. When his father finally did find out, there was no way Bobby could explain his abuse.

If Bobby's father saw him take a pill, the old man would tell him, "*Arrete ca!* For the love of God, stop that."

But it wasn't as simple as deciding to quit. Somehow, Bobby's bouts with alcohol and pills had not affected his bottom line. As the oilfield and the decade ascended, his revenues only climbed. When it came to business, not even the chemicals could stop him.

Chapter 17

The Succession

Post 1973

While the 1973–74 Arab oil embargo officially lasted only five months, the embargo's effect on the Gulf of Mexico would linger for years. The embargo had quadrupled petroleum prices and made the oil companies a little paranoid about their previous dependency on Middle Eastern oil. Consequently, they poured money into building surplus reserves, and in so doing, continued to push for development in the Gulf of Mexico.

Suddenly, all kinds of investors were trying to squeeze into the boat business. Doctors, lawyers, bankers, and other neophytes were throwing their money behind one limited partnership boat scheme or another. The oilfield expanded and exploded all over Louisiana, from New Orleans to Lafayette to Cameron. In Morgan City, workers stacked casing two stories high in the pipe yards, and giant cranes swung from shipyard to shipyard, building larger-than-life derricks and platforms. And as the oilfield grew, so did the population of oilfield characters, demanding more bars, cheap motels, and whorehouses.

With the infusion of deck-loads of cash into the economy, the physical face of south Louisiana began to change. Within a few years, the Cajunland started to look like the rest of America. The 1970s boom had accelerated the growth of typical Ameircan shopping centers in the bayou country. Up and down Bayou Lafourche, from Donaldsonville to Thibodaux to Galliano-Golden Meadow, strip malls replaced the downtown shopping areas and the quaint bayou roadside stores. In Houma, the city exploded with concrete parking lots and metal buildings, and developers there replaced the pastoral green space along Bayou Terrebonne with long chains of storefronts. Of course, this rectangular commercialization hadn't happened that long ago in other parts of America; it was just that it happened so *fast* in the bayou land, a place that had been so culturally separate from the American mainstream.

As south Louisiana erupted, so did the offshore planet. Propelled by the global push to develop reserves outside the Middle East, significant offshore fields developed in places like Atlantic Canada and Malaysia. The people developing these areas were Cajuns and Texiens. They took their oilfield skills, be they in boat-handling, drilling, or production, and their families to exotic locales. At one point in the 1970s, thousands of south Louisianians made their home in Singapore.

In Canada, the growth of the marine oilfield in Nova Scotia and New Brunswick would ultimately reunite many Cajun oilfield workers with their Canadian Acadian cousins.

And as the oilfield spread its reach from ocean to ocean, in Great Yarmouth, England, things finally stabilized for Pye Theriot. By March 1974, Pye was beginning to accept his role in the company and was looking forward to an upcoming visit by his father. But when Nolty arrived in England, Pye was taken aback. His father was far from his usual robust self and instead was pale and drawn. Although Pye had seen Nolty look tired and even stressed, he'd never observed him in a weakened state. He told him, "You don't look very well."

"I haven't been feeling well," Nolty admitted.

Pye asked more questions, but his father was vague. He downplayed his condition, saying only that he was going in for a checkup as soon as he returned to Louisiana.

Truth be told, Nolty didn't know what was inside of him, sapping his strength. Something was slowing him down and making him pass blood. When he arrived back in Louisiana and went in for his checkup, his doctor mentioned the possibility of stomach cancer. Nolty wasn't exactly surprised. At least two of his Theriot relatives had died of stomach cancer, and something had been gnawing at his insides all of his life. He'd always said that after he'd survived the firing squad, everything was *lagniappe*. Perhaps he was reaching the end of his *bonne chance*.

In May, Nolty checked into Baptist Hospital in uptown New Orleans for exploratory surgery, but the doctors found nothing.

While the news gave Nolty some relief, it was also unsettling. Although he was supposedly cancer free, he still felt feeble and fatigued.

And as his condition worsened, the perpetually booming North Sea oilfield began to slow down. Was this once-virgin territory turning into the Gulf of Mexico of the 1950s and 1960s? Nolty didn't believe that, but there were some discouraging signs.

For one, in the summer of 1974, there wasn't as much work. Two, for what pipelaying work there was, there was hell of a lot more competition than there had been in the late sixties. The British and Norwegian boat companies had learned how to outfit their vessels with anchor-handling systems, and their captains were becoming more and more proficient at handling anchors. Essentially, the Cajuns had taught the English, the Scots, and the Norwegians how to take their jobs.

Nolty suspected the competitors would come but believed it would take more than a little market downturn to knock him from the top. Nolty J. Theriot, Inc. was now the world's largest independently owned offshore tugboat company.

However, even if Nolty thought his company was indestructible, he knew his body was not. In July, he was still passing blood and having problems. Worse than anything, his weakened condition and all of his doctor visits were making it difficult for him to spend the time he needed running his company. He was trying to build boats and call on clients, but he could do neither very well now that his doctors were controlling his schedule.

By August 1974, everything was coming to a head. Nolty's body was doing nothing but deteriorating and another surgery was coming. Across the Atlantic, the North Sea tugboat market was showing no signs of an upswing, and even more confusing, Brown & Root had made a serious offer to buy Nolty J. Theriot, Inc. While Nolty had no intentions of selling, the offer complicated what was already a Byzantine picture.

Over in Great Yarmouth, Pye Theriot didn't know about Brown & Root's offer. He wasn't thinking about the business as much as he was concerned with his father's health. He'd been in New Orleans for the previous surgery, and when the surgeon had emerged, he'd told Pye, "Look, I was going in there expecting to find something. I couldn't find a thing."

But when Pye flew back to New Orleans for the second surgery, the news was entirely different. This time the cancer was not only there; it was all over the place.

As the doctors prepared Nolty for chemotherapy, the outlook was grim. They'd given him at the very most, two years to live.

When Pye saw his father after the surgery, Nolty seemed unaffected. If anything, he appeared to be frustrated because he was chained to a bed. Of course, he would find a way to work. One of his first tasks was to call a meeting right in his room.

Pye watched the room fill up with people—his mother, his uncle and company bookkeeper Jeff Alario, Jeff's assistant Benny Bourgeois, Charlie Sanders, and some of the company's attorneys.

Pye looked at his father sitting in his bed with his shirt off, sporting a fresh surgical scar across his stomach. Right after Nolty started the meeting, he told everyone about the cancer. Some of the people started crying, but Nolty never flinched. He simply segued right into the news of Brown & Root's offer to purchase the company. Then he stared right at Pye and asked him, "Do you want to run this company or not?"

Pye didn't initially respond. He'd just found out his father was dying of cancer. The company was the furthest thing from his mind. But he had to answer the question, and he had to do it in front of a room full of people. Perhaps, in a different setting, he might have said, "No. I'm proud of what you've done, but I don't want to spend my life doing something I don't want to do." But instead, being put on the spot, he said what came to him, which was, "Yeah," he did want to run the company.

"If you don't want it, I'm selling right now."

Apparently, that was why the lawyers were there. They were going to collect Nolty's signature and consummate the sale or some phase of it.

Sure, Pye was tempted. He knew his "yeah" had been half-hearted. He understood that if he agreed to the sale, he, his mother, and his sisters and all their immediate progeny would have some real security. He could then slip back into politics and look into other ventures.

Yet he also knew what a "no" would do to his father. It might kill him right there on that bed. Nolty didn't care about cashing in; he was obsessed with building and conquering. The more money he made, the more he'd give away. But if he sold the company, there would be nothing left to conquer, no important game left to play. His father's legacy was about much more than money. Nolty's mark was about continuing what the French Theriots, the Acadian Theriots, and the Lafourche Theriots had done in surviving the expulsion and enduring the odyssey, in riding out the hurricanes on Cheniere and Leeville, in taking *grandpere* Leon's simple *Petit Caporal* shrimping operation and building on Paris' multiple local businesses, and taking all of their collective experiences and molding the best boat company in the world. It was about combining his operational expertise with the Vizier brothers' boat-handling ability, with Dick Guidry's salesmanship, with Robert Alario's diplomatic skills to create a Cajun juggernaut.

If Pye encouraged his father to sell, Nolty's purpose and his dream would die. He knew with a fleet of vessels, his father saw infinity. But with a mere pile of millions in cash, Nolty faced only his mortality. Pye couldn't let that happen. He made up his mind that his father would die knowing his family still owned the company.

It was also clear to Pye that as long as Nolty was still alive, Nolty himself would run the business. He'd still call the shots in between chemo treatments and embarrassing moments of physical inertness. And Nolty would also soon take on another distraction. He told Pye he would run for the state representative's seat in 1975, even though he already held a public office, the presidency of the fledgling Lafourche Parish Port Commission. But the port presidency wasn't particularly time consuming, and while Nolty's political aspirations weren't as focused or as passionate as Pye's, Nolty had, to some degree, dreamed of a seat in the Louisiana legislature. Still, Nolty wouldn't have run had he not been urged by so many people to do so.

When he announced his candidacy on May 9, 1975, he told the press through a statement, "I have conquered an illness which has made me appreciative more than ever, of the worth of the future." Nolty, however, had not beaten the cancer; contrarily, the pictures he took for his campaign brochure showed that he'd lost weight and that his hair, which had recently been richly dark, was now solidly gray.

Also in his announcement to the press, Nolty said, "I have, in preparation for my candidacy, turned the reins of my business over to my son so that I might spend full-time in this undertaking."

His son knew this wasn't true, either. Pye had already clashed with his father over whether to retain some of Nolty's employees who weren't really needed; his father had made it clear these employees would stay. While Pye didn't want to argue with his dying father, he couldn't shake his sense that something disturbing was happening. It was counterintuitive to say that Nolty J. Theriot, Inc. was exploding and imploding at the same time, but that's exactly what was taking place.

The company was still growing, building boats and working them, creating enough of buzz to be sold at a ridiculously high profit. There was still more Title 11 money to spend and even more boats to build. By the same token, the North Sea work was becoming less and less available.

Not only was the pipeline construction market suffering, but the North Sea nations were beginning to nationalize coastwise trading. They were requiring vessels of their own flag with their own unionized crews. In Great Britain, the new Labour government was bent on having their own people on the tugs. The socialized Norwegians weren't much different. It was possible for Theriot to make adjustments and switch their flags to that of a North Sea nation; they were building British flag supply boats with the Rothschilds. But even if the Theriots made a complete conversion, it didn't take away from the fact that the North Sea was no longer a gold rush.

Moreover, some North Sea native mariners had mastered the art of anchor handling. Around this time, one day, Captain Tommie Vizier, the North Sea's seminal anchor handler, was now running his own ice-classed tug with his brother, Jimmie. As he worked that afternoon, he watched two Norwegian captains handle anchors alongside him. He couldn't believe their skill; it was as if they'd been born in Golden Meadow. He'd later confess that, "I couldn't do better than what they were doing."

Not only were the Norwegian skippers skilled, but they also had something that the Theriot tugs didn't have at the time—bow thrusters. A bow thruster was a side-mounted propeller on the boat's bow that could move the front of the boat from left to right. In a rough North Sea, a bow thruster could counterbalance a strong current and render it almost non-existent. That meant the tug could hold its position much, much longer. While some of the Theriot captains had pleaded with Nolty to install bow thrusters in his latest tugs, he'd decided the device was too expensive.

The Norwegian tug companies, though, had the money because they were government subsidized. Evidently, these subsidies were much more lucrative than even the sweetest Title 11 deal.

In any event, Pye could see that, in 1975, the factors and the forces were driving the Theriot fleet from the North Sea. But to his father, the planet's surface still contained more than a hundred million square miles of undeveloped water, and that meant he could still build more boats. So in 1975, he negotiated a $40 million contract with Avondale Shipyards to build ten more tugs. While Robert Alario warned him that the deal was probably a violation of his previous Title 11 loan covenants and that he needed the Mar Ad's and the banks' prior approval, Nolty waved him off and signed the contract anyway.

Pye also argued with Nolty about personnel at the marsh camp near Catfish Lake. But there was little Pye could do. His father told him point-blank, "Until I'm dead, this is my company. We're gonna do it my way."

And it was clear that Nolty's way was not as effective as it would have been had he been healthy. He was doing what he could to cope with the cancer. His wife had asked that he let a special priest known as a "healer" pray over him. Nolty agreed to do it only if the healing service could be kept secret. Family friend Archbishop Hannan had offered his private chapel, and Nolty accepted, not counting on the healer to work a miracle but doing his best to please his wife.

In fact, Nolty spent what were supposed to be his last months pleasing a lot of people. Ultimately, his decision to run for office was not so much to fulfill a personal dream as to do what many people expected him to do. The people of lower Lafourche knew full well he was dying of cancer and elected him anyway on December 13, 1975.

Yet their leader would never take his oath of office. Despite their pleas and prayers, the man who'd survived a firing squad couldn't beat cancer. Nolty Joseph Theriot died on March 14, 1976.

After Nolty's death, Pye Theriot's life was a blur of faces and issues. At his father's funeral wake, an unending stream of people approached him. The old timers said it was the most heavily attended burial mass in Golden Meadow history. Presided over by Archbishop Hannan, the audience included dozens of oilfield and political luminaries, including Louisiana Governor Edwin Edwards.

As the procession of mourners comforted the Theriots, in the days that followed, Pye had to deal with his own grief and move the company forward.

He also had to decide what to do about his father's vacant political positions. In Pye's heart, he wanted to run in the special election for his father's legislative seat. But his wife, Janet, didn't want him spending most of his time in Baton Rouge, especially considering what she'd heard about the state capitol's political entertainment scene, which in her mind, was even worse than the oilfield's. So Pye would run for the Port Commissioner position, and Dick Guidry decided to come out of political retirement and vie for his old legislative post.

The duo ran on one ticket, printing "Dick and Pye" bumper stickers. For Pye, the campaign was a nice diversion, and at times, comic relief. He enjoyed several lighter moments, including one when an elderly woman approached him at a "Dick and Pye" rally and said, "*Mais* I can eat the Pye, but I can't swallow the Dick."

Her message proved to be prophetic, as Pye won and Dick Guidry lost. But the victory didn't mean as much as his earlier one for police juror. In Port Fourchon's early days, the Port Commissioner's position carried little weight, and in truth, Pye was too busy to focus on politics.

Then in August 1976, his first child, Nolty II, was born, and Pye was determined to spend more time with his son than his father had spent with him. But just like his father, company obligations were pulling Pye. In fact, he was confronting a dilemma that his father had never had to face.

By the end of 1976, Theriot had lost all of its North Sea tugboat work. Faced with the prospect of pursuing Gulf of Mexico jobs for the first time in several years, Pye's problem was his father had given the Gulf work to Otto Candies and other operators. It wasn't like he could take back those jobs. He had to find other ones.

What he didn't realize was that he was losing the company's hold on its best client, Brown & Root. In the wake of Nolty's death, as Pye was busy tending to his family's grief, his father's estate issues, his wife's pregnancy, and campaigning for his father's old political seat, he started using his friend, Leslie Schouest, to help him make calls on customers. Leslie was a good salesman, and Pye in no way wanted to duplicate his father's practice of personally making all the calls and in doing so, taking time away from his family. So when a key Brown & Root man asked to see Pye, Pye, who was in the middle of other things, sent Leslie.

Pye didn't know that the Brown & Root man would be offended. He didn't realize the man wanted to see Nolty's son and only Nolty's son. He had no idea his lack of a personal appearance would ultimately erode the two companies' long-standing relationship. But that was precisely what it did.

Making matters worse was the $40 million dollar contract Nolty had signed with Avondale. Pye would have to negotiate a release from that contract, which he ultimately did, but the break cost him $1.5 million. Moreover, the company was still $30 million in debt and had not one job.

Although Pye didn't need any new vessels, he also didn't know what to do with his present ones. As he and Leslie started finding work for them, he soon realized that his tugs were a liability. The heavy North Sea boats burned too much fuel for working in the Gulf of Mexico, where their big hulls and railroad engines weren't necessary, and the lower day rates sometimes barely covered the operating costs.

Nonetheless, because the Gulf was still booming, Pye could hire out the big tugs. However, if the economy ever turned and the rates dropped, Pye would have to sell them. Perhaps he should start selling them now; there were, for the time being, available purchasers on the North Sea market. Maybe Pye should've also started letting go some of the men whom his father had hired mostly out of generosity or loyalty. The fact was he couldn't afford many of these men, and they weren't needed. But how could he do that to his father's memory? In all, the picture of this company that had landed in his lap was so messy he wasn't sure what to do. It wasn't as if he'd asked for the job. Then again, it wasn't as if he hadn't had his chance to bail out and ask his father to sell. Any way he looked at it was complicated, so very complicated.

For Lou Cheramie, things were equally as complex. It didn't matter what she did to her husband Minor; he wasn't going to change. She could take the wheel of his car and spin them into the marsh. But in time, his shock would pass, and he'd be back at the bar, getting loaded, fighting with some hard leg, and chasing a pair of tight shorts and high heels, some wavy-haired Farrah Fawcett look-alike.

He'd calmed some when Deanie had left the house in 1970 and was especially tranquil as long as his grandkids were around, which they often were. Watching him with them, no one could've believed he had a problem with violence, and to his credit, it was much less of a problem now. But all it took for him to turn back into Mr. Hyde was a round of drinking, and then he sometimes couldn't help himself.

In 1978, he turned fifty, and he arguably should have been too old to keep up his habits. One night when he'd done something to hurt Lou, either he'd been with some woman or called her some insulting name, she asked him a question that she'd asked before, but which seemed to wake him up this time. "Why," she said, "are you doing this to me?"

He stared at her with a lost look in his eyes. It was as if something in him was too sad and too forlorn to explain.

"Anything you want from me, you can get. So why are you doing this to me?"

"Because I'm no good," he said. "I'm no good."

Despite having tremendous confidence and charisma, did he really, down deep, lack self-worth? She didn't know, and it wasn't as if he was going to allow himself to be psychoanalyzed.

Of course, he was good to many, many people. But none of the benevolence excused his treatment of her. And none of it helped solve the riddle of his darker side.

A few miles down Highway 1, at MONTCO, Bobby Orgeron continued to battle his substances like Minor did his drink. The boom had led to binges, some wild swings through the Caribbean and the usual forays in the French Quartter. But as hypocritical as it might have appeared, he still said the Rosary every day and combatted constant guilt.

His only pure, guiltless fun was the building of the business. In little more than a year, he was going to build $16 million dollars-worth of cargo boats and tugs. This would be his first foray into the tug industry and a huge leap into the offshore cargo world. In 1977, he put two of these cargo vessels under construction at Halter Marine in Lockport. He was lucky to have secured the spots at a local shipyard, many of which had year-plus waiting lists for new construction. But when two men from New York came to Bayou Lafourche and asked if he wanted to sell his spots, he had no idea there was *that kind* of demand.

Bobby had no interest in selling them the space because he knew Atlantic Richfield was waiting for one of his 166-footers, maybe both. So he told them, "No, I don't want to sell my spots."

Then they started offering money and when the price climbed to $250,000, Bobby couldn't refuse it.

Of course, Bobby still needed his boats built, and luckily, he knew Halter's Floyd Naquin well, so he worked out a deal where he paid the yard $50,000 to put him high enough on the list so he could get his boats built on time.

In the late 1970s, it seemed as if Bobby could make no mistakes. In 1977, he had a new cargo boat, the *Joseph J. Orgeron*, that was about to leave the shipyard without a job. This was a strange predicament for him in the boom, and he thought he might be able to rectify things by calling his best client, Atlantic Richfield. He'd been working for Atlantic Richfield and its predecessor Atlantic Refining and their superintendent Dallas Melton since 1957. So he called Melton and said, "Hey, Slick, I got the *Joseph J.* coming out, and I ain't go no job."

"Let's see what we can do," said Melton. "Well, that *Atlantic Tide* is getting a little old. It's been there awhile."

The *Atlantic Tide* was a Tidewater vessel that Tidewater had named after Atlantic Richfield. When Bobby had originally watched the boat go to work for AR, he raised his eyebrows but shrugged it off. While he didn't like Tidewater moving in into his territory, he didn't need the job because all of his boats were working. Now, if one of his fellow independents had taken an AR supply boat job without brokering it through him, he would have been offended. But Tidewater? The company was hardly human to him.

Yet if Melton and AR were going to bump a Tidewater vessel for the *Joseph J.*, a boat named for his baby boy, well that was justice.

And sure enough, two days later, Melton let the *Atlantic Tide* go and replaced it with Bobby's boat.

Later, Bobby ran into Tidewater's John Laborde at an industry trade meeting. Laborde was hot, telling him, "You bumped me off that job."

"Wait a minute, John," said Bobby. "Hold on there. You were on my turf. I was with Atlantic Richfield long before you."

"You don't just build a new boat and bump us off. We'd even named that boat the *Atlantic Tide.*"

"You gonna have to talk to Dallas Melton about that, not me."

Whatever one's opinion of the incident, it proved the boat business was far from being controlled by the corporate titan. Unlike the many stock market-driven American industries, in the workboat world, the collective little men had as much power as the public giant.

As for the ever independent Bobby Orgeron, he kept the deals flowing. In June 1978, he formed THOR of Golden Meadow, Inc. with Leon Theriot. Before Leon's cousin Nolty Theriot had died in 1976, Bobby and Nolty had talked about combining the TH in Theriot with the OR in Orgeron to create a deck barge company. With Leon taking Nolty's place, THOR ordered two 1.2 million dollar deck barges from a shipyard in Braithwaite; the barges could load everything from oilfield tools to shipping containers.

With THOR's barges launching into the Mississippi River, Bobby felt as strong as the mythical Thor, the Norse god of thunder. The only thing that could have made him feel stronger in 1978 was if his eldest son, Lee, had showed more interest in the business.

But Lee was moving in the opposite direction. He was heading up the bayou to Nicholls State for college. He'd just graduated from high school, and following graduation, he had immediately married his long-time sweetheart Tammy Collins. During the summer of 1978, the newlyweds moved into an off-campus apartment in Thibodaux. They were focusing on school and distancing themselves from the boat business.

After Lee watched how the oilfield had kept his father away from home, he wanted nothing to do with the industry. As a child, he'd done his best to warm up to the family business. He'd quickly learned that the only way he could spend time with his dad was by following him to the office or jumping on a seaplane with him. As Lee got older, he began to pass his summers working as a gopher for the company's port captains, learning all about engines, and eventually, he worked some offshore as a deckhand. But he could hardly get past the waves at Belle Pass without feeling seasick. One year, while working on the *Myrtle C.* off of Trinidad, Lee had become so sick that he refused food for a week straight, and his father had to fly down and pick him up. On another occasion, off Cameron, Louisiana, Lee was on a boat headed out to assist a rig in trouble during a tropical storm when he got so nauseous and delirious he blacked out and lost memory of the entire day.

When Bobby realized his son's sickness was too severe to handle the seas as a deckhand, he put him back to work as an assistant to the port captains. After a day working on greasy engines, Lee would come home so covered in black grime all his father could see was a set of teeth and two eyeballs.

But it wasn't the grease, the sweat, or even the seasickness that kept Lee away from MONTCO. It was the extracurricular activity. Lee would not do to Tammy what his father had done to his mother, and when Tammy gave him children, Lee was determined to spend time with them.

So instead of jumping into the boat race, Lee would pursue a business degree and see where that took him.

In Bobby's mind, if Lee didn't want anything to do with the business, maybe the boats would interest Joseph, his youngest child and second son. If not, Bobby would just keep going. If he could buy a new Rolls-Royce, a sleek Ferrari, a condo in Aspen and another one on the Mississippi Gulf Coast, why not keep moving? If he could ring up all these party pads and toys and not even feel it, why should he stop? If he could net $200,000 from just taking his name off of a shipyard list, there was no way he could go wrong.

Yes, he was still drinking, and unfortunately, his pain pill intake was at an all-time high. And this time, the pills and alcohol *were* in the way. Bobby's chemical dependency was about to disrupt his son's education. One fall day toward the end of Lee's first semester in 1978, his mother called him and told her son with desperation in her voice, "I need you to come back and work in the business."

She told him how sick and strung out his father was, how the drugs had consumed him and were ruling him. Rehabilitation was inevitable, but by itself, Bobby's recovery would not solve the company's problems.

At the same time, longtime MONTCO employees were talking to Lee, too. They were concerned about the company's sudden $15–16 million new construction debt load and believed the company lacked direction and organization, particularly in the new tugboat side of the operation. And of course, they knew Bobby was not himself; the drugs had finally affected his ability to manage MONTCO.

The way Lee saw it, he had no choice. He couldn't abandon his family. He and Tammy would finish the semester, move out of their Thibodaux apartment, and head back down the bayou. By January 1979, young Lee would be running the entire company.

In retrospect, it was illogical that grown men and women would beg an eighteen-year-old to rescue a multimillion dollar, debt-heavy business. But in their judgment, Lee Orgeron was no ordinary eighteen-year-old.

With all the free spending and freewheeling of 1970s, few boatmen thought they could make a mistake. But there were some, like Sidney

Savoie, who'd decided to leave while the business was peaking. For Sidney, the gushing mid-1970s were such a relief from the litigious, politically corrupt, economically volatile rock and roll of the 1960s. By 1976, at age sixty-four, Sidney had made enough money to put away and live comfortably for the rest of his life. Of course, he wasn't materialistic; he never made a habit of coveting the sports cars, yachts, camps, and the like. He and Mathilde were still happily passing their days in the same house they built in 1948. They didn't need anything else. So Sidney was getting out. His son, Ted, and his son-in-law, Larbow, could fight the next downturn, whenever it was coming. Him, he was staying home with Mathilde.

Sidney's strategy was anomalous in the boat business. Most of the boatmen rolling along were riverboat gamblers like Minor Cheramie. Minor kept borrowing and building all through the 1970s and culminated his spending spree in December 1980 with an $11.9 million new-construction loan with a division of the Chemical Bank of New York. The loan's New Orleans closing was a highfalutin affair, held in a lordly conference room at the esteemed Milling law firm in the old Whitney Bank Building.

When Minor walked into the room with his entourage, including his brother, Lefty, and his attorney, Bill Porteous, he couldn't believe all the formality. The room was full of starched New York and New Orleans lawyers and paralegals. At the center, piles of documents sat atop a conference table. Minor had seen his share of legal paper, but he'd never witnessed anything like the two-foot high stacks that were in front of him.

As everyone gathered around the table and prepared for the signing, Lefty took a classic left turn when he looked at Minor and told him, "I ain't signing."

The lawyers froze. "What?" asked Minor.

"I ain't gonna sign til I get more salary," said Lefty.

Minor shook his head. If nothing else, his brother understood the art of leverage.

All Minor could do was usher the Cheramie clan out of the room and ask Lefty to take a walk. Eventually, the group ended up in the men's room and tried to come to terms. Lefty protested his "paltry" salary; while he was being paid no less than Minor, he was demanding an increase in pay of about $1,000 per month. Finally, Minor gave in to his brother, and the group walked back into the conference room, where the nervous members of the New York and Louisiana bar were waiting.

By this point, Minor had realized the absurdity of everything, and looking at the documents, he turned to his counsel and said loud enough for the entire room to hear, "Bill, you see all that damn paper? It don't mean shit."

"What you mean, Minor?" asked Porteous.

"It's simple. If I pay my note every month, they ain't gonna bother me. They won't give a damn what's in them papers. And if I don't pay my note, they gonna go on reading them damn papers til the cow come home, and it don't make no difference. If I ain't got any money, so what? Them papers ain't gonna give them any money. If I can't pay the note, I can't pay the note."

The lawyers dropped their jaws. They'd spent all of this time drafting important words on fine parchment, and this was how they were treated?

Ultimately, the attorneys and their bank client would receive Minor's and Lefty's signatures, but not necessarily their compliance. While L & M Botruc religiously paid the Chemical Bank's notes, one day, Minor decided he would violate "them papers."

He didn't particularly care for a loan covenant that limited his yearly capital expenditures, which basically meant he couldn't build more than one boat per year. Finally, Minor ignored the covenant and decided to build two boats.

The Chemical Bank learned of his transgression and called him on it. Minor responded by telling the bank representative, "What you gonna do about it?"

"What did you say?"

"What are you gonna do? You gonna foreclose?"

The banker was mortified. How could this Cajun say that to the corner office of the Chemical Bank?

But as the weeks passed, the bank did nothing, and Minor launched his new Botruc.

Apparently, not even a strict Manhattan financier could slow down the economy-charged verve of boatmen like Minor.

Across the bayou, Dick Guidry was equally confident. Despite suffering a North Sea plunge like Nolty J. Theriot, Inc., Dick had a much smaller fleet than Theriot and presumably, didn't take as big of a hit. Besides, all Dick had to do was look at what the Gulf was doing. If he couldn't make money out there now, then where could he? These days, even the amateur b.s. artists were making a killing in the Gulf. Boatmen were going to Las Vegas, blowing $20,000 and laughing it off.

As the 1970s drew to a close, Dick was talking about the current good times with Lawrence Mazerac at Main Iron Works south of Houma. But Maz wasn't so sure of things. He talked about the problematic signs in the business, particularly some of the policies of Jimmy Carter's presidential administration. In 1978, Carter had announced an ambitious government-backed synthetic fuels program. Additionally, the auto industry had begun making fuel-efficient cars. They'd started shrinking automobiles, and in some cases, replacing the gas-gulping V-8 engines with V-6s and even V-4s. Further, the masters of the tiny, fuel-efficient car, the Japanese, were now sending more of their Toyotas and Datsuns into the US market. Down in South America, the Brazilian government was reducing its fossil fuel needs by allowing gasoline to include alcohol made from sugarcane bagasse. The cane fuel, which could have just as easily been gleaned from the sugar mills along Bayou Lafourche, made up 20 percent of some Brazilian gasoline mixtures.

With the move toward alternative fuels and gasoline efficiency, the world wouldn't need as much fossil fuel, and with an oversupply, the price of crude oil and natural gas had to decrease. Moreover, in the boat business, with all these *couillon* doctors and lawyers funding limited partnerships run by rogue boatmen, there had to be a glut of vessels, too. What would happen to the boats when the price of oil finally dropped?

It was simply too much of everything. The decade was one of excess anyway—of long, wavy hair and wide collars, of high platform shoes and flowing bell-bottoms. To some, the 1970s had been long on strobe lights and purple smoke, Evil Knievel stunts and pharmaceutical illusion, but short on substance and reality. And this was about more than the awkward transition from dance halls to discotheques. It was, to some oilfield prognosticators, a gross overabundance, an impending implosion.

But Dick didn't see the negative. He'd had offers to buy his company that would have left him with a profit well into the millions. So how could times be bad?

Of course, he'd also heard, either from Lawrence Mazerac or from some other doomsayer, of the problems of rising interest rates. In December 1980, the prime rate hit 21 percent. Yes, 21 percent was a helluva high rate, but if the banks were willing to take the risk, so what? And besides, bankers from all over the country were calling on Dick's Galliano office and trying to lend him money. With all this activity and aggression, Dick didn't think anything bad could happen.

While there were plenty of boats in the Gulf, they were needed to service all those rigs, and *mon Dieu*, look at all those rigs.

V

Gravity

Cheramie Bo-Truc 36 servicing a rig in the Gulf of Mexico in 1982.
(Courtesy of L & M Botruc Rental, LLC)

V

Gravity

Chapter 18

The Empire Strikes Back

1982

———⟨∞⟩———

The galloping 1970s had produced rigs, rigs, and more rigs. Across the Gulf of Mexico, the monolithic, multilegged platforms echoed and clanked with work. They burned flames and puffed smoke, emitted strange-smelling gases and brimmed with men in hard hats. In nine years, the iron creatures had popped up so fast in the Gulf that they soon dominated parts of the shore front horizon. They weren't just isolated structures, but whole cities of steel. The rig clusters soon became known to the captains as constellations with Big Dipper-like nicknames. Approaching them from the water, the rigs loomed like steel monsters, resembling the gargantuan walking tanks in *The Empire Strikes Back*, the 1980 *Star Wars* sequel.

Although these leviathans appeared to threaten to come to life and start marching, as the months passed in 1982, a growing number of rigs became dormant. While many people in the oilfield couldn't yet see it, the steel giants had produced far more petroleum than the market needed. The oversupply of oil along with the move toward fuel efficiency had knocked back the price of crude, which had been climbing since 1973 but was now falling and falling.

Suddenly, there were too many boats running on banknotes with interest rates that their borrowers couldn't handle. In fact, the economy plunged so quickly that the ol' gambling boatmen could no longer employ their high-rolling methods. They could no longer make big bets with the Empire, which was the Arab-manipulated, Middle Eastern-controlled, whimsical global oilfield. If the Bobby Orgerons and the Minor Cheramies were going to survive, they had to do business in a different manner. They could no longer barrel their way onto Mineral Boards or barge into senators' offices and pull themselves out of messes. They couldn't just borrow *plus d'argent* and keep going. For one thing, no lender in their right mind was going to risk more money on a hopelessly red balance sheet.

As if the financial shortfalls weren't bad enough, business was also becoming more expensive. With boat companies forced to cut back on their vessel maintenance, the boats experienced more engine problems, which the boatmen couldn't always afford to properly redress. As the companies cut back on the number of crew to save money, the remaining crew members sometimes suffered from being shorthanded or too fatigued. The result was an increase in the number of accidents, some of them fatal. There was real gruesomeness out there—everything from drilling tools severing fingers to crane booms cracking skulls to falling loads crushing bodies. Even with the proper manpower, the oilfield was a dangerous place. In the understaffed, overstressed environment of the 1980s, the workplace was particularly hazardous.

As each accident occurred, insurance rates rose. With many of the claims being governed by the plaintiff-friendly Jones Act, the boatmen stood little chance of prevailing and lowering their insurance rates. In the past, if a maritime defense attorney beat the odds and won a Jones Act suit, a boatman might reward him with a brand-new car or a set of expensive golf clubs. Now, the same boatman could barely afford the insurance that ultimately paid for his defense. Some of the insurance brokers like Leon Theriot might spot their customers a few payments, but they couldn't carry them forever.

In many senses, the gamblers like Minor Cheramie had to rely heavily on their financial advisors. Number men like Minor's Woody Terrebonne became the saviors. While both Terrebonne and Minor knew that as the 1980s progressed it would've been much easier to file for bankruptcy, Minor refused to take that course. Instead, Terrebonne constantly talked on the phone with the fleet's financiers, with companies like GE Credit and Chemical Bank, convincing them to allow L & M Botruc to pay a reduced note; then, as times worsened, only interest and later, less than full interest.

Minor had also told Terrebonne that he wanted to keep as many employees as possible. That meant he had to put his office workers on a seven-days-on, seven-off schedule. He watched as Terrebonne advised him to cut salaries by 5 percent, then 10 percent. Later, they'd scale down on benefits and do anything to keep some money in the pockets of his most loyal people. Hopefully, the moves would help them live up to the oilfield's new saying, "Stay Alive 'Til '85"—a saying grounded more in hope than in fact.

At MONTCO, Lee Orgeron had been on a revival mission ever since he stepped into his father's seat as a green eighteen-year-old in 1979. Of course, until 1982, the economy was so healthy that Lee didn't have to worry about the availability of work, but he did have to contend with his father, a recovering substance abuser. Although Bobby's initial rehabilitation was successful, like any other addict, his battle was ongoing. He'd struggle with alcohol until he gave it up for good in 1989, but his aching body would always make it difficult for him to handle his craving for pain medication.

Bobby's passing of the gavel to Lee wasn't so much about Bobby's struggles with chemical dependency as it was a clash of personalities. Just as Bobby had argued with Juan, Lee quarreled up and down the office with Bobby. Sometimes, their spats were so heated the other office workers walked into another room or left the building altogether.

Unlike Bobby, when dealing with outsiders, Lee could remain level- and coolheaded. While Bobby was an emotional dice roller, Lee was a steady hand. Bobby pounced on instinct, whereas Lee moved methodically, taking action in small, carefully planned steps. Although Bobby was loud and in your face, Lee was quiet and poker-faced. Lee was every bit as tall, and even bigger than, his father, yet Lee didn't use his size to intimidate. He preferred to remain understated and, at times, completely mysterious. Unlike Bobby, who was famous for making brash proclamations, Lee became known as a young man who asked questions—lots and lots of them. If he didn't comprehend something, he researched it thoroughly, and, in so doing, he'd probe everyone he could find from Bobby to MONTCO employees to competitors, insurance brokers, bankers, and anyone else on any topic from liquid mud systems to natural family planning.

Most of the time, Lee's elders answered his questions. But occasionally, he'd encounter a competitor who wanted to take advantage of Lee's youth. Sometimes, the unfriendly competitor might try and jump MONTCO's position in a shipyard and attempt to have his boat repaired before Lee's, hoping to take a job that MONTCO had. This was the exception rather than the rule; most of the boatmen were willing to patiently listen to Lee's inquiries and give him real answers.

Usually, people wanted to help him. Chevron's Bob Looper often kept him abreast of the market from the oilman's side. Sometimes, if Tidewater was asking for rate increases, Looper would call Lee and tell him that Chevron was getting ready to grant the public giant's request, and that Lee should write him a letter and also ask for a rate increase.

Lee's education also came from experience. In 1982, his father convinced him to build two liftboats, telling him he'd lend him the $50,000 down payment and would cosign the note. Lee himself investigated the financing. In dealing with the banks, Lee researched every possible loan and rate structure available. In finding the best deal for construction of the liftboats, he learned that, overall, MONTCO's debt structure was muddled, problematic, and, frankly, wasteful. His father had never spent much time on learning the finer points of financing; Bobby had instead focused on getting boats built as fast as he could and then putting them to work. Because of this aggressive yet impetuous style, the Orgerons were paying far too much interest on a hodgepodge portfolio of high-risk loans.

Lee was starting to feel the debt load squeeze the Orgeron operation, which split into three companies, all of which Lee ran. One was Lee's own two-liftboat business; the other was Bobby's MONTCO, which owned three tugs, five supply boats, and two liftboats; the third was THOR, Bobby and Leon Theriot's company that owned two deck barges.

As 1982 shifted to 1983, Lee was finding it increasingly difficult to pay down all the debt. He believed there had to be a solution. Of course, he couldn't just bull and barter his way through this crisis the way his father had done in the past. He'd have to focus on the numbers. Somehow, he had to manipulate them.

By 1983, Nolty J. Theriot, Inc. had been stuck in a deep swell for quite some time. For Pye Theriot, the downturn of the 1980s had actually started in the mid-1970s when the North Sea nationals had begun to push the Theriot fleet from Europe. While Pye's fellow boatmen flourished in the late 1970s, Pye was stuck with heavy, high-horse tugs that burned too much fuel for the Gulf. Only five of his twenty-six tugs were fuel efficient enough to be truly profitable; the other twenty-one had three times the necessary horsepower and burned three times the fuel. Also, there was suddenly little need for Theriot's speciality, pipeline construction. While there was rig-moving work in the Gulf, it was temporary and mostly hourly work. It didn't compare to the steady, day-pay construction jobs, where the oil companies even absorbed the costly fuel. Instead of sitting back on a pipeline gig and raking in the profits, the Theriot men had to keep hustling and bidding work.

Moreover, the Gulf was an entirely different insurance climate than the North Sea. In Europe, Theriot had lost only one man, a Spanish deckhand who'd been swept overboard and had drowned. As tragic as that incident was, financially, it had no effect on insurance premiums. The deckhand's family didn't sue, and the only Theriot employee to file suit was a British engineer who'd lost his fingertip. The Brit sued in a US court, but the case was thrown out because of the Jones Act's exclusion of foreign seamen in foreign waters. The near claim-free North Sea environment meant Theriot had received a yearly *reduction* in insurance costs. But in the suit-happy Gulf in the early eighties, insurance premiums could increase from year to year by as much as 25 percent.

As the cost of doing business escalated, Pye started to move the company through the bust by selling some of his boats. Although he should've sold them sooner, the profits from the sales helped to retire some debt.

He still had several North Sea-class tugs, which weren't even fuel efficient enough to make a profit doing rig moving work, just sitting at the dock. Finally, it got to the point where Pye couldn't make his $800,000 quarterly payment on the Mar Ad–backed Title 11 loan. So Pye traveled to Washington and asked the Mar Ad to go interest only, which the company could handle. In south Louisiana, many of the banks had been allowing interest only, and many of them believed that they were lucky to even get the interest.

The Mar Ad officials accepted Pye's offer or, at least, that's what Pye thought. He flew back to Louisiana one Friday thinking he had a deal. He also believed he'd worked out a purchase agreement to sell four of his tugs to a Seattle company.

Then the shocker came on Monday morning, when Pye learned that *both* deals were off. The Seattle company that was supposed to purchase the four Theriot tugs had instead gone to the Mar Ad and talked to them about taking over Theriot's Mar Ad notes on the tugs, and the Mar Ad, rather than working with Theriot on an interest-only loan, had decided to work with the Seattle company.

Incensed, Pye decided to kill the Title 11 loan with a Chapter 11 bankruptcy. Before he had his lawyers file the petition, he took his remaining $400,000 in cash and paid off all of Theriot's unsecured creditors, showing up at the bankruptcy hearing with only one creditor, the Maritime Administration.

After discharging the Mar Ad loan in bankruptcy, Pye sold some more tugs and kept going. Even though he had enough cash to carry the company, the competition was starting to kill him. While he'd never had to worry about a price war in the North Sea, that's exactly what the eighties glut had created in the Gulf of Mexico. The price for moving a rig had gone from $360 an hour to $140 an hour, and a tug, depending on the amount of hours, needed to get about $250 an hour to break even. While every tug company knew this, they were clearly trying to sweat each other out. They weren't just violating the boatman's Code, they were flat out abandoning it and cutting one another's throats like pirates.

Pye knew it had gotten bad when Bobby Orgeron, who had three tugs operating in the Theriot fleet, walked into Pye's office one day and said, "Pye, I got heartburn."

"What are you talking about, Bobby?"

"I got them three damn tugboats sitting right here across my stomach. I got to do something with 'em."

What Pye, Bobby, and many other operators ultimately decided to do was call the first of several meetings in a back room at Erjy's, a bayouside Lockport restaurant. Every major operator was invited, including Tidewater, Claude Autin, Guidry Brothers (Bobby and Dickie Guidry were distant cousins of Dick Guidry), Otto Candies, and the Theriot group, which included, among others, the Vizier brothers, Dick Guidry, and Bobby Orgeron. The goal was to in some way get the price back up, because if it didn't come up, they'd all be out of business.

Tidewater didn't send a representative to the first meeting and, being a public company, had to be careful about getting into any discussions that could be seen as price-fixing. Really, the Tidewater executives didn't have as much to worry about as the others. They were working for a paycheck; if the company defaulted, the bank couldn't take their personal assets. If the independents failed to make it, they could lose their homes.

Ultimately, Tidewater did send a representative to some of the meetings, and its people did come to the understanding that at the market price, every hour their boat was working, the company was losing money. No one, not Tidewater, not the little man, wanted to lose. So they rallied together. All of the companies, private and public, somehow came to an understanding and the price went up. Whatever the legal definition of price-fixing, their actions were necessary. To them it was, in no way, collusion, but only survival.

It would take lots of meetings of the minds among the boatmen to pull through the 1980s. It helped to have a common trade organization, the Offshore Marine Services Association (OMSA) in New Orleans, which was now run full-time by Robert Alario, who'd helped to develop and manage the organization in the late 1960s when he was with Theriot.

While Tidewater was obviously a powerful presence in OMSA, the independents had their share of the clout, too. When Minor Cheramie threatened to quit the organization, none other than Tidewater's John Laborde told him, "Minor, you can't quit. You have to stay. If you want your problems addressed, you've got to come to the meetings and raise hell."

By 1984, Minor's hell raising had to give way to pure survival tactics. At this stage, he had only one weapon left in his arsenal, honesty. He, Woody Terrebonne, and their counsel Bill Porteous developed a policy of 100 percent truthfulness with all creditors—if the check isn't in the mail, don't say that it is.

The Cheramies also didn't, unlike some other boatmen, store cash in coffee cans and misrepresent their financial picture. Instead, Terrebonne invited the creditors to audit the company. It was company policy to treat all creditors proportionately alike. If they were paying 10 percent to a big bank, they were also paying 10 percent to a small welding company.

It boiled down to Minor Cheramie and Woody Terrebonne's reputation for integrity. For instance, back in the 1960s, Minor asked his son M. J. to take twelve postdated checks to Bollinger Shipyard to fund the construction of a Botruc. M. J. handed Dick Bollinger the checks, and Bollinger put them in his drawer. When a payment was due, Bollinger would take the check out, deposit it, and watch it clear.

With Minor now banking on his trustworthiness, he and his advisors still had to come up with new ideas on how to manage the daily bloodletting. One solution was for the L & M Botruc port captains to look into their stockrooms and decide what engines and parts they needed and which ones they could do without. L & M representatives would then take the unneeded ones to the machinery companies in exchange for credit against L & M's debt.

Despite all the effort, Minor still felt the weight of approaching insolvency. It got to the point where Bill Porteous told the Cheramie family members who had personally guaranteed the company loans that in the event of bankruptcy, there would be a conflict of interest between them and the company. Hence, he advised them to retain their own counsel.

When Minor heard Porteous utter the word bankruptcy, he blew up at him and shouted, "*We not going bankrupt!*"

In 1984, a climate of bankruptcy was beginning to settle over the Gulf South oilfield. At MONTCO, the Orgerons were losing command over their debt management. Their "profits" were simply rolling out in interest payments. The financials were mind-boggling; Lee could only shake his head as he watched one supply boat collect her day rate, which after paying the boat's note and costs, amounted to a net of -$400 per day. The company was quickly working itself broke.

Nevertheless, Lee felt like MONTCO was still well positioned in the market, and he didn't want to start liquidating equipment just to raise capital. Instead, he honestly thought he could refinance the entire fleet—his own two liftboats, supply boat, and tug and Bobby's six remaining boats—and start making real money again. Presently, many of the boats were on a prime plus rate, and Lee believed he could consolidate all of these single-boat loans into one fixed-rate, low-interest loan.

However, because the market and the company were still free-falling, Lee didn't have much time. Trying to create a presentation with pencils, an adding machine, and a stack of ledgers was taking far too long. There had to be a faster way.

By 1984, Pye Theriot had already survived some rough years, but his company still wasn't near the profit machine it had been back in 1975. Since his father's death in 1976, he'd been getting advice from all angles, from Nolty's trusted old lieutenants to new people trying to steer an impressionable young man. His critics claimed he didn't listen to the right people; had he paid attention to the older dogs like Charlie Sanders, Robert Alario, Tomey Doucet, and his insurance man Leon Theriot, they could've pulled him through the North Sea mess and the present Gulf bust. And, Pye should have first taken advice from someone else back in 1975—himself. Had he told his father to sell the company, he wouldn't have been in this pickle. Had he not been strapped with these big, fuel-burning tugs, he could've done well in politics because he was likeable and made people feel comfortable.

Now that a career as an elected official or as a lobbyist was improbable, Pye had to live by his 1975 decision not to sell. Unfortunately, Pye hadn't had the chance to watch his father run the company when Nolty was still healthy. By the time Pye got involved, he was an ocean apart from his father during a boom-boom North Sea cycle. He'd never had Nolty tell him things like Sidney Savoie had told his son, Ted, little pieces of wisdom like putting away money when times were good because you'd need that money when the times went bad.

Then again, Nolty had never been one to squirrel away money anyway. What Pye had seen his father do was give, give, give. Pye hadn't witnessed his daddy shave money by using cheap suppliers; he'd seen the opposite. By the same token, his father had, at times, been compelled to make some cuts. Pye hadn't been with the company when the 1960 recession had forced Nolty to lay off some of his most loyal employees. These were the type of cuts that Pye should've been making.

Nevertheless, some people in lower Lafourche would've criticized Pye no matter what he was doing because he wasn't his daddy, the war hero, the philanthropist, the North Sea conqueror, the man who could afford to live on *lagniappe* because *lagniappe* had been his life. Even when Nolty had no money, he'd had a passion for the business. He'd always had enough drive to will his way out of a downturn. Unlike his father, Pye had no love for tugs. In this economy, he couldn't just smile and say, "Don't worry about nothing" because he had too much to worry about and too little to give.

Moreover, while Pye didn't mind playing his beloved golf with clients, for the most part, he let his best friend, Leslie Schouest, handle the customers. Leslie had been running Offshore Tugs, Inc., Nolty's old brokerage group, and was having some success. Perhaps Leslie could push them through til 1985, when the oilfield would most surely revive.

But by 1985, the oilfield didn't come alive. If anything, it continued its plunge. The once gold-plated Golden Meadow was becoming a rusty boat graveyard. In many cases, the boatmen just didn't have the funds to do anything about the paint that was fading on their tied-up vessels. Across south Louisiana, start-up, get-rich-quick oilfield contractors were shutting their doors. Sometimes, employees would show up on a Monday morning for work and find the door to their workplace padlocked with a note on the door about where to pick up their last check. Sometimes, there were no last checks as oilfield companies choked up the bankruptcy court dockets all over the Gulf South.

Across south Louisiana, many of the new shopping centers of the 1970s were turning into vacant shells with hurricane tape on their windows, graffiti on their bricks, and weeds taking over the parking lots. The banks seized and shut down businesses up and down the bayous. In Lafourche parish, unemployment rose past 25 percent in 1985, the highest in the nation. With oil driving the entire economy, nearly every person, oilfield or non-oilfield, was affected, and for the first time in two hundred years, some Cajun families were faced with the prospect of leaving their homeland to find work.

In the boat business, even the healthiest companies struggled to survive. Unfortunately, Dick Guidry's once indomitable American Offshore, Inc. failed to make it. To save himself from bankruptcy, Dick had to sell his remaining boats for fifteen cents on the dollar. Like many others, he'd missed his chance at selling out in the 1970s for multimillions. At least he'd avoided the embarrassment of bankruptcy and had escaped with his dignity.

By 1985, Minor Cheramie's own escape was in serious jeopardy. Not only was he fighting for his company to stay afloat, he also learned that colon cancer was threatening his life. The first sign of cancer had been his passing blood, which led him to the Lady of the Sea Hospital in Galliano for an upper GI. The doctors found nothing and tried to schedule a lower GI. Minor, however, put off the exam because trawling season was about to start, and he wasn't about to miss it for some medical test. The lower GI could wait another six weeks or so. By the time Minor went in for the test, the cancer was everywhere.

He had no choice but to seek treatment at M.D. Anderson Hospital in Houston. While he'd try his best to save his life, he'd have no control over the attempt to rescue his company.

With Minor in the hospital, Woody Terrebonne and attorney Bill Porteous went up to New York City to meet with the Chemical Bank executives to convince them not to foreclose. Other South Louisiana boat companies were there, too, leading Porteous to call the affair "Cajun day before the firing squad." As the Cheramie crew waited for their meeting, they could overhear the bankers yelling at the owner of another boat company from the Lafayette area.

When Porteous listened to the bankers tell the boatman they were taking his vessels, Porteous prepared for a brutal round of brinksmanship. Sure enough, when the bank vice president called them into the room, Porteous believed the banker took on the persona of a "repo man for a used car lot."

As the banker badgered the Cheramie crew, Porteous said everything he could to dissuade the banker from repossession, telling him, "You don't understand the boat business. The country needs oil, which means this industry has to revive. And it will."

The banker threw up his arms. "I've had enough of all of this. Enough!" He looked at Porteous, held out his hand, and said, "Give me the keys to the boats."

The Cheramie crew smiled. Obviously, the banker had never heard that an offshore boat has a keyless ignition. Porteous licked his chops and said, "You see, I told you that you didn't understand the boat business. Boats don't have keys!"

The banker was speechless. He'd been more than one-upped. Perhaps he suddenly realized what Minor Cheramie knew all along. If Minor couldn't pay his note, the bank's mortgage documents wouldn't produce the money to pay those notes, either. This was especially true now, where the devalued collateral was worth very little in comparison with the debt. The bankers didn't have any choice; if they wanted their money, they had to back off of Minor and his boats and trust him.

However, as Minor's men valiantly fought off bankruptcy, he was having a difficult time saving himself. As the months passed in 1985, he was dying, and there was little the doctors at M.D. Anderson could do to save him.

Throughout his treatment, his wife had stayed by his side. As rough as their relationship had been, as Lou watched her husband suffer, she knew that she still loved him. In the hospital, he was stripped of his vices, and he was as blue-eyed and tender as he'd been at the moment she met him. One day, he told her, "I would have never done it without you. If I wouldn't have had a woman like you behind me, I would have done none of this. I wouldn't have made it."

Honest to his final hour, it was a good way for her to remember him. Minor Anthony Cheramie, Botruc visionary, devoted friend, loving father and grandfather, ever determined to fulfill his American dream, died on Flag Day, June 14, 1986.

As the summer of 1986 unfolded, the industry's death march continued. The price of oil hit absolute bottom, traveling from $40 a barrel in 1981 to less than $10 a barrel in 1986. As if the early 1980s hadn't done enough damage to the surviving boat companies, 1986 would knock out many of them. MONTCO was certainly absorbing its share of body blows. It had become so bleak that Bobby Orgeron had to take $1.2 million of his own personal money and pour it back into the company but, by itself, his hard-earned retirement stash wasn't enough.

The situation was far worse than it had been in the late 1960s, when Bobby and Nacis Theriot were a couple of hundred thousand dollars in the hole.

Now, Bobby and Lee Orgeron were in the negative for millions. Bobby admitted that he was in over his head; he fully believed that without Lee, the company wasn't going to make it. With him, at least they had a chance.

Back in 1984, Lee had believed the company's best chance was to refinance the fleet. After talking with his younger brother, Joseph, a college student at Nicholls and a technology buff, Lee learned of a way to efficiently prepare and make his loan presentation to the bank. Joseph convinced Lee to buy a personal computer, a Macintosh, and to install something called "software" into this convenient machine. The key program was Multiplan for the Mac, which had been created by an obscure independent company named Microsoft. In 1985, Multiplan would give way to Excel, and in 1986, Microsoft would go public.

But in 1984, Lee's discovery of Multiplan infused him with confidence and saved him precious time. He marveled at Multiplan's "spreadsheets," electronic ledgers that allowed him to change a number with a simple keystroke and instantly recalculate the bottom line. The spreadsheets enabled Lee to make extremely fluid loan projections. He could account for every contingency in the volatile market, where day rates and costs could vary week to week.

With the spreadsheets, Lee prepared his bank presentation much, much faster than he ever anticipated. Before he knew it, he was making a well-documented pitch to Premier Bank in Baton Rouge, the successor of Raceland Bank, which he had been dealing with since he joined the company in 1979. Ultimately, because of the strength of his personal relationship with the bank and the power of his numbers, Lee proved that, despite the market, MONTCO could handle a fixed-rate fleet loan. Such a loan, he demonstrated, would mean a healthy profit for Premier Bank in a market full of losses. In the end, the bank agreed to consolidate the Orgerons' debt with a $5.5 million loan at a manageable, fixed interest rate.

By 1986, Lee, who'd been deprived of a college education, had done his best to quench his thirst for knowledge by intimately studying his industry for seven years. In so doing, he'd obtained his own special degree, something arguably more valuable than the most hard-earned Harvard MBA. As Lee began to master the nuances of management, marketing, and finance, he also learned something about the oilfield ethics. Suddenly and surprisingly, things had changed.

Chapter 19

Independence

Post 1986

Lee discovered that what had been the business was not the business now. He had always been told that the only way for a boatman to survive was to booze and schmooze his clients, to pander to them, and philander with them. There was no way Lee was going to play that game.

Economically speaking, he learned that he didn't need to participate in all the bacchanalia to save the company. Part of the reason was that the lurid scene was fading. There was little money to fund the parties and the gifts, and many of the old oilmen who'd been on the entertainment dole had died or been forced into retirement. The ones who were still around didn't exactly feel comfortable hitting the bars with a young man in his twenties like Lee, who could've been their son and, in some cases, their grandson.

Moreover, the oil companies had made it clear to their employees that they had to avoid questionable practices. Whether this change resulted from the cutbacks or from a guilty conscience, the industry was undergoing a cleansing. It was arguably becoming "more moral." The payoffs, the gifts, and the prostitution drastically decreased. While there would always be men with their hands out, and there'd always be a rough, whoring segment of the industry, the oilfield would never again become a near universal bathhouse of illicit sex and graft.

Even if the oilfield hadn't purged itself, Lee still wouldn't have sold his soul to obtain contracts. What the oilman required, Lee learned, was impeccable service at a fair price. What they needed was a boatman they could communicate with and depend on. When it came to entertainment, Lee discovered it was much easier to win them over by taking them hunting or fishing with their wives or sons. A man's child was much closer to his heart than a new car or a cheap thrill could ever be.

Besides, Lee didn't have time for the partying. He didn't want a cloudy, throbbing head to make it difficult for him to function in the morning. He didn't want substances slowing him down. When the time came to make a decision, he had to make a clear, informed one.

The entire post-1986 movement was one of independence in two senses. It signified a freedom from an unethical way of doing business and from a reliance on a boom of false promise. While it did not mean an independence from the Empire and its Arab-driven swings, it at least meant a healthier, more educated respect for it.

During this period of change, all the transformation didn't affect the Code, which Lee valued deeply. He'd grown up with it, and in one particular instance in the late eighties, he witnessed how harshly it could be enforced. The incident began when a small utility boat operator asked Lee's father to help find a contract for him, and Bobby agreed. The Orgerons didn't have any more utility boats so Bobby was more than happy to help a friend and fellow Cajun. Bobby brokered the boat to an old client, UNOCAL, and took a relatively small fifty-dollar-per-day commission.

Six months later, the UNOCAL superintendent called Bobby about the utility boat operator and said, "You told me that guy was your friend."

"He is."

"Well, him and his brother came over here and told me they wanted to cut you off of the fifty dollars a day you're getting. They wanted to go direct with the company instead of working through you. What do you want me to do with that boat, Bobby?"

"Send it home," said Bobby, more saddened than angry. He couldn't believe a fellow bayou man would break the Code.

Eventually, and not surprisingly, the Code violator went bankrupt.

Of course, bankruptcy was something Bobby and Lee were trying to steer clear of in the 1980s, and it was Lee who was doing all the driving. Even though he'd cleaned up the company's financing, he still had to find work for their vessels; he now had four boats and his father had six. But there was no way he could put all ten to work in the oilfield. If the rig owners couldn't use his tugs, then where exactly was the opportunity?

Some of it was in the ocean towing market, pushing and pulling container barges, and that's where Lee found a willing Canal Barge Line and other clients. If his tugs could tow rigs on the Gulf, they could push and pull barges, too. Lee soon secured a steady gig towing container barges back and forth from Miami to Poncé, Puerto Rico. He and his sales staff also found exotic jobs, both geographically, pulling cargo to places like Cabinda, Africa; and cargo-wise, once towing a space shuttle fuel tank for NASA. The NASA job proved to be interesting but ultimately regrettable.

In November 1994, the *J.A. Orgeron* was under contract to tow a barge containing a $50 million space shuttle fuel tank, which was manufactured at the Lockheed Martin assembly at Michoud, just outside New Orleans. The *J.A.* would pull the valuable cargo down the Mississippi River across the Gulf and around the Cape of Florida to Port Canaveral. Unfortunately, during a violent storm, the *J.A. Orgeron* lost power in the Atlantic Ocean and sent out a distress signal. A supertanker, of all things, answered the call and dramatically rescued the *J.A.*'s crew and salvaged the boat, barge, and the mega-expensive space shuttle fuel tank. In consideration for salvaging the *J.A.*, MONTCO settled with the supertanker owner, captain, and crew for $220,000, but the tanker's claim against NASA went to trial in federal court in New Orleans. At trial, Judge Stanwood Duval made history with a $6.4 million salvage award. While the appellate court reduced the sum to $4.1 million, it was still the highest salvage award in US maritime history. For Lee Orgeron, the voyage was merely a short hurdle in his challenge to vault MONTCO into the next millennium. Lee had started to shape the company's future back in 1988, when he and Bobby decided to sell their collective five supply boats and focus on tugs and liftboats. The Orgerons had acquired their first liftboat in 1978, but that acquisition, made at Chevron's request, was mainly a

good boomtime gamble on a new gimmick. Although the liftboat concept had been around for years, first pioneered by Lynn Dean's prototype
and Nolty Theriot's closely related Purple People Eater submersible, the
vessel had yet to take off.

In the late 1980s, as Lee looked at the global oilfield picture, even
though he saw an oversupply of workboats, he didn't see many liftboats.
There were tens of thousands of tugs, crew boats, and supply boats; however, from what he could tell, there were hardly one hundred liftboats.
Not only was the market sparsely populated, but liftboats, looking more
like mobile rigs than boats, were loosely regulated. The manning requirements were next to nothing, and, unlike a traditional vessel, liftboats
were easier to repair. They didn't require an annual dry-docking. While
they, of course, needed maintenance, their uncomplicated propulsion
systems and efficient hydraulic jacking systems caused fewer problems
than those found on other vessel types.

Moreover, Lee realized that he could pitch his liftboats for just about
every facet of oil and gas well operations. From seismic work to well
workover, from platform installation to platform support, from pile driving to pipelaying, from rig repair to oil spill reclamation, the possibilities
were endless. Few people understood their potential. Later, in the 1990s,
Lee would watch admirably as Larose's Al Danos would turn a losing
year into a liftboat boom in Nigeria; back in the 1980s, the scarcity of
major liftboat players meant Lee could command a serious day rate, in
excess of $10,000 per day.

In the 1990s, in addition to Lee's liftboat success, he was still making money with tugs. He formed a tug marketing group with Tomey
Doucet and four other men. The group rivaled Theriot's Offshore
Tugs, Inc., which Lee had once made an unsuccessful offer to buy from
Pye Theriot, but the tug market was taking its toll on Lee. To stay
ahead, he had to constantly bid jobs. While he was spending 90 percent
of his time on the tugboat side of his business and only 10 percent on
the liftboats, tugs were producing only 35 percent of the company's
revenue.

It wasn't so much the slimmer profit margin that was souring Lee on
the tug market as it was the time away from home. The main reason he
had initially rejected the boat business was to choose a career that

allowed him some quality time with his wife and children. As a tug owner in the mid-nineties, Lee found himself away from his family— not partying and cavorting like the men of his father's generation, but grinding out bids—mostly in Houston. In 1996, Lee's wife, Tammy, pointed out to him that since their honeymoon in 1978, they'd never taken anything beyond a weekend together. Every vacation had either involved the kids or the clients. When Lee realized where all the tug toil had taken him, he sold his tugs to Kurt Crosby, a growing industry maven based in Galliano.

After the sale, Lee could focus on his family and his liftboats. He'd already positioned himself for the move. In 1988, he'd acquired a little shipyard on the Houma Navigation Canal and turned it into a liftboatonly repair yard so he could efficiently maintain his vessels. To minimize maintenance, he made sure his boats were well built. To that end, he decided to use the quality-driven and conveniently located Bollinger as his only liftboat builder.

After a few years of developing his fleet, Lee learned that he could do more than save his company. He could also buy his dream yacht, keep her docked off the coast of Mexico's beautiful Isla Mujeras, and, quite often, fly his wife and kids there on a whim for a long weekend. While coasting on the blue Mexican Gulf, Lee could take medicine that would help him deal with his tendency to get seasick as his petite Tammy, a passionate fisherwoman, fought one big yellowfin tuna after another.

As father Bobby watched Lee operate, he beamed in amazement. Bobby didn't think he could do what Lee was doing, and he was especially relieved that his son hadn't picked up his bad habits. He would say later about Lee, "I'm the happiest man in the world to see that he didn't turn out like me." While Bobby might've sparred with Lee here and there, mostly he listened to his son and signed his name wherever Lee pointed.

By the end of the terrible 1980s, Lee had not only saved MONTCO and made a name for himself; he'd also helped transform his father. In taking Bobby out of the business, Lee had, once and for all, indirectly caused Bobby to change his ways. By 1989, Bobby put an end to his drinking and womanizing. While he still had to cope with his chemical cravings for pain medication, he would now be what he'd been those first five years of marriage—a faithful husband. At least his grandkids would see only the best of him.

While Lee Orgeron had lassoed and streamlined the management of MONTCO, things weren't so clear in 1986 at L & M Botruc. Unlike MONTCO, where Lee was the obvious successor, when Minor Cheramie died, there were chiefs running all over the wigwam. Technically, Minor's brother, Lefty, had the most say-so with his 50 percent stake, but Lefty had never run the company and wasn't about to manage it now. Consequently, it was difficult to determine who was in charge, Minor's son M. J., son-in-law Pat, or office manager Woody Terrebonne. To further muddle matters, Lefty inserted his son, Steve, back into the business. Suddenly, the company, which had always only known one boss man in Minor, had several bosses.

Although Minor's passing had created this chaos and emotionally rocked his family and the company, financially, his death had initially helped the business by injecting it with $4 million in life insurance. While the cash in one sense saved L & M Botruc, it couldn't satisfy the company's debt service forever. For a spell, many of the employees, salesmen or not, hit the road and started selling.

But the team approach wasn't going to work with so many quarterbacks. Lefty's son, Steve, and Butch Danos couldn't get along, and Butch left the company to work for Bollinger Shipyard. M. J. and Pat wanted more control and more peace and agreed to buy out Lefty. The problem was that Lefty had personally guaranteed more than $20 million worth of notes. He couldn't sell his interest without relieving himself of all that debt. With the industry still unstable, the banks and finance companies didn't feel comfortable excusing any personal guarantors. In fact, when Terrebonne called the lenders and asked them to take Lefty's name off the note, most of them laughed.

As Terrebonne tried to figure out a way to make the buyout work, M. J. and Pat did their best to keep their boats working. Sometimes that meant finding work outside of the oilfield. In an extreme example of diversity, M. J. hired out the *C-Truc 3*, a 196-foot cargo boat, to run ammunition, rockets, and mortar shells to Pusan, South Korea. He was working through a bareboat charterer who couldn't disclose the ultimate purchaser of the munitions. Despite the potentially shady deal, M. J. had to take the job, for which he received half of the payment up front. For the trip to the South China Sea, M. J. hired a special captain out of Houston.

When the vessel hit the Pusan civilian harbor, unbeknownst to M. J., the captain put the entire mission at risk when he violated a South Korean military order by going ashore without a military escort. The Pusan harbormaster stopped the captain and told him that if he left the *C-Truc 3* again, he'd blow her up. Meanwhile, the vessel's engineer requested and received an escort to shore.

When the engineer returned to the civilian harbor, the *C-Truc 3* was gone. He ultimately found the vessel in the military harbor. The crew members told him that the captain had gotten drunk and had told the crew that the Russians were coming. To avoid a "Soviet attack," he snuck the *C-Truc 3* out of the civilian harbor and started doing antisubmarine maneuvers before the military corralled the vessel.

As the *C-Truc 3* arrived back on US shores in San Francisco, M. J. met her at the dock, listened to the engineer's story, and then told the crazy captain he was relieving him.

The captain laughed at him. "You can't relieve me," he said. "I can only be relieved by a licensed master."

M. J. pulled out his captain's license, which he'd kept up to date, even though he hadn't officially been behind the wheel in years. He held up the license and said, "Consider yourself relieved. Get your stuff off my boat and get the hell off."

M. J. then hired another captain to bring the boat home. While he'd saved the *C-Truc 3* from further tomfoolery and potential sabotage, he hadn't received the remaining half of his payment for the trip. In pursuing the money, his biggest problem was he didn't know the real parties involved in the munitions deal, and the bareboat charterer claimed he was working through someone with an undisclosed principal. M. J. hired an attorney but could never find the deal's source, apparently hitting a national security–type wall.

The Cheramies' lone foray into the munitions shipping business was a particularly maddening example of their frustration with the late 1980s. As the decade turned, the L & M Botruc picture started to clear. By 1990, Terrebonne had somehow convinced the banks and finance companies to excuse Lefty as a personal guarantor and replace him with M. J. and Pat as guarantors, making it possible for M. J. and Pat to buy out Lefty. There was no real explanation for this concession, other than the fact that Terrebonne had convinced them that the company stood a chance of being more successful if it could shrink its management. Terrebonne believed that the banks trusted him because he'd never led them astray throughout the 1980s, delivering on every payment he'd promised.

Whatever it was, in 1990 L & M Botruc had survived. M. J. and Pat were compatible partners. M. J. had the operations expertise, and Pat was the hungry, hustling salesman. Despite all the fear the 1980s had created, these two believed that, one day, they could build Botrucs together.

By 1987, Pye Theriot's outlook was also fairly positive. Many of the same people who had criticized him in the late 1970s for passing his work onto his friend, Leslie Schouest, now had a different opinion. Leslie was a lot like L & M Botruc's Pat Pitre, a young, energetic, but levelheaded go-getter who had learned how to effectively help run a boat company. With Leslie at the helm, Pye could afford to take a less active role and spend more time with his family.

But, in March 1988, a completely unexpected tragedy struck when Leslie Schouest was killed in a car accident on Highway 308 just south of Thibodaux. The death shook up the company and rocked Pye. In one instant, he'd lost his best friend and his trusted manager. After Leslie's passing, Theriot bookkeeper Benny Bourgeois echoed what many believed, "When Leslie died, the Theriot company died because at that point, Pye had no idea how to run the company." In truth, Pye's largest problem was probably his admitted lack of desire. After amassing fifteen years of experience, he still hadn't warmed up to the boat business. Given Pye's absence of passion, Bourgeois, who kept the company's balance sheet said, "The smartest thing Pye could've did at that point was sell. They had equity in the company. He should've salvaged what he could."

Instead of selling, Pye unwisely invested the company's profits in several losing nonboat business schemes. Ultimately, he threw the business's last million into a shipping venture that was supposed to take advantage of the growing Fourchon, the small port at the mouth of Bayou Lafourche. Coincidentally, Port Fourchon was something Pye's father, then later Pye, had helped to grow as members of the Lafourche Parish Port Commission. The commission had originally formed in 1960, when Senator A. O. Rappelet had convinced Governor Jimmie Davis to create it. At the time, Rappelet had wanted to make a leading banana port out of the place, which was then a near-deserted spit of land.

By the 1970s, the Port Commission embarked on another endeavor by attracting investors and oilfield lessees. One major player was a conglomerate of companies called the Louisiana Offshore Oil Port (LOOP). LOOP, which was located eighteen miles offshore, made it possible for deep draft tankers to unload their product into a deepwater pipeline terminal, which was completed in 1981. The product was then piped onshore to be stored in underground salt domes in Galliano.

Many people had said that if Nolty had lived, he would've obtained the lucrative, five-year-long, multivessel contracts to assist LOOP with line handling and maintenance. Nolty not only had connections with the Port Commission, he'd also done business in the North Sea with the company that constructed LOOP, the French contractor ETPM. When Nolty died, the Theriot company had lost its angle on the job. Instead, the contracts went up for bid and were won by the creative Edison Chouest Offshore, a company founded in 1960 by a former trawler, Edison Chouest, and subsequently taken over by his shrewd son, Gary. The LOOP contract helped vault Chouest into the 1980s, just as the other boat companies were sagging.

Nevertheless, LOOP would eventually help all of the Lafourche boat companies by centralizing the Gulf operations in their backyard. The process had begun as the eighties' crash forced many oil companies to downsize their operations and consolidate their Gulf support bases. Most of them began to select the Fourchon as their consolidated base site because of its deepwater port, proximity to the Gulf rigs, and its central Gulf location. Thus, as the oilfield dipped in the eighties, Port Fourchon soared.

With all of this growing activity at the port, Pye believed the shipping venture was a sound one; it was a way for him to capitalize on the Fourchon's growth but also get away from the oilfield. Despite all the promise, the venture suffered from mismanagement and, ultimately, failed, and in its failure, sucked away the cash Nolty J. Theriot, Inc. needed to thrive. The company would never recover. Before the turn of the next decade, Pye finally called it quits and sold the last of his tugs in 1999.

Nolty J. Theriot, Inc., once the world's largest independent offshore tugboat company, became only a nautical memory.

The liftboat *Myrtle* jacked up on her maiden assignment near Port Fourchon in 2002. (Courtesy of MONTCO, LLC)

Afterword

Summer 2016

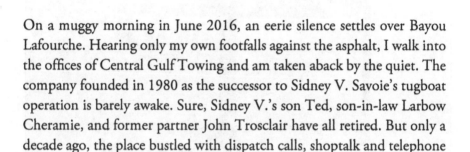

On a muggy morning in June 2016, an eerie silence settles over Bayou Lafourche. Hearing only my own footfalls against the asphalt, I walk into the offices of Central Gulf Towing and am taken aback by the quiet. The company founded in 1980 as the successor to Sidney V. Savoie's tugboat operation is barely awake. Sure, Sidney V.'s son Ted, son-in-law Larbow Cheramie, and former partner John Trosclair have all retired. But only a decade ago, the place bustled with dispatch calls, shoptalk and telephone rings. I wonder, *Where is everybody?*

I learn that a week ago, conditions forced Sidney V.'s grandsons, Central Gulf's managing partners Matt Cheramie and Sidney A. "Sid" Savoie, to lay off the company's personnel manager and sole remaining salesman. Matt and Sid have also had to trim the vessels' crews from a high of fifty-six to twenty-one and the office staff from seven to three. For those who remain, Matt and Sid have slashed their own salaries by a third, and everyone else's by 20–30 percent.

The emptiness of the present setting reinforces the numbers. Granted, I have had some warning. Ted Savoie told me on the phone, "It's worse than the eighties."

A little further down the bayou at L & M Botruc, Pat Pitre and M. J. Cheramie have both said, "This is worse than the eighties."

A few minutes ago, I passed Ted's home and noticed that across the highway on the bayouside, three of Central Gulf's signature red and white tugs are tied up, including the timeless *Susan G.* Once all reliable moneymakers, the tugboats have been sitting there, depending on the vessel, for years with no work in sight, simply waiting on a buyer.

About ten miles further north, two much larger supply vessels, *C-Trucs 3* and *5*, are moored against the bayouside in front of M. J. Cheramie's house, cold stacked. These are only a few of the more than 120 workboats tied up and gathering dust and rust against the banks of Bayou Lafourche from Leeville to Lockport. In the Bollinger Safe Harbor in Larose, there are another ninety or so in cold storage. Across Louisiana, there are hundreds more additional oilfield vessels, triple- and quadruple-side stacked, sitting dead on the water with little hope of awakening any time soon.

Back on the Lafourche, about three-dozen miles up the bayou at my law office in Thibodaux, signs of an oilfield crash first made their way into my door in early 2015. I started receiving some unusual phone calls after the price of oil, which had hovered north of $80 per barrel for most of ten years, began to fall in 2015 into the $40s. Clients, men with decades of experience in the oil and gas industry, were asking me to review severance packages. We received inquiries about wrongful terminations, collection claims against nonpaying workboat owners, and oilfield contractors breaching their office leases. In discussing the state of affairs with people in the oilfield hubs of Houma, Lafayette, and Morgan City, anyone, everyone, said, "It's bad."

Yet, the local economy as a whole, doesn't look so weak compared to the 1980s. In 1986, Lafourche Parish's unemployment rate of 25 percent led all of the nation's counties, yet in May 2016, unemployment in Lafourche was only at 6.3 percent, a point and a half above the national average. What is going on?

The explanation begins in the aftermath of two destructive super-storms. In 2005, Hurricanes Katrina and Rita ripped through the Gulf region, devastating cities and small towns from coastal Mississippi all the way to East Texas. The storms combined to kill nearly two thousand people, displace more than a million residents, and cause approximately $150 billion in economic damages. For more than two years in some of the Katrina-ravaged areas, particularly in the city of New Orleans, there were miles and miles of abandoned neighborhoods, casting the region in a film of gray filth and a pall of hopelessness.

Yet ironically, south of all the rot and ruin, the Gulf of Mexico gleamed with a golden oilfield opportunity. While the hurricanes caused billions of dollars in damage to oil rigs, pipelines, and other oilfield installations from Texas to Alabama, the storms also generated the necessity to repair all the damage and to reignite the Gulf oilfield. To accomplish this makeover, the industry needed fleets of workboats. In 2006, the demand caused workboat day rates to shoot through the deck, sometimes doubling the pre-Katrina rates, with the post-storm pay earning a prime lift-boat such as MONTCO's 2002-built *Myrtle* a daily gross in excess of $30,000.

The result once again gilded South Lafourche, which survived the storms without any significant flooding due to the fortune of being west of Katrina's eye and east of Rita's strongest outer bands. Also, Rita's surge was held back by South Lafourche's impressive levee system, while a weaker system in neighboring Terrebonne allowed Rita's waters to inundate thousands of homes and businesses south of Houma.

At first, the post-Katrina and Rita clean-up boom seemed temporary. Then in 2008, two more twin hurricanes, Gustav and Ike, wrecked the Gulf again, twisting more metal and knocking down more platforms. More destruction meant more work for workboats.

During this post-hurricanes heyday, Central Gulf Towing employed all nine of its tugs, working everything from salvage to anchor handling to rig moving. If the work wasn't offshore, it was onshore, as the inland bays still held promise.

Out in deeper water, L & M's Pat Pitre and M. J. Cheramie hired all fourteen of their Botrucs, amassing enough cash to slowly upgrade their fleet, improving *C-Trucs 6, 7,* and *8* by stretching their hulls, repowering their engines, and adding dynamic positioning. They also made plans to build two new, $20 million-plus vessels.

With the Gulf's boatmen helping the industry complete its storm repairs, a dip in the value of oil created a momentary reality check. The price, which had spiked to $151 per barrel in June 2008, fell steadily throughout the remainder of the year, all the way into the $40s by January 2009. This six-month drop was enough to tie up numerous vessels, including sending forty into the Bollinger Safe Harbor as of March 2009.

At Central Gulf, the partners permanently cold stacked two of their tugs, eventually selling one. The 2008 price plunge was the first sign that no matter what happened to the value of crude in the next decade, the oilfield had hit another 1970s-like peak. To some of the veterans, a 1980s-like free fall was inevitable, even as price climbed back into the $90s in March 2010. Ultimately, the bubble was going to pop.

Then on April 20, 2010, burst it did. On that night, forty miles below the mouth of the Mississippi River, the sky *boomed* and ignited into a giant ball of fire. The explosion turned the Gulf of Mexico into an ocean of flames. The cause was a massive well blowout on British Petroleum's (BP's) floating city of a platform, the *Deepwater Horizon*. The eruption's immediate human impact was devastating—eleven people died and seventeen others were seriously injured. The resulting environmental damage was staggering; nearly five million barrels of oil gushed into the sea for eighty-seven days, making it the world's largest-ever accidental oil spill. The casualties included oil-soaked wildlife, from lifeless endangered sea turtles to sludge-covered pelicans and porpoises. Some fish and other species that survived the flowing crude died en masse from the dispersants used to break up the oil. Due to the obvious health risks, for the entire summer of 2010, the government shut down fishing and beach going all along the Gulf coast.

President Barack Obama called the spill, "the worst environmental disaster America has ever faced."

Six years later, the BP spill's lasting effect on the Gulf's ecology and economy remains unknown. On the surface, the disaster's impact on the Gulf region seems measurable. Just after the spill, the prospects for those who make their living from the Gulf looked grim. There was no income during the summer of 2010 for marina operators, fishermen, beachside hoteliers, and others depending on the Gulf's bounty. In time, however, BP provided an opportunity for hundreds of thousands of residents of the Gulf states to recoup their losses. The words "BP claim" became common utterances not just for shrimpers, charter fisherman, and oystermen but for businessmen of all kinds with storefronts hundreds of miles away from the coast. Many of the claims were legitimate, others questionable at best. Whatever one's opinion of certain claimants or of BP itself, there is no doubting the mind-boggling amount of money spilling from the British giant's pockets. BP is expected to pay out a total of more than $20 billion in claims stemming from the 2010 spill.

So how would the spill change the lives of boatmen? In the very beginning, like wreckage from a hurricane, the disaster created immediate work. With oil slicks floating all over the Gulf, BP seemingly hired every motorboat available, including seafood vessels and many small pleasure craft. Among the larger vessels retained was the brand-new 234-foot-long *Botruc 40*, which Halter Marine in Pascagoula delivered five days before the spill. *Botruc 40's* job south of Mobile was to carry oil drums on its deck as smaller utility boats skimmed oil and transferred it to the *Botruc's* storage tanks.

In the same area south of the Alabama coast all the way across to Texas, Central Gulf Towing's tugs also aided the spill effort, helping to stage equipment and housing barges for the cleanup.

Despite creating some brief opportunities, the spill soon led to a work stoppage when on May 30, 2010, President Obama imposed a six-month moratorium on deepwater drilling, with deepwater federally defined as five hundred feet or greater below the water surface. The offshore industry responded with litigious outrage. After several oilfield companies filed suit, federal district Judge Martin Feldman ordered an injunction lifting the moratorium on June 22, and the Fifth Circuit Court of Appeals refused to reinstate the moratorium on July 8. The president then issued a second moratorium on July 12 on all drilling in the Gulf of Mexico, regardless of depth but vaguely based on an operator's equipment's ability to prevent a spill. Although the administration lifted the official suspension on October 12, oilfield insiders argued Obama only converted the moratorium into a "permitorium" because the government failed to issue a deepwater drilling permit until February 28, 2011, nearly eleven months after the spill.

The tightened regulatory climate discouraged future exploration and made it difficult for even the best new boats to find work. For instance, after spending more than $40 million on *Botrucs 40* and *41* (*Botruc 41* was delivered in the middle of the moratorium in August), the Cheramies and Pitres at L & M watched hopelessly as they were forced to pay a hefty banknote until their boats finally left the dock.

Nearing the one-year anniversary of the BP spill, as the permitorium ended, the tide began to turn, and for good reason: on April 1, 2011, the price of oil had climbed to $119 per barrel. But did the April Fools' Day zenith mean that the oilfield was really playing with fool's gold?

For three years, it didn't seem that way. The price per barrel bounced between the $80s and $110, and workboats' day rates jumped accordingly; a top end 220-plus foot supply boat hit $28,000 in day pay while the largest of lift boats earned a daily premium of $85,000. Money flowed across the Gulf oilfield, and it felt like a repeat of the 1970s.

To many, however, a rewind of the seventies could only be followed by a reliving of the eighties. At L & M, Tony Cheramie saw a disturbing trend taking place. From Katrina forward, he believed oilfield operators had "too much access to capital," which threatened to crowd the Gulf with an oversupply of rigs and boats once exploration slowed.

Elsewhere, new methods of drilling, particularly inland "fracking," resulted in oil gushing onto the international marketplace. As the months passed in 2014, the domestic fracking, along with the price-driven incentive to drill across the planet, poured far too much oil onto the worldwide market. With Saudi Arabia and other OPEC nations being able to produce oil more cheaply, they refused to cut back production to maintain a higher crude price. The result was a global glut of oil.

With the increased supply, the price plummeted, from $100 per barrel in June 2014 to the $40s by December. By the last quarter of 2015, oil's value descended into the $30s, bottoming out at $28.50 per barrel in January 2016. Workboat day rates followed suit, nosediving below break-even levels for many vessels. By the summer of 2016, there have been few signs of a recovery.

With the price too low to justify new exploration, the only index rising has been the number of insolvencies. From 2015 into the summer of 2016, eighty-five oil and gas producers and eighty-three oilfield service contractors have filed bankruptcy in the United States and Canada.

At L & M, Jacob Pitre notes that in addition to bankruptcies, mergers have also altered the face of the industry. "Within six months, our sixteen best customers dwindled to five, four."

Just as it is difficult to recognize who's left in the energy business, it is also hard to read and track the pages, chapters, and books of laws that the federal government continues to add to the maritime legal regime. When Central Gulf's Matt Cheramie is asked to sum up the industry in the last ten years, he gives a short answer: "Overregulated."

The vast and voluminous regulations differ depending on the size of the vessel and the waters they sail. Thus, on the one hand, the plights of smaller independent boat companies like L & M and Central Gulf seem very different; L & M is an offshore company while Central Gulf's specialty has become primarily inland waters. On the other, as their recent stories show, they must survive the game in much the same way.

When Pat Pitre learned that it would take more than $40 million to build *Botrucs 40* and *41*, something dawned on him. He realized that excluding the 2004-built *Botrucs 38* and *39*, the costs of *40* and *41* exceeded the expense of constructing every boat the company ever built through *Botruc 37*, including all the barges, deck barges, and any other vessels.

He couldn't help but wonder if L & M had taken too long of a leap; his fears were temporarily realized after *40* and *41* were released. "At the time the moratorium was going on, we'd look at our monthly financials, and I'd say, 'You know, if we wouldn't have those two boats, we wouldn't be doing bad.' Of course, all the other boats were paid, and they didn't make that much. Now (in only six years), it's just the opposite; if we didn't have those two boats, we'd be in trouble. It was just a 180-degree flip-flop."

The reason is twofold. One, the deepwater industry's demand is for the most updated, technologically advanced vessels. And two, Coast Guard and American Bureau of Shipping (ABS) regulations make it nearly impossible to keep a 1970s-built offshore boat in operation. "The boat cost you in 1978 $1.2 million to build, and you're going to spend $700,000 in dry docking it every five years." The docking expenses arise from the repairs and upgrades required by the government during these inspections.

Yet now, with his new state-of-the-art *Botruc*, he's watched the day rates decrease by more than 60 percent. When a competitor recently undercut his absolute minimum price for the same work, Pat had to tell the client that he was losing money at the current rate, yet at least he was keeping his people employed. He certainly couldn't come down any more. The client, having worked with L & M for years, decided to keep the *Botruc* on the job.

Yet it's work that only allows L & M to barely meet its margins. "I'm in the red every month almost," says Pat.

So how is L & M making it? Some of it is reducing its fleet and cutting payroll by as much as 40 percent. Part is the "cushion" that Pat and M. J. have always ensured was in the company accounts. Their cash and equipment equity allowed them to refinance their debt service into one low-interest note at the end of 2015 that saved the company about $200,000 per month.

Then there's diversity. In 2009, Pat, M. J. and their children formed a new company, Express Weld, originally intended to save L & M money by self-servicing the Botrucs that came in for supplies or repairs at Port Fourchon. Express Weld has certainly done that, allowing the Botrucs to run more efficiently. "You're not spending two thousand dollars just to tie up and throw trash away like you were before," says Jacob.

Additionally, Express Weld has become a profitable venture by servicing other vessels, including competitors' boats, providing them with needs that range from load-outs to welding and electrical repairs. Express Weld has also given L & M an advantage over a competing company who only has a supply boat and lacks a dock service. "The thing going forward is package deals," says Jacob. "People want to cut down their vendor lists. They're going to make you package stuff together. 'You got boats at Fourchon? You got a dock at Fourchon? Give me a package.'"

As oilmen look to cut costs, boatmen must deal with wages that have escalated well beyond inflation. In the boat business, a captain who used to make $200 per day in the 1980s is now making a day rate as high as $900; a deckhand's daily wage has risen from $25 to $220.

The 1980s' lower costs and more reasonable regulatory climate made it much easier to handle than the current downturn. "The business today is no fun like it was in the eighties," says Pat, "It was hard (in the eighties), but it was fun to run it. Now there's so many regulations."

The new laws range from increased security costs after 9/11 to a sailor's knots of captain's training requirements to President Obama's

Affordable Care Act, which has jacked up health insurance costs, making it difficult for many small businesses to operate.

With Pat cutting back his hours and M. J. already semi-retired, L & M's future rests with Jacob's and Tony's willingness to forge ahead. For now, they are committed to providing for their families and for the more than one hundred longtime employees who have made the company what is today.

Jacob says the downturn "made us better." In truth, it is the only conclusion he can make as a leaner L & M Botruc sails into further into the deep water.

In shallower depths, recent times have turned Central Gulf's name into a misnomer. Not only has much of the company's oilfield work been inland and not in the Gulf, most of its business now lies outside the oilfield. Depending on the month, 60 to 70 percent of Central Gulf's tugs are now working on dredging jobs, towing and anchoring dredge barges as they perform channel maintenance and beach restoration work from Brownsville, Texas, to Wilmington, North Carolina. Without the dredging work, there would be no Central Gulf Towing.

The company's other saving grace has been its conservative strategy; its boats are all paid for. "After Katrina, we didn't get stupid," says Sid Savoie. "Nobody went buy a camp on Grand Isle. Nobody went buy a big boat or a big car. We saved our money, and that's why we're here today."

It's not that Sid and his first cousin and partner, Matt, don't want to do more oil and gas business. Oilfield towing, which includes a lot of standby time, is much easier on a vessel than the constant twenty-four-hour churn of dredging. It's also more profitable when the price of oil cooperates.

For the future, Sid and Matt do not see many oil and gas opportunities for Central Gulf's type of towing operation. The BP spill may have occurred in deep water, but the spill perhaps did more damage to the shallow water Gulf and the inside waters market. "Over the past five years, we haven't touched a drilling rig," says Sid. As far as he's concerned, "there's still a moratorium," despite the 2010 moratorium technically applying only to deepwater drilling. "They don't want to issue the permits."

On the continental shelf, the statistics back up Sid's observation. Even when oil prices were at consistent highs, the number of shallow-water drilling permits issued dropped dramatically, from ninety-five in 2009 to twenty-six in 2013. In inland waters, the rig count has moved more predictably with the value of oil; hence, the number of working inshore rigs in Louisiana sunk into the single digits in February 2015 and in 2016 has hovered between a paltry monthly count of one to five.

With the shelf and inshore oilfield drying up, Central Gulf's work has varied; in addition to dredging, Matt and Sid have pursued various non-oil and gas towing work and in so doing, have motored through pages of new federal rules and insurance requirements. It was one particular job that helped send Ted Savoie into retirement.

In 2014, the task was to tow a casino barge from Greenville, Mississippi, down the Mississippi River into and across the Gulf of Mexico, up the Atchafalaya River and through a connecting channel to Amelia, Louisiana. Already, the job had opened a "box of Hula-Hoops," requiring Ted and his team to repeatedly jump through hoops thrown up by marine surveyors, insurance underwriters, and bureaucrats to ready their tugs for departure.

Central Gulf agreed to perform the job with two 2,400-horsepower tugs, with the *Judy Ann* towing the casino from its bow and the *Sidney V.* made up to the barge's stern to act as the brake. Finally, the two tugs were set to pull the casino away from the dock when a surveyor hired by the insurance company told Ted, "I don't think you have enough horsepower."

Ted wasn't sure how to react. He'd been pushing tows on the river since the 1950s. He explained to the man that with the Mississippi's current running strong, one 2,400-horsepower tug was more than enough to pull the barge with a second tug made up to the barge's stern to stop her, when necessary.

The insurance man insisted on a third tug of at least 1,200 horses, so Central Gulf had to send the *Helen* upriver, which took another five days. Although a third tug meant more profit for Central Gulf, it was a senseless, expensive move for the client.

Then, when Ted notified the Coast Guard of their departure, the officer in charge said, "Hold up! You can't come through Vicksburg with that thing. Does your captain know how to get through Vicksburg?"

"Well, we came up the river with a levee on both sides and came up all the way here."

"Well, we want someone who knows the current to come from Greenville through Vicksburg."

Knows the current? The same current we just rode up here? Ted took a breath. He had to hire a local pilot to stay on the tug for a day until they cleared Vicksburg. In the end, the pilot did nothing but stand in the wheelhouse, and for the duration of the trip, the third tug, the *Helen*, only rode along and watched.

"What got to me is you had people who weren't even born when I was doing this type of work telling me how to do the job."

On June 20, 2016, the instructions on towing have become even more minute, tedious, and arguably unnecessary through the passage of Subchapter M, an eight-hundred-page new set of federal rules governing seemingly every detail of towing vessels. Prior to Subchapter M's passage, Ted tried to make the rule makers understand their regulatory overkill and how different inshore oilfield tugs are from both deepwater vessels and push boats pushing giants flotillas of hopper barges on inland waterways. "We're not brown water," he'd tell them. "We're not blue water. We're brackish water."

Yet the fact that inland oilfield tugs worked mostly on open bays fell on deaf ears. Between Subchapter M and the ever-increasing, expensive licensing requirements for captains, the former and current partners at Central Gulf hardly recognize the business of their forbear Sidney V. Savoie. With Sidney's great-grandchildren having no interest in the company, his grandsons Matt and Sid will do their best to navigate their new normal.

For the last seventeen years, the concept of normality has taken on a different meaning for Pye Theriot. Paradoxically, Pye is a free man now. At age sixty-five, he's long since shed the tugboat shackles that harnessed and haunted him for most of his life. While people along the bayou may look at Pye and see a wasted opportunity, what some don't realize is that it was an opportunity he never wanted.

Today, Pye lives in Destin, Florida. It's his second residential stint on the Emerald Coast. He says he originally left the bayou for the white Floridian sands in the 1990s to provide better opportunities for his sons Nolty II and Robert. He didn't want his boys to be saddled with his sinking business or to feel the throes of an unsteady industry. Then, when he later returned to Louisiana to be closer to family, he chose Baton Rouge because, again, he thought the business and educational climates there were better for his children than the oilfield-controlled south Lafourche. It gave both his boys the opportunities to pursue professional prospects. Nolty II, a political aficionado like his father, benefitted from living in the hub of state government, and Robert, then a budding, passionate cook, gained culinary experience working at two of the area's fine restaurants.

The moves arguably paid off for Pye's sons. Nolty II is currently spending his fifteenth year on the Hill in Washington, DC, presently working for the US Chamber of Commerce, and Robert is also in DC as the chef in charge of opening new locations for an international restaurant group.

Pye's own career path was notably rockier. The prevailing opinion is that Pye could have done a much better job managing Nolty J. Theriot, Inc. The negative is he didn't do what he should've done—encouraged his father to sell the company in 1975 or sold it himself at other junctures—moves that would've given him a nest egg to pursue his real interest in politics. The positives are that Pye's lack of obsession over the business allowed him to spend more quality time with his children than his father spent with him and, by distancing his kids from the oilfield, he allowed them to live their own lives and establish their own identities. His sons live and work around people who have never even heard of the tugboat legend Nolty J. Theriot.

Yet Pye felt the burden of being the heir to Nolty's anchor-handling throne for years. When I interviewed him in April 2002, he and his wife, Janet, were living temporarily in the family's Grand Isle camp. She was a substitute teacher at Grand Isle High, and he was trying to cobble together a consulting career.

That same year, Pye's luck began to turn when his first big client, the Southeast Louisiana Economic Council (SLEC) asked him to assist with organizing the politics of introducing local companies to new foreign markets. He had the most success in Kazakhstan, the ex-Soviet, central-Asian nation. In the early 2000s, the former Communist country on the Caspian Sea began booming with new oil activity, resembling the Gulf of Mexico in the 1950s. While vast mineral reserves existed in the Caspian, the region lacked skilled oilfield service contractors, which the Cajunland, of course, had in great numbers.

Pye soon began paving the way for a Cajun-Kazakh governmental and business alliance. For most of the last decade, he traveled to Kazakhstan about four times per year. He worked mainly for US companies helping them to do business in the old Socialist republic. The more twenty-four-hour plane trips he made, the more ties he began to establish with the Kazakh government itself. In 2010, the Kazakhstan Minister of Foreign Affairs appointed him Honorary Consul for the states of Louisiana, Mississippi, and Alabama. Though the position was unpaid, it was a personal honor; it came with the distinction of being ratified by the US State Department. Pye's consulate also led to more business opportunities in Kazakhstan.

By 2014, the thirty or so trips to Kazakhstan began to take their toll on his health and quality of life. Having enough savings to work part-time, Pye decided to focus only on stateside work.

While he has thoroughly enjoyed his governmental and business consulting, he admits, "I've thought a lot about the mistakes I've made that I'd like to go back and change." He was initially understandably "reluctant" to relive his story in this book, yet the experience was "kind of cathartic." He is even pleased when often told by strangers, "You're the Theriot guy from *Cajun Mariners*."

His past narrative has helped him recently in advising current oilfield professionals. During the last couple of years, part of his mission has been to assess oilfield businesses for SLEC and Louisiana Economic Development to see how the state can help them. "I'm meeting twenty- and thirty-year-olds that weren't around in the eighties when we had our downturn," he says. "They want to learn from my experience, how we handled it back then."

Thinking back to his own missteps, he stresses the need to be "quick on your feet" when the recession comes. "If you need to divest some equipment and an opportunity presents itself, don't wait thinking you're going to get more money next week. It's all about cash."

He also notices that the relationships between boatmen and oilmen don't appear to be as strong as they were in his father's day; he observes that business now is "more a science than an art." Between the technology needs, cash requirements, and the mounting regulations, he can hardly imagine running tugs in the current market.

In "twenty-twenty hindsight," he knows what he could have done to change the outcome of the Theriot tale, yet he cannot argue with where life has taken him. As Pye and Janet celebrate their forty-third year of marriage in their Florida Panhandle home, he says, "If somebody would have told me when I was thirty years old in 1980 that when I was sixty-five, sixty-six years old, I'd be on the beaches of Destin, I think I would have signed the contract."

Of course, the contract ultimately ends for everyone, and since I conducted my first interviews for the book in 2001, many of my former interviewees have passed on, including the trailblazer Sidney V. Savoie and the matrons Mathilde Savoie, Lou Cheramie, and Bea Theriot. Others who have died since graciously giving me at least a part of their stories include Jeff Alario, Melvin Bernard, Luther Blount, Dick Bollinger, Benny Bourgeois, Paul Candies, Albert Cheramie, Edison Chouest, Al Danos, Butch Danos, Dick Guidry, Anthony Guilbeau, Bill Porteous, Nacis Theriot, Jimmie Vizier, and Tommie Vizier. For many of these pioneers, dodging death was a part of their lives on the high seas and the open roads.

After Bobby Orgeron walked away from nine serious automobile accidents, he took his final car ride on August 2, 2008. Since phasing out of the boat business years ago, Bobby had experienced the joys of retiring and traveling the world with Myrtle, only to lose her to liver cancer in 1999. After her death, he battled an intense loneliness, then remarried in 2002 only to struggle through his own maladies, including a kidney removal and the constant physical aches that had originally created his addiction to painkillers.

Hopefully, on Bobby's last Saturday afternoon in Galliano, he was at peace when driving his Lexus SUV along LA 1. He was operating the vehicle without any passengers when witnesses say he slumped forward against the wheel, apparently losing consciousness. His car drifted across the center line into an oncoming 18-wheeler. After the collision, "(Bobby's) car came off the ground, did a 360 in the air, and landed on the side of the road," a nearby motorist told the *Daily Comet*. "It was a hell of a lick."

An "explosion," said another man, who did not see but heard the crash from inside his house, thinking "something had blown up."

On that hot afternoon in 2008, something had definitely combusted— an era. With Bobby's tenth totaled automobile, the age of the wild and wide open Cajun mariner had detonated and evaporated into the sky.

Eight years later, if Bobby and his brethren were still alive, they would scarcely believe the appearance of their business.

One reason is there are fewer Cajun mariners out there now. The Central Gulf employee list is typical of today's boat companies; what used to be Cajun-only crews have transformed into mostly drawling "Texiens" from Alabama, Mississippi, and Florida.

Economically, the metamorphosis is healthy. A growing number of job classifications for Cajuns and a diversification of industries for the Cajunland is the reason why, despite the region's cornerstone industry suffering from a record slump, the southern Louisiana economy is much more vibrant than it was in the eighties.

Because so many oilfield contractors like Nolty J. Theriot, Inc. went down in the 1980s, the people of the Gulf South began to lose faith in the oilfield. In south Louisiana, many of the young people graduating from high school in the mid-to-late 1980s and early 1990s didn't trust the industry and didn't even consider seeking employment in it. They'd heard from too many people, "Look, you're young. You need to find something that's got nothing to do with the oilfield."

The region's refusal to rely on oil and gas resulted in a more diversified economy. The Lafourche-Terrebonne area, which at times has had one of the nation's highest concentrations of patenting activity, has added medical technology, environmental science, food processing, paper manufacturing, chemical resin production, and agricultural equipment fabrication to its proven expertise in the oilfield, marine, seafood, and sugar industries.

Throughout the fight to diversify the eighties' economy, the Cajuns learned that they were their own greatest assets. They discovered that people actually wanted to experience their unique way of life. This vibrant Cajun tourism industry began when Opelousas-born chef Paul Prudhomme accidentally burned a fish dish in the kitchen of his New Orleans restaurant in the mid-1980s. Prudhomme's renowned blackened redfish sparked a Cajun renaissance. Suddenly, everything Cajun was cool. People began to buy George Rodrigue's "Blue Dog" paintings, read James Lee Burke's books, laugh at Justin Wilson's cooking show, and watch South Lafourche's own Bobby Hebert throw touchdown passes for the New Orleans Saints. They started listening to traditional Cajun music and dancing to zydeco and swamp pop. And, of course, culinary enthusiasts everywhere began to eat what the rest of America called Cajun cuisine and the Cajuns only knew as mama's cooking. As Tabasco and Tony Chacheres spread their spices, and Frito-Lay served Cajun-flavored Ruffles and McDonald's fried up Cajun McChickens, Cajun culture, whether real or bastardized, became a hot commodity.

Nevertheless, oil and gas are still the region's most valuable resources, and to survive the eighties, the oilfield's leaders had to find ways to achieve intra-industry diversity, then grow through education and technology. In the mid-1980s, two Lafourche businesses, Edison Chouest Offshore and Bollinger Shipyards, did just that. At Bollinger, after Boysie Bollinger took over his father Donald's operation, the lack of 1980s orders for workboats forced him to seek and obtain government jobs, scoring Bollinger's first contract to build sixteen Coast Guard cutters in 1984 and securing several Coast Guard or Navy contracts thereafter.

As part of Bollinger's growth, the shipyard also built boats for Chouest—until Gary Chouest grew his fleet so quickly he needed to start his own yard to meet his demand. Like Bollinger, Chouest also made the government a primary client; the Galliano company provided the US military with its largest number of privately owned and operated vessels. The Chouests also laid claim to the planet's largest fleet of independently owned research and seismic vessels, which included a line of polar icebreakers, built in sweltering Larose.

As Chouest, Bollinger, and other companies grew before the latest downturn, so did Port Fourchon, which began as a small fishing wharf and mushroomed into an industrial mini-city of bustling docks, swinging cranes, hovering helicopters, rolling 18-wheelers, and motoring massive vessels constantly moving in and out. Perhaps the most significant oil and gas installation in the United States, Port Fourchon is the land base for LOOP, which handles 10–15 percent of the nation's intake of foreign oil and 10–15 percent of its domestic oil and is connected to 50 percent of the United States' refining capacity.

From Port Fourchon to Port Aransas, Texas, the oilfield's new millennium growth has also led to long leaps in technological improvements. On the most advanced vessels, a workboat captain can now navigate without a written chart (global positioning), steer with an ultraprecise device (joystick), stay in place without an anchor (dynamic positioning), turn without a rudder (z-drive propulsion), and program the boat so she guides herself (automatic pilot). Back on shore, the vessel's owner can use wireless Internet technology to track many of the boat's operations, from her geographic position to her fuel supply. The owner may also, in some instances, go online to an oil company website and bid for a job, using cyberspace to bypass the backroom and barroom "bidding" of the old days.

Despite the computerized advances of the marine oilfield, the fact remains that in 2016 there are billions of dollars worth of cold-stacked, technologically marvelous rigs and vessels that will cost untold sums to bring back online. Further, with so many of the Gulf's young people in other careers, where will the Gulf oilfield find its soldiers if it ever revives?

The answer to the oil business' future might lie in its present-day outliers.

One example is the plight of MONTCO, Bobby Orgerons' old company, led by his son Lee with his second son Joseph serving as second in command. In 2002, Lee lured the former physicist Joseph away from his six-figure salary at the M&M Mars candy company. After the move, Joseph, who has a Ph.D in high-energy particle physics, became MONTCO's chief technology officer.

In 2016, as Lee's and Joseph's fellow boatmen have cold stacked their vessels, the brothers Orgeron have employed 100 percent of their fleet.

As MONTCO's competitors have laid off scores of workers, the Orgerons have added dozens of employees. As some of MONTCO's fellow oilfield practitioners file bankruptcy, Lee and Joseph are making money from bankruptcy courts. Somehow, in perhaps the worst oilfield depression in history, MONTCO is having their "most active year" in 2016.

The seeds of the Orgerons' current success were planted in concerns Lee had during the post-Katrina boom. As the good times then rolled, he saw troubling signs. Because the Gulf of Mexico was the world's first offshore market, it was also the most developed, most competitive, most price sensitive, and most expected to have less work in the future.

Lee's worries would lead him to make several moves, the first being to look for a field that contained platforms more likely to need maintenance work without hoards of other vessel operators lining up to bid. He found one in the Middle East. Recent history had proven to him that the Arabian Gulf nations were hell-bent on production no matter the circumstances, pointing out that it was "obvious that the Middle East doesn't really care what the price of oil is."

Not knowing exactly where to start, he made his first trip to the Arabian Peninsula in 2008 and continued to visit as the years passed. He lined up meetings in the United Arab Emirates and Qatar "with anybody who [could] give [him] any information," including geologists who could show him photographs of the seabed, engineers who understood how to adapt a vessel's systems to temperatures exceeding 150 degrees, and anyone who could help him come up with a liftboat design and learn the culture.

From the beginning, the Arab oilfield executives impressed Lee. Usually dressed in traditional head scarfs and robes, the oilmen came across as warm and genuine. By 2013, Lee had made valuable Saudi, Qatari, and Emirati contacts, and he'd come up with a liftboat design adapted for every possible nuance of the Arabian Gulf, including some pure regional preferences. For instance, because the locals place more importance on cheaper labor and less on automation, Lee's designer drew tighter crew quarters with triple rather than double bunks. With the schematics in his hand, Lee remained unsure of the best way to enter the market.

Then just before the 2013 holidays, Lee met with a Gulf of Mexico competitor, SEACOR CEO Charles Fabrikant. Although the public company SEACOR had elevating vessels in its fleet, it lacked MONTCO's level of liftboat expertise. Yet SEACOR had a global footprint, offices already established in the Middle East and had relations with banks all over the world.

The two companies agreed to form a fifty-fifty joint venture called Falcon Global, LLC, and after vetting several shipyards in the Asian theater, the Falcon partners found one, Triyards in Ho Chi Minh City, Vietnam, that actually had experience building the elevating boats originally invented in south Louisiana. Delivery for the first two Falcon Global vessels are set for September and November 2016.

While Falcon Global's future in Arabia looks promising, the new liftboats have yet to produce any income for MONTCO. So how exactly are the Orgerons pulling off a banner 2016?

It's about Lee's prescient nature that keeps him always thinking about the future, particularly during a boom, when an abundance of work creates a tendency to be complacent.

At first, Lee and Joseph saw what everyone noticed after the 2005 and 2008 hurricanes—the Gulf of Mexico was full of "idle iron," non-working platforms that needed to be properly decommissioned. The storm damage proved that many of these structures lacked integrity. The post-storm cleanup demonstrated that it cost significantly more to remove a platform that had fallen into the water than one that was still standing. After the fallout from the BP spill, the derelict platforms' hazards became more publicly apparent.

On September 15, 2010, the Department of the Interior issued an "Idle Iron Guidance," requiring oil companies in the Gulf to "set permanent plugs in nearly 3,500 nonproducing wells" and "dismantle about 650 [idle] oil and gas production platforms." The new law made it clear that wells and platforms that had not been used for five years would have to be plugged and disassembled.

Of course, Lee and Joseph weren't the only liftboatmen to understand the potential of the Idle Iron initiative. To obtain an advantage, they had to upgrade their fleet to offer a liftboat their competitors could not. In 2002, they had already built, through Bollinger, what rigzone .com called the "next generation liftboat," the 137.5-foot *Myrtle*, named for their mother. Not only did the *American Ship Review* write that the *Myrtle* "raise[d] the sophistication of these vessels to a new level," but the liftboat's release was also featured in the mainstream *Popular Mechanics*. Yet now the brothers Orgeron planned a much larger, more powerful vessel than the *Myrtle* and her nearly identical twin, the *Kayd*. They wanted a boat that would allow a client to simultaneously perform all three phases of the decommissioning process. Normally, it occurred in three consecutive stages: the cementing of the well hole, the dismantling of the structure above the water, and the sending of divers below the surface to take apart and remove most of the platform's substructure. If the Orgerons could build a liftboat large enough to accomplish all three phases in parallel, MONTCO could cut the time needed to do the work in half.

The new boat would contain a deck double the *Myrtle's*, nearly as long as a football field, with quarters that could house 132 people. The planned mammoth vessel, though, did not fit into the current Coast Guard and ABS regulations, meaning building such a vessel was legally impossible.

Unsure of how to obtain unprecedented construction permits, Lee hired an old friend and well-known operative, Robert Alario. Robert worked his wonders in Washington, DC, meeting with and swaying the Coast Guard. He explained to the powers that be that they had nothing to worry about: MONTCO's new liftboat would not only be the world's largest, but it would also be extraordinarily safe.

Just as four decades ago Robert had made magic in Washington for his brother-in-law, Nolty Theriot, in 2010 and 2011, Robert helped MONTCO obtain all the necessary government approvals. As a result, MONTCO hired Gulf Island Fabrication in Houma to build the *Robert* in 2011–2012 (named not for Mr. Alario, but for longtime MONTCO Captain Robert McLuckie) and the *Jill* in 2014.

Around the time the *Robert* was under construction, Lee still saw problems ahead. Yes, the big boat gave him an edge, but the monolith would also be expensive to operate with her break-even rate somewhere north of $50,000 per day. What would happen when a downturn dropped day rates?

Lee saw his opportunity in an interesting industry trend: oil companies were slashing or eliminating their decommissioning staffs. Some of these oil producers had sold all their non-operable wells; now the government was telling them that they had to decommission their former properties because the wells' buyers had gone bankrupt, and as the prior owners, the well plugging responsibility reverted to them. In other cases, bankruptcy courts required a debtor oil company to set aside enough assets to plug a well and/or remove a platform.

If MONTCO could control the entire scope of the decommissioning, the Orgerons wouldn't have to sweat the next drop in liftboat day rates. To that end, when rates were still high, Lee decided to take a chance in 2011 and buy a company, Abandonment Consulting Services, LLC (ACS). The sale transferred no actual equipment assets but an invaluable knowledge from ACS' expert owner, Carroll Price, and his staff. By acquiring ACS and changing the name to Montco Oilfield Contractors, LLC (MOC) in 2012, Lee was no longer simply a boatman. He could approach clients with the capacity to do every step of the decommissioning.

With the former ACS engineers and other new hires, MOC could handle everything from design and permitting to performing the physical decommissioning. No other company, liftboat, or contractor, could offer the same level of service.

As MOC removes idle iron from the Gulf, MONTCO has also added a non-oilfield niche. This time, the client actually pursued the Orgerons, calling Joseph on the telephone and asking him a question he never saw coming.

Telephoning from the landlocked state of Utah, the caller worked for a nonprofit, and he wanted to look into hiring one of MONTCO's liftboats. His aim wasn't to extract oil and gas but to altruistically advance the cause of science.

A scientific not-for-profit retaining a multimillion dollar liftboat? It didn't seem realistic. The nonprofit, DOSECC, stood for Drilling, Observation and Sampling of the Earths Continental Crust. It consisted of a consortium of research laboratories, mainly located at universities across the United States with some in Europe. The DOSECC representative said Joseph's liftboat could act as a platform for some coring work off the East Coast.

The man sounded credible, yet at the time, Joseph could not have known how far down an alternative path the call would take MONTCO. He certainly didn't know that on June 25, 2009, Philadelphia's NBC 10 News would show video of MONTCO's *Kayd*, opening its story with, "From a hulking, three-legged liftboat forty-eight miles off the coast of Atlantic City, a massive drill digs deep into the ocean floor, pulling buried mysteries about the earth's past to the surface."

In time, the physicist/businessman Joseph would understand the project in depth, but at the moment, the scientific opportunity simply intrigued him. DOSECC was hired by the European Consortium for Ocean Researching Drilling.

Whomever the client, Joseph had to calculate a price. The scientific consortium had to pay MONTCO for the nearly two-week trip from Port Fouchon through the Florida Straits all the way up to the staging area in New Jersey. Joseph estimated some additional crew changes from Atlantic City and quoted a day rate about 5 percent higher than the prevailing Gulf oilfield day rates for the *Kayd*. The scientists agreed, and in late April 2009 at the Atlantic City Coast Guard Station near what was then Trump Marina, they began loading the *Kayd* with the coring unit and ten Conex shipping containers, each containing working laboratories. As twenty men and women of science in red jumpsuits and white lab coats boarded the boat, the *Kayd* motored offshore, jacked down its legs, and the coring began. The scientists' goal "was to estimate the amplitudes, rates, and mechanisms of sea-level change" in part to help predict the future rate of sea-level rise.

In and around the three-month period of crust extracting, Joseph got a good taste of work outside of oilfield country. When the *Kayd* was in port in Atlantic City, he walked into a restaurant, and the hostess asked him, "Are you from that funny looking boat over there?"

"Yeah, I am."

"What are you guys doing?"

"Scientific work."

"Not oil and gas?"

Judging by the look on her face, if he'd said yes, he didn't know if she'd have given him a table.

The casino-studded coast presented a scene quite different from the docks of Gulf oil ports. Once on shore, Joseph looked out his window and saw entrepreneur, reality TV star, and future president, Donald Trump emerging from a helicopter with what might have been Trump's hair flying in the wind.

Joseph's novel stay in Atlantic City soon became more profitable when DOSECC asked him about more core sampling for some potential "offshore wind mills" up the seaboard. The client, Deepwater Wind, claimed to be erecting America's first offshore wind farm off Block Island, Rhode Island. After Joseph worked a deal with the wind people, the *Kayd* headed further north for ten additional days of work.

Was offshore wind a viable pursuit? Joseph and Lee thought so. They discussed how President Obama had pushed alternative energy as a big part of his platform, and they believed there would be many windmills in the Atlantic's future. So Joseph attended wind conferences, renting booths, putting up backdrops, pressing flesh, and making a push for more windmill support work. The offshore wind developers responded to Joseph's not-so-soft sell by assuring him that they would need his big liftboats.

But for six years, nothing happened. Every time Joseph watched the weather and heard of a nor'easter battering the eastern seaboard, he sighed at the loss of potential energy. After each wind conference, he left with only hollow promises. "Let me tell you," he says, "I was called Don Quixote for quite a while." His doubters claimed he was just "chasing windmills."

Then in 2015, Joseph found out that the Block Island Wind Farm was back online. Deepwater Wind needed MONTCO's best, the *Robert*, and agreed to a profitable day rate that was higher than anything the *Robert* could have garnered as a liftboat-only operation in the recessed Gulf.

By fall of 2016, Block Island's gusts should be providing its residents with most of their electricity, reducing their utility costs by a projected 40 percent.

Meanwhile, MONTCO has continued to practice weird science. In Joseph's latest endeavor, he pursued dinosaurs.

Beginning in April 2016, MONTCO and DOSECC teamed up again to take core samples for their European consortium client. Their purpose was to retrieve sediment from an asteroid crater located off the coast of the Yucatan. The scientists were following up on the established theory that 66 million years ago, an enormous mass of fiery rock hurled toward the earth and struck with such force that it penetrated several miles into the crust, left a crater more than 115 miles wide, and set off a chain reaction of volcanoes, earthquakes, and other catastrophes that wiped out 80 percent of the planet's life, including most of the dinosaurs.

In search of understanding how the asteroid killed so many species, the scientific crew commenced a very unusual load-out for Port Fourchon, craning aboard portable labs and research gear before heading to the southern Gulf of Mexico, north of Progresso. The three-month overall job earned the *Myrtle* a much better day rate than the depressed economy's price for a similar boat in the Gulf oilfield.

In sum, science makes sense for MONTCO, as has the need to develop new business hypotheses. Whether pursuing dinosaur extinction, windmills, foreign oilfields, or new oil and gas services, Lee and Joseph have learned to listen to the changing political and socioeconomic winds.

Despite MONTCO's success, Lee doesn't pretend to understand the future of the Gulf of Mexico oilfield. He is especially concerned about the "liquidity constraints" of the smaller oil companies currently operating on the Gulf's outer continental shelf. In the 1980s crash, he drew confidence from the strong financial positions of the dominant shelf operators, big oil companies like Mobil, Gulf, and Chevron. "Now you have a downturn, and you have operators that don't have any cash and have huge credit restraints. So to be able to figure out exactly what's going to happen long term and how the banks are going to react, and how private equity is going to react is going to be an art form at best."

Nonetheless, it's not as if the Cajuns have given up on the Gulf. One example of the industry's response to the mounting regulations was to partner in 2013 with Nicholls State University to create a Maritime Management Concentration as part of the university's business curriculum. All of the program's funding comes from private donors, including MONTCO, L & M Botruc, Bollinger, SEACOR, Edison Chouest Offshore, and Otto Candies.

One of the program's lecturers is Joseph Orgeron, who has donated his time to teach one-third of the Introduction to Maritime Management class. "We saw we needed college educated people to help us with compliance," says Joseph. "We need businessmen to come out of Nicholls who already know port, starboard, bow, stern, propulsion systems, the twenty-four-hour operation of oil and gas business from drilling all the way up. As they're getting their education solidified in the business school, they're also getting a very good sampling of everything that's involved in the offshore industry."

The classes take the students from learning the marine oilfield basics to understanding obscure regulations. To give the future boatmen an appreciation of their roots, Joseph has titled his first lecture, "Rise of the Cajun Mariner."

Although the Cajun mariners rose long ago, their journey continues today. Having evolved from shrimpers and trappers like Juan Orgeron to the boating gamblers of Bobby's era, to the shrewd operators and scientists like Lee and Joseph, the Cajuns have always adapted to ever-changing seas. History has shown that they will emerge from the current depression, no matter how bleak the horizon. In some form, the Cajun mariners will ply the world's waters and boardrooms, building platforms of all kinds on the backs of their pioneers.

One of MONTCO's smaller lift boats, the 165-feet long *Paul* (far right), provides support in 2016 during the construction of America's first offshore wind farm off Block Island, Rhode Island. (Courtesy of Deepwater Wind)

Acknowledgments

Foremost, I thank Lee Orgeron. Without Lee, this story would never have made its way to my computer. His goal was for his children's and his grandchildren's generations to understand what their forefathers went through to create and develop an industry that meant so much to lower Lafourche.

With the book idea embedded in Lee's brain, he asked his boat builder and friend Boysie Bollinger if he knew of an author. Boysie, to my gratitude, mentioned me. During my initial meeting with Lee, he offered to put up the seed money for the research and writing of the book through the Nicholls State University Foundation. The Foundation, to which I am also very grateful, would then raise additional money, and I would have editorial control over the content.

During my first draft, that content ran wild. While I could never include every interesting character and every incredible tale, I sure tried to stuff them all into the first passes of my proposal. Luckily, my old writing group came to the rescue and helped me fix the name-choked drafts. For steering me straight, I owe the authors Rick Redmann Jr., Gloria Alvarez, and Joanna Wayne.

I am also indebted, of course, to the people who actually lived this story. This book is what it is because of their time, candor, and patient cooperation. I thank everyone who answered my questions and, in particular, I appreciate the assistance of the people who seemed to take the biggest interest in this project, including Ted Savoie, Pat Pitre, and Robert Alario.

In more ways than one, this is the people's story. In-person and tel-ephone interviews make up the book's overwhelmingly dominant source material. Supplementing these oral histories were many helpful works of nonfiction. I am especially grateful for the research of the Lafourche Her-itage Society. The two rich *Lafourche Country* volumes and the innova-tive *Stories My Grandparents Told Me* helped flesh out the historical background of lower Lafourche. It would have been difficult to put the boat business in a cultural context without the groundbreaking work of writers like Jeanne Rome, Robert Looper, John Doucet, Dale Rogers, Elton Oubre, and many other Lafourche area aces.

Three years after I had read and mined the Lafourche Heritage Soci-ety works, the society came through again in the summer of 2006. At the time, it had been a year and a half since my would-be publisher had withdrawn its contract offer. With the project stalled, I showed my com-pleted draft to the society board and some of the board members read and critiqued it, enthusiastically encouraging me to "get the book out there." Consequently, I appreciate the last minute push from Marge Barker, Marjorie Landry, John Doucet, and Elton Oubre.

As crucial as the Lafourche Heritage writers were in making the old days on the bayou come to life, oil industry historians were just as vital in supplementing and corroborating my interviewees' accounts of marine oilfield development. I found the most material in Joseph A. Pratt, Tyler Priest, and Christopher J. Castaneda's *Offshore Pioneers: Brown & Root and the History of Offshore Oil and Gas.* Their well-researched details assisted me immensely. For instance, their section on the North Sea added background and authentication to the stories told by the men of Nolty J. Theriot, Inc. In *The Color of Oil*, Michael Economides and Ron-ald Oligney gave a concise explanation of every facet of the oilfield. In the epic *The Prize*, Daniel Yergin put the industry in geopolitical perspective.

Then there were the probing researchers from the University of Ari-zona, led by Tom McGuire, who had the foresight to dig into the south Louisiana oilfield. If there were ever any doubts that the birth of Gulf of Mexico oil had a unique history worthy of documenting, Tom and his Tuscon-based team dispelled them by procuring grants totaling $850,000 from the Mineral Management Service to chronicle the industry's devel-opment. For anyone wanting to look beyond the boat business and peer deeper into the history of every facet of the oilfield, I recommend the MMS reports, which are cited below.

I must also acknowledge two authors for their profiles of historic figures that appeared in certain chapters of this book. In the chapter "Sovereign State," I pulled most of the background information about Leander Perez from James Conaway's revealing work, *Judge*. Mr. Conaway not only deserves full credit for the tales of Salvador Chiappetta, the National Guard, and the fort that became a prison, he also corroborated the Perez machine's sabotage of the non-parish workboat owners. In the chapter "Bobby Goes to Washington," I drew from Thomas Becnel's thorough portrait of *Senator Allen Ellender of Louisiana*. It was an unusual experience to hear Bobby Orgeron describe his dealings with Ellender and then see Bobby's descriptions match those of Dr. Becnel's. I am also grateful for Dr. Becnel, who was once a teacher at Golden Meadow High School in the 1950s, agreeing to read my book and approve my own sketch of the senator.

When it came to verifying dates, a great source was the shipyard hull lists, like those at Bollinger and Blount Boats, Inc. Another solid date determiner was the Louisiana Secretary of State corporations index website, which accurately records the names and dates of incorporations.

Because of all these wonderful resources, which are detailed below, I had plenty of material for the proposal and sample chapters. Nevertheless, I still needed help editing it all down into something readable. During this phase, my secretary at the time, Kendra Thomas, read and critiqued several drafts.

The most effective proposal editor was my former agent, John Ware, who died in 2013. John put me through a multiple-draft torture chamber, but in the end, the proposal came out as letter-perfect as possible. Like many of John's authors throughout his esteemed career, I appreciated every drop of John's blue ink.

When I finished a draft of the entire manuscript, several readers helped improve what was a monstrous mess. They included my brother-in-law Mark Gauthier, father-in-law Mike Gauthier, my sister Nicole Falgoust, her husband, my brother-in-law and fellow writer, J. Wesley Harris, and the manuscript's cleaner, my wife Susie. Additionally, Susie and my two daughters Grace and Celeste provided me with the love and comfort I needed to cope with a project that was much more challenging than I'd ever imagined.

During the fact-checking of the draft, I benefitted from several readers. Lower Lafourche historian and coastal crusader Windell Curole offered sound advice. Many of the people who appear in the book read certain sections for accuracy. In fact, at least two people from each of the four main families reviewed their families' excerpts. While I understand that it was painful at times for some of the subjects to read portions of the material, I appreciate their honesty and professionalism.

There were also dozens of people along Bayou Lafourche with whom I discussed my book. I could never remember the names of everyone who offered background and ideas, just as I could never include every Cajun who owned a workboat, but I acknowledge them all *en masse* and *in globo*. Many of them have their own boat stories. There could and should be other books on Gary Chouest's ability to turn an expensive, innovative idea into an international reality, on the socioeconomic and political influence of Boysie Bollinger and his talented extended family, on what Al Danos accomplished in Nigeria; on the multidimensional Callais clan, in particular on what Harold Callais did in expanding a boat company into banking, garbage collecting, and cable TV; on the three-generation Exxon magic of Otto Candies; and on many, many others.

Most practically, I thank the people responsible for publishing and publicizing the first, self-published edition of the book, particularly the turnkey production manager Lynne Johnson Evans and publicist Stephanie Barko and to everyone at my law office during the book's original 2006–2007 production and release, especially Roxanne Legendre, the self-publishing label Stockard James' marketing director, bookkeeper and delivery specialist. Then there are the people responsible for ensuring that the book endures: literary agent Regina Ryan, who secured a contract with Skyhorse, my editor Joseph Craig, my publicist Leslie Davis, and my highly cooperative law partner Cassie Rodrigue Braud.

Shifting back to sources, the people listed below provided valuable information through formal in-person or telephone interviews, and some graciously submitted to multiple interviews. Many of them shed light on more than one family and on general local history. Most, if not all, of the sources gave me insight into the boat business and the oilfield. Some, such as the insurance broker Lynn Pierce, were particularly good at helping me understand the reasons for and the effects of industry cycles. Consequently, even though I have included the sources' company affiliations next to their names, please note that each person provided me with a fair amount of *lagniappe*, too.

Jefferson Alario (Nolty J. Theriot, Inc.)

Robert Alario (Nolty J. Theriot, Inc., Executive Director of OMSA)

Melvin Bernard (Chevron)

Luther Blount (Blount Boats, Inc., Creator of the Botruc)

Donald "Boysie" Bollinger (Bollinger Shipyards, Inc.)

Richard "Dick" Bollinger (Bollinger Shipyards, Inc.)

Benny Bourgeois (Nolty J. Theriot, Inc.)

Albert Cheramie (C. & G. Boat Service, Inc.)

Lou Cheramie (L & M Botruc, Inc.)

Reed Cheramie (Huey J. Cheramie Marine, Inc., Schlumberger)

Minor "M. J." Cheramie Jr. (L & M Botruc, Inc.)

Paul Candies (Otto Candies, Inc.)

Dan Carroll (Baton Rouge C.P.A. of Nolty J. Theriot, Inc., and other boat companies)

Edison Chouest (Edison Chouest Offshore, Inc.)

Gary Chouest (Edison Chouest Offshore, Inc.)

Benton "Benu" Danos (MONTCO)

Louis "Butch" Danos (MONTCO, L & M Botruc, Inc.; Bollinger Shipyards, Inc.)

Rodney Gisclair (MONTCO)

Anthony Guilbeau (C. & G. Boat Service, Inc.)

Dick "Dickie" Guidry (Guidry Brothers, Inc.)

Richard "Dick" Guidry (American Offshore, Inc.)

Archbishop Philip Hannan

Bobby Orgeron (MONTCO)

Joseph Orgeron (MONTCO)

Lee Orgeron (MONTCO)

Nadine "Deanie" Cheramie Pitre (L & M Botruc, Inc.)

Patrick "Pat" Pitre (L & M Botruc, Inc.)

Lynn Pierce (The Insurance Agency of Theriot, Duet & Theriot, Inc.)

William "Bill" Porteous (Counsel for L & M Botruc, Inc., and other companies)

Linwood "Woody" Terrebonne (L & M Botruc, Inc.)

Bobby Savoie (Nolty J. Theriot, Inc.)
Mathilde Eymard Savoie (Guidry & Savoie, Inc.; United Tugs, Inc.)
Sidney Savoie (Guidry & Savoie, Inc.; United Tugs, Inc.)
Ted Savoie (Guidry & Savoie, Inc.; United Tugs, Inc.; Central Gulf Towing, Inc.)
Gladys "Bea" Theriot (Nolty J. Theriot, Inc.)
Livingston Theriot (Nolty J. Theriot, Inc., Theriot Brothers, Inc.)
Nacis Theriot (Nolty J. Theriot, Inc.; MONTCO; Theriot Brothers, Inc.)
Paris "Pye" Theriot (Nolty J. Theriot, Inc.)
Jimmie Vizier (Nolty J. Theriot, Inc.; Vizier Offshore Towing, Inc.)
Tommie Vizier (Nolty J. Theriot, Inc.; Vizier Offshore Towing, Inc.)

Other sources providing corroboration and insight include Donald Ayo, Thomas Becnel, Charlotte Bollinger, Eric Bollinger, Ben Bordelon, Robert Boughamer Jr., Huey J. Cheramie, Minor "Tony" Cheramie III, Laney Chouest, C. J. Christ, Al Danos, Theresa Rebstock Dobard, Iris Doucet, Beryl Theriot Duet, Mary Foret, Michael Gauthier, Mike Gautreaux, Renée Gautreaux, Vic Lafont, James Leonard, Joyce Williams Leonard, Lincoln Martin, Glen Pitre, Charlotte Randolph, Eva Theriot Shaner, Scott Theriot, Lonnie Thibodeaux, Wayne Tyler, and many others.

Bibliography

Books

Becnel, Thomas A. *Senator Allen Ellender of Louisiana: A Biography* (Baton Rouge, Louisiana: Louisiana State University Press, 1996).

Berard, Dudley J. *This Cajun Ain't Bashful: The Outspoken Views of an Industrialist* (Lafayette, Louisiana: Jim Bradshaw Limited, 1986).

Brasseaux, Carl A. *"Scattered to the Wind:" Dispersal and Wanderings of the Acadians, 1755-1809* (Lafayette, Louisiana: The Center for Louisiana Studies, 1991).

Brasseaux, Carl A. *The Founding of New Acadia: The Beginnings of Acadian Life in Louisiana, 1765–1803* (Baton Rouge, Louisiana: LSU Press, 1987).

Callow, Clive. *Power from the Sea: The Search for North Sea Oil and Gas* (London: Victor Gollancz Ltd., 1973).

Cheniere Hurricane Centennial (Windell Curole, Chairman, Robert Looper, Editor), *Reflechir: Les Images Des Priries Tremblantes: 1840–1940* (Thibodaux, Louisiana: Portier Gorman, Inc., 1994).

Cheniere Hurricane Centennial (Windell Curole, Chairman, Robert Looper, Editor), *Reflechir II: Les Decades* (Thibodaux, Louisiana: Portier Gorman, Inc., 1995).

Conaway, James. *Judge: The Life and Times of Leander Perez* (New York: Alfred A. Knopf, 1973).

Economides, Michael, and Ronald Oligney. *The Color of Oil* (Katy, Texas: Round Oak Publishing Company, Inc., 2000).

Falls, Rose C. *Cheniere Caminada or The Wind of Death?: The Story of the Storm in Louisiana* (New Orleans: Hopkins Printing Office, 1893).

Franks, Kenny A., and Paul F. Lambert. *Early Louisiana and Arkansas Oil: A Photographic History, 1901–1946* (College Station, Texas: Texas A&M University Press, 1982).

Halberstam, David. *The Fifties* (New York: Random House Value Publishing, 1996).

Kane, Harnett T. *Bayous of Louisiana* (New York: William Morrow & Company, 1943).

Lafourche Heritage Society, Inc. Doucet, John P. and Stephen S. Michot, Editors. *The Lafourche Country II: The Heritage and its Keepers* (Thibodaux, Louisiana: Lafourche Heritage Society, Inc., 1996).

Lafourche Heritage Society, Inc. Landry, Marjorie, Editor. *Stories My Grandparents Told Me: Student Essays on Lafourche Heritage* (Thibodaux, Louisiana: Lafourche Heritage Society, Inc., 1993).

Lafourche Heritage Society, Inc., Uzee, Philip D., Editor. *The Lafourche Country: The People and the Land* (Lafayette, Louisiana: Center for Louisiana Studies, 1985).

Looper, Robert B., with John B. Doucet and Colley Charpentier. *The Cheniere Caminada Story, A Commemorative* (Thibodaux, Louisiana: Blue Heron Press, 1993).

Pickens, T. Boone. *Boone* (New York: Houghton Mifflin, 1998).

Pratt, Joseph A., Tyler Priest, and Christopher J. Castaneda. *Offshore Pioneers: Brown & Root and the History of Offshore Oil and Gas* (Houston: Gulf Publishing Company, 1997).

Rome, Jeanne. *History of Golden Meadow* (Revised Edition, Self-Published, 1994).

Ross, Sally, and Alphonse Deveau. *The Acadians of Nova Scotia, Past and Present* (Halifax, Nova Scotia: Nimbus Publishing, 1992).

Schlosser, Eric. *Fast Food Nation: The Dark Side of the American Meal* (New York: Perennial, 2002).

Strong, Skip, and Twain Braden. *In Peril: A Daring Decision, A Captain's Resolve and the Salvage that Made History* (Guilford, Connecticut: The Lyons Press, 2003).

Wiggins, Melanie. *Torpedoes in the Gulf: Galveston and the U-Boats, 1942–1943* (College Station, Texas: Texas A&M University Press, 1995).

Writers' Program of the Work Projects Administration in the State of Louisiana. *Louisiana: A Guide to the State, American Guide Series* (New York: Hastings House, 1941).

Yergin, Daniel. *The Prize: The Epic Quest for Oil, Money and Power* (New York: Touchstone, 1991).

Special Reports, Government Publications and Booklets

Kochman, Ladd. *Economic Impact of Nicholls State University on the Local Economy* (Thibodaux, Louisiana: Nicholls State University, 1987).

Lindsedt, Dianne M., Lori L. Nunn, Joseph C. Holmes Jr., and Elizabeth E. Willis. *History of Oil and Gas Development in Coastal Louisiana*, Louisiana Geological Survey, 1991, Baton Rouge.

McGuire, Tom. *History of Offshore Oil and Gas Industry in Southern Louisiana, Interim Report*, "Volume II: Bayou Lafourche—An Oral History of the Development of the Oil and Gas Industry," OCS Study MMS 2004-050 (New Orleans, Louisiana: US Department of the Interior, Mineral Management Service, July 2004).

McGuire, Tom, Diane Austin, and Andrew Gardner. *Captains of the Road and Sea: Providing Transportation for the Gulf of Mexico Oilpatch, Part IV of Social and Economic Impacts of OCS Activities on Individuals and Families: A Four-Part Interim for the Participating Communities*, Bureau of Applied Research in Anthropology, University of Arizona, Tuscon, Arizona, September 30, 2000.

McGuire, Tom, Diane Austin, Bob Carriker, Joseph Pratt, Tyler Priest, and Allan G. Pulsipher. *History of Offshore Oil and Gas Industry in Southern Louisiana, Interim Report*, "Volume I: Papers on the Evolving Offshore Industry," OCS Study MMS 2004-049 (New Orleans, Louisiana: US Department of the Interior, Mineral Management Service, July 2004).

McGuire, Tom, and Diane Austin. *History of Offshore Oil and Gas Industry in Southern Louisiana, Interim Report*, "Volume III: Bayou Lafourche—Samples of Interviews and Ethnographic Prefaces," OCS Study MMS 2004-051 (New Orleans, Louisiana: US Department of the Interior, Mineral Management Service, July 2004).

Special Report on The Petroleum Industry in Louisiana, Prepared by Louisiana State Department of Labor, Division of Employment Security, September 1953.

US Bureau of the Census. *County and City Data Book, 1988* (Washington, DC: US Government Printing office: 1988).

Newspaper and Magazine Articles

"Bollinger Delivers New Liftboat," *Waterways Journal*, August 12, 2002, p. 5.

Christ, C.J., "War in the Gulf: Bad weather sends Naval blimp on unusual journey," *The Courier* (Houma, Louisiana), March 18, 2001.

Colomb, Beverly. "Man Who Played Dead Tells How Nazis Shot at Prisoners," *Times- Picayune*.

The Courier. "War in the Gulf: Cruise was a 'bad trip' for the *Robert E. Lee*," March 4, 2001.

The Courier. "War in the Gulf: Oil tanker sinking barges brings war close to Grand Isle Shore," February 18, 2001.

The Courier. "War in the Gulf: Rumors Abound of Gulf Spy Activity," April 29, 2001.

The Courier. "War in the Gulf: Shrimpers assisted in saving lives after torpedo attacks," February 4, 2001.

The Courier, "War in the Gulf: 'Swamp Angels' conducted rescues in south Louisiana marsh," April 1, 2001.

The Courier, "War in the Gulf: WWII German prisoners were housed in area POW camps," April 15, 2001.

Daily Comet, "Vessel may be the largest ever built locally," (Thibodaux, Louisiana, New York Times Regional Newspapers), April 2, 2003, p. 4A.

"Freight Trucks of the Oil Patch," *Marine Log,* September 2002, p. 51–54.

Gresham, Matt. "Bollinger completes boat for Lafourche firm," *Bayou Business Review,* p. 14.

Hall, Jesse. "C-Port brings efficiency to supply operations," *Bayou Business Review,* p. 12.

"Janis(et) Bergeron Wed Paris Theriot III," *Lafourche Gazette,* January 17, 1973.

King, Wayne. "Bad Times on the Bayou." *New York Times Magazine,* 11 June 1989, p. 56–59.

"Leggy Liftboats," *Popular Mechanics,* November 2002.

McKnight, Laura. "Project documenting offshore history on exhibit," *Courier,* January 23, 2005.

"Nolty Theriot Dead at 51," *Daily Comet,* March 15, 1976. "Nolty Theriot Enters Race," *Daily Comet,* May 9, 1975.

O'Brien, Keith. "War in the Gulf of Mexico," *Times-Picayune,* p. E-1, E-4, E-5.

Pearson, Larry. "Liftboat reaches a new level of sophistication," *American Ship Review,* 2002-2003, p. 45–47.

Schulz, William. "Portrait of a Mobster." *Reader's Digest,* August 1970, p. 59–62.

"Sidney Savoie," Obituary, *Daily Comet,* June 10, 2004.

Statutes and Jurisprudence

The Jones Act, 46 USC § 688.

Continental Casualty Co. v. Associated Pipe & Supply Co., 279 F Supp 490 (ED La 1967) and 310 F Supp 1207 (ED La 1969), affirmed in part and vacated in part 447 F 2d 1041 (5 Cir 1971).

Johnson v. Offshore Express, Inc., 845 F 2d 1347, 1352 (5 Cir), cert. denied, 488 US 968, 109 S Ct. 497, 102 L Ed 2d 533 (1988).

World Wide Web

"144 Year Old Converted Sailboat! The '*PETIT CAPORAL,*'" www.bertaut.com/sail1854.html.

"Alden J. 'Doc' LaBorde: The Man Behind the Rig," www.rigmuseum.com.

"Cover Story: Yearbook," http://www.workboat.com/archives/06jun/coverstory.htm. Gresham, Matt.

"Danos & Curole: Celebrating 50 Years, June 30, 1997," http:// www.businessnew-sonline.com/20Web20Site20Files/Feature_Business/ Danos_Curole.html

"Estimated 500,000 Need Mental Help a Year After Katrina," http://www.forbes. com/ forbeslife/health/feeds/hscout/2006/08/01/hscout534146.html, August 1, 2006. "Katrina and Rita One Year Later: Ecological Effects of Gulf Coast Hurricanes," http:// www.sciencedaily.com/releases/2006/08/060807155009. htm, August 7, 2006.

Louisiana Secretary of State, Commercial Division, www.sec.state.la.us.

"LRA Releases Estimates of Hurricane Impact," http://www.lra.louisiana.gov/ pr_1_12_impact.html, January 12, 2006.

McNamara, Dave, "Thunder in the Gulf," www.cdnn.info.

"Offshore Milestones," *Ocean Resources*, wwww.ocean-resources.com/backissues/ print-article.asp?ID=97.

Schleifstein, Mark. "Hurricanes claimed 217 square miles of state's coast," http:// www.nola.com/newslogs/tpupdates/index.ssf?/mtlogs/nola_tpupdates/ archives/2006_10_10.html, October 10, 2006. "THERIOT FLEET," www. tugtalk.co.uk. http://www.workboat.com/news/dayrates.asp. http://www.work-boat.com/news/stats_05.asp.

Generally:
www.bollingershipyards.com
www.botruc.com
www.chouest.com
www.dailycomet.com
www.danos.com
www.gulfoil.bara.arizona.edu
www.houmatoday.com
www.gomr.mms.gov
www.montco.com
www.ocean-resources.com
www.offshoremarine.org
www.tugtalk.com
www.workboat.com

Miscellaneous

Shipyard Hull Lists:
Bollinger Shipyards, Inc., Hull Listing, 1953 to 1996.
Blount Boats, Inc., Boat List, March 1, 1949 to July 22, 2003.

Films:
Zewe, Charles. *Cajuns on the Queen Sea* (WWL-TV, 1973).

Others:
Archives, Sacred Heart Church, Cut Off, Louisiana.
Inscription on Tombstone of William Riley Williams, Williams Cemetery, Golden
    Meadow, Louisiana.
Theriot, Nolty. *Campaign Brochure, Nolty Theriot for State Representative*, 1975. Suc-
    cession of Nolty J. Theriot, 17th Judicial District Court, Probate No. 9559,
    Thibodaux, Louisiana.

Bibliography for the Afterword

In southern Louisiana, the state of the oilfield is part of our daily discourse. Those of us who live and work on Bayou Lafourche have witnessed the economic swings of the hurricanes, the boom, the BP spill, the moratorium, permitorium, and the recent downturn. Consequently, the Afterword includes some of my personal observations.

That said, almost all of the Afterword's content comes from others. In some cases, it's my talks over the last decade with clients, friends, and people on the bayou of all walks. The meat of the information, however, originates from June and July 2016 interviews of the following family members of the story's four original pioneers: Pye Theriot, M. J. Cheramie, Pat Pitre, Tony Cheramie, Jacob Pitre, Ted Savoie, Larbow Cheramie, Sidney A. Savoie, Matt Cheramie, Lee Orgeron, and Joseph Orgeron.

Additional data about the BP spill comes the web articles cited below and from the book, *Blowout in the Gulf: The BP Oil Spill Disaster and the Future of Energy in America* by William R. Freudenburg and Robert Gramling (MIT Press 2010). The court case that litigated the resulting drilling moratorium is *Hornbeck Offshore Servs., L.L.C. v. Salazar, 696 F Supp 2d 627, 638–39 (ED La 2010) appeal dismissed as moot, 396 F. App'x 147 (5 Cir 2010)*.

I also drew from the following periodicals, which were either released in print, digital, or video and stored on the websites noted below. Some of the articles updated information from what I wrote about in the book's original Epilogue and Postscript.

Alford, Jeremy. "Paris Theriot new American Consul for Kazakhstan." March 15,
    2010. www.bestofneworleans.com.
Bayles, Cara. "New liftboat billed as world's largest." April 2, 2012. www.dailycomet.
    com.
Bell, Julia and Bradley, Brendan. "One Year Later, Lack of GOM Permits = Lack of
    Gulf Coast Jobs." Independent Petroleum Association of America. October 20,

2011. http://www.ipaa.org/friday-fact-checks/one-year-later-lack-of-gom-permits-lack-of-gulf-coast-jobs/.

"Block Island Wind Farm." http://dwwind.com/project/block-island-wind-farm/.

Broussard, Ben. "State of the Industry: Louisiana. Louisiana Oil & Gas Association." www.slideshare.net/laoilandgasassoc/gsrms-ben-broussardCrude Oil Prices - 70 Year Historical Chart.

Conca, James. "US Winning Oil War Against Saudi Arabia." *Forbes.* July 22, 2015. http://www.forbes.com/sites/jamesconca/2015/07/22/u-s-winning-oil-war-against-saudi-arabia/#411b2ba97876.

"Crude Oil Prices - 70 Year Historical Chart." Macrotrends. http://www.macrotrends.net/1369/crude-oil-price-history-chart.

Day Rates, https://www.workboat.com/resources/reports/2016-day-rates/.

Decision Memorandum, Department of Interior, to Bureau of Ocean Energy Management, Regulation and Enforcement. " Decision memorandum regarding the suspension of certain offshore permitting and drilling activities on the Outer Continental Shelf." July 12, 2010. https://www.doi.gov/sites/doi.gov/files/migrated/deepwaterhorizon/upload/Salazar-Bromwich-July-12-Final.pdf.

Greenberg, Jerry. "OSV Day Rates." *Workboat.* June 11, 2012. https://www.workboat.com/archive/osv-day-rates/.

Greenberg, Ted. NBC 10 News, Philadelphia. June 25, 1999. Video found ateNew Jersey Shallow Shelf: IODP Expedition 313, www.dosecc.org/index.php/projects/continental-margins/25-new-jersey-shallow-shelf-expedition-313.

"Haynes and Boone LLP Oil Patch Bankruptcy Monitor, June 30, 2016." www.haynesboone.com.

"Haynes and Boone, LLP Oilfield Services Bankruptcy Tracker, July 20, 2016." http://www.haynesboone.com.

"Interior Department Issues 'Idle Iron' Guidance." September 15, 2010. www.doi.gov/news/pressreleases/Interior-Department-Issues-Idle-Iron-Guidance.

Kirk, Donald. "How Fracking Contributes To Oil Glut, Cheap Fuel For You And Me." *Forbes.* January 26, 2015. http://www.forbes.com/sites/donaldkirk/2015/01/26/how-fracking-contributes-to-oil-glut-cheap-fuel-for-you-and-me/#74a5ce8b2699.

LOGA Data & Statistics, http://loga.la/gulf-of-mexico/data-statistics/.

"Maritime Management Concentration," https://www.nicholls.edu/management/degree-plans/maritime/.

Moss, Laura. "The 13 largest oil spills in history." Mother Nature Network. July 16, 2010. http://www.mnn.com/earth-matters/wilderness-resources/stories/the-13-largest-oil-spills-in-history.

"Oil and Gas Journal Rig Counts – Reported by Baker Hughes." http://dnr.louisiana.gov/assets/TAD/data/drill_weekly/ogj_rig_count.pdf.

"Oil Price Drop Sinks Offshore Supply Vessel Market: Lower Global Oil Prices Make OSV Fortunes Flounder." January 2016. http://www.alixpartners.com/en/LinkClick.aspx?fileticket=nJhG6itDWdA%3D&tabid=635.

Plyer, Allison. "Facts for Features: Katrina Impact." August 26, 2016. http://www.datacenterresearch.org/data-resources/katrina/facts-for-impact/.

"Port Facts," http://portfourchon.com/seaport/port-facts/.

"Preliminary Report, Integrated Ocean Drilling Program, Expedition 313," http://publications.iodp.org/preliminary_report/313/313pr_4.htm.

Stefani, Robert J. "Offshore Supply Vessel Market Turnaround May Be In Sight, But You Need a Long Telescope to See It." March 7, 2016. http://www.king-krebs.com/news-253.html.

"The Subchapter M Final Rule Review." *MarineCFO*. June 15, 2016. http://www.marinecfo.com/2016/06/15/the-subchapter-m-final-rule-review/. The law is found at *46 CFR*. For a more detailed explanation, see the *Federal Register* at https://www.uscg.mil/hq/cg5/TVNCOE/Documents/SubM/SubchapterMFinalRule.pdf.

Generally:

www.botruc.com

www.centralgulftowing.com

www.dosecc.org

www.montco.com

www.workboat.com

Three generations of Savoie boatmen aboard the *Susan G* in 1998.
From left, Ted, Sidney V., and Sidney A. The boat, which was originally built in 1951, worked through the 2000s. Due to poor economic conditions as of 2016, the boat is currently cold stacked and for sale. (Courtesy of Ted Savoie.)